Youth, Alcohol, and Social Policy

Youth, Alcohol, and Social Policy

Edited by

Howard T. Blane

University of Pittsburgh
Pittsburgh, Pennsylvania

and

Morris E. Chafetz

Health Education Foundation
Washington, D.C.

Plenum Press · New York and London

Library of Congress Cataloging in Publication Data

Youth, Alcohol, and Social Policy Conference, Arlington, Va., 1978.
Youth, alcohol, and social policy.

Papers presented at the conference organized by the Health Education Foundation and held Oct. 18–20, 1978 in Arlington, Va.
Includes bibliographical references and index.
1. Alcohol and youth–United States–Congresses.
2. Alcoholism–United States–Prevention–Congresses. 3. Liquor problem–United States–Congresses. I. Blane, Howard T. II. Chafetz, Morris E. III. Health Education Foundation, Washington, D.C. IV. Title.
HV5135.Y68 1978 362.2'92'0973 79-9094
ISBN 978-1-4684-8540-0 ISBN 978-1-4684-8538-7 (eBook)
DOI 10.1007/978-1-4684-8538-7

Softcover reprint of the hardcover 1st edition 1979

A Division of Plenum Publishing Corporation
227 West 17th Street, New York, N.Y. 10011

We dedicate this volume to the memory of John H. Knowles, friend, colleague, and health visionary, whose career was suddenly and tragically struck down by cancer. The example he set as Director of the Massachusetts General Hospital, of sometimes irreverent but always pointed criticism of medical conventionality, of the dehumanization of health care, and of the need for health promotion and disease prevention, has never left us. We hope this volume will, in at least a small way, serve as a reminder of his example and as a tribute to the memory of a man larger than life—a largeness inseparable from the inner strength and inspiration of his wife, Teedy.

Contributors

Howard T. Blane • School of Education, University of Pittsburgh, Pittsburgh, Pennsylvania

Lawrence W. Green • School of Hygiene and Public Health, The Johns Hopkins University, Baltimore, Maryland

Thomas C. Harford • Department of Health, Education and Welfare, National Institute of Alcohol Abuse and Alcoholism, Rockville, Maryland

Richard E. Horman • National Psychiatric Institutes, Washington, D.C.

John E. Killeen • Major, USAF, Office of the Assistant Secretary of Defense (Health Affairs), Department of Defense, Woodbridge, Virginia

David P. Kraft • Mental Health Division, University Health Services, University of Massachusetts, Amherst, Massachusetts

Peter M. Miller • Department of Behavioral Medicine, Hilton Head Hospital, Hilton Head Island, South Carolina

J. Michael Polich • Social Science Department, The Rand Corporation, Santa Monica, California

Reginald G. Smart • Program Development Research, Addiction Research Foundation, Toronto, Ontario, Canada

Henry Wechsler • Director of Research, The Medical Foundation, Inc., Boston, Massachusetts

Richard W. Wilsnack • Department of Sociology, University of North Dakota, Grand Forks, North Dakota

Sharon C. Wilsnack • Division of Psychiatry and Behavioral Science, Department of Neuroscience, University of North Dakota School of Medicine, Grand Forks, North Dakota

Robert A. Zucker • Department of Psychology, Michigan State University, East Lansing, Michigan

Foreword

Anxiety about "alcohol and youth" has been excited by shocking events and reports. Events are exemplified by multiple deaths of adolescents in automobile crashes after drinking parties. Reports are exemplified by the conclusion, from a national survey, that more than one fourth of youngsters aged 13 to 18 are already problem drinkers. Response provoked by these events and reports has taken the form of proposed or enacted legislation in several states to raise the so-called legal drinking age from 18 to 19, or 20, or 21.

The confusion around the alcohol-and-youth problem is manifest in the fact that no one can be sure that raising the legal drinking age will make any difference. The legislation may be tilting at windmills; and it is doubtful even that the windmills exist. (But the legislative windmills are whirling.) The confusion is clearly manifest in the fact that the legal-drinking-age legislation does not deal with a drinking age.

A fantastic situation: newspapers report the debate about the proposed legal-drinking-age bills. TV newscasters report on the votes for and against the new legal-drinking-age bills. Legislators argue over whether the legal drinking age should be raised, and whether to 19, or 20, or 21. (But no one proposes to raise it to 25, though—as you will learn herein—it is the age class 21 to 25 that experiences the most drinking troubles.) And finally new laws are enacted in some states, and governors then pose before TV cameras solemnly explaining why they are signing the bill to raise the legal drinking age. It is fantastic because it is as though no one—no one—has bothered to read the legislation, which does not say a word about drinking. The new law, like the older law, only forbids purchase of liquor by the designated underaged, or sale to them, or furnishing to them (except by parents or guardians), and sometimes sale or transportation by them, or even possession by them in a public place. It does not forbid them to drink.

Why does everybody persist in talking about a legal drinking age when there is no such thing? Why are all the adults kidding themselves?

The kids could not care less. (Exception: Some civil-liberties-conscientious young people, indifferent about alcohol, have protested being discriminated against by the age legislation.) They were drinking before the alcohol-age was lowered to 18. And they will still drink where the alcohol-age is raised above 18.

The adults are kidding themselves because they are worried and they do not know what to think.

Alcohol is a dangerous drug. But unlike other dangerous drugs, it has been domesticated by traditions that predate history. It is intimate with our social life. It is the ravening wolf that became our pet dog, a dear and useful pet. With value as food, as medicament, as euphoriant, as soothing-syrup and consoler, even as helper and protector, alcohol is too agreeable a dangerous drug for people to be willing to give it up. They remember that although it harms some who are reckless, or unlucky, or sick, it comforts the most. Yet, if it is not to be abolished, how do we keep it for ourselves—for us, the entitled adults—while denying it to the untrustworthy, undeserving young? Or, if the prematurely adultified young are not to be denied (indeed, no—not by legislative fiat), how can they be safeguarded from harm?

Whatever was done up to now has not worked very well. The youth-and-alcohol relationship has been worsening. We are enacting laws, but who can say that they will make any difference?

The confusion of ideas around alcohol-and-youth issues, the self-kidding of adults, was dramatically demonstrated at the symposium which is the basis of the present book. A question by a member of the audience started a discussion of what turned out to be an exciting issue: Baby Beer. That was the name given by the news media to a beverage newly marketed, as an experiment, by one of the great national breweries—a beer free of alcohol! "Baby Beer" they called it because, being nonalcoholic, it must be weak, like a baby; and because it was intended for those presumed too young to drink adult beer—the strong kind. But Baby Beer quickly evoked a loud, horrified, widespread public clamor: "Why, this was nothing else than a plot by those wicked brewers to entice our innocent youth, our babies, to learn to like beer!" This idea was expressed with concern and with indignation by several members of the audience when—a miracle! An officer of the brewery that had put out the nonalcoholic beer was attending the symposium. He rose and announced that he had received word from his company that very morning that the Baby Beer project was being discontinued, in deference to public opinion. *Applause! Cheers!* What a victory for the protection of the young! The concerned citizens were elated.

In my observer's corner I sat reflecting: a brewer had at last had the brilliant idea of offering the young an alternative to alcohol, the safe beer, the beverage of total moderation. The alcohol-concerned citizens had denounced it. As if the youngsters were not nearly all drinking beer anyhow—the alcoholized beer, of course—a fact revealed in all the surveys reported at this very symposium! So they might have had the choice—at least some of them some of the time—to drink the beer without the alcohol. But no more choice. Their concerned elders, ignoring the reality, had frustrated that chance. (And I indulged another reflection: Had the company abandoned the Baby Beer business in deference to public opinion, or had their marketing tests shown that the kids were not going to buy the Baby Beer?)

Clearly, new thinking is wanted. New thinking ought to be based on better knowledge. That, then, is the aim of this book. In this collection of essays by earnest thinkers, who are also original researchers and outstandingly knowledgeable in their several special fields, a bold effort is made to rethink the issues around drinking by the young. The newest knowledge is presented straightforwardly, and the knowledge and the thinking are expertly synthesized so as to open up prospects of fresh approaches with a brighter promise of working solutions than we have seen hitherto.

Lovers of paradoxes should find this book entertaining too. These authors are not afraid to surprise. One who has carried out some of the most sophisticated and successful survey studies warns not to take the results of such research too seriously. (They are not all that consistent.) Another, who comes out of a medical environment, warns against "the medical model" and asserts that the young problem drinkers do not have a disease, but he nevertheless concludes that they do represent a health problem.

All these clever authors have some ideas, and they expound them cogently. I might agree with all of them—but I have some ideas of my own. I admit, however, that my own ideas have been stimulated, moderated, and refined by the ideas set forth in this book. That, I think, will happen to all thoughtful readers who are—as we all should be—uneased by the waxing alcohol-and-youth problems.

MARK KELLER

Contents

Chapter 6
Sex Roles and Adolescent Drinking
Sharon C. Wilsnack and Richard W. Wilsnack

Chapter 7
Priorities in Minimizing Alcohol Problems among Young People
Reginald G. Smart

Chapter 8
The Impact of Sociopolitical Systems on Teenage Alcohol Abuse

Richard E. Horman

Chapter 9
Toward National Policy for Health Education

Lawrence W. Green

Chapter 10
Strategies for Reducing Drinking Problems among Youth: College Programs

David P. Kraft

Introduction

One of the most noteworthy social developments of the past decade, manifest in the United Nations' recent call for 1979 as the International Year of the Child, is society's increased attention and focus on youth. Young people today confront a world made more complex by virtue of kaleidoscopic exposure to differences in moral vision, that is to say, what men in different places and at different times have conceived to be right and wrong, good and evil. An almost unrestricted exposure to every facet of our world has become possible by increasingly more efficient and comprehensive technological advances in the fields of communications and transportation. This exposure has brought with it problems and demands, opportunities and challenges. While the problems of the past—educational deprivation, malnutrition, inadequate health care, job discrimination, substance abuse, and so on—remain, they have assumed a new coloration brought about by popular awareness of the tremendous variety of human experience. Every facet of existence is defined and acted upon differently by different societies and different subcultures. Once-unnoticed discrepancies in having and not having can lead to a renewed and integrating sense of purpose but perhaps more often result in impotent frustration and rage. Whether for this reason or others—such as the new hedonism or problems in the home—adolescents and young people today are turning in distressing numbers to ways of using alcohol that have the net effect of increasing its hazards. The trend is upward for social and personal problems related to the use of alcohol among young people, and unless responsible intervention occurs, serious life problems will result for a significant portion of them.

With considerations such as these in mind, the Health Education Foundation, in the fall of 1978, undertook the organization of a national conference that would bring together the diverse body of information dealing with alcohol use and alcohol-related problems among youth. We wished to provide a forum in which facts and ideas could be reexamined and recent developments presented and debated in a manner suitable to the needs of all professionals concerned with youth and alcohol, from the practitioner to the scientist. We also wished, in an area in which moral sentiment runs high, to help to distinguish fact from fiction, myth from reality, with regard to youthful drinking behavior. Finally, we wished to examine the issues in a way that could lead to responsible development of social policy with regard to alcohol and that would, in turn, lead to programmatic action that would serve to reduce alcohol problems among youth.

In order to present the latest in the way of factual information, based upon the most recent and the best research investigations, we called upon social scientists and epidemiologists who have been in the forefront of research concerning youthful drinking practices, including high school and college drinking and drinking among youth in the military and in the work place. It is necessary to provide a topography that shows the peaks and valleys of drinking behavior according to sex, age, and other demographic characteristics. Any such topography is incomplete unless it includes the dimension of time, the manner in which drinking behavior among young people has changed over the years. A map such as this provides the interested person a guide to chart a course in understanding youthful drinking behavior.

While the empirical picture is a first step toward understanding any social phenomenon by itself, it is not sufficient to lead to the fullest understanding of the phenomenon. For such understanding to occur, it is necessary to turn to those scholars and researchers who have constructed conceptual frameworks that serve to explain the various aspects of drinking behavior among youth. The development of theoretical structures dealing with the complex genetic, biochemical, psychological, social, and cultural factors that intertwine to affect drinking behavior and that, in turn, can explain problems around drinking behavior is a basic requirement in any comprehensive understanding of youthful drinking practices.

Knowledge of facts and the manner in which they are conceptualized, especially with regard to socially problematic behaviors, is a necessary step in developing effective and consistent social policy. With this in mind, we undertook to review the current state of the art with regard to public policy formulation as it impacts on alcohol and youth and to explore the new directions in policy development.

Policy is the forerunner of social action. Conceptually sophisticated programs for reducing problem behaviors concerning drinking among youth are relatively recent developments. The effectiveness of these programs in minimizing problems is still open to question. Until recently, attempts to evaluate such programs were inadequate to the task, and at this point, it is too soon to tell how effective such programs are. Nevertheless, a great deal is occurring at the program level and we wish to summarize and describe the state of the art.

In essence, then, we attempt to provide in this volume the most recent and up-to-date statement of the epidemiology of drinking behavior and drinking problems among young adults and late adolescents, theories that attempt to explain youthful drinking behavior and the problems associated with such behavior, the social policy implications of youthful drinking practices and problems, and, finally, a review of programs designed toward reducing problems associated with alcohol among young adults and adolescents.

We commissioned 12 experts, 3 in each of the four areas covered by this volume, to prepare background papers on topics relevant to each section. At the conference itself, we asked each author to present a concise summary of the major points made and the conclusions drawn in the background paper. The papers themselves, in published form, were to serve as the fleshed-out empirical and conceptual backup for the summary statements presented at the conference.

This volume, *Youth, Alcohol, and Social Policy*, represents the first in the Health Education Foundation monograph series. Each monograph and publication of the Health Education Foundation will highlight a crucial public and social health area of concern in contemporary society. The series is consistent with the foundation's assumption that the prevention of illness, disease, and premature death and the promotion of socially and physically healthy behaviors can be accomplished through the comprehensive and sophisticated employment of health education strategies and tactics, that is, supplying the public with the awareness and tools that will enable it to choose the lifestyle, job style, and family-style behaviors that will be most health promoting. The evolution of the nature of the foundation is noteworthy in this connection. Many of its members have been responsible for creating and implementing major governmental policies and programs in the health and social welfare field. At the time of its conception, the foundation recognized that the day of innovative government programs had passed and that the future of health care and individual well-being had to come from broader initiatives. The foundation sees its role as a catalyst in mobilizing and bringing together diverse constituencies from the private, public, and voluntary sectors. Concerning the potential value of health education and communications in prevention, the foundation views itself as an independent bridge between the public and the private sectors.

The Youth, Alcohol, and Social Policy Conference—and this volume, therefore—represents the first in a series of monographs on important public health issues and social problems. The reader may wonder about our choice of alcohol and youth as the topic for our first conference and monograph. We elected to call national attention to this issue because of new data available in this area of universal concern. Also, several members of the foundation have had a long history of involvement with alcohol problems and alcohol-related issues as they affect the body politic. Moreover, we know that when federal programs have focused on youth, they have focused primarily on high school students and teenagers of high school age, with a much smaller thrust at youth of post-high-school age, who, by best available evidence, consume the heaviest amount of alcohol and have the highest incidence of alcohol-related problems of any age group. Governmental programs for post-high-school youth have shown some concentration on college programs but not upon the young adults in the work place or in other sectors of society.

Although young adults are a major target for concern, they have not generated a concomitant public or private response to that concern. The continuing and sometimes hysterical alternative emphasis on high school youth occurs for several reasons. High school students and teenagers of high school age are still at least partially dependent on adults. They beg for our attention and provoke our guilt. They also happen to be a captive audience without an organized voice about what happens to them. Further, we find it relatively simple to attribute the sins of the father to the child. Finally, the conflict between legal status of younger adolescents with regard to alcohol, on the one hand, and the normative behavior that violates this legal status, on the other, complicates the situation, making it more ambiguous and subject to emotional reaction rather than rational assessment. As for post-high-school youth, they are on their own and assert their independence and identity in no uncertain terms. They are less dependent, less to be understood, and less helpless, and while they may need our attention, they are often beyond our appeal. Also, for post-high-school youth—in most jurisdictions within this country, at least—the legal status is clear and unambiguous. Young people are entitled legally to drink. Finally, drinking, and heavy drinking in particular, is valued and socially supported behavior among the majority of young people in the United States.

Considering the general absence of interest in alcohol problems among young adults, it is hardly surprising that no clear and coherent policy has been articulated about alcohol in relation to young adults. Among the purposes of the conference and this volume is the exploration of policy potentials. At the conference itself, we noted an excitement from the moment it began that continued through to its closing session. For once, in a field replete with conventional catechisms, a new perspective and potential were being explored. The conference demonstrated that opportunities regarding health issues lie more in our hands than we had realized. We hope that the reader of this volume will learn from the materials as much as the editors did, and that the reader will experience the excitement that prevailed at the conference itself.

The conference could not have been conducted, nor could this volume have appeared, without the broad support and sponsorship of a number of individuals and groups. It is noteworthy that many of these groups and individuals have had no previous association with issues that involve alcohol. The reason is that the issues and answers in the conference and in this volume go beyond a parochial concern with alcohol. In addition to sponsorship by the Health Education Foundation, the Rockefeller Foundation of New York, whose president, John H. Knowles, is a member of the Health Education Foundation Advisory Board, served as a co-sponsor. The second co-sponsor was the Center for Metropolitan Planning and Research of the Johns Hopkins University, under the direction of Jack Fisher.

Those groups that contributed financial backing to the conference are to be thanked for their generosity and support. The Public Welfare Foundation, a charitable organization in Washington, provided a challenge grant that was the financial impetus for creating, organizing, and implementing the concept of the conference. Although the Public Welfare Foundation does not generally support conferences or work on alcohol, its president, Davis Haines, and its board member, Edgar Berman, accommodated their priorities when they recognized an obvious social need that had to be met.

The kindness and responsive concern of the following individuals and organizations to match the challenge grant made the conference a reality: Lucian Wulsin, Chairman of the Board of Baldwin-United, and an advisory board member of the Health Education Foundation; Rudi Vignone, Director of Governmental Relations of Goodyear Tire and Rubber; John Dilucca, President of the Wine Institute; Gene Hollen of Johnson and Johnson; Henry King of the United States Brewers Association; and John Keller and Joan Kroc of Operation Cork. In addition to those who contributed direct financial support, other individuals and organizations provided support services of one sort or another. We are particularly indebted in this regard to the Psychiatric Institutes of America for staff support, Diana MacArthur of Consumer Dynamics, Inc., for advice in conference planning, and Kathleen Lipnicky of the University of Pittsburgh, for her secretarial services.

We are also indebted to Mark Keller, Editor Emeritus of the *Journal of Studies on Alcohol* and noted scholar in the field, and Maureen Carroll, Director of the National Center for Alcohol Education, for their thoughtful comments and adherence to rules of order during the sessions they chaired during the conference.

Finally, and leaving the best to the end, we are totally indebted to Marion Chafetz and Gail Dickersin of the foundation, whose devoted services in developing, planning, carrying out, and managing the complex day-to-day operations involved in the conduct of any conference cannot be fully enough acknowledged. They handled the plethora of details attached to running such a conference with skill, responsibility, and conscientiousness, providing a model for all to follow. We cannot thank them too much.

I

Epidemiology of Drinking Practices among Adolescents and Young Adults

Investigations of drinking practices and associated behaviors among young people have typically been conducted in settings convenient to the social scientist. Thus, studies of adolescents have usually been conducted in high schools, with their captive populations; studies of young adults have, for the most part, been conducted in college settings, which in addition to containing captive populations, have the advantage of being the researcher's home territory. Relatively few studies of young people in the general population exist, and we know of none in the work place. In recent years, drinking among military personnel has been surveyed, and since men and women in the service are relatively young on average, the results provide another source of information about drinking among young adults.

The three chapters that constitute Part I cover the research that has been conducted in each of these areas. Howard Blane contrasts the drinking characteristics of late adolescents and young adults with those observed among middle-aged alcoholics. He draws heavily on research examining drinking among 18- to 24-year-old men and women in college, military, and general population surveys and contrasts the rates of alcohol-related problems in young people and older adults. Henry Wechsler presents recent findings from studies that he and his research team at the Medical Foundation have carried out with high school, college, and general population samples in the Greater Boston and New England area. Much of this work represents new information. J. Michael Polich discusses past research in military samples, particularly those from the U.S. Army and U.S. Navy studies conducted by the Social Research Group in Washington and Berkeley, reanalyzing these previous data and comparing them with more recent findings obtained from surveys of U.S. Air Force personnel.

The conclusions that may be drawn from the three chapters are amazingly consistent and convergent, demonstrating a high rate of adverse consequences from drinking among young adults. The normative pattern appears as one of frequent drinking occasions with large amounts of alcohol consumed per occasion, thus increasing the overall level of risk for the occurrence of alcohol-related problems.

This is not to say that divergences in the data and in the interpretation of results do not occur. Nevertheless, all agree that heavy drinking in late adolescence and young adulthood has no strongly predictable linkage to later problem drinking or the development of alcoholism. That is to say, many of the alcohol-related problems of young adulthood are circumscribed and do not manifest themselves later in life. This observation is, of course, offset by research that shows that a certain proportion of youthful problem drinkers do indeed mature into alcoholics in later adulthood. The review by Blane suggests that young women do not have the level of problems that characterize young men. However, the studies that Blane reviewed suggest that women may be prone to alcohol problems associated with frequent heavy drinking somewhat later in life, but still before middle age. Blane's conclusions regarding sex differences differ from those of Wechsler, whose more recent data suggest that young women may indeed be becoming more prone to the kinds of problem consequences of heavy drinking that characterize young men. Polich, on the basis of an analysis of U.S. Air Force data and a reanalysis of U.S. Army and U.S. Navy data, suggests that the high problem-drinking rates observed among young military men are more attributable to sex and marital status than to age *per se*. When Polich controlled for marital status and sex, he found that age differentials in problem rates went down considerably. Nevertheless, there is no question that rates among the military are generally higher than those among civilian young adults.

Other factors that cut across all chapters include the need for careful definitions and the need to develop common means of measuring both alcohol use and problems associated with alcohol. The failure to have a common frame of reference with regard to definitions and measurement opens the door to misinterpretations of data or interpretations of data based on unscientific criteria. One of the most needed methodological refinements is a consistency of measurement across high school and post-high-school investigations, so that the degree of continuity or discontinuity in drinking problems can be studied empirically. As things stand now, it is extremely difficult to make direct comparisons across high school and post-high-school samples, because the criteria for heavy drinking or problem drinking differ so much between high school and post-high-school studies.

Although commonality of definition and measurement is largely lacking, it does appear that drinking levels and problems associated with drinking are less in high school than in post-high-school youth. Blane attempts to account for this by arguing that alcoholic beverages are not as readily available to high school as to post-high-school youth, that high-schoolers spend most of their lives in settings in which drinking is not permitted, and that the average high school student lives in a world in which the psychological and moral force of adult authority is still extremely compelling. Each of these brakes on drinking behavior fades rapidly when the student graduates or leaves high school.

Another theme that emerges from each of the chapters is the salience of drinking among late adolescents and young adults. They clearly form the core of a society that values drinking behavior, and not simply drinking itself but frequent drinking in relatively large amounts, that is to say, four or more drinks at least once a week. This prevailing attitude signifies that any policy development about alcohol among young adults must take into account the fact that fairly heavy, frequent drinking is normative and positively valued. Thus, any direct attempts to modify drinking behavior at this population level are doomed to an untimely end.

Both Polich and Wechsler make pleas for caution in interpreting findings from survey data concerning the drinking behavior of young adults. Despite this caveat, each concludes that the weight of the evidence, even when its methodological and conceptual limitations are taken into account, indicates a dangerously high level of problems associated with the use of alcohol among late adolescents and young adults.

The general outlines of the descriptive epidemiology of youthful drinking practices as presented in these chapters are reasonably well established. Obviously, a great deal needs to be done in terms of analytic and experimental epidemiology, but the general parameters of the phenomenon are well identified.

1

Middle-Aged Alcoholics and Young Drinkers

Howard T. Blane

1. Introduction

The ideas and research put forth in this volume depart dramatically from traditional approaches to alcohol problems. They reflect a new sociopolitical consciousness of the interdependent economic, social, behavioral, and medical importance that alcohol, drinking, and behavior coincident with drinking assume in American society. In this chapter, I argue that alcoholics are not the only population with high rates of socially costly alcohol problems: another population shows equally high problem rates entailing equally high social costs. The second population consists of frequent heavy drinkers, drawn largely from among young adults between their immediate post-high-school years and their middle 20s. Many specific problems and conditions characterize both groups, a fact offset partly by disinctive differences in some problems, but mainly by the way problems cluster within or across individuals in each group and, most significantly, by differences in social perceptions concerning alcoholics and frequent heavy drinkers. Despite high problem rates, no public resources have been allocated to the frequent heavy-drinking population; on the contrary, nearly all available resources have been funneled to alcoholics. The wisdom of this *de facto* policy has not been debated.

After describing key features of the alcoholic and the frequent heavy drinker, I will, using available knowledge, explicate the kinds, magni-

Howard T. Blane • School of Education, University of Pittsburgh, Pittsburgh, PA 15260.

tudes, and rates of alcohol-related problems manifested by each and examine methodological, research, and conceptual issues raised by this analysis. There follows an outline of implications that the foregoing analysis has for policy about alcohol and suggestions about program directions.

The sources of the data for the chapter include a comprehensive review (Blane & Hewitt, 1977) of research conducted over the past 30 years concerning alcohol and youth generally; surveys of national, state, and community household samples of the general population; surveys of military samples; and reanalyses of statistical compilations of national health, crime, traffic safety, and population characteristics. The data presented here do not include new findings presented elsewhere in this volume, particularly in Chapters 2 and 3. The chapter, then, may be viewed as a general introduction to our current state of knowledge in the area and a prelude to the chapters to follow.

2. Two Alcohol Problem Populations

2.1. Alcoholics

Traditionally, the frame of reference for alcohol problems has been alcoholism. Even the occasional sorties into the study of drinking behavior in nonalcoholic populations usually have either had an explicit alcoholism focus or held a promise for furthering the understanding of alcoholism. Although alcoholism is viewed as a unitary condition, it, like cancer, has been internally differentiated by a variety of diagnostic and clinical subtypes (e.g., essential versus reactive; addictive versus neurotic; dependent versus counterdependent; Jellinek's alpha, beta, gamma, delta, and epsilon "alcoholisms"). Generally considered to be of complex multifaceted origin, alcoholism has been conceptualized in terms of physiological, genetic-constitutional, psychological, and sociological constructs and theories. In the United States, alcoholism is predominantly perceived within a medical framework. The disease model of alcoholism has had a profound pervasive influence on public policy concerning alcohol, so that the predominant orientation toward alcoholism is treatment and rehabilitation within a health services context. Such an orientation not only results in exorbitant financial costs but is restricting with regard to treatment and rehabilitation since alcoholic individuals or treatments not legitimized by the health service model fall outside the scope of the policy. Further, policy based on a disease model is narrow when viewed from the perspective of the range of functions and effects that alcoholic beverages have in contemporary society. A disease model, for example, is little concerned about such alcohol-related problems as traffic safety or domestic violence or about the complex dynamics involved in the economics of the production, sale, and advertising of alcoholic beverages and the public revenues derived therefrom. Finally, since vested interests established by the implementation of a policy serve to reinforce and solidify that policy, there is no reason to suppose that the adherents of a disease model are likely to provide much of the impetus that would be required to broaden its focus.

Most available information about the alcoholic population is based upon cases identified in treatment and law enforcement settings. The population is known to be middle-aged and predominantly male, although it appears that both mean age and male:female ratio are declining gradually. For persons making initial contacts in 1976 at federally supported alcoholism treatment centers serving the general public (n = 61,208), the mean age was 41.8 years with no age difference between men and women; the sex ratio was 3.62 (Reed, 1978). These figures are somewhat lower than those reported in other studies using smaller samples, an observation that may be attributed to the recency of the Reed data compared with those presented in the professional literature or to the fact that the national figures are based on initial contacts, which may include alcoholics *and* nonalcoholics. Presumably, many of the nonalcoholics are spouses of alcoholics; since there are more male than female alcoholics, a majority of the spouses are likely to be wives, and since wives are usually younger than husbands, the mean age of initial contacts would tend to be lower overall; further, the sex ratio would be lower than expected.

Changes over time in age and sex ratio may also be observed in the national statistics, although there are not enough data points to draw definite conclusions. For the three-year period 1975–1977, the mean age of initial contacts has declined steadily each year, with a total decrease of 3.2 years for both men and women (Reed, 1978). An overall decline in the sex ratio may also be observed, but here the decrease is not consistent, being lower in 1976 than in 1977. These shifts over time, particularly in age, appear to be reliable and stable estimates, barring changes from year to year in the requirements for reporting ages.

In addition to being a male disorder of middle age, alcoholism is characterized by a concentration in the affected individual of multiple, longstanding problems that pervade all aspects of his life. These psychological, social, interpersonal, economic, and medical problems are so well known that we do not need to recatalog them here. There are, however, three aspects of the alcoholic's condition that are important for the present discussion; the first has already been mentioned: the pervasiveness and chronicity of the alcoholic's condition. A predictable, unremitting cycle of negative behaviors and occurrences characterizes the life of the alcoholic, combined with activities that are in one way or another increasingly self-destructive. Even the remissions of the binge drinker are fraught with expectations of another dreaded bout. Second, alcohol is a governing force in the alcoholic's life, centralizing and organizing the routine of daily existence. All duties and responsibilities as well as leisure and recreation are secondary to the apparent preoccupation with alcohol. This seems to be the case regardless of the individual's drinking pattern, whether it be steady, episodic, or binge. A third feature of alcoholism involves its consequences for physical health, especially among those alcoholics who have been daily or near-daily consumers of large amounts of absolute alcohol (i.e., five or more ounces) for periods of 10–15 years or longer. Liver disease occurs among 20% of alcoholics; many other physical illnesses have also been implicated, but their rates are generally considerably lower. Nevertheless, a mounting body of evidence indicates that chronic, regular intake of large amounts of alcohol is deleterious to physical health. The most dramatic evidence may be found in the lower life expectancy rates for alcoholics (de Lint & Schmidt, 1977; Schmidt & Popham, 1976).

2.2. Frequent Heavy Drinkers

The data base for identifying frequent heavy drinkers is at once less certain and more comprehensive than that for alcoholics: less certain because its investigations have not covered the possible range of the phenomenon, and more comprehensive because its principal methodological technique, the survey, has been applied to random samples of the general population. The data base has the additional advantage of using measures that are comparable across studies. Generally speaking, frequent heavy drinking refers to a pattern of drinking in which relatively large amounts of alcohol are consumed per occasion and occasions are spaced relatively frequently over time. A standard technical definition is drinking five or more drinks of any alcoholic beverage at least as often as once a week (Room, 1972). This frequent heavy drinking index, developed by Cahalan (1970) and later refined by Blane (1977), is a major component of Cahalan's Index of Frequent Intoxication, which has been used as an indicator of potential drinking problems. In its general sense, frequent heavy drinking may also be indicated by any one of a number of related measures, some of which use more severe and some less severe criteria than the index of frequent heavy drinking.

Heavy intake (Cahalan & Cisin, 1975) and very heavy intake (Durning & Jansen, 1975) are more stringent measures; peak drinking (Blane, 1977), high maximum, and high volume (Cahalan, Cisin, & Crossley, 1969) are less stringent measures. Further, there is a series of measures that connote the general meaning of frequent heavy drinking and may, therefore, be taken as indirect measures of it. These include such measures as frequency of intoxication, frequency of hangovers, binge drinking, and symptomatic drinking (Cahalan & Cisin, 1976b).

Frequent heavy drinking, like alcoholism, occurs more often among men than among women but, unlike alcoholism, finds its highest rates among young adult males, 18–25 years old. Further, as we shall see, it appears that frequent heavy drinking peaks in the 18- to 20-year age range. In the sections below, I present the evidence for these assertions, based upon results of surveys of general population samples, college youth, military personnel, and ethnic subgroups. While there are gaps in the available information, the convergence of estimates from different sources is impressive and lends support to these conclusions.

Before proceeding to this evidence, however, there are several characteristics of frequent heavy drinking among young adults that may serve both to distinguish it from and relate it to alcoholism. The first three of these characteristics may be placed in counterpoint to the three aspects of alcoholism discussed above: chronicity and pervasiveness, alcohol as a life-centralizing theme, and the physical health consequences of prolonged and steady drinking.

Frequent heavy drinking is not chronic in the sense of being continuous nor pervasive in the sense of affecting all spheres of the individual's life. Heavy drinking may occur several times a week, and the consquences of drinking may indeed affect a person's life, but intake is episodic and occurs within a more-or-less conventionally ordered lifestyle. More critically, perhaps, alcohol is not a guiding principle in the frequent heavy drinker's life. Drinking episodes are self-limiting and circumscribed events that occur independently of other significant life events. Important for the moment, they recede into the background of one's existence as other activities come to the fore. Further, the consequences to physical health of frequent heavy drinking stem from the acute consequences of alcohol intake, such as hangovers, blackouts, and gastritis. Except for fatal overdose and the fetal alcohol syndrome, these are all temporary and as far as is known not ultimately hazardous to health, unless they occur in the context of heavy, almost daily intake over many years.

Another aspect of frequent heavy drinking is that it appears largely as a self-limiting condition that moderates with age, probably peaking at 18–20 years of age and declining steadily thereafter. The question of the relationship between youthful heavy drinking and later alcoholism is important in this connection, and relevant research is discussed in Section 3.3. For present purposes, it is important to note that considerable overlap exists between the behavioral manifestations of chronic alcoholism and those of frequent heavy drinking. On the variable of drinking alone, one could well argue that frequent heavy drinking is at best a special case of alcoholism, since all alcoholics would be classed as frequent heavy drinkers by the technical definition. Making a distinction between the acute and the chronic effects of alcohol is useful in this regard. Traditional definitions of alcoholism stress the social, behavioral, and physical effects of repeated use of alcohol in large amounts over long periods of time; single large doses of alcohol are also considered but are insufficient for a diagnosis of alcoholism. Frequent heavy drinkers are a group at risk for suffering acute physical effects of alcohol, behavioral concomitants of intoxication (incoordination and disinhibition, including belligerence, crying, "silliness," raucousness, impulsive behavior, poor judgment), and negative social and interpersonal consequences (fights, impaired driving ability, fractured relationships with friends and relatives, destruction of property, job difficulties, arrests or other involvement with police). Some of the behaviors enumerated are identical to behaviors that contribute to a diagnosis of alcoholism, particularly those in the area of social and interpersonal consequences. Given this partial coincidence of acute and chronic behavioral signs, it becomes only too easy to confound them in attempting to distinguish alcoholics from frequent heavy drinkers who are not alcoholic. In applying clinical definitions of alcoholism to young adults, particular care is required not to confuse occasional with regularly repeated social and interpersonal consequences. A positive diagnosis of alcoholism can be made only in the presence of substantial chronic effects; acute effects in the absence of chronic effects do not warrant a diagnosis of alcoholism.

These considerations of similarity between alcoholism and frequent heavy drinking bring into focus another set of conditions that distinguish the two. In alcoholism, many problems and adverse consequences of drinking manifest for long periods of time are concentrated in a single individual; that is, the alcoholic shows many of the psychological, physical, and social concomitants of alcoholism. The young frequent heavy drinker, on the other hand, consistently shows one or a few adverse consequences, but typically a great many signs, each persisting over time, do not cluster in a single individual. It appears that there are many more frequent heavy drinkers than alcoholics in the general population. Taking this disparity and the differential clustering of problems, it would appear that the prevalence of problems related to acute effects of drinking is at least as great if not higher among frequent heavy drinkers than among alcoholics. In later sections (3.1 and 3.2) that examine prevalence rates for selected alcohol-related problems, this hypothesis concerning problem rates for the two populations is tested. In the immediately following sections (2.2.1.–2.2.5.), research relating to the age and sex distribution of frequent heavy drinking is reviewed.

2.2.1. *General Population Surveys*

Combining data from two national surveys of 1,561 men aged 21–59 years conducted in 1967 and 1969, Cahalan and Cisin (1976b) found that the proportion of 21- to 24-year-old men reporting heavy intake and binge drinking was as high as and in most instances higher than any other age group. The sharpest declines occurred between the 21- to 24-year-old and the 25- to 29-year-old groups for binge drinking (10% versus 3%). The effects for heavy drinking were less marked but in no other age group exceeded the percentage of 7% noted in the 21- to 24-year-old group. Similarly, Schaps and Rubin (1975), in a 1973 survey of Pennsylvania respondents, found that 12% of 20- to 24-year-old men and women reported drinking an average of four or more drinks per day, a rate higher than found for any other age group. And a 1975 household survey (Wechsler, Demone, & Gottlieb, 1978) of metropolitan Boston adults 18 years of age or older reported the highest proportions of heavy drinkers in the 18- to 24-year-old group for both men and women; however, the criteria used in this study to classify respondents as heavy drinkers, identical to those of Cahalan, Cisin, and Crossley (1969) in their 1967 national survey, are considerably less rigorous than the criterion of five or more drinks at least once a week that defines frequent heavy drinking.

Two separate surveys (Cahalan & Treiman, 1976) of California and San Francisco residents showed somewhat different results. Intoxication experience (drunk at least once a month) was higher among 25- to 29-year-old men than 18- to 24-year-old men in both studies (40% and 45%, respectively, versus 37% and 43%). However, these rates of intoxication were higher than for any older age group. Women 18–24 years old, on the other hand, showed the highest intoxication rates (13% and 25%, respectively) among women. It is interesting to note the higher San Francisco rates, which support the concept of urban–rural differences in drinking practices.

Other findings of the San Francisco survey relative to frequent heavy drinking are also less consistent with results of the other studies, cited above, for both men and women. Thus, while more young men

(18–24 years) obtained high symptomatic-drinking scores (26%) than older men (21%), more 30- to 59-year-old men had high heavy-intake scores (37%) than young men (32%) and more 40- to 49-year-old men had high binge-drinking scores (8%) than young men (6%). A similar result obtains for women, with a higher percentage of 30- to 39-year-old women falling into the high intake-, binge-, and symptomatic-drinking categories (20%, 3%, and 21%, respectively). Parenthetically, it should be remarked that the scoring criteria used in the San Francisco survey are not as severe as those used in the national survey data cited above, so that percentages based on the scores are not directly comparable.

With regard to sex differentials, frequent heavy drinking is more characteristic of men than of women, although sex ratios tend to be lower among younger age groups. Room (1972) examined the prevalence of frequent heavy drinking among several general population samples; secondary analysis of his findings reveals sex ratios ranging from 2.5:1 for the Pacific coastal states to 7.5:1 among "middle Americans" (white, married Christians) in inland cities. Schaps and Rubins (1975) reported a 4.6:1 ratio for drinking an average of four or more drinks per day in Pennsylvania. While neither of these studies presents data on age separately for men and women, results of other studies (Cahalan *et al.*, 1969; Wechsler *et al.*, 1978; Cahalan & Treiman, 1976) indicate lower sex ratios among young adults. Ratios for heavy drinking were 2.4:1 for 21- to 24-year-olds nationally in 1964–1965 (Cahalan *et al.*, 1969) and 2.6:1 for 18- to 24-year-olds in Boston in 1975 (Wechsler *et al.*, 1978). For monthly intoxication, Cahalan and Treiman (1976) reported ratios of 1.7:1 among San Francisco residents in 1975 and 2.9:1 for California residents in 1974. All these ratios are lower than those reported for the entire sample; further, other measures of drinking practices related to frequent heavy drinking showed similar trends.

2.2.2. *Studies of College Drinking*

Blane and Hewitt (1977) reviewed 68 surveys of college drinking practices conducted between 1936 and 1975. None of the studies conducted in recent years (since 1966) assessed drinking practices in a manner that permits direct comparison with surveys of the general population. The one measure that casts some light on frequent heavy drinking is intoxication experience. The average prevalence of one episode of intoxication during college is 55% for five surveys (Bowers, 1971; Sanford & Singer, 1968; University of Massachusetts Alcohol Task Force, 1975). This estimate is conservative since it includes some studies that used period prevalence rates for the past month or year rather than for the entire college career, which averages out to approximately two years. For example, one study (University of Massachusetts Alcohol Task Force, 1975), conducted in 1974, found a prevalence rate of 58% for a one-month period.

Since the Blane and Hewitt review, a report by Engs (1977) has appeared with data on 1,128 college men and women from 13 institutions of higher learning across the country. Engs's definition of heavy drinkers coincides exactly with that employed here for frequent heavy drinking: drinking five or more drinks more than once a week. She reported that 20% of the men and 4% of the women fell into the heavy drinker category. Engs also reported lifetime prevalence rates and one-year–period prevalence rates for hangovers of 58% and 74%, respectively. These indirect indicators of frequent heavy drinking are comparable to average intoxication experience as reported in the Blane and Hewitt review.

Generally speaking, these figures are somewhat higher than the general population rates cited above for California and San Francisco, but differences in sampling, methodology, and scoring criteria make hard-and-fast comparative statements hazardous. More recent data on college drinking, based on a large sample of regional institutions of higher learning, are presented in the next chapter.

2.2.3. *Military Samples*

Only one study (Durning & Jansen, 1975) of military personnel has reported findings on frequent heavy drinking variables separately for young servicemen. Durning and Jansen surveyed 2,045 male naval recruits (mean age = 19.3 years; 90% of the sample fell between the ages of 17 and 20) in 1973–1974. Of these recruits, 46% reported heavy intake, 27% binge drinking, and 35% symptomatic drinking, each following the definitions used by Cahalan and Cisin (1976b) in the 1967–1969 national surveys. It may be noted that civilian rates for 21- to 24-year-old men are considerably lower on all three indices (heavy intake: 7% for civilians versus 46% for naval recruits; binge drinking: 10% versus 27%; symptomatic drinking: 26% versus 35%).

These major discrepancies are subject to at least three nonmutually exclusive interpretations: (a) changes in drinking practices between 1967–1969 and 1973–1974; (b) heavier drinking in 17- to 20-year-old men; (c) heavier drinking among enlisted military men than among men in the general population. Analytic reviews of changes in drinking practices over time among high school and college students conducted by Blane and Hewitt (1977) suggest that major increases in drinking practices between 1966 and 1975 are unlikely. With regard to age-linked differences in frequent heavy drinking, however, I have already noted findings that indicate that post-high-school youth contribute most heavily to this pattern of alcohol consumption, and, subsequently, I will present additional data on the point. Furthermore, other evidence indicates heavier drinking among servicemen and servicewomen than among civilians, differences particularly noticeable within younger age ranges.

Other surveys (Cahalan & Cisin, 1975; Cahalan, Cisin, Gardner, & Smith, 1972) of military personnel have presented composite classifications of drinking problems by age that enable direct comparisons between military groups and between military and civilian samples (allowing for slight variations in criteria for classification from study to study). The current problem-drinking index developed by Cahalan and Cisin (1976b) is one such classification based on self-reported interpersonal, health, or financial problems consequent to drinking. While not a direct measure of frequent heavy drinking, the index does presuppose episodic heavy consumption. The results of studies using this index are summarized in Table 1 for males and in Table 2 for females.

Table 1 shows a clear-cut regression in problems by age for both U.S. Army and U.S. Navy enlisted men, with the highest rates in the 17- to 20-year age range and the lowest in the oldest age group. In addition, military rates are considerably higher than civilian rates,

Table 1. Male Current Problem Drinkers by Age (in Percentages)[a,b]

	Naval enlisted 1974		Army enlisted 1972		Civilian national survey 1969		Civilian San Francisco 1975	
Age group	*n*	%	*n*	%	*n*	%	*n*	%
17–20	788	46	1,007	53	—	—		
							73	21
21–24	1,167	43	1,942	42	130	34		
25–29	624	32	898	37	117	17		
							110	7
30–34	523	30	625	30	122	19		
							139	12
35–39	457	29	573	26	124	15		
40–44	116	24	316	25	133	18		
							86	14
45–49	31	10	81	20	114	13		
50 +	6	—	43	7	238	16	89	9

[a] Sources: Cahalan and Cisin (1976b), Table 3, p. 544; Cahalan and Treiman (1976), Table 8, p. 26.
[b] Percentages are based on the past three years for the first three samples and on the past year for the San Francisco sample.

Table 2. Female Current Problem Drinkers by Age (in Percentages)[a,b]

	Naval enlisted 1974		Civilian, national survey 1969		Civilian San Francisco 1975	
Age group	*n*	%	*n*	%	*n*	%
17–20	514	20	—	—	95[c]	5
21–29	626	19	92	3	145[d]	8
30–39	67	12	129	6	153	9
40–49	11	—	157	5	94	5
50–59	6	—	106	2	131	10

[a] Sources: Cahalan and Cisin (1975), Table 36, p.107; Cahalan and Treiman (1976), Table 8, p. 26.
[b] Percentages are based on the past two years for the first two samples and on the past year for the San Francisco sample.
[c] 18–24 years.
[d] 25–29 years.

except at 45 years and older. The consistent decline with age noted in the military samples does not hold for either civilian sample, but peaking in the youngest age group characterizes both civilian and military groups. The female military sample (Table 2) shows a pattern similar to the men's, but it is much weaker and problem drinking does not drop off markedly with age. Both female civilian samples show a pattern dissimilar to the male pattern, with problem drinking peaking in early or late middle age, although the absolute level of problem drinking is so generally low that conclusions must be qualified. These findings suggest that behaviors associated with frequent heavy drinking manifest themselves differently for women than for men. The usual kinds of sex ratios are also apparent, ranging from 2.3:1 for young naval personnel to 4.2:1 and higher for young civilians.

The evidence reported here concerning military samples indicates an extremely high rate of frequent heavy drinking among enlisted personnel, strikingly apparent among young servicemen and possibly among young servicewomen as well. More recent data on drinking practices in the military, with new and recent findings on the U.S. Air Force, are presented in Chapter 3.

2.2.4. *Ethnic Subgroups*

Blane (1975) conducted surveys of drinking practices among 1,473 Italian-Americans and 1,529 Irish-Americans during 1972–1973 in an eastern seaboard city. Frequent heavy drinking, as defined by Cahalan

(1970), was measured for each group by sex and age. The findings (Table 3) show the expected kinds of age differences for both Irish and Italian males and Italian females. Irish females, however, show a pattern more like that inferred from the results of the 1969 national survey (Cahalan *et al.*, 1969) and the San Francisco study (Cahalan & Treiman, 1976) presented earlier, namely, that frequent heavy drinking among women may persist over age or even increase, although this is clearly not the case for Italian females in Blane's study. Findings on sex ratios for frequent heavy drinking are consistent with data from general population, college, and military samples, the overall ratios for Irish (5.8:1) and Italians (5.0:1) being quite similar. Taking age into account, sex ratios for Irish are for the most part lower in the 26- to 40-year age range than in early adulthood, whereas for Italians they are lower in the 18- to 25-year age range.

It may further be noted that frequent heavy drinking rates are much higher generally for Irish than for Italians, particularly among males, and also that frequent heavy drinking is almost nonexistent among Italian females over the age of 40, with only 3 (1%) frequent heavy drinkers out of 327 women interviewed. These national ethnic differences are quite congruent with other research on drinking practices among Americans of Irish or Italian descent. Cahalan and Cisin (1976b), for example, summarized data showing that Irish are higher and Italians lower than general population samples on such measures as symptomatic and binge drinking and on other indices of problem drinking.

These data on ethnic subgroups further support the thesis that frequent heavy drinking characterizes young adults more than other age

Table 3. Irish-American and Italian-American Frequent Heavy Drinkers by Sex and Age (in Percentages)

	Irish-American				Italian-American			
	Male		Female		Male		Female	
Age Group	*n*	%	*n*	%	*n*	%	*n*	%
17–20	64	58	45	11	131	30	95	10
21–25	152	68	99	7	166	21	106	8
26–30	111	51	71	14	87	29	45	4
31–40	136	50	112	13	119	11	82	5
41–50	161	51	158	9	106	22	138	0
51–60	114	42	107	6	108	10	93	2
61–70	80	35	67	10	70	19	64	0
70 +	11	46	41	5	31	13	32	3
Total	829	52	700	9	818	20	655	4

groups in our society. But the finding of marked differences between the two groups highlights the importance of other mediating factors. Not only is national-ethnic background important, but current life status (college, working, military service, unemployed), race, marital status, socioeconomic status, geographic region, and urbanization have all been shown to be related to the patterning of frequent heavy drinking and related behaviors among young adults.

In addition to the survey findings on various types of samples noted in the preceding sections, further support is available in studies (e.g., Cosper & Mozersky, 1968; Harford & Mills, 1978; Vogel-Sprott, 1974) that demonstrate that the amount of alcohol consumed per drinking occasion decreases linearly with age from the middle and late teens onward. With regard to the frequency with which drinking occasions occur, Cosper and Mozersky (1968) and Vogel-Sprott (1974) reported a curvilinear relationship to age showing that frequency increases and then declines with age. Harford and Mills (1978), on the other hand, reported a linear increase in frequency with age; this discrepant finding may reflect the fact that Harford's adult sample consisted of at least monthly drinkers, thereby truncating the distribution of frequency of drinking occasions. Nevertheless, drinking occurs often enough among young adults (according to Harford and Mills, 6–11 times a month among males aged 16–25 years) so that, taken in combination with typically large quantities consumed at a sitting, one can infer high levels of frequent heavy drinking.

2.2.5. *Empirical and Conceptual Issues*

This brief review of frequent heavy drinking among young adults raises both empirical and conceptual questions. It (a) points out gaps in the research evidence concerning youthful drinking; (b) raises the question of the relationship of drinking behavior among high school students to frequent heavy drinking among post-high-school youth; and (c) highlights the use of age as a variable in attempts to understand a behavior with obvious developmental features.

Concerning the need for additional information, it is clear that the extent and the generalizability of the evidence on the peaking of frequent heavy drinking in the late teens is not all that one would desire, being based largely upon surveys of the military and ethnic subgroups and on indirectly applicable data from college surveys. Indeed, one of the two general population surveys (Cahalan & Treiman, 1976) that included 18- to 20-year-old respondents reported data not entirely consistent with the thesis of frequent heavy drinking among late adolescents; and Blane's survey (1975) of two national-ethnic groups also shows some inconsistencies. Surveys of drinking behavior, using comparable measures, are needed on young adults in the general population, in the work place, and in colleges and universities. Further research is also needed to obtain information other than that derived from surveys about relevant drinking-related behaviors, including observational data on actual drinking behavior in bars, at parties, and in other settings; sales data; blood alcohol concentration levels; and careful estimates of the role that drinking effects have in problems that are usually thought to be closely linked with alcohol use (e.g., automobile accidents, domestic strife, violence).

In the foregoing, I have concentrated on demonstrating that frequent heavy drinking is most prominent among young adults from their post-high-school years through their mid-20s, with peaking occurring in the late adolescent years. Generally, when drinking problems and youth are juxtaposed, one's mind fixes upon high school drinking. Although comparable information is not readily available, a tremendous amount of research has been conducted over the years concerning high school drinking. A thoroughgoing review of this body of research by Blane and Hewitt (1977) indicates that while frequent heavy drinking indeed occurs among high school youth, its prevalence is considerably less than among post-high-school youth. In most instances, heavy drinking episodes do not occur often enough to qualify as frequent heavy drinking. Harford and Mills's (1978) study of age in relation to frequency of drinking occurrences and quantity consumed per occasion supports such a conclusion. While average quantity per occasion is high among older high school students, frequency of drinking occasions does not rise sharply until 18 years of age.

The conditions of being a high school student probably influence and shape the quality of drinking, tending to keep it more moderate than not. Alcoholic beverages are not as readily available to high school as to post-high-school youth, by virtue of economic and legal constraints: high-schoolers don't have as much money, and their purchase of alcoholic beverages is against the law (these are, of course, relatively inhibiting factors; for the person determined to drink, questions of cost or legality form no barrier). Also, high-schoolers spend much of their daily lives in settings in which either drinking itself is taboo (the school) or heavy drinking is not permitted (the home). Further, and independent of formal and informal controls, the high school student lives in a world in which the psychological and moral force of adult authority is still extremely compelling. These general social conditions that surround the role of high school students tend to reinforce not drinking at all or drinking moderately and to inhibit heavy drinking. That other powerful forces are also operative is obvious from the fact that high-schoolers do drink excessively and sometimes do so repetitively. The point is that these brakes built into the high school student's life either disappear or fade considerably after he leaves high school, allowing for greater play in drinking behavior.

For the person who enters the military service, the status shift with regard to controls over drinking is probably the most extreme. After an initial period of enforced abstinence, drinking is not only legitimate but virtually obligatory. Learning how to hold one's liquor is a highly valued goal among servicemen and provides a commendable reason for drinking more than one can handle. In addition, the recruit has money to buy alcoholic beverages, which are themselves cheaper in the military. Under these conditions, it is little wonder that the highest rates of frequent heavy drinking are observed among the youngest members of the armed forces. At the opposite extreme is the person who continues to live at home and either works or commutes to college. Though the home still exerts a conservative influence, the power of adult authority represented in the parents changes mutually with the person's newly conferred adult status. Correspondingly, ranges of behavior that were previously less acceptable now become more acceptable. Further, the values of the work place or the college, which are oriented to the person as an adult with adult prerogatives, such as drinking, complement the changes within the home. While the young person in this situation does not have an open invitation to drink heavily, previous constraints are much reduced. It remains to be determined empirically, but frequent heavy drinking rates in this group would presumably be among the lowest. Between these two extremes are those young adults who leave home to go to college, to get an apartment, to work in another region, or to establish a family. All of these alternatives carry with them more opportunity and more freedom to drink heavily.

This discussion of the lesser role of frequent heavy drinking among high school students than among post-high-school young adults raises the question of the role of age in relation to drinking. Much of the analysis conducted in this chapter relies on age as a critical independent variable. It needs to be stated that age as an independent variable is no more than a convenient index or marker and does not carry the causal implications usually associated with independent variables. This distinction is obvious from the preceding paragraphs, in which the concepts of role, status, and role transition were viewed as useful in establishing a broad set of social conditions that influence changes in drinking behavior. An explanatory analysis, as contrasted to the descriptive analysis presented here, would, to be fruitful in advancing our understanding, focus not on age as a critical variable but on concepts such as role, status, and transition or some other set of variables in which the linkages between the concepts and the behavior could be specified in sufficient detail so that differential predictions could be made; in the area of development of drinking behavior see, for example, Jessor and Jessor (1975), Riester and Zucker (1968), and Chapters 4–6 in this volume.

3. Problem Rates in Young Adulthood and Middle Age

In a preceding section, the hypothesis was advanced that prevalence of alcohol-related problems dependent on the acute effects of drinking are just as great if not greater among frequent heavy drinkers than among alcoholics. Ideally, a direct test of this hypothesis would identify random samples of nonalcoholic frequent heavy drinkers and alcoholics and compare the prevalence of problem rates between the two samples. For purposes of this presentation, another approach was adopted. National statistics on selected problems were used to establish age- and sex-specific rates per 100,000 population for 18- to 24-year-old and 35- to 54-year-old males and females in the general population. These groups were chosen on the assumption, empirically supported by data presented in Sections 2.1 and 2.2, that frequent heavy drinking is concentrated in the younger age range, while alcoholism is concentrated in the older age range. Actually, we know that neither range is "pure"; that is, the younger group contains some alcoholics and the older group contains some nonalcoholic frequent heavy drinkers. The proportions are uncertain but may be estimated to be between 5% and 10% for alcoholics in the younger group (Reed, 1978; Smart & Finley, 1978) and around 10% for frequent heavy drinkers in the older group (Blane, 1975).

Two sets of alcohol-related problems were distinguished, those that could be directly attributed to alcohol or the effects of drinking and those in which the relationship to alcohol is more tangential and not necessarily causative, but in which alcohol or drinking is known to be frequently implicated. Problems directly attributable to alcohol include cirrhosis mortality, inpatient–outpatient episodes of care for alcohol abuse, drunkenness, fatal injuries among drunken drivers, driving while intoxicated, and liquor law violations. Problems not directly attributable to alcohol include disorderly conduct, vandalism, serious crimes against persons (murder, manslaughter, aggravated assault, and robbery), other assaults, rape, sex offenses, prostitution and commercialized vice, offenses against family and children, divorce, accident mortality (including motor vehicle fatalities), and suicide. The selection of these problems was largely a function of the availability of aggregate information about them; clearly, other problems might have as great importance as the ones selected but, in the absence of large data bases, were not included. The operational definitions of these problems and the procedures followed in collecting information about them are described in the following sections.

3.1. Problems Directly Attributable to Alcohol

Of the six problems directly attributable to alcohol, three predominantly reflect acute effects of alcohol (drunken-driver crash mortality, drunkenness, and driving while intoxicated), two reflect the chronic effects of alcohol or alcoholism (liver cirrhosis mortality, inpatient admissions for alcohol abuse), and one (liquor law violations) is a highly age-linked variable. Information about these problems was gathered for the year 1976, the most recent year for which data were generally available; when information is from another year, it is so indicated. When the source of information categorized age differently from the 18- to 24- and 35- to 54-year age ranges, I adopted various conventions, depending on how the information was reported; these variations are noted.

Precise definitions, source of information, and quality of estimate for each of the six problems are as follows:

(a) Liver cirrhosis mortality: deaths in 1975 caused by cirrhosis of the liver (U.S. Bureau of the Census, 1977); reporting is complete with fairly standard criteria.

(b) Fatal injuries among drunken drivers: a complex national estimate of the total number of fatally injured drivers in 1975 with blood alcohol concentrations (BACs) of 0.10% or higher (Jones, 1977); the estimate is based on three studies conducted in three states in about 1970, studies considered among the "more reliable epidemiologic studies." Jones reported data for 16- to 19- and 20- to 24-year-old age groups. For purposes of the present report, I assumed that fatalities and number of licensed drivers were equal for each year of age in the 16- to 19-year-old group; this assumption permitted me to estimate rates for 18- to 19-year-olds, incorporate them with rates for 20- to 24-year-olds, and so obtain an estimate for the 18- to 24-year-old group. Given the rather extensive chain of manipulations that led to the final estimates, results based on them should be viewed with caution.

(c) Inpatient–outpatient episodes of care for alcohol abuse in all psychiatric facilities: patient care episodes for 1971, the most recent year available for patients having alcoholic diagnoses, that is, alcoholism, alcoholic psychosis, or nonpsychotic organic brain syndrome with alcohol (National Institute of Mental Health, 1973). Information is available for the 18- to 24-year age group, but the presentation of data for older age groups does not conform to the 35- to 54-year age range used in the present report, and there was no satisfactory way of creating a reliable estimate. Therefore, the data in Table 4 for the older age group covers 25- to 44-year-olds. It may be noted that the 45- to 64-year-old rates are higher than those for 25- to 44-year-olds and that there is a sharp drop in the last age group, 65 years and older. Except for outpatient psychiatric services of Veterans Administration hospitals, the reporting is fairly complete, with reasonably standard criteria.

(d) Drunkenness: arrests for drunkenness in 1976 as reported to the Federal Bureau of Investigation by the uniform crime reporting system (Federal Bureau of Investigation, 1977; U.S. Bureau of the Census, 1977); reporting does not cover all jurisdictions, but the criteria are fairly standard.

(e) Driving while intoxicated (DWI): as for drunkenness above.

(f) Liquor law violations: as for drunkenness above. Violations of liquor laws may involve any of a wide range of activities ranging from smuggling and illegal production to purchase or possession by a minor; it appears that infractions involving minors comprise the bulk of the liquor law violations.

Table 4 shows age- and sex-specific rates per 100,000 population for each of the six problems for males and females in the 18- to 24- and the 35- to 54-year age ranges. Of the three problems related to acute effects of alcohol, two (drunken driver mortality and DWI arrests) conform to expectations, both being greater in the young adult than in the middle-aged population. Drunkenness arrests, on the other hand, show higher rates in the middle-aged population. Cirrhosis death rates and psychi-

Table 4. Age- and Sex-Specific Rates for Selected Problems Directly Attributable to Alcohol among 18- to 24- and 35- to 54-Year-Old Males and Females (per 100,000)[a]

	Males		Females	
Problem	18–24	35–54	18–24	35–54
1. Liver cirrhosis mortality	<1	36	<1	18
2. Drunken driver mortality	37[b]	26[b]	—	—
3. Care episodes for alcohol abuse	117	520[c]	18	131[c]
4. Drunkenness	1,542	1,727	120	125
5. Driving while intoxicated	1,728[b]	1,276[b]	123	92
6. Liquor law violations	772	109	128	17

[a] See text for sources.
[b] Rates per 100,000 licensed drivers.
[c] Rates for 25- to 44-year age group.

atric care episodes, both reflections of chronic alcoholism, have higher rates, as expected, among the older population. Arrests for liquor law violations have a much higher rate among young adults, reflecting the age-linked characteristics of this measure. The rates throughout are higher for men than for women, in accord with what we know about sex differences in alcohol problems generally. It is of interest, however, to note that the population ratios of young adults to people of middle-age for each problem (except drunken driver mortality, where an estimate for females was not available) are approximately the same for men and women, suggesting that although the level of prevalence of problems differs markedly between sexes, the structure according to age is stable.

It has been argued previously that high school students do not contribute as much to the frequent heavy drinking population as post-high-school young adults. It follows that their problem rates should also be lower. Where possible, we have calculated rates for 16- and 17-year-olds, on the assumption that most will be in high school and with the caveat that for problems involving arrests, there may be some underreporting since 16- and 17-year-olds are treated as juveniles in some jurisdictions. Rates for 16- and 17-year-olds for drunken driver mortality, drunkenness arrests, and DWI arrests are all lower by a considerable margin than for the 18- to 24-year-old population. Thus, the average rate for drunken driver mortality for 16- to 17-year-old males is 17, compared to 37 for 18- to 24-year-olds; for drunkenness arrests, it is 650 versus 1,542; and for DWI arrests it is 486 versus 1,728. Further examination by year shows that 16-year-olds have lower rates than 17-year-olds. Arrests for liquor law violations, on the other hand, have considerably higher rates among 16- and 17-year-olds (1,644 versus 772), as one would expect given the fact that all 16- and 17-year-olds are minors with regard to liquor laws, whereas only some 18- to 24-year-olds fall into that category.

Questions may also be raised about rates in the 25- to 34-year-old range. In this group, cirrhosis mortality rates rise gradually with age. Rates for arrests for liquor law violations, DWI, and drunkenness in the 25- to 34-year-old population are each lower than in the young adult, 18- to 24-year-old population. Compared to the older 35- to 54-year-old population, the mid-age group shows lower rates of arrest for drunkenness and, among men, for DWI; liquor law violations, on the other hand, are higher in the mid-age group than in the older population.

The age distribution of mortality among drunken drivers deserves special comment since it follows a shape somewhat different from the predicted. Rates are low for 16- to 19-year-olds (17 per 100,000), rise very sharply among 20- to 24-year-olds (44 per 100,000), and then gradually decline over the remaining age range, with a very sharp dropoff after 65 years. Available information does not allow us to examine the 16- to 19-year group year by year, but data on DWI arrests would suggest increases in mortality among 18- and 19-year-olds, with a peak occurring between the ages of 20 and 21 years. Also, the DWI arrest rate for 16- to 17-year-olds, as noted above, is lower than that for 18- to 24-year-olds by a factor of one to four.

In summary, the national data presented and analyzed for problems directly attributable to alcohol and drinking conform to the hypothesis that rates for these problems are at least as great or greater among the young adult population, which contains a disproportionate number of frequent heavy drinkers, than among the middle-aged population, which proportionately contributes more than its share to the total number of alcoholics.

3.2. Problems Indirectly Attributable to Alcohol

Twelve problems indirectly attributable to the use of alcohol were selected for study. All are related to the acute effects of alcohol consumption, although at least two—divorce and suicide—are also traditional concomitants of alcoholism. We used the same conventions here as with direct alcohol problems regarding the year (1976) for which information was gathered, variations from it, and variations in age categorizations.

Precise definitions, source of information, and quality of the estimate for each of the 12 problems are as follows:

(a)–(h) Disorderly conduct, vandalism, serious crimes against persons, other assaults, rape, sex offenses, prostitution and commercialized vice, and offenses against family and children (including nonsupport, neglect, desertion, or abuse): arrests for each of these classes of offenses in 1976 as reported to the Federal Bureau of Investigation by the uniform crime reporting system (Federal Bureau of Investigation, 1977; U.S. Bureau of the Census, 1977); reporting does not cover all jurisdictions, but the reporting criteria are fairly standard. The category of serious crimes against persons includes murder, nonnegligent manslaughter, negligent manslaughter, robbery, and aggravated assault. Unlike the uniform crime reporting system's violent crime index, it does not include rape but does include negligent manslaughter. The sex offenses category does not include rape or prostitution, which are detailed separately.

(i) Divorce: divorce rates for 20- to 24-year-olds in 1970, the most recent year available (Plateris, 1978); no means was available to estimate rates for 18- to 24-year-olds; reporting is complete with standard criteria.

(j) Accident mortality: death due to all types of accidents, including motor vehicle fatalities, in 1976 (U.S. Bureau of the Census, 1977). For the young adult age group, data were available only for 15- to 24-year-olds, inclusive. Estimates cannot be made for 18- to 24-year-olds. Reporting is judged to be complete with fairly stable reporting criteria.

(k) Motor vehicle fatalities: pedestrian and nonpedestrian deaths occurring in motor vehicle accidents in 1972 (U.S. Department of Transportation, 1975); data for the younger group are presented in 15- to 19- and 20- to 24-year-old categories, with no valid means of separating out 18- and 19-year-olds. Results are tabulated for 15- to 24-year-olds combined, and findings for the groups separately are discussed in the text. All data are based on the number of licensed drivers in each age and sex category. Three different estimates of accident mortality related to motor vehicle involvement have been presented, because all estimates are complex, involve different criteria, and are based on data collected at various points in time, ranging from the 1960s to 1976. It was hoped that a more comprehensive and convergent picture would emerge as a consequence of using this approach.

(l) Suicide: suicide rates in 1975 were available for 15- to 24-year-olds, with no feasible way of making an estimate for 18- to 24-year-olds (National Center for Health Statistics, 1977). The level of reporting and the criteria for defining suicide are thought to result in underestimates, but there is no reason to assume an age bias.

Table 5 presents age- and sex-specific rates per 100,000 population

Table 5. Age- and Sex-Specific Rates for Selected Problems Indirectly Attributable to Alcohol among 18- to 24- and 35- to 54-Year-Old Males and Females (per 100,000)[a]

	Males		Females	
Problem	18–24	35–54	18–24	35–54
1. Disorderly conduct	1,239	325	245	60
2. Vandalism	249	37	23	3
3. Serious crimes against persons	715	188	87	25
4. Other assaults	684	254	113	39
5. Rape	60	12	<1	<1
6. Sex offenses	97	43	10	4
7. Prostitution and commercialized vice	72	7	176	15
8. Offenses against family and children	118	56	14	6
9. Divorce	3,360[b]	1,275	3,330[b]	1,020
10. Accident mortality	97[c]	36	24[c]	11
11. Motor vehicle fatalities	96[c,d]	36[d]	35[c]	18
12. Suicide	19[c]	26	5[c]	12

[a] See text for sources.
[b] Rates for 20- to 24-year age group.
[c] Rates for 15- to 24-year age group.
[d] Rates per 100,000 licensed drivers.

for each of the 12 problems for males and females in the 18- to 24- and 35- to 54-year age ranges. All problems except suicide exhibit higher rates among young adult men and women than among middle-aged men and women, thus strongly supporting the expectation that problems indirectly attributable to alcohol show high rates among young adults. Also, for the eight problem areas for which information about 16- and 17-year-olds was available, six showed lower rates at these young ages (arrests for disorderly conduct, other assaults, rape, sex offenses, prostitution, and offenses against family and children). Only arrests for vandalism and serious crimes were higher among 16- and 17-year-olds; vandalism appears to peak at 15 years of age and serious crimes at 17 years. Each of the other categories peaks between 18 and 21 years. Further, for these eight arrest variables, rates are lower for all age categories 25 years and older. Finally, the results follow essentially the same age pattern for women as for men, although women show consistently lower rates (except for prostitution and commercialized vice) than men.

Despite the extremely regular and convincing pattern of these findings, alternative explanations exist. A major flaw in interpretation consists in a missing piece of crucial evidence, namely, the extent to which alcohol is implicated in each of the problem categories and the way in which it interacts with other factors to produce the behavior. While we know there is a considerable amount of alcohol involvement in violence (Pernanen, 1976), family disturbance (Ablon, 1976), suicide (Miles, 1977), and accidents (Jones, 1977), the range of involvement reported in the literature is extremely variable (Aarens, Cameron, Roizen, Roizen, Room, Schneberk, & Wingard, 1977), appearing to reflect the level of methodological sophistication of research conducted in given casualty areas. Estimates of alcohol involvements in motor vehicle fatalities, a topic that has received considerable research attention, vary within a relatively small range. For example, 22 studies of driver fatality reported that alcohol involvement at the time of the accident (as measured by BACs, police reports, and/or witness reports) ranged between 35% and 59% (Aarens *et al.*, 1977). In studies of nontraffic accidents, on the other hand, an area in which sophisticated research procedures are not so fully developed, estimates of alcohol involvement range widely. For instance, in studies of accidental drowning, alcohol involvement was as low as 4% and as high as 83%, and in fire fatalities the range was 9–83%. Even when stable estimates are available, as in the case of motor vehicle fatalities, virtually no models exist to enable us to ascertain the ways in which alcohol and other factors interrelate to form a causal network. Research is badly needed in this area.

Another difficulty is that we have little knowledge of the way in which contributing factors may shift with age. For instance, the data on vandalism, which show high rates beginning at ages 11 and 12 with peaking at age 15, suggest that alcohol involvement at those ages is probably minimal; however, vandalism at age 20 or at age 45 may be related to the use of alcohol. Further, many of these problems may decline with age independent of alcohol involvement; an obvious case in point is prostitution.

An additional difficulty is posed by the fact that many of the problems we are dealing with involve complex forms of social processing known to be highly selective with regard to age, sex, race, socioeconomic status, and other variables. Information on arrests, in particular, is prone to such bias. The actual levels of the activities in question may differ substantially from those that ultimately show up on a police blotter. Finally, the decrease in rates with age may reflect not a reduction in alcohol-related problems but a more sophisticated capacity to modulate the behaviors in question so that they don't come to the attention of those whose function it is to identify such behaviors. That is to say, people may drink just as frequently and heavily but become more practiced in handling the consequences in a socially acceptable manner with age. Findings from surveys (Cahalan *et al.*, 1972) point to this possibility.

In light of the considerations noted in the previous paragraph, it cannot be definitely concluded that alcohol problem rates are higher, or as high, among young as among middle-aged adults. The *prima facie* case is, however, a strong one, and it finds additional support in levels of problem behaviors found in surveys of populations that include young adults. In the 1967–1969 national sample of 21- to 59-year-old men, Cahalan and Cisin (1976b), for example, found that the highest rates for problems directly related to drinking occurred in their youngest age group (21- to 24-year-olds); the problems included belligerance, problems with wife, problems with friends or neighbors, job problems, police problems, health problems or injuries from drinking, and financial problems. Similar patterns were obtained in studies of army and navy personnel for 17- to 20-year-olds (Cahalan & Cisin, 1975; Cahalan *et al.*, 1972).

3.3. Do Frequent Heavy Drinkers Become Alcoholics?

I should now like to turn to the relationship frequent heavy drinking and its associated complex of adverse consequences bear to the subsequent development of alcoholism. It can be stated at the outset that both continuities and discontinuities exist and that no straightforward linear model is likely to connect the two conditions in a way that accounts for the diversity of the information available about them. In a general sense, it does appear that problems with drinking in early adulthood are linked with alcohol problems in middle age, but the linkages are so weak that no reliable predictive statement can be made about a given individual even in the presence of extensive information about the person's drinking behavior, personality, and life history. What seems to occur is that young adults in their late teens and early 20s who drink heavily and with negative consequences constitute a pool from which middle-aged alcoholics will be selected by criteria that are as yet almost completely unknown. This phenomenon is complicated by two other observations: (a) it seems that lower but nevertheless substantial proportions of young adults who drink moderately or who do not drink at all become problem drinkers in middle age, and (b) frequent heavy drinking and its associated behaviors, as noted earlier, show a general decline with age. In what follows, I examine some of the evidence for these generalizations.

Concerning the observation that frequent heavy drinking is a self-limiting condition for a majority of young adults who exhibit it, most of the research cited earlier indicates a steady decrease in the proportions of individuals who fall into frequent heavy drinking categories at each successive age level. The trend is most clearly delineated for men. Women, on the other hand, may maintain or increase frequent heavy drinking as they get older, but the absolute level never appears to be high. For both men and women, the frequency of drinking occasions increases with age; for men, the quantity per occasion declines, whereas for women, it may stay the same or increase.

The factors underlying declines in frequent heavy drinking among men are not at all understood. General explanations, like "burning out," or "settling down," are not satisfactory. One alternative is that frequent heavy drinking has symbolic associations with significant developmental markers of young adulthood, such as, for example, establishment and consolidation of adult identity. Once these developmental tasks have been accomplished and the stage in which they are rooted passes, symbolic connections to heavy drinking become weaker and less compelling. Frequent heavy drinking may have instrumental value in gaining entry to valued social organizations and groups; fraternities and other social clubs are examples.

Another alternative has to do with the aversive consequences of frequent heavy drinking. Anecdotal report suggests that single instances of negative effects from drinking can be sufficient to effect substantial changes in drinking behavior. Such one-trial learning probably occurs most frequently among persons who are not frequent heavy drinkers to begin with, but singular episodes among frequent heavy drinkers undoubtedly have the same effect. Very little is known about the naturally occurring aversive effect of normal drinking, and it is a fertile area for future research.

Finally, evidence, particularly from military surveys, indicates that heavy intake may continue well into middle adulthood, while the negative social and behavioral consequences associated with heavy intake decrease with age. In the U.S. Army survey (Cahalan *et al.*, 1972) the percentage of male heavy drinkers having no negative consequences increased up to 30–33 years and then stayed approximately the same throughout the remaining age range; heavy drinking with negative consequences, on the other hand, showed a steady decline with age. Navy enlisted men remained at the same level for heavy intake without problems throughout the age range of 21–49 years after a higher proportion at 17–20 years but showed a consistent decrease over the entire age range for heavy intake with problems. These findings suggest developmental shifts over the adult age range in the behaviors elicited by alcohol, shifts that may have to do with adaptation to drinking, changes in activity levels, the typical settings in which drinking occurs, or the ways in which individuals habitually drink (i.e., spacing of drinks, sip frequency, and size).

The evidence for the decline with age of frequent heavy drinking and the associated problem behaviors is based almost exclusively on data from cross-sectional surveys and national statistics on the prevalence of alcohol-related problems. Information from cohorts followed over time is the best means to determine the extent to which youthful drinking problems predict later drinking problems. Only one such longitudinal study exists (Fillmore, 1974, 1975). Fillmore examined problem drinking longitudinally from young adulthood to middle age by comparing reports by the same individuals ($n = 206$) during college and middle age. Since her study did not seek to classify respondents as alcoholic or nonalcoholic, it cannot provide a direct answer to the nature of the relationship between frequent heavy drinking and alcoholism, but it does provide valuable information about problem drinking. Of 31 persons classified as problem drinkers in college (Fillmore, 1974), 9 (29%) were classified as problem drinkers in middle age; the remaining 22 individuals (71%) were either nonproblem drinkers ($n = 21$) or abstainers ($n = 1$) in middle age. Clearly, in this study, the predictive utility of problem drinking at an individual level is not great (although from a statistical point of view, the correlation between problem drinking at Time 1 and Time 2 is significant). Nevertheless, the finding that a substantial proportion of youthful problem drinkers continue to be problem drinkers later in life is congruent with the notion that frequent heavy drinkers form a pool from which alcoholics will be selected. The picture is complicated by Fillmore's (1974) finding that some college nonproblem drinkers and abstainers are classified as problem drinkers in middle age and in roughly equal proportions. Out of 84 nonproblem drinkers in college, 8 (10%) were problem drinkers in middle age; the corresponding percentage for college abstainers is 12% (8 out of 91).

Fillmore's (1974) results indicate that there is considerable movement in and out of problem drinking. Cahalan and Cisin (1976b) reported similar studies conducted over shorter time spans.

The results of other analyses by Fillmore (1975) also further our understanding of the relationship of youthful drinking to later problem drinking: frequent intoxication in college, a variable similar to frequent heavy drinking, showed little predictive utility for men but was the best single predictor for women's later problem drinking; binge drinking in college, another variable related to frequent heavy drinking, showed little predictive value for either men or women; and symptomatic drinking in college (blackouts; drinking before a party if not sure of getting any drinks or enough to drink; liking to be one or two drinks ahead without others' knowing it; drinking before or instead of breakfast) was the best single predictor for men but a poor predictor for women; however, symptomatic drinking occurred at much lower levels in middle age than in college, an observation consistent with national survey findings (Cahalan & Cisin, 1976a,b).

Taken together, these findings indicate that direct predictive relationships between young adults' frequent heavy drinking and middle-aged alcoholic drinking are not strong. That they are complex, differentiated by sex, and probably consist of several subtypes is amply demonstrated by Fillmore's work. The relationships she found also support the notion that we are dealing with two sets of alcohol problems, which, though related, are basically different. A major connecting link between the two may be symptomatic drinking. Since, however, it is clear that few of the many young drinkers who qualify in this regard become problem drinkers later in life, other refinements in conceptualization are needed before this lead is pursued.

4. Social Considerations and Policy Implications

Historically, the alcoholism movement has necessarily been concerned with the severe casualties of alcohol use, chronic alcoholics. While this single-mindedness of purpose gave the movement vitality, a dedicated sense of purpose, and political effectiveness in advocacy for alcoholics, it tended to obscure the consideration of other aspects of the complex relationship that exists between alcohol and a host of social and economic factors in contemporary society. Now that treatment and rehabilitation facilities for alcoholics are generally available, and major strides have been made in creating support systems for ensuring the accessibility of services without prejudice, there is a heightened sensitivity and turning of attention to the broad and complex role that alcohol plays in society, of which alcoholism is just one, albeit an important, component. It is within this general context that we can begin to appreciate how the issue of alcohol-related problems among young adults has not received a great deal of attention in the past in terms of policy formulation and concomitant social action, even though the basic dimensions of the phenomenon have been known for some time.

There are, of course, other social forces that have kept this issue out of the limelight. Among these is a preoccupation with high school drinking, which obscures recognition of the magnitude of the problem consequences of frequent heavy drinking among young adults. Another has to do with the positive value that alcohol assumes as one part of sociability and recreation for a majority of young adults, and the reinforcement of this importance by a wide variety of social influences. A third factor is a general societal tolerance of behaviors in young people that in older people might be perceived as deviant. And finally, with the exception of highway fatalities, there is little public awareness of the contributory role that alcohol plays in various social problems; that is to say, society at large invokes "causative" factors other than excessive drinking to explain these problems.

Whatever the reasons for the low public recognition of the demonstrably high prevalence of alcohol-related problems among young adults, the mere fact of low recognition has distinct advantages for those whose interest lies in the formulation of policy. The range of options to choose from is very broad, since *ad hoc* social structures designed willy-nilly in response to the issues and fixed positions held by vested interests are relatively lacking. In fact, it becomes possible to include among the options a policy of no policy, a point of view defensible on several grounds that merit further consideration:

(a) Since heavy drinking among young adults is, as we have seen, a positively valued behavior, in itself largely harmless, it can be argued that adoption of a policy to reduce it would constitute an infringement of rights, would be politically unsound, and would very likely be ineffective.

(b) Although many socially deleterious consequences ensue from frequent heavy drinking, formal and informal mechanisms for reducing and coping with these consequences already exist; adding to these mechanisms or creating new ones would be costly and possibly duplicative and would result in a situation of diminishing returns.

(c) Available evidence, reviewed in the foregoing pages, indicates that frequent heavy drinking is a self-limiting condition, especially in regard to the problems that proceed from it, and further, is not highly predictive of alcoholism. That is, it passes of its own accord without intervention; also, there seems to be little percentage in reducing it as a means of preventing alcoholism.

In light of these considerations, it might be more costly than not to initiate a policy of programmatic action against frequent heavy drinking.

The first principle of this approach has much to recommend it and should be a cornerstone of any sound policy. The other two justifications suffer in that the former assumes that existing mechanisms have effective alcohol components, while the latter assumes that because the condition is self-limiting, the problems that occur during its course are not in themselves threats to public health and do not have a continuing impact after the condition has ceased, both of which points are arguable.

Concerning the first principle, of infringing on individual rights, it would appear that any policy directed toward frequent heavy drinking among young adults needs to make extremely careful distinctions between drinking, on the one hand, and its positive and negative consequences, on the other. Policy should not be directed toward a general redefinition of the value of drinking but toward reducing problems in which heavy drinking, along with other contributing factors, assumes a more-or-less causal role. Concentration on problem behaviors rather than upon frequent heavy drinking has several beneficial consequences. There is more public agreement about the need to minimize the negative behaviors associated with drinking than there is about the need to minimize drinking. A valued behavior does not become the focus of public concern and action. Also, focusing on the consequences of drinking is consonant with public attributions of cause to the drink rather than to the drinker and the low probabilities involved in the connection between drinking and the occurrence of a problem. Further, if frequent heavy drinking is not center-stage, then frequent heavy drinkers are also in the background, thus reducing the possibility of labeling, with its often pejorative effects. Finally, since problems are not indissolubly linked with the consumption of alcohol, this approach minimizes constraints against invoking non-alcohol-specific conceptual models and allows for freer play for programmatic emphasis on other contributing factors. This approach is consistent with current thinking about the multifactorial causal chains that mediate social problems and with the need for the broadest possible scope in programs.

A corollary to the principle of separation of heavy drinking and its associated problems is the need for a policy that locates responsibility for programs outside the health and welfare services delivery systems. When program responsibility lies within these systems, programmatic action inevitably becomes "medicalized": costs go up, effectiveness (especially with behavior problems) goes down, recipients are identified as being "sick" or deviant, and the specter of chronicity is always present. To the extent that policy is preventive in purpose, it runs the danger of co-option by the rehabilitative services when embedded only in the health delivery systems (Blane, 1976).

Another corollary to the idea that policy needs to focus on alcohol-related problems rather than on drinking itself is the notion of piggybacking, that is, coordinating efforts so that alcohol components are introduced into already existing programs directed toward social problems. This approach presupposes a careful analysis of the problems imputed to bear some relationship to drinking, in order to determine the extent and nature of drinking involvement. Piggybacking also requires a thorough examination of the current mechanisms for reducing problems and carefully thought-out means for introducing alcohol components. There are several manifest advantages to piggybacking: lower costs, no appreciable rise in autonomous bureaucratic structures, and no direct attack on valued behaviors. Possible disadvantages include (a) turf problems and vested interests that resist the introduction of change or the recognition of alcohol as contributing to problems and (b) the loss of programmatic initiative and control as a result of the decentralization inherent in piggybacking. Both potential difficulties are management issues that require sensitivity to the importance of human and organizational factors in programming.

Two examples of piggybacking are the mutual involvement of the National Highway Traffic Safety Administration and the National Institute of Alcohol Abuse and Alcoholism (NIAAA) in drinking–driving programs and NIAAA's investment in the alcohol and drug abuse education program emanating from the U.S. Office of Education. Neither of these efforts has been documented in detail, but careful analyses of the issues and problems involved in each would provide extremely useful case studies in planning future initiatives.

Given a policy toward heavy drinking among young adults that does not focus on drinking behavior *per se* but on alcohol-related problems, that is not locked into the health and welfare service delivery systems, and that relies heavily on piggybacking, what are some of the kinds of programming one might anticipate? It goes without saying that a central program element would of necessity be research and evaluation, but research and evaluation with highly specific aims: (a) to map frequent heavy drinking and to monitor changes in it; (b) to determine the causal role that drinking plays in each alcohol-related problem; (c) to anticipate the consequences of social trends in problems related to frequent heavy drinking and alcohol (e.g., there will be more women drivers in the next 10 years; how will highway crash statistics be affected?); (d) to evaluate changes in the incidence and prevalence of alcohol-related problems and to relate program activities to those changes; and (e) to conduct biochemical research that has immediate application, for example, the development of amethystic (sobering-up) agents.

As for program elements beyond research and evaluation, the possible directions are numerous. Some examples are:

(a) Linkages with sex education and counseling programs to introduce the effects of drinking on dating and marital relationships and its relationship to unwanted pregnancies, rape, incest, and homosexuality.
(b) Linkages with parent-effectiveness training groups to include an alcohol awareness component.
(c) Coordination with social skills and assertiveness training groups on the assumption that improved social skills reduce reliance on alcohol as a social facilitator.
(d) More pinpointed emphasis on alcohol in weight reduction and other dietary programs.
(e) Inclusion of information on drinking effects in physical fitness and health promotion programs.

Drinking-specific program elements framed in terms that do not create negative labels may also be included, for example:

(f) Drinking-control programs patterned after weight-control and smoking-control programs; frequent heavy drinkers often drink more than they plan to or feel guilty or ashamed about the things they do when drunk. Drinking-control programs, based on self-monitoring, self-evaluation, and self-control techniques, can help individuals drink as they plan to (see point g, as well as Chapter 12 for a fuller treatment of this topic).
(g) Related to drinking-control programs are how-to-drink programs, which, for instance, teach people how to drink without getting a hangover. Such programs include drinking sessions in which drink size, spacing of drinks, sip frequency, sip size, and other drinking behaviors are measured in relation to body weight, blood alcohol levels, food intake, mood, and other

situational factors. Program elements with specific goals can be devised for drinking–driving programs, work place settings, and military settings.

5. Summary and Conclusions

In this chapter, it is argued that there are two "alcoholisms," the one referring to traditional clinical, diagnostic, and treatment nomenclature, the other to the transitory social and behavioral consequences of the episodic consumption of relatively large amounts of alcohol at a single sitting. Traditional alcoholism clusters in middle age (35–55 years), whereas the new "alcoholism," termed *frequent heavy drinking*, is most common among post-high-school adults between the ages of 18 and 24 years, especially males. Problems associated with alcoholism tend to be cumulative and chronic and to pervade all aspects of the afflicted individual's life. Problems associated with frequent heavy drinking tend to be directly linked to drinking events, circumscribed within the individual's life, and usually self-limiting. Alcoholism is confined to a smaller proportion of the population than frequent heavy drinking, the latter being normative among some groups (e.g., young military personnel). Alcoholism may indeed be conceived of as a special extreme case of frequent heavy drinking.

Analysis of national data bases indicates that for problems directly attributable to alcohol, middle-aged males and females have higher rates than young adults of liver cirrhosis mortality, inpatient–outpatient care episodes for alcohol abuse, and arrests for drunkenness. Young adults have higher rates for drunken driver mortality, arrests for driving while intoxicated, and arrests for liquor law violations.

For problems indirectly attributable to alcohol, young adults have higher rates than middle-aged adults of all problems examined, except suicide. These problems include motor vehicle fatalities, other accident mortality, divorce, arrests for disorderly conduct, vandalism, serious crimes against persons, other assaults, rape, sex offenses, prostitution and commercialized vice, and offenses against family and children.

These findings suggest that the social and human costs associated with alcoholism, on the one hand, and problems stemming from frequent heavy drinking, on the other, probably do not differ greatly. Nevertheless, current social policy concerning alcohol problems focuses almost exclusively upon alcoholism and its treatment. The policy and programs regarding frequent heavy drinking among young adults are notable for their absence rather than for their presence, although some college and military efforts have been mounted.

Alcohol-related problems among young adults have little salience in the public mind. Rather, popular views of youthful drinking problems concentrate on high school rather than post-high-school youth, even though the facts do not agree with these views. Except for vandalism, alcohol-related problems are uniformly lower for high-school–aged young people than for their post-high-school counterparts. These findings suggest that the public is misinformed about youthful alcohol-related problems and argue that public information efforts in the area are needed. An informed public can make wiser input concerning policy about alcohol.

References

Aarens, M., Cameron, T., Roizen, J., Roizen, R., Room, R., Schneberk, D., & Wingard, D. *Alcohol, casualties and crime* (Final Report, No. C-18, NIAAA Contract ADM-281-76-0027). Berkeley: Social Research Group, University of California, Nov. 1977.

Ablon, J. Family structure and behavior in alcoholism: A review of the literature. In B. Kissin & H. Begleiter (Eds.), *The biology of alcoholism* (Vol. 4). New York: Plenum, 1976.

Blane, H. T. *Cross-national drinking practices* (Final Progress Report, NIAAA Grant No. AAOO4011). Pittsburgh: University of Pittsburgh, March 1975.

Blane, H. T. Acculturation and drinking in an Italian American community. *Journal of Studies on Alcohol*, 1977, *38*, 1324–1346.

Blane, H. T. Issues in preventing alcohol problems. *Preventive Medicine*, 1976, *5*, 176–186.

Blane, H. T., & Hewitt, L. E. *Alcohol and youth: An analysis of the literature, 1960–1975* (Final Report, NIAAA Contract ADM-281-75-0026). Pittsburgh: University of Pittsburgh, 1977. (NTIS No. PB-268-898).

Bowers, W. J. Trends in college campus deviance. *College Student Survey*, 1971, *5*, 20–30.

Cahalan, D. *Problem drinkers: A national survey*. San Francisco: Jossey-Bass, 1970.

Cahalan, D., & Cisin, I. H. *Final report on a service-wide survey of attitudes and behavior of naval personnel concerning alcohol and problem drinking*. Washington, D.C.: Bureau of Social Science Research, 1975.

Cahalan, D., & Cisin, I. H. Drinking behavior and drinking problems in the United States. In B. Kissin & H. Begleiter (Eds.), *The biology of alcoholism* (Vol. 4). New York: Plenum, 1976. (a)

Cahalan, D., & Cisin, I. H. Epidemiological and social factors associated with drinking problems. In R. E. Tartar & A. A. Sugerman (Eds.), *Alcoholism: Interdisciplinary approaches to an enduring problem*. Reading, Mass.: Addison-Wesley, 1976. (b)

Cahalan, D., & Treiman, B. *Drinking behavior, attitudes, and problems in San Francisco*. Report prepared for the Bureau of Alcoholism, Department of Public Health, City and County of San Francisco, Jan. 1976.

Cahalan, D., Cisin, I. H., & Crossley, H. M. *American drinking practices: A national study of drinking behavior and attitudes*. New Brunswick, N.J.: Rutgers Center of Alcohol Studies, 1969.

Cahalan, D., Cisin, I. H., Gardner, G. L., & Smith, G. E. *Drinking practices and problems in the U.S. Army, 1972* (Report No. 73-6). Arlington, Va.: Information Concepts, 1972.

Cosper, R., & Mozersky, K. Social correlates of drinking and driving. *Quarterly Journal of Studies on Alcohol*, Supplement No. 4, 1968, 58–117.

de Lint, J., & Schmidt, W. Alcoholism and mortality. In B. Kissin & H. Begleiter (Eds.), *The biology of alcoholism* (Vol. 4). New York: Plenum Press, 1976.

Durning, K. P., & Jansen, E. *Problem drinking and attitudes toward alcohol among navy recruits* (Report No. TR77-21). San Diego: Navy Personnel Research and Development Center, 1975.

Engs, R. C. Drinking patterns and drinking problems of college students. *Journal of Studies on Alcohol*, 1977, *38*, 2144–2156.

Federal Bureau of Investigation. *Crime in the United States, 1976*. Washington, D.C.: U.S. Government Printing Office, 1977.

Fillmore, K. M. Drinking and problem drinking in early adulthood and middle age. *Quarterly Journal of Studies on Alcohol*, 1974, *35*, 819–840.

Fillmore, K. M. Relationships between specific drinking problems in early adulthood and middle age. *Journal of Studies on Alcohol*, 1975, *36*, 882–907.

Harford, T. C., & Mills, G. S. Age-related trends in alcohol consumption. *Journal of Studies on Alcohol*, 1978, *39*, 207–210.

Jessor, R., & Jessor, S. Adolescent development and the onset of drinking. *Journal of Studies on Alcohol*, 1975, *36*, 27–51.

Jones, R. K. Alcohol and highway crashes: A projection for the 1980s. *HSRI Research Review*, 1977, *7*, 1–16.

Miles, C. P. Conditions predisposing to suicide: A review. *Journal of Nervous and Mental Disease*, 1977, *164*, 231–246.

National Center for Health Statistics. *Vital statistics of the United States, 1975. Vol. 2: Mortality, Part B*. DHEW Publication No. PHS-78-1102. Hyattsville, Md.: National Center for Health Statistics, 1977.

National Institute of Mental Health. *Utilization of mental health facilities, 1971*. DHEW Publication No. NIH-74-657. Washington, D.C.: U.S. Government Printing Office, 1973.

Pernanen, K. Alcohol and crimes of violence. In B. Kissin & H. Begleiter (Eds.), *The biology of alcoholism* (Vol. 4). New York: Plenum, 1976.

Plateris, A. *Divorces and divorce rates, United States*. DHEW Publication No. PHS-78-1907. Hyattsville, Md.: National Center for Health Statistics, 1978.

Reed, P. *Age and sex distributions for initial contact form data for cross-population grantees (1976 and 1977) and alcoholism treatment centers (1975, 1976, and 1977)*. Rockville, Md.: National Alcoholism Program Information Service, National Institute on Alcohol Abuse and Alcoholism, May 1978.

Riester, A. E., & Zucker, R. A. Adolescent social structure and drinking behavior. *Personnel and Guidance Journal*, 1968, *47*, 304–312.

Room, R. Drinking patterns in large U.S. cities: A comparison of San Francisco and national samples. *Quarterly Journal of Studies on Alcohol*, Supplement No. 6, 1972, 28–57.

Sanford, N., & Singer, S. Drinking and personality. In J. Katz, H. A. Korn, V. Ellis, P. Madison, S. Singer, M. M. Lozoff, M. M. Levin, & N. Sanford (Eds.), *No time for youth: Growth and constraint in college students*. San Francisco: Jossey-Bass, 1968.

Schaps, E., & Rubin, E. L. A study of the prevalence and intensity of drug and alcohol use in the Commonwealth of Pennsylvania. In *The Pennsylvania alcohol abuse prevention plan 1975, Governor's Council on Drug and Alcohol Abuse*, Harrisburg, Pa., 1975.

Schmidt, W., & Popham, R. E. Heavy alcohol consumption and physical health problems: A review of the epidemiological evidence. *Drug and Alcohol Dependence*, 1976, *1*, 27–50.

Smart, R. G., & Finley, J. Increases in youthful admissions to alcoholism treatment in Ontario. *Drug and Alcohol Dependence*, 1976, *1*, 83–87.

U.S. Bureau of the Census. *Statistical abstract of the United States: 1977* (98th ed.). Washington, D.C.: U.S. Government Printing Office, 1977.

U.S. Department of Transportation. *Traffic Safety '74*. Washington, D.C.: U.S. Government Printing Office, 1975.

University of Massachusetts Alcohol Task Force. *Progress report, NIAAA grant*. Unpublished manuscript, University of Massachusetts at Amherst, 1975.

Vogel-Sprott, M. Defining "light" and "heavy" social drinking: Research implications and hypotheses. *Quarterly Journal of Studies on Alcohol*, 1974, *35*, 1388–1392.

Wechsler, H., Demone, H. W., & Gottlieb, N. Drinking patterns of Greater Boston adults: Subgroup differences on the QFV index. *Journal of Studies on Alcohol*, 1978, *39*, 1158–1165.

2

Patterns of Alcohol Consumption among the Young: High School, College, and General Population Studies

Henry Wechsler

1. Introduction

Today, the drinking of alcoholic beverages is a popular and generally accepted social activity in American society. Although widespread throughout the population, the extent and frequency of alcohol consumption is known to differ among population subgroups. One of the findings in epidemiological studies of alcohol use is that young adults exhibit the highest frequency and the greatest quantity of alcohol consumption of all age groups (Room, 1972: U.S. Department of Health, Education, and Welfare, 1975).

This paper provides information about the extent of drinking among young persons in high school and junior high school, and in college, as well as among young adults in the general population. All the studies that I report on were conducted in the same geographic area—Greater Boston and New England—which has been found to have higher

Henry Wechsler • Director of Research, The Medical Foundation, Inc., Boston, MA 02116.
The research on which this report is based was supported in part by grants 1 RO1 AA 00318–01 and 1 RO1 AA 02679–01 from the National Institute on Alcohol Abuse and Alcoholism and Grant 1 RO3 MH 19838–01 MSM from the National Institute of Mental Health—Center for Studies of Narcotic and Drug Abuse.

proportions of heavy drinkers than other regions, such as the South (Cahalan, Cisin, & Crossley, 1969).

2. Use of Alcohol among High School Students

2.1. Method

In November 1974, we conducted a questionnaire survey of a sample of approximately one-fifth of the students in grades 7 through 12 in two eastern Massachusetts communities (Wechsler & McFadden, 1976). The selected communities differed in size and socioeconomic characteristics. One was a semi-industrial city with close to 90,000 residents, with a predominantly middle- and lower-middle-class population. The other, with a population of about 60,000, was more residential and predominantly middle to upper middle class. In each community, a random sample of classrooms was selected at each grade level.

Students were asked to complete anonymous self-report questionnaires, which were a revised version of an instrument used in 1970–1971 in the same two communities. The students were assured of the anonymity and the confidentiality of their responses. They were told that their participation was voluntary and were asked to work individually. Of 1,751 students present in the sample classrooms on the day of the questionnaire administration, all but 14 turned in completed questionnaires.

The students were asked to indicate how often during the year they drank beer, wine, and/or hard liquor and how often they had become intoxicated on these beverages. We analyzed responses to these questions separately for students in grades 7–8 (junior high school) and for those in grades 9–12 (senior high school) in each community.

2.2. Results

As shown in Table 1, over three-quarters of both boys and girls in the senior high schools had had beer during 1974, and more than two-thirds reported the use of hard liquor at least once during the year as well as the use of wine, with the exception of boys in City A. The reported use of alcoholic beverages was considerably lower among the junior high school students.

Among the junior high school students in both communities, the proportions of boys who reported drinking beer or wine at least once during the year were significantly greater than the proportions of girls. However, when reports of drinking these beverages more than 10 times during the year were examined, the only sex difference was found in the use of beer in one of the communities (City A). In the reported use of liquor, there were no significant differences between the sexes in either community.

Similarly, among the senior high school students, no significant differences appeared between the sexes in reported use of hard liquor, although, unlike the findings at the junior high level, the proportion of girls exceeded that of the boys in two instances: in Town B, those who reported consuming liquor one or more times during the year and, in both communities, those who reported consuming it more than 10 times. Girls also exceeded boys in reporting drinking of wine more than 10 times, and in City A, the difference was significant among those who reported consuming wine at least once during the year (75% versus 60%). Boys exceeded girls, on the other hand, in reported drinking of beer: in City A, significantly more boys than girls reported drinking beer at least once, while in Town B, significantly more boys than girls reported drinking beer more than 10 times.

The data presented in Table 2 reveal that close to half the senior high school students reported at least one episode of intoxication on either beer or hard liquor, while intoxication from wine was reported by about one-third. The reported intoxication at the junior high level was, in most instances, less than half that reported at the senior high level.

Table 1. Drinking and Frequent Drinking among High School Students by Sex, in Percentages

	Grades 7–8				Grades 9–12			
	City A		Town B		City A		Town B	
	Boys	Girls	Boys	Girls	Boys	Girls	Boys	Girls
Drank one or more times in 1974	(N=192)	(196)	(144)	(128)	(339)	(350)	(193)	(174)
Beer	61[a]	50[a]	60[b]	40[b]	89[b]	82[b]	80	77
Wine	58[a]	46[a]	71[c]	35[c]	60[c]	75[c]	76	71
Liquor	39	32	39	35	74	72	68	70
Drank more than 10 times in 1974	(N=187)	(190)	(138)	(124)	(332)	(341)	(184)	(172)
Beer	15[a]	8[a]	8	5	45	39	37[a]	26[a]
Wine	4	3	17	9	6	8	21	24
Liquor	6	5	2	1	18	22	14	18

[a] $p < .05$.
[b] $p < .01$.
[c] $p < .001$.

Table 2. Intoxication and Frequent Intoxication among High School Students by Sex, in Percentages

	Grades 7–8				Grades 9–12			
	City A		Town B		City A		Town B	
Intoxicated one or more times in 1974	Boys (N=198)	Girls (197)	Boys (146)	Girls (128)	Boys (342)	Girls (355)	Boys (197)	Girls (174)
Beer	33	25	16	14	68	62	52	45
Wine	16	12	10	13	24	29	28[a]	39[a]
Liquor	25	19	14	12	56	63	42[a]	53[a]
Intoxicated five or more times in 1974	(N=196)	(196)	(144)	(128)	(339)	(350)	(196)	(173)
Beer	12	10	2	2	47[a]	38[a]	26	21
Wine	2	2	0	1	5	6	7	10
Liquor	9	6	2	3	23	29	15	19

[a] $p < .05$.

Among the junior high school students in both communities, there were no significant differences between the sexes in reported intoxication on either beer, wine, or hard liquor. For the most part, the proportion of boys who reported intoxication was greater than that of girls. An exception to this was in Town B, where 13% of the girls reported being intoxicated on wine one or more times during the year, compared with 10% of the boys.

Reports of intoxication among the senior high school students revealed a number of significant differences between the sexes. Intoxication from beer was reported by higher proportions of boys than girls in both communities; in City A, this difference was significant among those who reported being intoxicated five or more times. Intoxication on wine or hard liquor, on the other hand, was more frequently reported by girls than boys in both communities; in Town B, this difference was significant for at least one episode of intoxication during the year on wine and for reports of becoming intoxicated on hard liquor one or more times.

Finally, all students were classified into one of six categories on the basis of whether they drank, what type of beverages they drank, and whether they had been intoxicated in 1974. Based on this classification, no statistically significant differences were found between the sexes among the junior high school students. Among students in the senior high school, the only significant differences found between the sexes were in those reporting being drunk on hard liquor five or more times: in City A, 30% of the girls versus 23% of the boys fell into this classification ($p < .01$), and in Town B, the respective figures were 19% and 14% ($p < .05$).

This study of alcohol use among high school students in two Massachusetts communities showed few significant differences between the sexes in patterns of alcohol consumption. Those differences that did appear among the junior high school students were largely confined to the occasional use of beer or wine, where boys exceeded girls. Where differences existed among senior high school students, boys exceeded girls in the use of and intoxication from beer, while girls generally exceeded boys in the reported use of both wine and hard liquor as well as in reports of intoxication from these substances.

A unique opportunity existed that allowed us to compare these findings with those of earlier studies to examine possible change over time. In 1970–1971, we had conducted a similar survey of alcohol use among high school students in the same two communities (Wechsler & Thum, 1973), and in 1965, Demone (1966, 1973) had conducted a survey in three other eastern Massachusetts communities, which were of the same general size and proximity to Boston as those represented in the 1970–1971 and 1974 resurvey studies (Demone & Wechsler, 1976). Although identical questions were not asked in the three studies, direct comparisons could be made on certain items for at least two of the studies. Rather than comparing any use of alcoholic beverages by high school students, I have chosen to present findings representing more extensive involvement with alcohol, namely, the proportion who reported intoxication.

As indicated in Table 3, it is interesting to note that among the junior high school students, frequent consumption of each alcoholic beverage decreased considerably for both sexes over the decade between

Table 3. Frequent Use[a] of Alcohol among High School Students by Sex, 1965 and 1974, in Percentages

	Grades 7–8				Grades 9–12			
	1965		1974		1965		1974	
Report frequent use of	Boys	Girls	Boys	Girls	Boys	Girls	Boys	Girls
Beer	32	16	11	6	41	16	41	36
Wine	20	14	10	5	23	15	11	14
Liquor	16	8	4	3	26	13	15	20

[a] The percentages for 1965 are based on those who reported consuming the beverage 12 or more times during the year and, for 1974, on those who reported 11 or more times.

1965 and 1974. In 1965, boys were twice as likely as girls to report the frequent consumption of beer or liquor. Although the percentages are small, by 1974 girls had almost equaled boys in reported frequent consumption of hard liquor, while for beer, the difference between the sexes remained stable over the 10-year period. The difference between the sexes in wine use increased, with boys in 1974 being twice as likely as girls to report frequent consumption of this beverage.

At the senior high school level, among the boys the reported frequent use of beer remained the same, while, as in the junior high school, the frequent use of wine and of hard liquor decreased. By contrast, the proportion of girls reporting the frequent consumption of beer more than doubled between 1965 and 1974, and the frequent use of hard liquor also increased among the girls. Although the reported frequent use of wine remained essentially the same for girls, in 1974 they exceeded the boys in the use of this beverage as they also did in the frequent use of liquor.

The data in Table 4 indicate a substantial increase in reported intoxication among high school students, particularly at the senior high school level, even though different wording of the question in the three surveys should have resulted in the highest rates being reported in 1965, the next highest in 1974, and the lowest in 1970–1971. At both the junior and senior high school levels, the sharpest increases in reported intoxication are seen between the 1965 and the 1970–1971 studies, and the 1974 rates are even higher than those in 1970–1971, with the exception of the rate for junior high boys. Boys in 1974 were about twice as likely as in 1965 to report intoxication, whereas, for the girls, the rates of reported intoxication increased three times at the junior high school level and five times at the senior high school level. In 1974, girls at the senior high level equaled boys in reported intoxication, while at the junior high level, boys slightly exceeded girls.

In summary, the comparison of the 1965, 1970, and 1974 results

Table 4. Drunkenness[a] among High School Students by Sex, 1965, 1970–1971, and 1974, in Percentages

	Grades 7–8			Grades 9–12		
Subjects	1965	1970–1971	1974	1965	1970–1971	1974
Boys	14	32	33	34	61	70
Girls	8	23	27	14	59	69

[a] In 1965, *drunk* was defined as "drunk ever." In 1970–1971, *drunk* was defined as "hard liquor users who were also drunk on any alcoholic beverage in the past year." In 1974, *drunk* was defined as "drunk on any alcoholic beverage in 1974."

indicates an increase in alcohol use and frequent alcohol use among high school girls and in intoxication among both boys and girls.

3. Use of Alcohol among College Students

In their extensive analysis of the literature appearing between 1960 and 1975 on alcohol and youth, Blane and Hewitt (1977) commented:

> Our review of college age drinking practices reveals that information about drinking behavior among today's college and noncollege youth is extremely limited and . . . has little value for informing program and policy decisions. This gap in our knowledge is all the more striking since the little evidence available to us clearly indicates that the post-high school years—18–25 years—are those in which alcohol consumption is higher than at any other time during the life span. . . . Studies specifically directed toward in-depth investigations of representative samples of college and noncollege youth are badly needed.

In their analysis of drinking practices by college students, Blane and Hewitt cited a number of methodological problems with the studies and particularly criticized sample size, pointing out that of the 68 surveys they chose to report on, only 4% involved over 5,000 respondents and the majority had fewer than 1,000 (one had as few as 24). Since we have just completed an extensive survey of drinking among college students that included a final study sample of 7,083, we believe our findings will serve to fill some of the gap in knowledge referred to above.

3.1. Method

In the spring of 1977, we conducted a survey of alcohol consumption among students at 34 New England colleges. The schools, located in five of the New England states, included both state-supported and private institutions; colleges in urban, suburban, and rural settings; coeducational and all-women colleges; and large- and small-sized colleges. All were four-year institutions offering programs leading to bachelor's degrees.

At each of the colleges, a random sample of full-time undergraduate students was selected, including both commuting and resident students. The number of students chosen at a college ranged from 50 to 400, depending on total enrollment, whether the college was coed, and the ratio of men to women. The final study sample included 5,000 men and 5,500 women.

A 15-page questionnaire seeking information on alcohol use, the use of substances other than alcohol, and on a number of social and demographic variables was sent to each student. The questionnaire was accompanied by a letter explaining the reason for the survey, the sampling techniques, and the procedures to safeguard the respondents' anonymity as well as the confidentiality of their responses. The letter also explained that participation was voluntary and that the students were free to disregard questions they did not wish to answer. Two follow-up mailings to nonrespondents were later conducted.

From the original sample, 263 students were eliminated because they were no longer at the college (they had transferred, graduated, or dropped out) or because their correct addresses could not be obtained. Questionnaires were returned by 7,345 students (7,170 responses were received from the first and second mailings, 175 from the third), providing a total response rate of 72%. For the data analyses, we restricted the sample to respondents to the first and second mailings. These included 3,185 college men and 3,898 college women. Not included were an additional 87 respondents for whom information on sex was not available.

3.2. Results

This study of drinking among college students revealed a number of statistically significant differences between the sexes. To begin with, men differed significantly from women in reported frequency of drinking, as shown in Table 5. Among the men, more than two out of three reported drinking alcohol at least once a week, and the reported frequency increased at each class level to the point where as many as one out of eight seniors reported drinking nearly every day. Frequency of drinking was not as great among women, nor were substantial increases found by class level. Half the women reported drinking at least once a week: only 2% reported drinking nearly every day.

For each type of beverage (beer, wine, and liquor), statistically significant differences beyond the .001 level were found between the sexes in all instances of frequency and quantity usually consumed. As shown in Table 6, beer was reported consumed more frequently and in greater quantity by men than by women. Wine was the least commonly consumed alcoholic beverage among college students; only 12% of the men and 18% of the women reported drinking wine at least once a week. While the women were significantly more likely than the men to report drinking wine, the men surpassed the women in the quantity usually consumed. Similarly, significantly higher proportions of women reported drinking liquor, yet less than half reported usually having more than two drinks, compared with almost 6 out of 10 men.

Table 5. Frequency of Drinking Any Alcohol by Sex and Year in College, in Percentages[a]

		Year in college			
	Totals	Freshman	Sophomore	Junior	Senior
Men	(N=3,122)	(781)	(745)	(747)	(849)
Never, not in 1976	3.4	2.9	4.0	3.6	3.2
Less than weekly	27.2	31.7	28.4	26.5	22.3
1–2 times a week	39.9	41.9	43.4	37.2	37.5
3–4 times a week	20.9	18.1	17.0	23.6	24.6
More than 4 times a week	8.6	5.4	7.2	9.1	12.4
	$\chi^2 = 63.17$, 12 *df*, $p < .001$.				
Women	(N=3,830)	(1,043)	(949)	(899)	(939)
Never, not in 1976	4.0	4.3	3.8	4.0	3.9
Less than weekly	45.6	43.4	46.4	46.4	46.6
1–2 times a week	38.1	41.5	37.8	38.9	33.7
3–4 times a week	9.9	9.1	9.3	8.7	12.6
More than 4 times a week	2.4	1.7	2.7	2.0	3.2
	$\chi^2 = 24.66$, 12 *df*, $p < .02$.				

[a] Men versus women: totals, $\chi^2 = 429.47$, 4 *df*, $p < .001$; freshman year, $\chi^2 = 64.09$, $p < .001$; sophomore year, $\chi^2 = 75.46$, $p < .001$; junior year, $\chi^2 = 141.58$, $p < .001$; senior year, $\chi^2 = 163.50$, $p < .001$.

Among the college students responding to this survey, drunkenness was not a rare occurrence. Explaining that "by drunk we mean when alcohol causes you to lose control of physical activities, or to get very unsteady, aggressive, or sick to your stomach," we found (as presented in Table 7) that more than five out of six men and close to three out of four women reported having been drunk at least once. While the numbers are small, the present survey also indicated that in terms of frequency, 9% of the men and 3% of the women reported being drunk at least once a week.

In addition to reporting on drunkenness, students were presented with a list of other consequences of drinking and asked how often they had experienced each. As seen in Table 8, among the men nearly one-quarter (24%) had been in trouble with authorities and one-fifth (21%) reported that they had been in physical fights after drinking. About 10% also reported that drinking had caused them to have an automobile accident, and similar proportions said that they had been in other alcohol-caused accidents in which someone was hurt and/or had seriously damaged a friendship as a result of drinking. Nearly one-fifth (19%) of the men reported having gone without other things because of the cost of alcohol; 43% said they often or sometimes did or said something when drinking that they would not otherwise do or say: and 15% said that they often or sometimes forgot where they had been or what they had done.

In contrast, reports of adverse consequences of drinking were relatively rare among women. Only 7% of the women had ever been in trouble with authorities as a result of drinking, and less than 5% had ever lost a friend, been in physical fights, had an automobile accident,

Table 6. Type of Alcohol: Frequency of Intake and Quantity[a] Usually Consumed by Sex, in Percentages[b]

Type of Alcohol	Men (*N*~2,811)	Women (*N*~3,251)
Beer		
Frequency		
Never, not in 1976	4.8	23.1
Less than once a week	32.2	49.0
Once a week or more	63.0	27.9
Quantity		
1–2 12-oz cans or bottles	34.5	59.6
3–4 cans or bottles	33.6	29.6
More than 4 cans or bottles	31.9	10.8
Wine		
Frequency		
Never, not in 1976	13.7	8.7
Less than once a week	74.2	73.4
Once a week or more	12.1	18.0
Quantity		
1–2 6-oz glasses	64.5	69.0
3 glasses	20.7	21.0
More than 3 glasses	14.7	10.0
Liquor		
Frequency		
Never, not in 1976	7.7	4.7
Less than once a week	65.5	67.5
Once a week or more	26.7	27.8
Quantity		
1–2 drinks[c]	42.9	54.4
3–4 drinks	38.7	38.3
More than 4 drinks	18.4	7.3

[a] Percentages are based on those who reported consuming the beverage.
[b] For each variable, χ^2 analysis revealed statistically significant differences between men and women beyond the .001 level.
[c] Containing at least 1.5 oz of straight liquor.

or had another accident in which someone was hurt; 36% said that they often or sometimes did or said things when drinking that they would not otherwise do or say, and 8% reported often or sometimes forgetting where they had been or what they had done.

Men and women differed significantly ($p < .001$) on each of the adverse consequences listed in Table 8, with two or more times as many men as women reporting involvement in six of the eight items.

Two aspects of drinking have been viewed as signs of possible problem drinking: drinking alone and drinking before noon. Of the men, 42% compared with 26% of the women reported drinking alone at least once in a while. As for drinking before noon, only 8% of the men and 4% of the women reported doing so some or most of the time. Both these differences were statistically significant at the .001 level.

Thus far, individual components of the drinking patterns of New England college students have been described. Now the question arises of how these students can be grouped into some classification by alcohol consumption. For this study, we devised a drinking typology based on quantity and frequency.

In terms of quantity, students were classified as drinking a "heavy" amount if they reported that during one sitting, they usually drank more than a six-pack of beer, five or more glasses of wine, or five or more drinks with 1.5 ounces of straight liquor in them. Students were said to drink a "medium-heavy" amount if they usually drank five or six cans of beer, four glasses of wine, or four drinks with liquor; or a "medium-light" amount if they usually drank four cans of beer, three glasses of wine, or three drinks with liquor. Students were classified as drinking a "light" amount if they usually drank no more than three cans of beer, two glasses of wine, or two drinks with liquor during one sitting.

In terms of frequency, students were divided into four groups based

Table 7. Frequency of Drunkenness[a] by Sex, in Percentages

Frequency	Men (N=3,065)	Women (3,733)
Never	15.6	29.1
Not in 1976	13.2	16.4
Less than monthly	36.8	37.7
1–3 times a month	24.9	14.1
Weekly or more often	9.4	2.6
	$\chi^2 = 382.05$, 4 *df*, $p < .001$.	

[a] The students were told: "By *drunk* we mean when alcohol causes you to lose control of physical activities, or to get very unsteady, aggressive, or sick to your stomach."

on how often they usually drank any type of alcohol: (1) less than monthly (but on at least one occasion in 1976); (2) one to three times a month; (3) one to two times a week; and (4) more than twice a week. Those students who said they never drank alcohol, or who did not drink any alcohol in 1976, were classified as abstainers.

Based on a combination of these quantity–frequency measures, we arrived at six categories of drinking: abstainers, infrequent-light, frequent-light, intermediate, infrequent-heavy, and frequent-heavy drinkers. This classification of students resulted in a statistically significant difference between the sexes (see Table 9). In both sexes, 3–4% were classified as abstainers, while alcohol consumption by 15% of the men and 29% of the women fell into the infrequent-light category. In contrast, 29% of the men fell into the frequent-heavy category, compared with 11% of the women. Thus, men exceeded women in the frequent-heavy drinking category by about three to one, while women exceeded men in the infrequent-light category by about two to one.

Of all variables examined in relation to this classification by drinking typology, students' reports of drinking in high school showed the highest levels of significance (see Table 10), thereby indicating that the students in our survey established their patterns of drinking before they entered college. For example, of those college students classified as current abstainers from alcohol, 53% of the men and 75% of the women never drank in high school. By contrast, less than 3% of the college men

Table 8. Adverse Consequences of Drinking by Sex, in Percentages[a]

Consequences	Men (*N*~3,005)	Women (*N*~3,682)
Those who often or sometimes:		
Forgot where they were or what they did	15.3	7.6
Did or said something they would not otherwise do or say	42.5	36.1
Those who ever:		
Went without other things because of the cost of alcohol	18.8	11.2
Lost a friend or seriously damaged a friendship	9.8	4.7
Got in trouble with authorities	24.3	6.7
Got into physical fights	20.6	2.1
Had an automobile accident	9.6	2.2
Had any other accident in which they or someone else was hurt	9.8	4.1

[a] For each consequence, χ^2 analysis revealed statistically significant differences between men and women beyond the .001 level.

and women classified as frequent-heavy drinkers reported never drinking in high school; in fact, more than half reported drinking at least once a week while in high school. The overall findings from the present survey indicate that 93% of the men and 89% of the women had had their first drink *before* college. These findings contrast sharply with those of the often-cited national study by Straus and Bacon (1953) conducted in 1949–1951, when 21% of the men and 35% of the women had their first drink in college.

Experience of the adverse consequences of drinking was examined in terms of this drinking typology. As one might expect, students in the frequent-heavy drinking category were significantly more likely than those in the lighter drinking categories to report adverse consequences, and this holds for both men and women.

Among men in the frequent-heavy drinking category, the range of involvement in drinking-related problems was from 17% who reported they had had an accident in which someone was hurt to 67% who said they often or sometimes said or did something they would not otherwise do as a result of drinking. One-third or more of the male frequent-heavy drinkers also said they had gone without things because of the cost of alcohol, had been in trouble with authorities, had been in physical fights, or had often or sometimes forgotten where they had been or what they had done after drinking. In contrast, no more than 5% of the men categorized as infrequent-light drinkers reported drinking-related problems, with the exception that 13% admitted to often or sometimes doing or saying something they might not otherwise do or say as a result of drinking.

Similarly, women in the frequent-heavy drinking category were more likely than those in the lighter drinking categories to report adverse consequences of drinking. Among female frequent-heavy drinkers, the proportion reporting drinking-related problems ranged from 7% who

Table 9. Drinking Typology by Sex, in Percentages[a]

Type of drinker	Men (N=3,160)	Women (3,873)
Abstainers	3.4	4.0
Infrequent-light	15.3	29.0
Frequent-light	20.3	18.5
Intermediate	28.7	35.1
Infrequent-heavy	3.0	2.4
Frequent-heavy	29.3	10.8

[a] $\chi^2 = 481.82$, 5 df, $p < .001$.

Table 10. Drinking in High School by College Drinking Typology and Sex, in Percentages[a]

	Abstainers	Infrequent-light	Frequent-light	Intermediate	Infrequent-heavy	Frequent-heavy
Men	(N=107)	(479)	(636)	(895)	(93)	(917)
Never	53.3	13.6	4.1	3.8	8.6	1.7
Less than once a month	27.1	54.3	20.0	22.7	28.0	7.3
1–3 times a month	11.2	25.7	41.3	43.7	34.4	31.1
More than 3 times a month	8.4	6.4	34.6	29.8	29.0	59.9
χ^2 = 1110.34, 15 df, p < .001.						
Women	(N=157)	(1,113)	(712)	(1,340)	(92)	(417)
Never	75.2	12.9	4.9	4.1	7.6	2.6
Less than once a month	19.1	55.6	23.4	29.7	35.9	10.3
1–3 times a month	3.8	24.3	44.1	42.2	28.3	30.4
More than 3 times a month	1.9	7.1	27.5	24.0	28.3	56.6
χ^2 = 1558.86, 15 df, p < .001.						

[a] Men versus women: χ^2 = 190.92, 3 df, p < .001.

had been in physical fights or who had ever had an automobile accident to 71% who said that they often or sometimes did or said something they would not otherwise do. In contrast, among women in the infrequent-light category of drinkers, only 12% reported this latter problem, and less than 3% reported drinking-related problems in any of the other areas examined. For the most part, however, women in all categories of drinking were less likely than men in the same categories to have experienced drinking-related problems. This was most evident for the "acting-out" consequences, where, for example, in the frequent-heavy drinking category, 7% of the women compared with 37% of the men reported having been in physical fights and, for trouble with authorities as a result of drinking, the respective figures were 20% and 44%.

In addition to categorizing drinkers on the basis of quantity–frequency typology, we attempted to identify a group of students that most people would agree contains a high proportion of problem drinkers. As has been pointed out by other researchers, one cannot assume that regular drinking of large quantities automatically constitutes problem drinking. For example, it should not be construed that all the students included in our "frequent-heavy" drinking category were either alcoholics or were on their way to becoming alcoholic. However, within this category, we identified a smaller group who reported becoming drunk at least once a week. This group included 244 men (8% of the men whose drinking typology could be classified) and 68 women (2% of the women)—in other words, the men were four times as likely as the women to fall into this group. Although this group was small (only 4.5% of the students responding to this survey) it should be noted that if this same proportion were projected onto the total population of approximately 173,000 full-time undergraduate students attending the 34 colleges included in this survey, it would mean that 7,785 students fall into this group.

Adverse consequences reported by this group of problem drinkers were more the rule than the exception. Among both the men and the women categorized as problem drinkers, more than half said that they often or sometimes did or said something that they otherwise would not and often or sometimes forgot where they had been or what they had done as a result of drinking. Equal proportions (56%) also admitted that they had at least once gone without something because of the cost of alcohol. Furthermore, over half the men reported that they had gotten into trouble with authorities or into physical fights after drinking. In fact, none of the adverse consequences was reported by less than one-quarter of the male problem drinkers.

In summary, this survey of New England college students indicates that the drinking of alcoholic beverages is a common activity: nearly all students drank alcohol, and regular drinking (at least weekly), drinking in sizable quantities, and drunkenness were not at all uncommon. In almost all instances, differences between the sexes were found. The men tended to report a greater frequency of drinking, the consumption of larger quantities, and more drinking leading to intoxication than the women. Also, the men appeared to drink more frequently as they progressed through college. A similar increase was not found among the women, perhaps because beer drinking is such a popular activity among college students and beer was clearly the beverage of choice among the men: it was selected as the favorite beverage by half the men and only 13% of the women. Furthermore, men were as likely to report drinking in groups with other men as in groups with both sexes. Women, on the other hand, most frequently reported drinking in the company of men—either in groups or on a one-to-one basis. The college survey, then, indicated that there were strong differences between the sexes in alcohol use that were not apparent in our studies of drinking among high school students.

4. Use of Alcohol among Young Adults

4.1. Method

We recently had the opportunity to analyze the extent of alcohol use in a survey of the general population in the Boston metropolitan area. The survey, conducted in 1975 by the United Community Planning Corporation and the Combined Jewish Philanthropies, employed an area probability sample of all housing units in the Boston Standard Metropolitan Statistical Area (SMSA). At each of the 3,800 housing units selected, an enumeration of all household members was obtained. Subsequently, approximately one in three of these housing units was designated for the final study sample. By random selection, respondents were chosen from all adults, 18 years of age or older, within each household, and detailed interviews were held with 1,043 persons in 52 cities and towns in the Boston SMSA.

The survey instrument included two questions on alcohol use that were derived from the quantity–frequency–variability (QVF) index of Cahalan, Cisin, and Crossley (1968, 1969). One question asked how often the respondent drank alcoholic beverages of any kind. The other question asked how often the respondent drank different quantities of alcohol at one time. For different specific quantities, ranging from more than eight drinks at one time to one or two drinks at a time, respondents were asked whether they consumed that amount nearly every time they drank, more than half the time, less than half the time, once in a while, or never. Each individual was categorized on the basis of the average amount consumed (Q), how often he drank (F), and the largest quantity of drinks consumed (V).

This adaptation of Cahalan *et al.*'s classification system enabled a comparison between the Boston study and others conducted previously in Boston, San Francisco, and nationwide. We were able to categorize the drinking behaviors of 984 adults on a scale ranging from abstainers to heavy drinkers, with each progressive category entailing more alcohol involvement than the previous one (Wechsler, Demone, & Gottlieb, 1978). Although some of the categories bear the same labels as those developed for the college study, the findings are not directly comparable between studies because the drinking typology used in the college study examined usual quantity and frequency, without incorporating the dimension of variability.

4.2. Results

As shown in Table 11, the findings indicate that the highest proportion of heavy drinkers was in the youngest age group among both men and women, with the proportions decreasing with increasing age. In comparison with the oldest age group (those 55 years of age or older), the proportion classified as heavy drinkers was more than two times

Table 11. Drinking Typology by Sex and Age,[a] 1975, in Percentages[b]

	18–24	25–34	35–44	45–54	55+
Men	(N=69)	(110)	(59)	(62)	(119)
Abstainers	2.9	8.2	15.3	14.5	19.3
Infrequent drinkers	7.2	6.4	10.2	8.1	16.8
Light drinkers	20.3	22.7	20.3	12.9	29.4
Moderate drinkers	15.9	15.5	18.6	30.6	10.1
Heavy drinkers	53.6	47.3	35.6	33.9	24.4
	$\chi^2 = 48.30$, 16 *df*, $p < .001$.				
Women	(N=81)	(130)	(77)	(78)	(188)
Abstainers	13.6	6.9	13.0	19.2	32.4
Infrequent drinkers	17.3	17.7	23.4	25.6	22.3
Light drinkers	30.9	39.2	42.9	35.9	31.9
Moderate drinkers	17.3	19.2	7.8	10.3	7.4
Heavy drinkers	21.0	16.9	13.0	9.0	5.9
	$\chi^2 = 62.16$, 16 *df*, $p < .001$.				

[a] Information on age was not available for 11 respondents.

[b] For each age category, χ^2 analysis revealed statistically significant differences between men and women.

greater among the young adult men and almost four times greater among the young adult women. Although the number of respondents in the young adult age category (18–24) was small, what is particularly striking about these findings is that more than half the male respondents were classified as heavy drinkers. In addition, abstention was the exception rather than the rule, with less than 3% of the men under 25 classified as abstainers.

These findings replicate the findings of other studies, which show that heavy drinking tends to peak in young adulthood and to decline subsequently (Room, 1972). However, unlike other studies, which suggest that the differences observed between men and women in drinking behaviors may be disappearing (Wechsler & McFadden, 1976; Becker & Kronus, 1977), this survey of drinking among the general population revealed that there still remain statistically significant differences between the sexes at all age levels. This difference ranges between two and a half times as many heavy drinkers among men than women in the youngest age group to four times as many in the oldest. We also found that this sex difference held up when social class, race, ethnicity, and marital status were controlled.

More recently, we surveyed adults in four Greater Boston suburban communities (Wechsler, Bovey, Gottlieb, & Reed, 1979). While the data were not analyzed separately for young adults, results from this survey indicate that the proportion of heavy drinkers was almost three times greater in the youngest age group (those under the age of 35) than in the oldest age group (those 55 years of age or older). Similarly, it was found that men were heavier drinkers than women in all age groups but most so in the youngest.

This then is the general pattern of drinking practices in the Greater Boston area: heaviest drinking among adults in the youngest age group (18–24), particularly among men. In this group, there are almost no abstainers, and a sizable proportion are classified in the frequent-heavy drinking category.

5. Conclusions

It is not the purpose of this paper to become unduly alarmist about drinking patterns among the young in the United States and among populations in high school and college. Survey data of the nature we have reported do not permit judgments of how much alcohol is too much. Nor do we claim that drinking patterns established initially among the young will continue into middle age or lead for many to alcoholism. Moreover, we are well aware of the many arguments against making such evaluative statements from normative data. Such factors as body weight, time duration over which drinking occurs, and the amount of alcoholic intake among others should be considered in assessing the drinking behavior of any single individual.

However, our zeal to be scholarly and to consider all such factors should not induce us to miss the forest while concentrating on the trees. There are danger signals in all of these data. When 50% of the young adult males in a metropolitan area fall into a "frequent-heavy" category, when over two-thirds of both high school boys and high school girls report drunkenness during the year, when 8% of college men and 2% of college women fall into a problem drinking category on the basis of being "frequent-heavy" drinkers and being drunk at least weekly—we are faced with a sizable number of potential drinking problems. An examination of the kinds of adverse effects associated with such regular drinking in terms of trouble with authorities, physical fights, and automobile accidents serves to define current drinking practices among the young as an important public health issue—not to be denied or ignored with a "boys will be boys" philosophy.

ACKNOWLEDGMENT

The author wishes to acknowledge the assistance of Joanne D. Bovey in the preparation of this manuscript.

References

Becker, C., & Kronus, S. Sex and drinking patterns: An old relationship revisited in a new way. *Social Problems*, 1977, *24*, 482–487.

Blane, H. T., & Hewitt, L. E. Alcohol and youth: An analysis of the literature 1960–75. Prepared for National Institute on Alcohol Abuse and Alcoholism. (Report No. PB–268 698). Springfield, Va.: U.S. Department of Commerce, National Technical Information Service, 1977.

Cahalan, D., Cisin, I. H., & Crossley, H. M. Measuring massed versus spaced drinking. *Quarterly Journal of Studies on Alcohol*, 1968, *29*, 642–656.

Cahalan, D., Cisin, I. H., & Crossley, H. M. *American drinking practices: A national study of drinking behavior and attitudes*. New Brunswick, N.J.: Rutgers Center of Alcohol Studies, Monograph No. 6, 1969.

Demone, H. W., Jr. Drinking attitudes and practices of male adolescents. Doctoral dissertation. Waltham, Mass.: Brandeis University, 1966.

Demone, H. W., Jr. The nonuse and abuse of alcohol by the male adolescent. In *Proceedings of the Second Annual Alcoholism Conference of the National Institute on Alcohol Abuse and Alcoholism*. Washington, D.C.: U.S. Government Printing Office, 1973.

Demone, H. W., Jr., & Wechsler, H. Changing drinking patterns of adolescents since the 1960s. In M. Greenblatt & M. A. Schuckit (Eds.) *Alcoholism problems in women and children*. New York: Grune & Stratton, 1976.

Room, R. Drinking patterns in large U.S. cities: A comparison of San Francisco and national samples. *Quarterly Journal of Studies on Alcohol*, 1972, Supplement No. 6, 28–57.

Straus, R., & Bacon, S. D. *Drinking in college*. New Haven, Conn.: Yale University Press, 1953.

U.S. Department of Health, Education, and Welfare, National Institute on Alcohol Abuse and Alcoholism. *Second Special Report to the U.S. Congress on Alcohol and Health, from the Secretary of Health, Education, and Welfare*. (DHEW Publication No. (ADM) 75–212.) Washington, D.C.: U.S. Government Printing Office, 1975.

Wechsler, H., & McFadden, M. Sex differences in adolescent alcohol and drug use: A disappearing phenomenon. *Journal of Studies on Alcohol*, 1976, *37*, 1291–1301.

Wechsler, H., & Thum, D. Alcohol and drug use among teenagers: A questionnaire study. In *Proceedings of the Second Annual Alcoholism Conference of the National Institute on Alcohol Abuse and Alcoholism*. Washington, D.C.: U.S. Government Printing Office, 1973.

Wechsler, H., Bovey, J. D., Gottlieb, N. H., & Reed, R. B. Social class and life-style: Health-related behaviors in four Massachusetts communities. Boston, Mass.: mimeographed report, 1979.

Wechsler, H., Demone, H. W., Jr., & Gottlieb, N. Drinking patterns of Greater Boston adults: Subgroup differences on the QFV index. *Journal of Studies on Alcohol*, 1978, *39*, 1158–1165.

3

Alcohol Problems among Civilian Youth and Military Personnel

J. Michael Polich

1. Introduction

It is widely recognized that problems caused by alcohol are pervasive and costly in American society. Accompanying this recognition is a conviction, growing stronger in government circles, that young people are especially exposed to risks of harm from alcohol misuse (USDHEW, 1978). Yet there remain many unresolved questions connected with estimating such risks. Definitions of precisely what constitutes an "alcohol problem" are controversial. Data relating to the general youth population are scant. Little is known about the actual economic impact of the myriad disruptive behaviors linked to excessive drinking. These circumstances complicate the answers to a very basic prevalence question: How widespread and how serious are alcohol-related problems among young people?

This paper suggests certain avenues of approach to that question and reports relevant results from recent survey data. The task necessarily begins with a review of the varied traditions of theory and research that identify "alcohol problems." From these traditions, a small set of fundamental variables can be extracted, providing behavioral measures along which the general population can be arrayed. The data reported here include several recent surveys of the U.S. household population

J. Michael Polich • Social Science Department, The Rand Corporation, Santa Monica, CA 90406.

and three companion surveys of the military services that together permit a head count of persons with identifiable alcohol problems. Such data do not allow a full quantitative assessment of the "seriousness" of alcohol problems since they omit measures of impaired economic productivity and deteriorated physical functioning. However, they provide a start in answering the basic prevalence question for the young adult population.

Our interest here focuses on young adults. This is in contrast to most studies of youthful alcohol problems, which generally deal with adolescence rather than young adulthood. Indeed, these studies often concentrate on a very restricted youth population, such as high school students or those under the legal age of majority (Blane & Hewitt, 1977). The reasons for this preoccupation are instructive. Public interest in adolescent behavior is intense, reflecting the apprehensions of both parents and community concerning all forms of youthful deviance. However, when adulthood is reached, the simple use of alcohol is no longer deviant in itself. Consequently, less attention is paid to the same adolescents after they become adults, even though it is then that they enter situations where regular use of alcohol is both normative and unrestricted.

Another source of the inattention paid to young adults is the common tendency among the public to view "alcohol problems" as coextensive with "alcoholism." Numerous studies of clinical alcoholics confirm that alcoholism is a disorder that typically comes to medical or psychiatric attention in middle age rather than in youth. Accordingly, prominent conceptual schemes for explaining alcoholism posit that many years of heavy drinking are required before the disorder takes firm root (Edwards, 1976). Although a well-designed prevention effort might attempt to correct such problems in the developmental phase rather than waiting until the culmination, as a practical matter resources usually follow the visible manifestation of the problem and therefore focus on treatment, that is, treatment of older alcoholics.

On the other hand, if one defines alcohol problems as more inclusive than alcoholism, the prominence of young people becomes greater. Reports of national surveys dealing with "problem drinking" suggest that occasional or intermittent problems, as opposed to chronic alcoholism, are commonly found among young adults (Cahalan, 1970; Cahalan & Room, 1974). As one might expect, mildly damaging or disruptive episodes linked to drinking, such as gross intoxication or trouble with the police, are concentrated among young men.

These observations point up the fact that definitions have a great deal of influence on our understanding of alcohol problems, among youth and elsewhere. Yet a lack of precise definitions, coupled with conceptual confusion, characterizes alcohol research. Different studies may appear to be dealing with the same phenomenon, yet one may identify the phenomenon by excessive alcohol consumption, another by the immediate adverse effects of alcohol on social functioning, and still another by the long-term development of addiction or dependence. Some studies, in particular those dealing with teenagers, identify the problem simply in terms of the "use" or the "nonuse" of alcohol, so that most of what we know about adolescent alcohol problems centers on the prevalence of the simple use of alcohol.

Our objectives are concerned with sorting out these conflicting conceptions of alcohol problems and with applying the resulting ideas to general population data. We first review the multiplicity of alcohol problems and the primary dimensions of alcohol-related behavior that emerge from the literature. Then we report the evidence from recent surveys showing prevalence rates for such behaviors, with particular attention to alcohol consumption patterns and the diverse consequences of excessive consumption. Following that, we examine a special category of young adults, members of the military services, to determine whether their alcohol behavior is discernibly different from that of their civilian counterparts. Finally, we summarize the implications of these results for research and policy.

2. The Multiplicity of Alcohol Problems

The term *alcohol problems* includes a broad range of human behaviors, and the scientific literature is characterized by a vast array of definitions and measures that fit the term. Most definitions reflect a judgment that alcohol problems are "problems" because they are injurious, that is, because they reflect damage or disruption to the individual or his associates. Beyond that basic notion, authorities diverge on the question of what should be included. There is a striking range of behaviors that could be classified as injurious. At one extreme are those behaviors that are clearly dangerous to health. In this class are such patterns as consuming alcohol at an extremely high rate over a long period, leading directly to liver disease (Wallgren & Barry, 1970). At the other extreme are behaviors that may have no determinate damaging consequences for the individual but are viewed as socially unacceptable by associates (e.g., spouse or friends). Compounding this diversity is the fact that many kinds of alcohol-related behavior are viewed as injurious only in certain situations; for example, drinking any alcohol on the job is usually proscribed in the United States but not in many other countries.

By far the greatest amount of attention has been given to the most severe manifestations of alcohol problems, those that go by the name of *alcoholism, alcohol addiction,* or *alcohol dependence.* Most information that reaches the public and most government expenditure in the alcohol area come about because of concern with this severe condition. Proponents of the disease concept of alcoholism traditionally distinguish alcoholism from less serious and less chronic problems associated with alcohol (Keller, 1976). In part, this approach reflects the long struggle by treatment practitioners to remove the moral stigma from alcoholism and to gain acceptance for its reality as a psychophysical disorder. In earlier times, alcohol problems were treated simply as "drunkenness." In the modern tradition, however, theory focuses on the apparent compulsion of some drinkers to consume large amounts of alcohol in spite of their desire to refrain or stop. Thus has arisen a conception of alcoholism as a psychiatric or physical disorder characterized by a "morbid insatiable craving" for the drug ethanol (Paredes, 1976). In the elaborate theory constructed by Jellinek (1960), this inability to control drinking became the hallmark of a chronic and progressive disorder, though the term used was often changed to *addiction* or *dependence* to distinguish it from other types of adverse effects due to alcohol. Within this tradition, a long list of symptoms has been developed to indicate the presence of the underlying condition. Proposed by Jellinek and eventually formalized into a diagnostic scheme for alcoholism (National Council on Alcoholism, 1972), this list includes not only loss of control but also the withdrawal syndrome, the maintenance of high blood alcohol concentrations, blackouts, secretive drinking, and a host of less specific behavioral indicators.

These notions have been enormously influential in achieving recognition of alcoholism as a specific syndrome of severe and chronic problems. In Jellinek's time, the World Health Organization granted official status to the disorder by defining alcoholics as

> those excessive drinkers whose dependence upon alcohol has attained such a degree that it shows a noticeable mental disturbance or an interference with their bodily and mental health, their interpersonal relations, and their smooth social and economic functioning. (WHO, 1952)

This definition, although frequently criticized for vagueness, clearly set out to distinguish alcoholics from the many other people who experience adverse effects of alcohol ("interference with functioning," etc.) but who do not habitually drink excessively or who do not exhibit dependence symptoms. A more recent WHO group has reemphasized this distinction, suggesting that persons with the "alcohol dependence syndrome" be isolated among those with "alcohol-related disabilities" and affirming that alcoholism and alcohol dependence are essentially similar (Edwards *et al.*, 1977). This leaves, of course, a potentially large group of persons whose functioning has been impaired without their experiencing alcohol dependence.

The numerical importance of the nondependent group has been estalished beyond argument by the survey work of "problem drinking" researchers. In a series of important books (Cahalan, Cisin, & Crossley, 1969; Cahalan, 1970; Cahalan & Room, 1974), these researchers have shown that dependence symptoms are much less frequently encountered in a general population sample than are the many other adverse consequences of heavy drinking. Far from resembling a coherent syndrome such as that observed in clinical alcoholism treatment, the cases of "problem drinking" uncovered in these surveys show patterns of diverse and fragmented difficulties, often linked to periods of acute intoxication rather than to continuous heavy alcohol intake. Moreover, longitudinal study of these persons over time shows that many of the less severe cases underwent "natural remission," in contrast to the chronic, progressive deterioration of functioning that would be predicted by traditional theories of alcohol addiction (Roizen, Cahalan, & Shanks, 1978).

This set of findings has placed the problem drinking conception of alcohol problems to some extent at odds with the proponents of traditional alcoholism models. In the view of the former group, alcohol problems are identified principally by the adverse consequences that alcohol produces. Such events as intoxication incidents, marital discord, law enforcement encounters, accidents, and absenteeism from work figure prominently in their measures of the impact of alcohol on individuals and on society. The existence or nonexistence of an underlying dependence condition is largely irrelevant to the measurement of consequences, and the tendency is for problem drinking researchers to deny that, in most cases, any such integrating condition exists (Clark, 1975). The contrast between this picture of disjointed, intermittent problems and the clinical appearance of alcoholism is stark enough to strike the observer as representing "two worlds of alcohol problems" (Room, 1977). The implication is that however important the dependence syndrome may be among the relatively few cases in clinical settings, the prevalence rates for alcohol problems in the general population will be dominated by instances of adverse consequences of drinking without identifiable dependence symptoms.

There is a third influential school of thought that highlights alcohol consumption rather than dependence or adverse consequences in order to assess the prevalence of alcohol problems. Loosely known as the *single-distribution theory,* this conception derives its force from the strong correlations across populations between cirrhosis mortality rates and average per capita alcohol consumption. Both cross-sectionally and longitudinally, numerous studies have demonstrated that as per capita consumption in a population rises, so too does the rate of mortality from cirrhosis of the liver (Schmidt, 1976). Moreover, the distribution of alcohol consumption among individuals in surveys typically follows an invariant distribution conforming to the lognormal curve with near-constant variance (Bruun, Edwards, Lumio, Mäkelä, Pan, Popham, Room, Schmidt, Skog, Sulkanen, & Oesterberg, 1975). As a result, the cirrhosis mortality rate and the mean consumption rate are directly related to the number of heavy drinkers in the population (i.e., those who consume more than a given amount). From these facts, it is a short conceptual step to the theory that higher *average* consumption in a population leads to higher rates of heavy drinking in the population and thence to higher rates of cirrhosis. The inference can be buttressed with the findings of many studies of individuals showing significantly elevated mortality or morbidity rates, particularly for liver diseases, among very heavy drinkers (Schmidt & de Lint, 1972; Lelbach, 1974). The theory thus focuses attention on the physical risks of heavy alcohol consumption and suggests that heavy consumption itself should be viewed as the alcohol problem *par excellence*.

For our purposes, the single-distribution theory is inapplicable as a device for prevalence assessment because it cannot be used directly to estimate the heavy-drinking segment of a subpopulation such as young adults. However, it serves to reinforce the notion that the original source of all adverse effects—heavy intake of alcohol—needs to be considered in its own right as a potential alcohol problem. This notion in turn implies that consumption should be treated separately from adverse consequences or dependence, since surveys have shown that the social correlates of consumption are quite different from the correlates of other drinking problems. For example, persons of higher socioeconomic status tend to drink more than those of lower status, but the latter tend to experience more adverse consequences of alcohol use (Calahan, 1970; Armor, Polich, & Stambul, 1978). It is also well to remember that heavy consumption occurs in different patterns. Among clinical alcoholics, the common pattern is that of exceedingly heavy consumption every day, often continuously throughout waking hours (Schmidt & de Lint, 1970; Armor *et al.*, 1978). Problem-drinking surveys, on the other hand, have noted that occasional heavy-drinking episodes without sustained high consumption are common among problem groups (Cahalan & Room, 1974).

A diagrammatic summary of the interrelationships among these concepts is shown in Figure 1. The upper portion of this figure depicts a simple causal relationship that might represent the milder forms of problem drinking where dependence is not present. Here the typical pattern of drinking is that of repeated episodes of heavy drinking, at least one of which results in an event that seriously affects the individual's status or functioning (for example, an arrest for driving while intoxicated or the loss of a spouse because of the person's heavy drinking). Such events can obviously be seriously damaging to the individual affected, but the future recurrence of such events may be improbable because the individual is not necessarily heavily involved with alcohol. The lower portion of the figure, in contrast, depicts the typical situation when alcohol dependence is present. Here high alcohol consumption is linked to the dependence syndrome so that dependence, once established by heavy drinking, itself causes the maintenance of high consumption in an interactive relationship. Likewise, dependence may imply that drinking occupies a preeminent position among daily activities, leading to serious adverse consequences that themselves reinforce the dependence by isolating the individual from social networks and non-drinking-related environments. In this situation, the person tends to increase consumption, partly as a response to increasing tolerance and partly to avoid withdrawal; thus, high daily consumption rates replace intermittent episodes of heavy drinking. Physical damage to bodily organs may ensue after years of such high intake. It is this tangle of pathologies, in the extreme, that is derived from clinical experience and that guides traditional concepts of alcoholism.

Unfortunately for research on prevalence, national data appropriate for assessing the syndrome of alcohol dependence are not available. Ideally, detailed data on the frequency and the intensity of dependence symptoms should be used to judge whether an individual shows sufficient evidence to warrant a classification of dependence or a certain degree of dependence (Edwards, Gross, Keller, Moser, & Room, 1977). National surveys to date have not included such measures, although

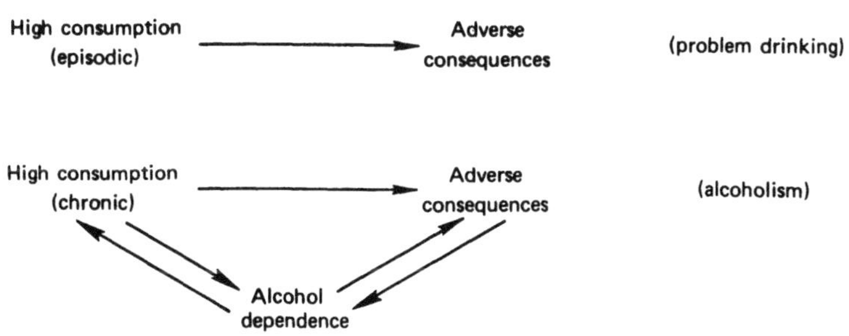

Figure 1. Patterns of alcohol problems.

they have included detailed measures of consumption quantity and adverse consequences. One recent study of the U.S. Air Force has obtained such information via survey, however (Polich & Orvis, 1979). The results showed that there is a very large overlap between the set of dependent persons and the set of persons experiencing any adverse consequence during the past year. Hence, we may be reasonably confident that we are including almost all dependent or "alcoholic" persons when we isolate persons with consequences, even though the specifically alcohol-dependent subgroup cannot be reliably distinguished.

It is also important to recognize that no survey—perhaps no systematic measurement process—is likely to include the full set of alcoholic or alcohol-dependent persons actually present in the population. Most surveys utilize a household sampling frame, which explicitly excludes those persons living in group quarters (who will be disproportionately alcoholic). Even if the frame is expanded to attempt full population coverage, nonresponses are likely to include disproportionate numbers of alcoholics and other lower-status and less-integrated individuals. In the case of a military or other employed population, this is not an issue since a comprehensive list of population members can be obtained and used to determine the degree of nonresponse bias. For the general civilian population, however, the possible omission of alcohol-dependent persons may be significant. These considerations merely reemphasize the fact that survey methods, of necessity, are better suited to measuring the broad rates of commonly occurring characteristics (such as heavy drinking or adverse consequences) than to isolating very small groups that are far "out on the tail" of a distribution (such as highly dependent, extremely impaired alcoholics).

3. Alcohol Consumption Patterns

It has been argued that the amount of alcohol consumption is a crucial variable in explicating the process of alcohol problems. Accordingly, let us examine some recent national data on the types of consumption patterns and the total amount of alcohol consumption, both in the general population of the United States and among young people. Table 1 shows some basic information about drinking practices based on four surveys of the national household population between 1972 and 1974. These surveys were originally commissioned by the National Institute on Alcohol Abuse and Alcoholism to obtain reaction to public education campaigns, but they also included specific questions on the respondent's use of alcoholic beverages during the past 30 days (Harris,

Table 1. Typical Alcohol Consumption, U.S. Population, 1972–1974

Group[a]	Percentage of drinkers[b]	Median frequency of drinking among drinkers (days per month)[c]	Median consumption among drinkers (number of drinks per drinking day)[d]			N
			Beer	Wine	Liquor	
Males, 18–24	80	5.6	2.8	1.8	1.1	573
Males, 25–39	79	5.1	2.2	1.3	1.0	867
Males, 40–59	65	6.2	2.1	1.2	1.0	1,088
Males, 60 and over	44	5.4	1.2	1.2	.8	566
Females, 18–24	58	2.2	1.0	1.3	.8	495
Females, 25–39	56	2.9	1.0	1.1	.8	1,094
Females, 40–59	44	3.4	.9	1.1	.8	1,146
Females, 60 and over	27	2.0	.7	1.1	.7	425

[a] Four combined sample surveys of U.S. national household population, 1972–1974, conducted by Louis Harris and Associates (Harris, 1975).
[b] Percentage of designated group who reported consuming any alcoholic beverage during the "past 30 days" (30 days before the interview).
[c] Number of days when any alcoholic beverage was consumed during the past 30 days.
[d] "Typical" amount of the designated beverage that was consumed during a day when the beverage was drunk, during the past 30 days. One drink was defined as one 8-oz glass of beer, one 4-oz glass of wine, or one 1-oz shot of liquor.

1975). No differences of any significant magnitude were found among the four surveys, so they were combined into one data base to provide large numbers of cases for analysis. Identical drinking items appeared in each questionnaire.

The table demonstrates that there remains a very wide discrepancy between the sexes despite the widespread public impression that male and female drinking practices have been converging in recent years. Males of all ages are much more likely than females to be drinkers (i.e., to have consumed any alcoholic beverage in the past 30 days), and if they do drink, their frequency of drinking is likely to be two or three times as great. (These results hold up both for the 18- to 20-year-old group and for the 21- to 24-year-old group.) When one considers *quantity* of consumption on a drinking day, these disparities remain. For example, the median female drinker aged 18–24 reported consuming about one glass of beer on days when she drank beer, whereas the median male drinker of the same age group reported almost three glasses on such an occasion. The table also illustrates the continuing concentration of heavier drinking rates among the youngest cohorts. Drinking rates for beer are particularly elevated for young males (18–24).

These statistics apply to the median or average person. Therefore, they serve to remind us that typical drinking behavior is quite moderate even among the demographic groups that consume the most alcohol. However, they tell us little about either the atypical heavy-drinking individual or about the individual who typically drinks moderately but occasionally experiences a high-consumption episode. Table 2 shows more complete information about the distribution of individuals according to total consumption amounts. The measure tabulated here (labeled as "Daily Consumption Level") is a quantity–frequency index of total ethanol intake in ounces per day. It is computed by multiplying the typical quantity of each beverage consumed on a drinking day (stated in ethanol content) by a frequency factor for that beverage and then summing across all three beverages. This, of course, is only one method of estimating total consumption, and experience shows that survey techniques sometimes underestimate actual consumption by considerable amounts (Pernanen, 1974). Observers differ on the degree to which such techniques yield biased estimates; one study (Room, 1971) estimates that compared to beverage sales, perhaps two-thirds of actual consumption is covered by survey methods, while in at least one case (Polich & Orvis, 1979), a survey appeared to account for about 85%. In view of the possible role of defects in sampling frame or response rates in reducing the sample's coverage of all consumers, it is possible that the coverage rates for the actual sample could be even higher than these estimates. In any event, it should be borne in mind that the statistics reported here could show somewhat lower rates, in absolute terms, than the actual population parameters. In relative terms, nevertheless, there is little reason to question the validity of the data, so that the rank order of groups may be assumed to be correct (Cahalan & Room, 1974).

Table 2. Alcohol Consumption Distribution

Daily consumption level[a]		Distribution in percentages[b]				
		Males		Females		
Ounces of ethanol	Number of drinks (approximate)	18–24	25 and over	18–24	25 and over	All persons
None	None	20	34	42	54	42
0.1–1.0	1–2	54	49	53	42	47
1.1–2.0	3–4	13	10	3	3	7
2.1–3.0	5–6	6	3	1	1	2
3.1–5.0	7–10	4	2	1	0	1
Over 5.0	11 or more	3	2	0	0	1
Total over 2 oz	—	13	7	2	1	4
N		573	2,521	495	2,665	6,254

[a] Quantity–frequency index of average daily ethanol consumption (ounces consumed per calendar day during the past 30 days). For computation methods see Armor, Polich, and Stambul (1978).
[b] Four combined sample surveys of U.S. national household population, 1972–1974.

The distributions in Table 2 confirm that young males are by far the population group most subject to high alcohol consumption, whatever standard one wishes to use. The cutoff used here is 2 ounces of ethanol (approximately 59 10^{-3}l), which roughly corresponds to four average-sized drinks if a drink is taken to be a bottle of beer, a glass of wine, or a shot of distilled liquor. According to this standard, 13% of males aged 18–24 engage in daily high consumption (five or more drinks per day), as contrasted with only 7% of other males and very small percentages of females regardless of age group. Compared to the general population, the category of young males stands out as the single deviant group in this table. Although we use the 2-ounce limit as a device for presentation, this table illustrates the fact that young males are exposed to the greatest risks from alcohol consumption regardless of the particular level of consumption selected.

Figure 2 demonstrates the special importance of the mid-20s age threshold among males. Here are plotted the percentages of each sex and age group who report high consumption rates using more detailed age categories than shown in Table 2. The figure makes it clear that

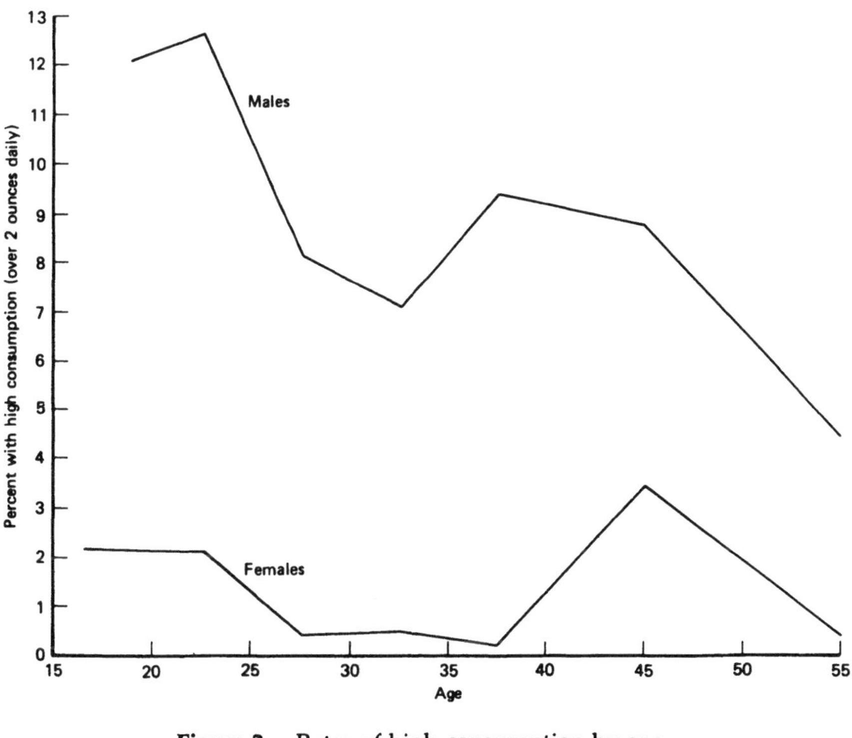

Figure 2. Rates of high consumption by age.

consumption drops off very sharply among males as they move from the early 20s into the late 20s and early 30s. The levels for females are uniformly much lower than for males, but there is also a slight drop in the mid-20s among females. The data do show somewhat higher rates for middle-aged females than for younger females, but even in these age groups, the percentage of high consumers is less than half that among males. These patterns are entirely consistent with the reported rates of high consumption encountered in studies from the previous decade (Cahalan, 1970). More than anything else, they provide strong evidence that alcohol problems are likely to be concentrated among young males. Examined another way, these data imply that males aged 18–24 account for about 30% of the heavy consumers of alcohol, while they account for only 9% of the population. No other group carries such a disproportionate load of risks due to alcohol.

By the time these surveys are executed, collated, analyzed, and reported, a period of several years has elapsed. One may wonder, are these behavior patterns still characteristic of the population, or could secular trends imply that the rates in Table 2 should be adjusted upward for an estimate of today's or next year's situation? This question is specially important in light of the long-term trend exhibited in Figure

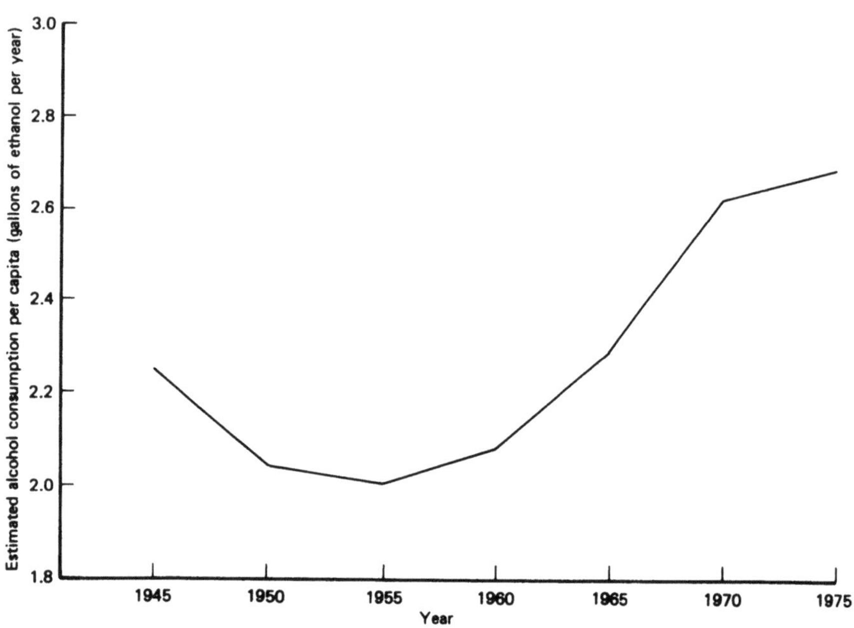

Figure 3. Trends in alcohol consumption in the United States, 1945–1975.

3, which shows apparent per capita consumption (from beverage sales taxes) over the period from 1945 to 1975. There was clearly a substantial upward trend in per capita consumption from 1955 onward, although it appeared to level off in the last five-year period. Given the known relationships among mean consumption, proportion of high-consuming individuals, and cirrhosis mortality, such a trend can appear quite ominous. Moreover, we intend to examine several data bases (including military surveys) with slightly shifting time periods of measurement during the past few years. Therefore, it is important to examine more carefully the behavior of such consumption trends over the very recent past.

Very recent trends for both apparent consumption per capita and survey reports (from our identical survey items across four years) are shown in Table 3. The line dealing with apparent consumption shows that the fairly steep upward trend of the 1950s and 1960s appears to have been arrested in the 1970s; no discernible change is present since 1971 (and there is no statistically significant linear trend). The self-reports of survey respondents likewise show that there has been no trend in mean consumption quantity over the four years for which comparable survey data are available. It is, of course, technically possible that the means could remain the same while the proportion of heavy drinkers increases, although this possibility would contradict the empirical generalizations supporting the single-distribution theory and

Table 3. Recent Trends in Alcohol Consumption, Total U.S. Population

	Year				
Item	1971	1972	1973	1974	1975
Apparent alcohol consumption per capita (gallons)[a]	2.68	2.63	2.69	2.66	2.69
Mean alcohol consumption reported in survey (oz ethanol/day)[b]	[c]	.52	.49	.52	.49
Percentage of survey respondents reporting consumption over 2.0 oz/day[d]	[c]	4.3	5.5	5.6	4.8

[a] Tax-paid withdrawals (presumptive beverage sales), from U.S. Department of Health, Education, and Welfare, *Alcohol and Health* (1978).
[b] Mean quantity–frequency index, national sample surveys (minimum N = 873).
[c] Not available.
[d] National sample surveys (minimum N = 873).

would require some fairly peculiar changes at the low end of the distribution in order to maintain constant means. This possibility cannot be tested using gross totals for per capita consumption, but it can be addressed using the survey data. The third line in Table 3 shows that this technical possibility has in fact not occurred; the proportion of survey respondents reporting high consumption rates has remained virtually constant over the period. A more detailed trend analysis conducted for NIAAA (Johnson *et al.*, 1979) among age and sex groups suggests that there were also no trends within demographic subgroups, although the sample sizes are limited for such analyses. Altogether, then, the available data imply that the survey results from the late 1960s through the mid-1970s are probably unaffected by possible trends in consumption.

The above results are concerned with the *typical* behavior of individuals, that is, with the frequencies of drinking and the amounts drunk on typical days. An unexplored area, as yet, is the issue of atypical or episodic heavy consumption. The national surveys that have been shown thus far, unfortunately, have no information on atypical high consumption. There is, however, an available survey from 1969 covering a representative sample of civilian males aged 21–60 with such information. Table 4 shows the patterns of episodic high consumption for various age groups from this survey. Once again, the youngest age group (21–24) exhibits the highest rates of heavy consumption. This table sets off frequencies of once per week or more often as "episodic heavy consumption," though this cutting-off point is essentially arbitrary. If one uses this criterion, the proportion of men in the youngest age group who drink heavily on a relatively frequent basis is about three

Table 4. Frequency of Episodic Heavy Consumption by Age

Frequency of episodic heavy consumption past year[b]	Percentage distribution by age[a]				
	21–24	25–29	30–39	40–59	All ages
Never	51	64	65	79	70
Less than once per month	17	9	18	7	11
Once per month	8	10	6	5	6
2–3 times per month	13	12	8	5	7
Once per week or more	11	4	3	5	6
N	130	117	246	485	978

[a] U.S. national household survey, 1969, males only.
[b] Frequency with which the respondent reported consuming eight or more drinks on a single occasion during the past year.

times as great as that among the other groups. Perhaps of more interest is the fact that heavy drinking—here defined arbitrarily as days when eight or more drinks were consumed—is a fairly common event among males. If one loosened the criterion and designated as a "frequent heavy drinker" anyone drinking at that level at least once a month, fully 32% of the 21–24 age group would qualify. If such drinking took place within four hours, a 165-pound man would exceed a blood alcohol concentration of .100, which would make him legally liable for prosecution for driving while intoxicated in most United States jurisdictions. In short, even though the modal drinking patterns of young adults are basically moderate, episodes of fairly heavy drinking with substantial known risks are fairly common among the young male population.

4. Adverse Consequences of Alcohol Consumption

As noted earlier, most survey studies of alcohol problems have dealt with the consequences of drinking rather than with the amount of consumption. Such an approach has numerous practical advantages; rather than becoming bogged down in the complexities of measuring actual drinking behavior, the researcher can simply use the subject's report of adverse effects to infer a deviant pattern of drinking. Furthermore, defining an "alcohol problem" according to manifest incidents of damage or disruption that are consequential to drinking minimizes the subjective intrusion of the researcher into the measurement process (although it also shifts some subjective burdens to the survey respondent). On the other hand, relying exclusively on consequences tends to restrict attention to those persons whose alcohol problem behavior has already reached a fairly advanced state, ignoring high consumers whose problems are only incipient. These considerations suggest that although adverse consequences clearly need to be considered, they should be seen in the context of multiple measurements drawing on other approaches.

A set of serious adverse consequences drawn from the 1969 national survey is presented in Table 5, along with the prevalence rates for each. These items are among the most prominent measures included in the problem drinking indices developed by Cahalan (1970). Each item covers a particular event that survey respondents were asked to affirm or deny as having happened to them during the past three years, a period sufficiently long so that fairly rare events would be registered. In some cases, the consequential character of the relationship to drinking is obvious (e.g., "arrested for driving while intoxicated"), but in many instances, the respondent is required to make the causal link himself (e.g., a spouse threatened to leave "because of drinking" as opposed to some other reason). There are many other questionnaire items used by Cahalan and his associates to indicate milder drinking problems, such as being told by someone to cut down on drinking, but such items did not appear to represent definite, serious adverse consequences and therefore were not included here.

The reporting rates in Table 5 may seem to imply that serious adverse consequences of drinking are rare in the general population, since in no instance does any item reach much above 5% of the sample. The fact that the rates for these events are individually low, however, does not imply that alcohol problems are infrequent when considered in the aggregate. The reason is that the events are not all concentrated in a small group of individuals with chronic problems (such as alcoholics). Many persons experience just one such consequence during a three-year period. Thus, those who reported incidents of work impairment during the period are not necessarily the same people as those who were hospitalized or involved in an accident. To a considerable extent, adverse consequences tend to be disjointed events, often devoid of a pattern or linkage that would suggest persistent, continuous drinking or alcohol dependence (Cahalan & Room, 1974; Polich & Orvis, 1979).

Table 5. Adverse Consequences of Drinking[a]

Adverse consequence	Percentage reporting[b]
Serious work impairment	
Lost a job	1.8
Drinking hurt promotion opportunity	1.9
Was off work for one week because of drinking-related illness	1.5
Less serious work impairment	
Told to cut down on drinking by others at work	2.8
Off work because of a hangover	5.3
Drinking harmed work (in general)	3.4
Family problems	
Spouse threatened to leave or left	2.0
Health impairment	
Hospitalized because of drinking	1.2
Involved in an accident	1.7
Law enforcement incidents	
Involved in drinking and driving incident	2.9
Involved in nondriving alcohol incident	2.4
N	978

[a] U.S. national household sample, 1969 (males only).
[b] Percentage reporting one or more occurrences, past three years.

Table 6. Rates of Adverse Consequences by Age

	Percent reporting designated consequence[a]			
Adverse consequence	21–24	25–39	40–60	Total, all ages
Serious work impairment[b]	3.8	2.5	4.1	3.5
Family disruption[c]	3.8	2.2	1.4	2.0
Health impairment[d]	8.5	3.3	4.1	4.4
Law enforcement incidents[e]	10.8	4.1	2.7	4.3
Any serious consequence[f]	19.2	9.1	6.8	9.3
N	130	363	485	978

[a] Percentage reporting any occurrence of any one of the designated consequences during the past three years. U.S. national household sample, 1969, males only.
[b] Lost a job, drinking hurt promotion opportunity, or missed one work week because of drinking.
[c] Spouse threatened to leave or actually left because of drinking.
[d] Was hospitalized, ill one week, or involved in an accident because of drinking.
[e] Involved in DWI (driving while intoxicated) or nondriving infraction because of drinking.
[f] Any of the consequences listed in above footnotes (*b*) through (*e*).

Table 6 shows several indices of adverse consequences that illustrate this situation. Clearly, there is considerable overlap among the incidents considered. However, the overlap is by no means complete, since over 9% of the sample reported one or more incidents. Once again, we see that alcohol problems tend to be more frequent among the youngest age group. This concentration is particularly notable for law enforcement and health incidents, where the consequence rate among the 21–24 age group approaches two and one-half times the rate of the 25–39 group.

Although these results are themselves important as indicators of alcohol problem prevalence rates, they may also be used for a different purpose. The occurrence of any one of the adverse consequences listed in Table 6 may be considered as confirmation of a hazardous drinking pattern that the individual has developed. Looked at in this way, a given pattern of alcohol consumption may be interpreted as constituting a "risk" according to the probability that the pattern will eventuate in one of these adverse events. Table 7 shows that the amount of alcohol consumption, as measured by the daily consumption index, does indeed entail quantifiable risks. As consumption rises even slightly above one or two drinks per day, there are steep increases in the risk of an adverse consequence. In the U.S. Navy survey from which these data are drawn, persons who reported levels of only 1–2 oz of ethanol daily (three to four drinks) faced an absolute risk of almost 20%, a level elevated above that of the minimum consumption group by a factor of two and one-half.

The right-hand portion of Table 7 shows a very crude measure of possible dependence symptoms that is also strongly related to consumption. Significantly, the risk rates for alcohol dependence symptoms do not reach very high absolute levels until fairly extreme daily consumption levels occur. Despite the rarity of the individual adverse events that we have examined, a moderately high level of consumption is much more likely to culminate in such an event than to appear as an identifiable instance of the dependence syndrome. It must be noted in passing that the available national data do not really afford much opportunity for in-depth examination of dependence symptomatology. Only one national survey in the past 10 years had included any sort of frequency questions on symptoms, and that instrument was quite thin in other respects (Johnson *et al.*, 1979). In a U.S. Air Force environment, certain survey measures have been shown to be successful discriminators of a group with characteristics similar to those of alcoholics (Polich & Orvis, 1979), but no comparable assessment of the civilian population is available.

One reason that adverse consequences, as opposed to dependence symptoms, begin to appear at relatively low levels of average daily consumption is that a low rate of *average* consumption may hide a pattern of very heavy episodic consumption. Table 8 confirms the importance of frequent heavy drinking, as opposed to daily consumption, as a risk factor for adverse effects. It is notable that persons who report drinking heavily as infrequently as twice a month still report very

Table 7. Risk Rates for Varying Consumption Levels

Consumption level (ounces of ethanol)	Rate of adverse consequences[a] (percent)	*N*	Rate of dependence symptoms[b] (percent)	*N*
0.1–1.0	7.3	5,080	1.3	1,761
1.1–2.0	19.5	1,210	7.5	418
2.1–3.0	35.3	363	8.8	181
3.1–5.0	47.8	364	18.0	128
Over 5.0	55.0	231	47.7	111

[a] U.S. Navy survey, 1974. Includes any person reporting disciplinary action, illness causing a week's loss of work, hospitalization, accidents, arrest, serious marital disruption, or impaired promotion opportunity due to drinking.

[b] U.S. Air Force survey, 1977. Includes any person reporting regular occurrence of one or more of the following: morning drinking, tremors, inability to stop drinking, or blackouts.

Table 8. Risk Rates by Episodic Heavy Consumption

Frequency of episodic heavy consumption, past year[a]	Rate of adverse consequences[b] (percent)	*N*
Never	4.1	683
Less than once per month	11.7	111
Once per month	11.9	59
2–3 times per month	29.6	71
Once per week or more	40.7	54

[a] Frequency with which the respondent reported consuming eight or more drinks on a single occasion during the past year.
[b] U.S. national household survey, 1969, males only. Includes any person reporting disciplinary action, illness causing a week's loss of work, hospitalization, accidents, arrest, serious marital disruption, or impaired promotion opportunity due to drinking.

substantial rates of adverse consequences. While none of the existing surveys permits a simultaneous control for both daily consumption rate and frequency of heavy drinking, it is clear from the relative prevalence rates for these behaviors that there exists a large group of persons, particularly young males, who on frequent occasions drink very heavily even though their average total volume may be quite modest.

5. Alcohol Problems in Civilian and Military Contexts

The data presented thus far establish that alcohol problems are substantially concentrated among young adults. Although the recent consumption trends do not necessarily indicate that problem rates are increasing, young men stand out as especially subject to the risks associated with heavy alcohol use. These results are derived from civilian survey samples, but several recent studies indicate that the same patterns appear among members of the military services (Cahalan & Cisin, 1975; Cahalan *et al.*, 1972). Because the members of the services are disproportionately male, young, and unaccompanied by spouses, they would be expected to be especially subject to risks from alcohol simply because of demographic characteristics. However, the reports from the above studies suggested that the rates of problem drinking, broadly defined, might be several times higher for enlisted personnel than for civilians, even when demographic characteristics are controlled. Such findings seem to imply that there is something unique about military service or its environment that plays a causal role in alcohol problems. Such influences could easily be conjectured if one notes that military personnel

Table 9. Alcohol Consumption in Civilian and Military Samples[a]

Age Group	U.S. civilians 1972–1974	Military personnel 1974–1977
Age 18–24	13.0	18.0
N	573	6,356
Age 25–60	7.4	11.4
N	1,955	12,041
All ages	8.7	13.8
All ages, adjusted to civilian age distribution	8.7	12.4
N	2,528	18,397

[a] Percentage consuming over 2 oz/day (males only).

are more subject than civilians to such disruptive events as relocation overseas, work aboard ship, and separation from family.

The data now available permit a more detailed examination of these issues. Since the time of the first published military studies, which concerned the Army and the Navy, several recent civilian surveys cited earlier and a comprehensive Air Force survey have become available. Although the U.S. Marine Corps has still not been covered by such a study, a combination of the Army, Navy, and Air Force data covers over 90% of armed forces personnel. More detail concerning the nature of the samples and interservice comparisons may be found in the Air Force report (Polich & Orvis, 1979). For our purposes here, it suffices to note that all the military data are based on anonymously administered questionnaires from large random probability samples of the entire service populations.

Table 9 exhibits a summary of results comparing the daily alcohol consumption rates of civilians and military personnel. The military data are combined from the three service surveys and are weighted to represent the aggregate of the Army, Navy, and Air Force populations. Each military survey contained questions on the frequency with which various amounts of alcohol were consumed, using the format of Cahalan *et al.* (1975). A quantity–frequency index of daily consumption was developed from these measures and was compared against a different quantity–frequency index employed in the civilian surveys, using an Air Force survey containing both types of questions. The two measures proved to be highly related ($r = .70$) and showed almost the same percentage distribution, implying that aggregate comparisons should yield about the same results with either index. The results of applying these indices to the civilian and military groups, as shown in Table 9, confirm that heavier drinking is more common in the military services, particularly among the 18–24 age group. However, the differences are not as extreme as might have been expected; the overall rate of high consumption in the military is about five percentage points higher than among civilians, a figure that drops to under four points when the age differences in the two populations are taken into account.

These modest differences may seem puzzling to one acquainted with the implications of the U.S. Army and the U.S. Navy studies. Although the relative ratio of military to civilian consumption rates shown here is not far from the ratios for problem-drinking rates reported in these studies, the impression given is quite different. Accordingly, we have also examined the rates of adverse consequences of drinking using both the "tangible consequences" measure of Cahalan and the adverse consequence measure developed earlier in this paper. Table 10 displays the tangible problem rates according to the Cahalan measure.

Several aspects of the data presented here require comment. The civilian surveys of the 1970s did not include a comprehensive set of consequences, so we must rely on the earlier civilian survey conducted by Cahalan and associates. This survey, it must be remembered, excluded both females and 18- to 20-year-olds. For military comparisons of

Table 10. "Tangible" Problem Rates in Civilian and Military Samples[a]

	Civilian[b]		Military[c]	
Subgroup	Rate	*N*	Rate	*N*
High school education	23.4	608	32.8	6,004
College education	10.9	369	19.8	10,482
Age 21–24	33.8	130	34.7	4,463
25–60	16.4	847	21.8	12,023
Total	18.7	977	26.6	16,486
Total, standardized for education and age[d]	18.7	977	24.9	16,486
Total, standardized for education, age, and marital status[d]	18.7	977	23.7	16,486

[a] Percentage with any "tangible alcohol problem" in the past three years, males only, as defined in Cahalan *et al.* (1975).
[b] U.S. national household sample, 1969, males only.
[c] Weighted results from representative samples of the U.S. Army (1972), the U.S. Navy (1974), and the U.S. Air Force (1977), adjusted to represent the true age and education distributions of the three military services (except for last two rows).
[d] Standardized to the civilians' joint distribution on the demographic variables.

prevalence rates, the exclusion of females is relatively unimportant, since they represented only a very small fraction of total military personnel during the period covered. The omission of the 18–20 age group is a little more troublesome because this group has one of the highest problem rates and it accounts for about 23% of the armed forces. A second point to bear in mind is that the Cahalan tangible consequences measure covers a very broad set of potentially adverse effects, from arrests and marital dissolutions down to "spending too much money on drinks" or finding that one's drinking is "very displeasing to a relative." The originators of the index emphasize that its chief utility lies in making relative comparisons across groups rather than in fixing an absolute prevalence rate.

The results in Table 10 indicate that broad classes of difficulties connected with drinking are more frequently found in the military services than among civilians but that a considerable portion of the discrepancy is due to the demographic characteristics of military personnel. Younger people and people without college education are considerably more subject to alcohol problems than their opposites. Partly because the military contains more people with such high-risk characteristics, the total military rate is several percentage points higher than the total civilian rate. However, when these demographic differences between the two groups are controlled, the rates converge by about three percentage points, leaving only a modest estimated difference between the two. It is this difference, at a maximum, that could be due to nondemographic factors such as location, working conditions, or differences in customs and attitudes. Of course, not all individual background factors have been controlled in this analysis, so it is possible that the military–civilian difference after adjustment for such other factors would be even smaller.

Nonetheless, the military rates for special subgroups—in particular, the high-school-educated—are somewhat higher than civilian rates. It is these differences that captured attention in the previous analysis of Army and Navy samples. The U.S. Navy report took note of the large difference between enlisted personnel and all civilians, showing that the age differences in these groups did not explain the discrepancy away. The data in Table 10 show essentially this same difference, which can be seen by contrasting high-school-educated military personnel, who are virtually all enlisted, with the total civilian group. (In the services, virtually all officers are college-educated, whereas the overwhelming majority of enlisted personnel are not.) However, such a comparison is not entirely suited to the questions we have posed because it leaves the education factor uncontrolled; high-school-educated military personnel are being compared with a civilian group containing a large admixture of college-educated people. To avoid such an uncontrolled comparison, we have standardized the samples simultaneously on both age and education and then on those factors plus marital status. These results, exhibited in the bottom lines of Table 10, imply that when the two groups are comprehensively matched on the most relevant demographic characteristics, the differences become relatively modest.

In order to obtain a reading of the relative rates of quite serious drinking problems, we also analyzed the adverse consequence index presented earlier for civilians. This index simply measures the presence of any of the serious work, family, law enforcement, or health problems discussed in Section 4. Table 11 shows comparisons and analyses using this index as the dependent variable. The results parallel the results just obtained for the Cahalan tangible consequence measure, except that the absolute rates are much lower. The military–civilian differences are accordingly even smaller than those in the previous table. The demographic factors still make a substantial difference in problem rates, showing the robustness of those basic variables. In terms of serious adverse consequences, there is almost no difference between the military and the civilian samples after basic demographic characteristics are controlled.

Table 11. Adverse Consequence Rates in Civilian and Military Samples[a]

	Civilian[b]		Military[c]	
Subgroup	Rate	N	Rate	N
High school education	10.9	608	16.3	6,004
College education	6.8	369	7.6	10,482
Age 21–24	19.2	130	16.7	4,463
Age 25–60	7.8	847	9.4	12,023
Total	9.3	977	12.1	16,486
Total, standardized for education and age[d]	9.3	977	11.3	16,486
Total, standardized for education, age, and marital status[d]	9.3	977	10.4	16,486

[a] Percentage with any serious adverse consequence in the past three years, males only, as defined in Table 6.
[b] U.S. national household sample, 1969, males only.
[c] Weighted results from representative samples of the U.S. Army (1972), the U.S. Navy (1974), and the U.S. Air Force (1977), adjusted to represent the true age and education distributions of the three military services (except for last two rows).
[d] Standardized to the civilians' joint distribution on the demographic variables.

The outcome of these analyses, taken in the aggregate, suggests that alcohol-related behavior in the military services is not so very different from the behavior of comparable civilians. In general, the consumption rates of military personnel are greater than those of civilians. However, the differences in absolute terms are in the neighborhood of a few percentage points. A similar difference between military personnel and civilians appears with the use of the Cahalan problem-drinking index. Because of its inclusiveness, that index shows high rates of problems for both military and civilians, but as before, the difference between the two is confined to a few percentage points when matched demographic groups are compared. If attention is focused on very serious and concrete adverse consequences, represented by the special index proposed here, the civilian–military difference almost disappears after matching. A large part of the explanation for the seemingly higher military rates of alcohol problems lies with the demographic makeup of the military services: Compared with civilians, military personnel tend to be younger, less educated, and less often accompanied by spouses at their duty stations. It appears that after these demographic factors are taken into account, only a small discrepancy remains that could be attributed to unique characteristics of the military.

6. Implication for Research and Policy

The traditions of both research and policy in the field of alcohol problems have been preoccupied with the phenomenon of alcoholism. It has been only in the fairly recent past that even the research community has come to recognize the diversity of alcohol problems, which range over a wide territory. That territory encompasses not only chronic alcoholism, or the "alcohol dependence syndrome," but also various forms of heavy ethanol consumption, intoxication, and adverse consequences. The available evidence suggests that these other forms of alcohol problems occur more often in the *absence* of alcohol dependence than in its presence. That is to say, more people are seriously affected by alcohol problems without dependence than are affected by the chronic, debilitating disorder identified as alcoholism. Nevertheless, treatment of alocholism continues to absorb the great majority of research, public attention, and national effort devoted to alcohol problems.

Among young adults, the prominence of alcohol problems, as opposed to alcoholism, is not to be doubted. All of the data we have examined show that young adults, especially young males, face risks from alcohol that are higher than those faced by any other demographic group. Young males drink more frequently, drink higher amounts per occasion, and get into serious trouble because of drinking at rates that range from two to three times as high as those in other segments of the population. A very important question, as yet unanswered, is the extent to which those young people engaging in heavy drinking are also placed at risk of developing alcohol dependence. At this point, we lack the longitudinal studies necessary to isolate those behaviors that would indicate such a developmental path as opposed to a temporary phase of heavy drinking.

The available evidence suggests that the principal immediate risks for young people are probably not those of dependence in any event. Instead, the risks appear to be concentrated in the increased probabilities of accidents, law enforcement incidents, impaired productivity, and marital disruption. There is, of course, no disputing the fact that long-term excessive consumption of ethanol leads to liver damage and other organic pathologies. Nevertheless, the general-population surveys show that very few individuals approach the extreme daily consumption levels identified with organic damage. At the same time, the surveys confirm that consumption levels commonly found among young males do imply significant risks of more immediate economic and social problems. Thus, the fact that there are very few individuals reporting extreme levels of consumption is little reason for complacency.

The immediate effects of heavy drinking may be assessed by our measures of serious adverse consequences. According to these relatively crude measures, 9% of the male population, but 19% of males aged 21–24, are affected by adverse consequences of drinking during a three-year period. However, the general importance of this percentage to society is uncertain; in particular, the impact of these events on physical health and economic productivity cannot be measured with the available data. Such an assessment would seem to be an important area for future research. Rational decisions about the amount of national resources appropriately invested in combating alcohol problems should depend on an assessment of the cost of such problems in the first place.

The concentration of alcohol problems among young males makes it natural to examine more carefully particular segments of the population where they are heavily represented. The armed forces constitute such a segment, not only because of their demographics but also because military service entails certain conditions, such as transfer to remote locations, that might be linked to alcohol problems. Added to such conditions is the fact that military personnel generally consume more alcohol than civilians. Yet a review of the available data indicates that the prevalence rates for adverse consequences of drinking are only slightly higher among the military after the background characteristics of individuals are controlled. Even the very inclusive Cahalan problem-drinking index shows only a modest civilian–military discrepancy after controlling for age and education. Although the data are not completely definitive, they suggest that the somewhat higher rates of alcohol problems in the military are due largely to basic demographic variables rather than to anything unique about the military.

The accumulation of research on alcohol problems in youth serves to reemphasize the need for greater impetus in certain policy directions. The utility of policies that focus the overwhelming majority of resources on chronic alcoholism is clearly called into question by these data. The magnitude of alcohol problems not connected with alcohol dependence is certainly great enough to warrant further attention, particularly among the younger cohorts. The data also imply that males, not females, are the primary risk population for all types of alcohol problems, including alcoholism. The general-population data decisively demonstrate that the female segment of the problem-drinking group is small in proportion to the male segment. As important as it may be to identify and ameliorate the alcohol problems experienced by women, the bulk of the resources devoted to intervention should presumably be targeted on males, except where unique risks for females can be shown, such as the fetal alcohol syndrome. Finally, the nature of problem development and the payoffs to "early intervention" need to be evaluated. If early intervention is intended to prevent the immediate consequences of excessive drinking among youth, it requires justification by the demonstration that rates of adverse consequences are reduced by intervention programs. If intervention is to be based on a model concerned with preventing the development of future alcoholism, even more evidence is needed since the parameters of such a developmental process are unclear and the ability of intervention to forestall the process is uncertain. The imperatives of both research and policy suggest that better understanding of such developmental processes should be a singular priority in the area of youth and alcohol problems.

References

Armor, D. J., Polich, J. M., & Stambul, H. B. *Alcoholism and treatment*. New York: Wiley, 1978.

Blane, H. T., & Hewitt, L. E. *Alcohol and youth: An analysis of the literature, 1960–1975.* Washington, D.C.: National Institute on Alcohol Abuse and Alcoholism, 1977.

Bruun, K., Edwards, G., Lumio, M., Mäkelä, K., Pan, L., Popham, R. E., Room, R., Schmidt, W., Skog, O., Sulkunen, P., & Oesterberg, E. *Alcohol control policies in public health perspective.* Helsinki: Finnish Foundation for Alcohol Studies, 1975.

Cahalan, D. *Problem drinkers.* San Francisco: Jossey-Bass, 1970.

Cahalan, D., & Cisin, I. *Final report on a service-wide survey of attitudes and behavior of naval personnel concerning alcohol and problem drinking.* Washington, D.C.: Bureau of Social Science Research, 1975.

Cahalan, D., & Room, R. *Problem drinking among American men.* New Brunswick, N.J.: Rutgers Center of Alcohol Studies, 1974.

Cahalan, D., Cisin, I. H., & Crossley, H. M. *American drinking practices.* New Brunswick, N.J.: Rutgers Center of Alcohol Studies, 1969.

Cahalan, D., Cisin, I. H., Gardner, G. L., & Smith, G. C. *Drinking practices and problems in the U.S. Army, 1972.* Washington, D.C.: Information Concepts, 1972.

Clark, W. B. Conceptions of alcoholism: Consequences for research. *Addictive Disorders,* 1975, *1,* 395–430.

Davies, D. L. Definitional issues in alcoholism. In R. E. Tartar & A. A. Sugerman (Eds.), *Alcoholism: Interdisciplinary approaches to an enduring problem.* Reading, Mass.: Addison-Wesley, 1976.

de Lint, J., & Schmidt, W. Alcoholism and mortality. In B. Kissin & H. Begleiter (Eds.), *Social aspects of alcoholism. Vol. 4: The biology of alcoholism.* New York: Plenum Press, 1976.

Edwards, G. The alcohol dependence syndrome: Usefulness of an idea. In G. Edwards & M. Grant (Eds.), *Alcoholism: New knowledge and new responses.* Baltimore: University Press, 1976.

Edwards, G., Gross, M. M., Keller, M., Moser, J., & Room, R. *Alcohol-related disabilities.* Geneva: World Health Organization, Offset Publication Number 32, 1977.

Harris, L. *Public awareness of the National Institute on Alcohol Abuse and Alcoholism advertising campaign and public attitudes toward drinking and alcohol abuse.* Overall study final report, prepared for the National Institute on Alcohol Abuse and Alcoholism. New York: Louis Harris and Associates, 1975.

Jellinek, E. M. *The disease concept of alcoholism.* New Brunswick, N.J.: Hillhouse Press, 1960.

Johnson, P., Armor, D. J., Pollich, S., & Stambul, H. B. *U.S. adult drinking practices: Time trends, social correlates, and sex roles.* Report distributed by the National Technical Information Service, prepared under Contract ADM–281–76–0020. Washington, D.C.: National Institute on Alcohol Abuse and Alcoholism, 1979.

Keller, M. The disease concept of alcoholism revisited. *Journal of Studies on Alcohol,* 1976, *37,* 1694–1717.

Lelbach, W. Organic pathology related to volume and pattern of alcohol use. In R. J. Gibbins, Y. Israel, H. Kalant, R. E. Popham, W. Schmidt, & R. G. Smart (Eds.), *Research advances in alcohol and drug problems* (Vol. 1). New York: Wiley, 1974.

National Council on Alcoholism. Criteria for the diagnosis of alcoholism. *Annals of Internal Medicine,* 1972, *77,* 249–258.

Paredes, A. The history of the concept of alcoholism. In R. E. Tartar & A. A. Sugerman (Eds.), *Alcoholism: Interdisciplinary approaches to an enduring problem.* Reading, Mass.: Addison-Wesley, 1976.

Pernanen, K. Validity of survey data on alcohol use. In R. J. Gibbins, Y. Israel, H. Kalant, R. E. Popham, W. Schmidt, & R. G. Smart (Eds.), *Research advances in alcohol and drug problems* (Vol. 1). New York: Wiley, 1974.

Polich, J. M., & Orvis, B. R. *Alcohol problems: Patterns and prevalence in the U.S. Air Force.* Santa Monica: The Rand Corporation, 1979.

Roizen, R., Cahalan, D., & Shanks, P. Spontaneous remission among untreated problem drinkers. In D. B. Kandal (Ed.), *Longitudinal research on drug abuse.* Washington, D.C.: Hemisphere, 1978.

Room, R. Survey vs. sales data for the U.S. *Drinking and drug practices surveyor,* 3, 15–16. Berkeley: University of California, 1971.

Room, R. Measurement and distribution of drinking patterns and problems in general

populations. In G. Edwards (Ed.), *Alcohol-related disabilities*. Geneva: World Health Organization, Offset Publication Number 32, 1977.
Schmidt, W. Cirrhosis and alcohol consumption: An epidemiological perspective, In G. Edwards & M. Grant (Eds.), *Alcoholism: New knowledge and new responses*. Baltimore: University Park Press, 1976.
Schmidt, W., & de Lint, J. Estimating the prevalence of alcoholism from alcohol consumption and mortality data. *Quarterly Journal of Studies on Alcohol*, 1970, *31*, 957–964.
Schmidt, W., & de Lint, J. Causes of death of alcoholics. *Quarterly Journal of Studies on Alcohol*, 1972, *33*, 171–185.
U.S. Department of Health, Education, and Welfare. *Alcohol and health: Third speical report to Congress*. Washington, D.C.: U.S. Government Printing Office, 1978.
Wallgren, H., & Barry, H. *Actions of alcohol* (Vol. 2). Amsterdam: Elsevier, 1970.
World Health Organization. *Report of the second session of the Alcoholism Subcommittee, Expert Committee on Mental Health*. Geneva: World Health Organization, Technical Report Series Number 48, 1952.

II

Theoretical Models of Drinking among Adolescents and Young Adults

Historically, careful conceptualization in the field of alcohol studies has been the exception, not the rule. Much of the research reported in the literature proceeds from an empirical and atheoretical orientation. Further, the literature, as abundant as it is, is essentially nonscientific in character. That is to say, there has been little building of a cumulative data base that would add to our knowledge, guide our thinking, and so further our understanding of alcohol problems. Given the embryonic nature of the field in its early days, some of the first single-factor theories were fitting. From a current perspective, we can see that these early models were overly simple in formulation. They often grew out of a misperception of the experimental tradition of science as applied to social problems, which may foster single-factor explanations of a complex phenomenon. For example, one early formulation of problem drinking placed almost exclusive emphasis upon the nature and quality of the first drinking experience. More complex, but nevertheless still basically univariate models, include dependency-conflict formulations and power-inhibition models.

Another difficulty with these early theoretical attempts is that they fit only too well with popular conceptions of drinking behavior among young people. Popular conceptions are basically nonexplanatory and often pejorative and value-laden. To attribute drinking and its problems, for instance, to peer influences in an unelaborated manner does not further understanding but translates only too readily into a "bad companions" model of drinking behavior.

The growing maturation of the social-behavioral sciences in recent years, accompanied by major advances in analytic methods that permit examination of the effect of several variables simultaneously, has begun to become apparent in efforts at conceptualizing drinking behavior. Theoretical sophistication and subtlety are far more apparent than they used to be in models put forth to explain drinking behavior in general and among youth in particular. The chapters in this volume reflect this more complex conceptual approach.

Robert Zucker provides a broad and comprehensive, yet detailed, discussion of the manifold factors that need to be taken into account before a truly general theory of drinking behavior can be formulated. He adopts an essentially developmental point of departure that covers the span of the life cycle from infancy to old age. Within this framework, he examines the interactive influences of distant and immediate (distal and proximal) social and situational factors as well as internal personality and physiological factors (such as activity levels and levels of arousal). Zucker's model further permits us to begin to delineate the relative influence on drinking behavior of factors specific to alcohol and those that are nonspecific. For example, he examines the relationship between parental drinking behavior, on the one hand, and parental child-rearing patterns, on the other, as they in turn affect the child's drinking behavior and its consequences.

A problem with much of the research about drinking behavior and youthful alcohol problems is that it is for the most part correlational and does not deal conceptually or empirically with antecedent–consequent relationships. Its explanatory value, therefore, has been extremely limited. Zucker's model promises to change this conceptual stagnation by stimulating research oriented toward elucidating causal relationships.

Thomas Harford, in his chapter, provides a provocative new approach as he outlines an ecological perspective on drinking. Like Zucker, Harford points out the need for comprehensiveness in explanatory models. By novel use of case history vignettes of normal drinking behavior during a four-week period, he demonstrates the complexity of interaction among variables that determine drinking practices, simultaneously showing the richness and variety of the situational and objective environmental variables involved. The notions he puts forth concerning objective and perceived environments, internal and external environments, recast the traditional equation of personality × environment = behavior in an entirely new mold. Harford's theoretical stance and the evidence he advances for it complement Zucker's presentation, in that Harford expands upon the role of environmental factors in determining drinking behavior without losing sight of the importance of the dynamic interplay between the environment, on the one hand, and intra- and interpersonal dimensions, on the other, as they shift and change throughout the life span.

The contribution of Sharon and Richard Wilsnack on sex roles in relation to adolescent drinking behavior at first appears to stem from a differing posture concerning the role of theory in explaining drinking behavior. That this is a misperception soon becomes apparent and depends on distinguishing between the level of analytic inquiry that each author has chosen to adopt. Both Zucker and Harford make macrolevel statements about an important aspect of human behavior. Their formulations are heuristic in the sense that they guide and stimulate research and further conceptual inquiry. The Wilsnacks, on the other hand, choose a molecular approach to a specific but important dynamic in the development of drinking behavior. They present new findings, using a sophisticated multivariate analysis of a large body of empirical data collected in the national study of adolescent drinking conducted in 1974–1975 by the National Institute on Alcohol Abuse and Alcoholism. Their conceptualization and analysis of sex role presupposes a broader theoretical framework not unlike that presented by Zucker.

The contributions in Part II are important on several counts. They represent a new sophistication current in the social and behavioral sciences in thinking about drinking. Also, they promise to stimulate research and refined conceptualizations that will build cumulatively and add to our understanding of alcohol problems. This approach may be contrasted with the current atheoretical accumulation of facts that adds little to knowledge or to furthering the understanding of a complex problem. These theoretical contributions are further significant in that they stress the importance of environmental influences in shaping and molding behavior. This stress tends to redress an emphasis on intrapsychic and interpersonal dimensions in shaping drinking behavior; perhaps more important, inclusion of an environmental approach implies directions for control in order to minimize alcohol problems. Internal states and interpersonal behavior are much more difficult to modify than environmental factors.

These contributions are important and sufficiently justify the presence of these three chapters in this volume. There is, however, an even more important consideration, and that has to do with the fact that these contributions signify a movement to bring drinking behavior into the mainstream of current theoretical developments in the social and behavioral sciences generally. This represents an entirely new development in the field of alcohol studies, which has traditionally borrowed, with considerable time lag, from the mainstream of psychology, sociology, anthropology, and other disciplines. This phenomenon is not atypical for categorical concerns that do not flow from a parent discipline (for example, schizophrenia, juvenile delinquency, and other social and mental health problems). In specific problem areas, developments of theory and methodology are usually not implemented until some time after they have become common intellectual currency within a discipline. Examples abound in the area of alcohol studies. Little research has been conducted concerning attribution theory; this is surprising, given the importance that responsibility for behavior assumes in regard to alcohol problems. Locus of control, which would seem to be similarly important, became a hot issue in the alcohol studies area considerably after it had lost its theoretical and explanatory glow as a burning issue in social and clinical psychology. Studies of Machiavellianism have never been conducted with alcoholic samples. Social learning methods and techniques have been used for a number of years in the modification of habits (for example, obesity and smoking) but are just beginning to be applied in the alcohol area (see Chapter 12 for an exposition of the possible use of behavioral methods in modifying drinking behavior among young adults). Thus, the fact that these chapters bring drinking behavior into the mainstream of theory and thinking within the social-behavioral sciences is a hallmark in the field of alcohol studies. The significance of this development cannot be overestimated.

4

Developmental Aspects of Drinking through the Young Adult Years

Robert A. Zucker

1. Introduction

The consumption of alcoholic beverages at any point in the life span of the individual may be viewed from a variety of perspectives. It may be seen as an attribute of *personality*, in which case the investigator's primary concern is the stability and predictability of drinking behavior as a function of intraindividual factors. These may be traits, attitudes, motives, or habits whose presence (or absence) or relative degree of strength leads to a greater likelihood that drinking behavior will occur (cf. McClelland, Davis, Kalin, & Wanner, 1972; Williams, 1976). Such a perspective usually implies the presence of some stability of the behavior both across situations and over periods of time.

Drinking and its various sequelae may also be viewed as an attribute of situations (*situational influences*). From this point of view, the individual act of drinking is seen as the product of extraindividual characteristics, whether they be availability of alcohol, social support pressures for drinking and deviance among peers, presence of other drinkers, or such environmental factors as time of day, setting, and type of community where the drinker lives or does his drinking (cf. Snow, 1975; Sommer, 1965). Here again, the model presumes that regularities in

Robert A. Zucker • Department of Psychology, Michigan State University, East Lansing, MI 48824.

behavior can be demonstrated, but their source is ecological rather than personal.

A related but more strictly interpersonal perspective is contained within *sociocultural theories* of drinking activity. Here also, individual behavior is examined and explained by way of contextual impacts, but the content of the variables is restricted to the social environment and those nonsocial elements (e.g., biological age, sex, setting) that have social representations. These representations take the form of attitudes about such elements and norms regarding what are appropriate and inappropriate types of behavior (Cahalan, 1970; Field, 1962; Bacon, Barry, & Child, 1965). From this perspective, drinking behavior is governed by group processes; it "reflects the institutionalized behavior patterns of the significant social groups with which he [the individual] is identified and mirrors the complex cultural traditions of American society" (Maddox, 1964, pp. 37–38). Drinking behavior is learned, it is regulated by cultural traditions, and even deviations from the social norms are guided by social controls and social roles (Bales, 1962; Maddox & McCall, 1964; Snyder, 1962).

At the opposite end of the spectrum, *biologically* and *biochemically oriented investigators* (e.g., Mendelson, 1971; Goodwin, 1976b), focusing more on the pathological end of the drinking continuum, are concerned with the *pharmacological actions* of alcohol. This theoretical position is concerned with differences in initial response to the drug and with individual biochemical differences in both the metabolism and the metabolic by-products of alcohol ingestion. The understanding of these processes is deemed to be a vital link in explaining individual differences in alcohol consumption, in tolerance, and in understanding the mechanism of the presumptive additive disorder found among long-term, heavy consumers of the drug. Within this framework, disturbances of alcohol consumption are viewed as the manifestations of a medical (i.e., biological) disease process that remains to be charted physiologically. The organism of those specially afflicted with the disorder is presumed in some basic way to be wired differently, whether it be via genetic factors or prenatal influences, which lead to a biologic unfolding that produces both greater risk for and susceptibility to alcohol effects, once exposure to the drug has been effected. Behavioral effects are important but are presumed to be consequences rather than causes of the disturbance.

All of the above points of view are best characterized as monist positions, advocating a "simple and sovereign" theory (Allport, 1954) of the acquisition and maintenance of alcohol consumption and its related behaviors. From what we know of the complex nature of alcohol-related behavior, all are incomplete as overarching theories. Nevertheless, such positions are appropriate at early stages in scientific inquiry. They allow the investigator who embraces a particular one to push it as far as it will go, without having to be preoccupied with levels of data and explanations that the model and the conceptual language cannot handle. While such views are appropriate at early levels of empirical inquiry, they have serious defects as our data base expands. We are beginning to develop *interactional* theories (e.g., Kissin, 1977; Jessor & Jessor, 1977) at varying levels of sophistication and integration of sources of effect; where such integrations are not present, there is at least increasing attention given to the reasons for avoiding them (e.g., Cahalan & Cisin, 1976; Goodwin, 1976b). These efforts and my own reading of the empirical sophistication of the late 1970s suggest that the time for early-stage interactionist explanations is at hand if we are to develop conceptual models that will adequately predict and allow for the modification of drinking behavior.

The present review both openly advocates and is organized around such an interactionist perspective. Obviously, this perspective must traverse a number of data languages, ranging from the physiological (insofar as constitutional factors are represented) to the sociocultural (as it impinges on the biological organism by way of learning and socialization). In addition, if this perspective is to be truly representational, it must encompass organismic time as it relates not only to the learned history of drinking but also to the unfolding and maturation of the organism, leading to differing degrees of readiness for and attraction to alcohol consumption. Such a perspective is a *developmental* one. To paraphrase Kessen (1960), my concern is to establish a developmental model of drinking that is able to link age to drinking phenomena in an orderly way. Such ordering implies a clearer understanding of acquisition and maintenance processes, as they relate to maturation (unfolding), to learning, and to the specified time points where the impact of agents or agencies in the environment are felt.

In elaborating this process, the present review examines the time frame up through young adulthood (the early 20s). The organization of the review is as follows: (1) some conceptual distinctions are made among types of drinking phenomena as these relate to possible developmental process; (2) a conceptual structure is given, around which both longitudinal and cross-sectional research on drinking can be organized; (3) within this structure the available evidence on developmental processes in drinking is reviewed; finally, (4) a section is devoted to issues of continuity and discontinuity in developmental process as these relate to the available data and to current theories about drinking and problem drinking.

2. Some Conceptual Distinctions

2.1. Issues of Continuity–Discontinuity in Developmental Processes

In asking the question "How does drinking develop over time?" we might naively assume that drinking at developmental time point A is similar to, or identical with, drinking at a later developmental time point B. This may conceivably be the case but it must be established.

To highlight the implications of this issue, such a position would argue that factors relevant to the onset or acquisition of drinking are similar to those involved in the shift from moderate levels of drinking to more problem-related levels (or types) of drinking. While such an argument at a theoretical level is plausible, it presumes a continuity in the drinking process—from no drinking through nonproblem-related drinking through problem drinking, all the way to alcoholism (conceived of here as a chronic form of alcohol abuse)—that may or may not be there in reality and at the very least must be demonstrated empirically. In fact, when our area of discourse is early drinking, some investigators argue that problem drinking at this developmental time point is, by definition, not the same phenomenon as problem drinking and alcoholism in middle adulthood (cf. Bacon, 1976; Marden, Zylman, Fillmore, & Bacon, 1976; Rachal, Hubbard, Williams, & Tuchfeld, 1976). The position we take here is a simple one: the problem is ultimately not so much definitional as empirical–historical. When we can adequately map out the types of developmental course for types of drinkers, then the continuity-of-process issue can be resolved.

A related issue is the definition of alcoholism as a chronic and progressive disorder (e.g., National Council of Alcoholism, 1972; Jellinek, 1960). To take this position is to presume continuity in developmental process. This is another issue that needs to be closely examined.

To summarize then, our questions here concern (1) the extent to which there is evidence that the same factors are responsible for transition-related phenomena (from nondrinking to drinking) as are responsible for later transitions (from nonproblem drinking to problem drinking and from problem drinking to alcoholism); (2) the extent to which there is evidence (or not) for continuity within persons, over time, in "severity" or "extremes" of drinking behavior.

2.2. Issues of Behavioral Focus

As we noted in the introductory section, some perspectives on drinking emphasize the processes as they occur within individuals, both biologically and as social beings, and others focus more on the situational, social, and cultural aspects of drinking. From these contrasting standpoints, drinking may be seen as either an attribute of persons or, conversely, as a type of behavioral event. While this may not seem to be a terribly important observation to alcohologists, sociologists, or epidemiologists, it happens to be a vitally important distinction that is more peculiar to alcohol-related phenomena (and the theories used to account for them) than it is to other forms of psychopathology, such as depression and antisocial behavior.

In the conceptualizations of other forms of psychopathology, our primary focus is on the individual and the meaning context of the particular symptom within the framework of a style of life. In contrast, where drinking is concerned, we can adopt a similar focus, in which case our explanations are then usually labeled as theories of alcoholism or problem drinking, or alcohol abuse. Or we can focus on the act itself, how it is learned, how the probabilities of increased occurrence are likely to come about, what the situational contexts are in which problem sequelae are likely to emerge, etc. Such theories typically are situational or epidemiological. The point we make here is that the difference in such theories implies a primary distinction between focus on the *drinker* as compared to focus on the *drinking*. Differences in these theories lead us to different models of etiology, intervention, and prevention. We will have more to say about this in the latter part of the chapter.

2.3. Drinking-Specific versus Nondrinking-Specific Theories

Related to the issue of focus on the act versus focus on the actor, we can identify two types of theory about the development of drinking. One is a *drinking-specific theory* (Zucker, 1976), a conceptualization of drinking phenomena in terms exclusively related to alcohol variables. The specifics of learning to consume alcohol, learning the activities connected with drinking, and maintaining drinking behavior are presumed to be best understood by examining drinking influences both within the subject and within his environment. Thus learning to drink could be dealt with in terms of the amount of drinking in the subject's environment, the availability of alcohol, attitudes toward alcohol prior to drinking, etc. This is very much a behavioral theory, although within the alcohol field it is espoused by others as well as by behaviorally oriented treatment researchers.

In contrast, *nondrinking-specific* theories conceptualize the process in terms that include alcohol consumption, but that first concern behaviors and need patterns more central to human functioning, and not directly related to the drinking act and its sequelae. From this perspective, drinking is conceptualized as one alternative behavior that emerges given the presence of the necessary biological, psychological, or social preconditions. For example, if heightened aggressiveness were conceived of as a necessary precondition for earlier drinking, a complete conceptualization would include initial temperamental differences in activity level, parental modeling of aggression as a stimulator of heightened aggressive drives, cultural tolerance of aggressive behavior, and the like. These factors, in turn, should lead to greater aggression-related needs in the child. If alcohol consumption allowed for the heightened display of aggressive behavior and/or aggressive fantasies, then earlier and/or heavier drinking would be construed as one potential outcome of the matrix of these nondrinking-specific elements, provided that alcohol were available in the environment.

From a developmental standpoint, nondrinking-specific theories have a potentially greater ability to map continuities in process over longer periods of the life span, insofar as they allow for varied phenotypic expression of underlying and presumably more enduring characteristics. In these respects, they provide a conceptual framework that traces underlying continuity in the face of manifest transition and discontinuity. One note of caution is needed, however. While such theories may be heuristically more useful, they still need to be put to the test of empirical usefulness. In this regard, by the very nature of their broad base, they may in fact be less powerful predictively than are the narrow-based drinking-specific theories.

2.4. Psychopharmacology and Developmental Explanations of Drinking Behavior

> Drinking behavior among teenagers, wherever it is found, will typically be associated with the increasing identification of the young person with adult status if adulthood is perceived as involving some use of beverage alcohol. It is important to note that the hypothesis does not state that a teenager will come to drinking simply as a result of growing up. His drinking behavior is associated with growing up in an environment in which an important status to which he legitimately aspires, that of becoming an adult, is perceived typically as involving alcohol use.
>
> An adolescent does not have to invent the idea of drinking; he learns it. Some alcohol use is probably involved in growing up in a society in which most adults drink. (Maddox & McCall, 1964, p. 106).

While this statement is true within the framework of the data base generated by the authors, the reader should also be aware that we regard it as outdated, and in a sense provincial, because of the special nature of the drinking act being considered here, namely, the consumption of ethyl alcohol. This particular substance, unlike some others, has special pharmacological properties that lead to fairly immediate and somewhat specifiable changes that involve perception, fantasy, and mood and that vary as a function of how much of the substance is ingested (Carpenter & Armenti, 1972). This complex set of changes is a function, in part, of set, setting, and prior history of exposure to the drug (Kalin, 1964). Any developmental explanation of drinking behavior needs to take at least some account of the psychopharmacological aspects of the behavior in question and must detail the role that experience with the drug plays in either enhancing or changing the learning experiences of drinking. This point is especially relevant in adulthood when drinking involves a long history of drug use, as in cases of chronic alcoholism. (See also, Goodwin, 1976b; Nathan & Lansky, 1978.)

2.5. Variance

Although not strictly a conceptual issue, one other point needs attending to that ultimately relates very directly to the conceptual structures of our theories: the amount of variance accounted for separately and in interaction by different conceptual frameworks. One has only to peruse the abstract sections of the *Journal of Studies on Alcohol* for the last few years to be struck by the overwhelming number of concepts and variables linked to alcoholism and drinking etiology. Not all of them are important, even when they have proved themselves to be real in the sense that they account for statistically significant and replicable differences between drinking groups and their appropriate controls. As we move toward multilevel causal explanations, both developmental and cross-sectional, it becomes increasingly important to make sound judgments, based on the evidence, about the impact of the variables we include in our conceptual structures. My position is that, in general, characteristics that account for a larger proportion of the variance related to drinking are more important in ultimately tracing out the mechanism and the etiology of drinking than are those of small account; the latter are statistically significant but are practically insignificant.

3. An Organizational Framework for Developmental Processes Related to the Acquisition and Maintenance of Drinking Behavior

An earlier paper outlined a heuristic model for pathways of family influence upon the child's drinking (Zucker, 1976). It included sociocultural, parental, peer, and intraindividual levels of influence. The model is expanded here, to take account of interaction across the multiple data bases that the evidence suggests are important in accounting for drinking behavior. Figure 1 depicts the basic cross-sectional structure of the model. Class I influences, those concerned with the impact of the culture and the immediate community, include both drinking-specific and nondrinking-specific elements. They set the stage for possible drinking behavior in the sense that they have only indirect impact upon the person during early developmental periods, hence the unidirectional arrows. They very directly influence the Class II variables insofar as they

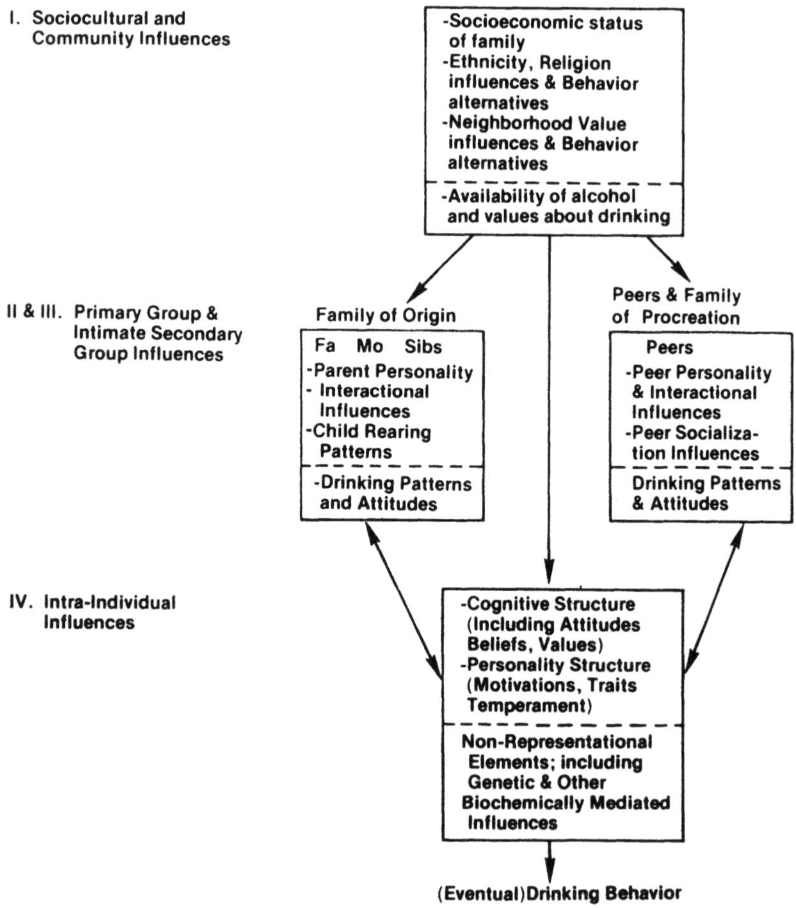

Figure 1. An organizational structure for classes of influences upon drinking behavior.

specify the groupings of work, play and intimacy, and the freedom of movement in such groupings that both family and the peer group have available to them in socializing the individual. They clearly have very direct influence in the sense that individual drinking cannot occur if beverage alcohol is unavailable.

Classes II and III are concerned with the effects of primary-group and intimate secondary-group members upon drinking behavior. Class II focuses on the primary socialization agency, the family, and its multiple levels of influence. These include both drinking- and nondrinking-specific variables and both direct and indirect effects. Direct influences are primarily those relating to socialization to alcohol use and to types of behavior acceptable within and outside of the family unit. Indirect effects occur via the parents' modeling of their own adaptations to alcohol and their indirect communication, via their own behavior, of standards of acceptable conduct.

Class III elements parallel family processes in that they also can be direct socialization effects, can produce change via modeling, and relate to both drinking experience and nondrinking-specific behavior. Both types of influence are depicted with arrows showing effects in two directions; we conceive of these effects as being interactional or, more appropriately, as transactional in the sense that both the child and the other parties to the influencing process have a mutual impact (cf. Sameroff, 1975).

Class IV elements are concerned with within-the-individual influences. They cut across a number of data levels, including (a) psychological structures such as attitudes and personality patterns; (b) temperament, which encompasses behavioral style and might, on the one hand, be considered a personality variable, yet, on the other, is clearly also a partial representation of constitutional factors; and (c) physiological influences insofar as they may determine predisposition to alcohol use and/or individual differences in the way it is absorbed and metabolized and the effects it has on central nervous system functioning.

The organizational framework outlined so far simply details the interrelation of influencing structures at a single time point. For a thorough developmental explanation, the structure needs to account for possible changes in the salience of these influences over organismic time. Figure 2 is a representational attempt at depicting this; it illustrates how the structure might change as the person matures. Classes of influence not relevant at one point (e.g., peer influences at birth and in early childhood) come into play at another point (e.g., adolescence); others, such as family effects, lose their importance as developmental time increases. For the purposes of illustration, only three time points are depicted here, although in actuality, the structure is a continuous one, with the relative contributory strength of influencing variables and classes represented by greater or lesser areas of each of the rectangles. Also, for purposes of convenience, prior (historical) influences of any of the classes are presumed to be transmitted via intraindividual learning or structural change. This may not necessarily be the case, as, for example, when early family influences continue to maintain their effect by way of sustained contact with family members.

4. Developmental Aspects of Drinking from Birth through the Young Adult Years

4.1. Introduction

In examining the substantive data on the acquisition and maintenance of drinking behavior through early adulthood, we need to bear in mind that the large majority of studies related to alcohol use start after the drinking behavior has commenced. The data base we have to work with in attempting to trace the developmental process is occasionally replicated, more often based on one or two studies, and sometimes

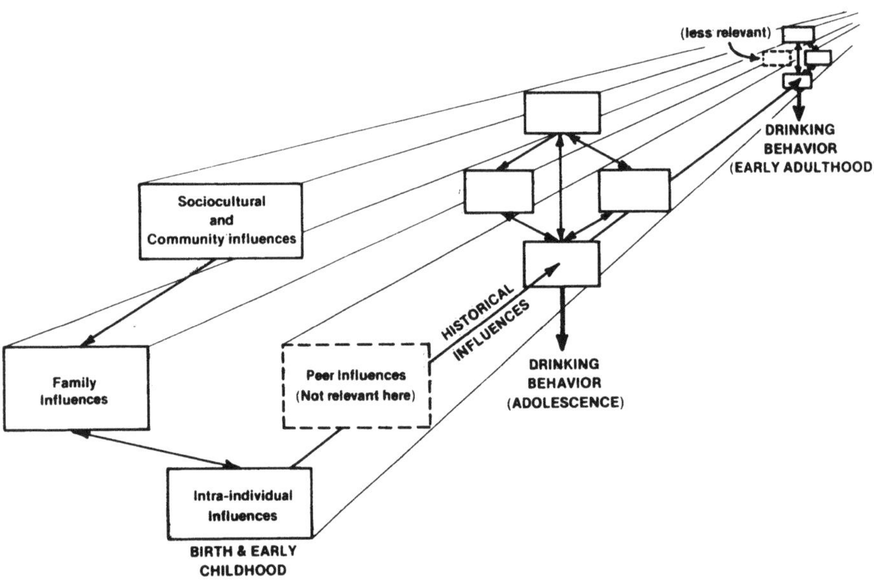

Figure 2. A heuristic model for changes in influencing structures affecting drinking behavior over developmental time.

requires a good deal of inference to fill in the gaps. This review is organized around three developmental periods: (1) conception through early childhood; (2) middle childhood through adolescence; and (3) young adulthood and beyond. Within each period, the literature is organized by way of the model just presented.

4.2. Conception through Early Childhood

The effects of sociocultural background and immediate community influences upon the early behavior of the child, as these relate to the later development of drinking behavior in its normal and more abusive forms, remain undocumented at this time. However, on the basis of what we know about normal developmental processes and about later drinking, there is every reason to suspect that these factors have some indirect, long-term influence on drinking and may in addition have a direct impact on the learning-to-drink process.

Early in adolescence, when drinking behavior first overtly emerges, small but consistent social-class differences separate those who drink from those who do not; persons from white-collar backgrounds are somewhat less likely to be abstainers than those from blue-collar backgrounds (Rachal, Williams, Brehm, Cavanaugh, Moore, & Eckerman, 1975). There is also strong evidence from other sources that religious and ethnic backgrounds differentiate those with a greater number and severity of alcohol problems in both adolescence and later life (Cahalan & Room, 1974; Jessor, Graves, Hanson, & Jessor, 1968; Rachal *et al.*, 1975). Explanations of these effects are usually couched in drinking-specific terms; as such they can be expected to have a most immediate effect upon the person when he or she becomes aware of beverage alcohol and contemplates using it . . . certainly long after early childhood.

What is left out of such explanations (with the exception of Jessor's work) is the ecological influence of socioeconomic and ethnoreligious factors on the family at earlier time points, insofar as it sets the climate and the opportunity structure within which the child is conceived, cared for, and socialized. We will see later that both mood (depressed) and behavioral style (impulsive) are related on an intraindividual level to the production of alcohol problems. Once this is accepted, it becomes a very reasonable first step to look for the development of such behaviors out of an ecological climate—of lack of opportunity—that encourages them. On an even more direct level, it is by now well documented that income level and racial and ethnic background are related to the greater infant mortality, prematurity, and physical and neural defects in offspring among the more deprived social groups (Birch & Gussow, 1970; Knoblock & Pasamanick, 1966; Pasamanick & Knoblock, 1966; White House Conference on Children, 1970). At least some of these mishaps are the direct effect of the lack of available facilities, support systems, adequate diet, and prenatal care. Once the chain of physical deprivation and developmental deficit starts, the opportunity structure makes it even less likely that the child will mature out of it (cf. Sameroff & Chandler, 1975). The point is that even in very early development, social structure may have a direct and possibly enduring effect on the biology of the child and the physical and emotional well-being of the mother. There is scant evidence at this point to document such effects (see the discussion of Class IV influences below), but the matter is well worth pursuing.

Class III influences—secondary-group relationships outside the family—upon later drinking are probably unimportant in any direct sense in early childhood. Play relationships with others are primarily noninteractive (e.g., parallel play) and move toward cooperative interaction only toward the very end of this developmental period.

In contrast, Class II (within-family) influences would be expected to play a significant role. The existing evidence is scanty, but with varying degrees of inference, it is suggestive of early family effects. The most direct data are concerned with family social-structural characteristics. Several studies have linked later alcoholism to larger family size (Koller & Castanos, 1969; Smart, 1963). One set of explanations for this effect is artifactual. Catholics are more likely to become alcoholics and are also more likely to have large families. Thus, the association is not a causal one. A contrasting view ties this phenomenon to family interaction. With a greater number of siblings around to compete for parental time and to dilute child-rearing effects, these families resolve the problem by more authoritarian patterns of interaction and discipline, looser parental control, and less attention giving. Insofar as these behaviors lead to a greater likelihood of problem drinking (as we will see that they do), the connection between family size and alcoholic disorders is clearly a structural one (Clausen, 1966; Hetherington & Parke, 1975; Wahl, 1956). Although little attention has been paid to the details of when this process is most likely to have its greatest impact, there is good reason to believe that the effect starts early and continues at least through middle childhood.

A related family structural factor frequently linked to alcoholism is birth position. The weight of studies show that consistently more last-born than first-born male children later become alcoholic; family size potentiates this effect. These results are present but weaker in studies of female alcoholics (Blane & Barry, 1973). Mechanisms evoked to explain these findings range from later childhood effects related to the increased probability of early exposure to parental loss (de Lint, 1964), to early childhood effects such as greater experience of dependency conflict by the family "baby," greater severity of weaning, and a greater likelihood that the child is unwanted, hence experiences greater affective deprivation and/or rejection (Smart, 1963; Blane & Barry, 1973). Related more to Class IV influences is the possibility that greater pregnancy and birth complications and congenital abnormalities—associated with greater maternal age and therefore with last-born birth position—lead to greater risk of a poor mother–child attachment and less effective impact of later child-rearing attempts. We are aware of no investigation dealing directly with this issue, although one researcher (Goodwin, 1976a) has proposed such a study and also has reported some equivocal retrospective data in this area (Goodwin, Schulsinger, Hermansen, Guze, & Winokur, 1975).

All of these family structural influences are clearer for later-to-be alcoholics than they are for later-to-be more normal drinkers. This is especially true when the relationship connection is between ordinal position and adolescent drinking of both normal and problem kinds (Barry, Barry, & Blane, 1969; Wechsler & Thum, 1973a; Zucker & Van Horn, 1972). The existing evidence makes it impossible to evaluate whether these effects are very attenuated with younger drinkers because they need a longer developmental course to unfold fully, or whether they are relevant only to later-to-be alcoholic samples.

Early emotional deprivation has already been mentioned as a potential corollary of last-born birth position and as a possible intervening early family influence upon later drinking. Other data collected from child abuse cases (Gil, 1971) and from alcoholic families (Fox, 1956; Jackson, 1962; Jacob, Favorini, Meisel, & Anderson, 1978; Mayer & Black, 1976; Spieker & Mouzakitis, 1976) inferentially suggest quite early parental unavailability as a contributory factor to later abusive drinking by the child. Insofar as parental alcohol abuse is one of the risk factors for later problem drinking in the child, these studies suggest that it is worthwhile to look to early parental emotional withdrawal as a nondrinking-specific early interactional phenomenon. What few data there are suggest that parental withdrawal is a more common sequel of abusive drinking than is the more infrequent, physically abusive episode. Mayer and Black even observed that during periods of drunkenness, the father may turn to his wife as a hostile target, as a way of avoiding abuse of the child. Another recent clinical report documents the children's experience of terror and panic during times when the father is drinking and assaults his wife, even though the children themselves appear to be in no immediate danger (Wilson & Orford, 1978).

The research done so far directly implicates only alcoholic parents, and the evidence is largely gleaned from considerably older ages than are our present focus. Nonetheless, the matter is worthy of pursuit in the sense that one would logically expect greater impact of parental affective deprivation in the early years, which in turn would have strong nondrinking-specific effects upon the temperament and the mood structure of the child. We take particular note of these influences at this juncture rather than waiting for a later time frame precisely because they have been neglected. Unfortunately, even major reviews on the subject (Ablon, 1976; Jacob *et al.*, 1978) at best only indirectly and in cursory fashion take account of that critical developmental variable of age of major effect. Given the presence of major family interactional disruptions over long periods of time, one is tempted to infer that earlier effects will be most potent. But the lack of evidence makes this only a speculation.

Class IV influences—concerned with cognition, personality, and temperament, as well as with more directly physiological variables—are most directly represented by temperamental characteristics and biological influences at this early developmental period. Influences that are cognitively mediated become salient only when a linguistic structure has developed.

Three types of evidence, although at present quite limited, bear directly on this time period. All have more to do with later alcoholism than with later patterns of normal drinking and nondrinking. One is the heightened frequency of neural disorder (including EEG abnormalities) observed among later-to-be alcoholics (McCord & McCord, 1960). While these evaluations were made around age 10, one clearly verifiable hypothesis is that barring unusual physical injury in earlier years, these defects were also present at birth.

A related line of investigation is the attempt to link up hyperactivity with later alcoholism via genetic mechanisms. Several reports have linked hyperactivity in male children to the presence of alcoholism in biological parents as well as in other blood relatives (McCord & McCord, 1960; Morrison & Stewart, 1971; Cantwell, 1972). In addition, two studies comparing rates of alcoholism in adoptive versus biological parents of hyperactive children suggest a genetic mode of transmission, given that rates of alcoholism were significantly higher among the biological parents (Morrison & Stewart, 1973; Goodwin *et al.*, 1975). Here again, data are based on comparatively small samples, age of assessment of hyperactivity is middle to late childhood or older, and most of the work is based upon a retrospective report of earlier behavior. Nonetheless, the possibility of biologically mediated behavior traits at these later ages leads us to include them among potential early childhood indicators, which at the very least interact with other social and biological influences to create a propensity for severe and chronic alcohol problems.

Even more directly related to a genetic hypothesis for alcoholism transmission—and therefore also implicated in presumed early developmental characteristics—is the work of Goodwin and his colleagues (Goodwin *et al.*, 1973; Goodwin, Schulsinger, Moller, Hermansen, Winokur, & Guze, 1974) utilizing a subject pool from the adoption studies being carried out at Copenhagen's Psykologisk Institut. The earlier study compared rates of alcoholism among male adoptees with biological parents who had been hospitalized for alcoholism against a suitable adoptee control group without the possible genetic background in their family history. Almost four times as many of the children of alcoholics, reared apart from their biological parents, were diagnosed as alcoholic. The second study examined drinking patterns and other information in a subgroup of the adopted sons of alcoholics, where there were also siblings still living who had been reared in the home of the biological parent (most usually the father), and where there had been no subsequent contact between them. Here also, the findings strongly supported a genetic hypothesis; the two groups had comparable alcoholism rates. The nonadopted son's length of exposure to the alcoholic parent was not associated with the development of alcoholism, but the severity of the parent's drinking problem was, in both nonadopted and adopted groups.

There are a number of problems with this work. Some of them are conceptual and have already been dealt with (see Tolor & Tamerin, 1973; Goodwin, 1973). But what the studies fairly straightforwardly show is that some biologically mediated characteristics relate to the development of those chronic and severe forms of drinking we call alcoholic. The mechanisms of this genetic linkage are as yet quite unclear, as is the issue of "what" is inherited (Cadoret, 1976). The Goodwin group data favor an alcoholism-specific mechanism that is unrelated to less severe forms of drinking and problem drinking. Other research by Partanen, Brunn, and Markkanen (1966), using a considerably more broad-based and therefore more population-relevant sample and a twin study methodology, found that heritability estimates were significant for amount of alcohol consumed and for abstinence but not for the measures of loss of control and social complications of drinking (e.g., arrests for drunkenness) that are traditionally necessary for a positive alcoholic diagnosis. Other data from Kaij (1960) support a complex notion of the transmission process, insofar as this twin study of alcoholics showed that social and intellectual deterioration was more heritable than was extent of drinking. Lastly, the Goodwin *et al.* (1973) adoption study data themselves raise questions about details of mechanism insofar as the one characteristic other than alcoholism that showed differences between adoptees of alcoholic biological parents and control parents was divorce. Insofar as this is an indicator—at least, in part—of interpersonal dysfunctions related to intimacy, it lends some support to the Kaij findings and leaves open the question of what the core biological nature is of the behavioral disorder that leads to alcoholism.

At the very least, the weight of evidence points to some biologically regulated process, more clearly established for later-to-be-alcoholics than for the normal range of drinking patterns. Should this process be tied more to social behavior than to drinking, it makes considerable sense to look for quite early manifestations of it in the developmental histories of children at higher risk for alcoholism. This issue is being pursued currently in a Michigan State University pilot study.

To conclude this section, we note that a number of lines of evidence point to potential developmental manifestations of later alcohol abuse. Insofar as these relate to hyperactivity, neural deficit, and biologically mediated behavioral characteristics, we are also dealing with classes of behavior that are in part constitutionally determined and that refer to the style or "how" of behavior rather than the "what." Within a psychological framework, such characteristics have been referred to under the rubric of *temperament*, and a good deal of largely nonpsychopathologically oriented developmental research has been conducted to trace out their vicissitudes (Thomas, Chess, Birch, Hertzig, & Korn, 1963; Thomas & Chess, 1977). Characteristics such as intensity of response, activity level, and mood are distinguishable within the first year of life; show moderate stabilities over periods as long as five years; and are also predictive of behavior disorder. This is especially true when such behaviors are found in conjunction with parenting that takes no account of the child's individual differences (Thomas, Chess, & Birch, 1968; Graham, Rutter, & George, 1973; Scholom, Zucker, & Stollak, in press). While it is a big jump from the psychiatrically nonspecific research connecting adverse temperamental characteristics with behavior disorders in children of early and middle childhood to that connecting temperament with severe alcohol problems in adulthood, we would point out that temperament variables emerge later on, in characterizations of mood and tempo, in at least one later developmental study linking adolescent behavior to alcohol abuse in adulthood (Jones, 1968, 1971). Such characterizations are at this time provocative, and the links to early development are speculative. But they need to be checked out.

4.3. Middle Childhood through Adolescence

This section treats the data relating to middle childhood through adolescence. This age period, roughly, age 6 to age 18, is clearly differentiable by at least one milestone developmental marker, the onset of puberty. The two periods are grouped together here because the studies on middle-childhood functioning are exceptionally rare; findings tend to be consistent with adolescent data, perhaps because they are, but possibly because we know so little about this time period from the perspective of drinking development. In any case, where differentiations are possible, we will make them.

Studies are also separated into two groups: (1) those concerned with the acquisition of drinking behavior and the development of normal drinking patterns; and (2) those concerned with the development of problem drinking and alcoholism.

4.3.1. *Transition to Drinker Status and the Development of Normal Drinking Behavior*

Sociocultural and community influences related to family of origin remain a constant throughout childhood with two provisos: (1) that the culture and the community remain stable through the approximately 12-year time span we refer to here, and (2) that the family remain within the same social and ecological space—being neither upwardly nor downwardly mobile. Both of these caveats are questionable for different reasons.

The first condition is unlikely to be met in any modern, postindustrial society, although it may be approximated on the community level if the individual is growing up in a small, largely rural, and fairly self-contained area (cf. Jessor *et al.*, 1968). In all other cases, there is ample evidence, at a variety of different levels, that the world is changing. Jack Block in his follow-up report on men and women originally seen in the two Berkeley-area longitudinal projects in the 1930s, vividly described the ways in which Berkeley changed from a fairly self-contained university town to a cosmopolitan suburb of the San Francisco area during the late 1930s and early 1940s (Block, 1971, pp. 24–26). Both ecological changes (the opening of the San Francisco–Oakland Bay bridge, the gradual increase in population density) and sociopolitical ones (the advent of World War II) had their impact on the morale of the people growing up there, in terms both of changes in available opportunities and of changes in life problems as a function of the issues that the culture required its members to come to terms with.

At a level closer to home, the Research Triangle adolescent drinking survey shows that older observations of urban–rural differences have disappeared in recent years and that regional differences in rates of drinking and problem drinking in older adolescents approximate the rates found among young adults in those areas (Rachal *et al.*, 1975). Data from a variety of sources confirm that these patterns reflect increases in drinking rates nationally (U.S. Department of Health, Education, and Welfare, 1974). Parallel national surveys of adults between the period

1964–1965 and 1972–1974 also show slight increases in consumption, although the proportion of abstainers seems to have remained constant. Insofar as drinking practices are consistently embedded in a cultural context and reflect the values of that period (Cahalan & Cisin, 1976), these data also show that sociocultural context can and does change in American society over a shorter period than the time it takes to traverse childhood to adolescence. There are longitudinal designs that allow one to take systematic account of these generational changes as separate from ontogenetic effects (Baltes, 1968; Schaie, 1965). None has yet been applied to longitudinal alcohol research. It should be. In the meantime, all we can do is recognize that some developmental change may be both age- and generation-specific; perhaps we also need to keep track of generational shifts as we evaluate the impact of sociocultural variables reported in the literature.

The second issue—the constancy of sociocultural influence on the family from middle childhood through adolescence—is probably an appropriate assumption for children socialized to normal patterns of drinking (see below), but it is unquestionably inappropriate for those who, during adolescence and thereafter, show patterns of alcohol abuse. There is considerable evidence among heavy drinkers (Wechsler & Thum, 1973a,b), among pathological drinkers (Demone, 1973), and among later-to-be alcoholics (McCord & McCord, 1960; Robins, 1966) that such families are beset with divorce, parental loss, and parental discord. All of these elements make it far more likely that the family will itself be the originator of social mobility (downward) and will be subject to differing sociocultural forces along the way.

Within this same context, it is important to note that what I referred to earlier as sociocultural and neighborhood influence actually comes closer to school influence during the preadolescent and adolescent years. Where available, drinking data in adolescent surveys that are broken down by school or community even within the same geographical area show substantial across-community differences (Wechsler & Thum, 1973a). The school and the peer culture within it (i.e., Class III influences) are probably the most important matrix, within which the larger cultural influence is transmitted, yet little work has been done to map out the details of this process. Riester and Zucker's (1968) report of clique structure in the high school setting, as it relates to drinking behavior, is one start in this direction. It details the interplay between social subgroup membership and patterns of alcohol use–abuse. Other work on clique and friendship choice as these are associated with drinking practices indicates that the peer group serves useful insulating functions against parental disapproval of drinking (Alexander & Campbell, 1967).

On a more interactional level, a by-now large body of data implicates peer-group influences (Class III) as the (possibly) most potent extraindividual set of determinants of the transition to drinker status. A number of studies have dealt with this issue both cross-sectionally and longitudinally. In evaluating the impact of peers upon the individual, the distinction needs to be drawn between the influence of peer pressure and the influence of peer behavior. The former is concerned with the maintenance of adolescent groups, the development and upholding of group norms by members. For example, one individual may give concrete suggestions to another within the group that he/she should behave in ways that are indicative of group solidarity; such behaviors are typically construed by the recipient of the message as pressures toward conformity. In contrast, peer behavior influences can occur on other than social levels of influence. Peer behavior serves as a model for the observer. In addition, peer drinking may make alcohol simply more readily available within the environment. Peer drinking may also change the perceiver's attitudes toward drinking, which in turn may lead to his/her own increased likelihood of taking a drink, and so forth. Our point is simply that different types of peer effect imply a different influencing process; not all of these processes are simple and straightforward "peer" causes.

Cross-sectional studies in this area clearly point to an association between a subject's drinking or nondrinking and his/her friend's drinking (i.e., presumed behavioral influences) (Rachal *et al.*, 1975; Globetti, 1964; Alexander & Campbell, 1967). These studies also point to the significant, phenomenologically experienced pressure that nondrinkers report when a significant number of their close friends are drinkers.

One might be tempted to conclude, as an easy next step, that peer pressure causes the nondrinker to make the transition to drinker status. Recent longitudinal evidence suggests that the process is a more complex one. A recent study of drinking onset phenomena finds that perceived peer behavior (drinking and other legal drug use) and involvement in peer activities (e.g., dating, parties) in fact anticipate (predict) later use of distilled spirits by earlier nonusers (Margulies, Kessler, & Kandel, 1977). Nevertheless, other aspects of the external environment (e.g., paternal drinking) and the internal one (the adolescent's own earlier involvement in minor delinquent activity or prior use of other drugs) are equally if not slightly more powerful in predicting onset. This study also found clear developmental effects. Breaking down their data by class in school, they found that friends' influences become increasingly influential as students progress through high school, while parent modeling effects remain steadily influential rather than decreasing with maturation. Lastly, the Margulies *et al.* data show striking sex differences. Parental influences (father's drinking, closeness to father) and perceived environmental pressure (modeling effects based on the perceived extent of friends' drinking) predicted onset in girls but not in boys. Among the latter, the respondent's involvement in peer activity (dating and the like) and participation in politics were more powerful variables.

So far, we have dealt primarily with Class III influences as these relate to drinking acquisition. The data first presented call attention to the fact that these are not pure effects but are moderated and intertwined with parental (family) influences, already ongoing behavioral tendencies (i.e., within-subject characteristics), and developmental differences in the types of influence that are most prepotent in determining the transition to becoming a drinker. More generally, model building in this area has been limited in the past to theories involving single classes of variables. The Margulies *et al.* report illustrates how limiting such approaches can be; their particular way out of this dilemma has been to assign weight to influencing elements on the basis of amount of variance contributed to the predictive regression equation. This is a major step forward, but it still leaves unsettled the spelling out of details of the across-class interactive process. It remains for future work to elaborate this.

We turn now to consider other Class II (family) and Class IV (intraindividual) influences related to transitional phenomena of the period through adolescence. Most of the work in this area has been cross-sectional rather than longitudinal. Therefore, we are left here, as in earlier parts of this review, with the same persistent question: To what extent are the replicated findings concerning drinker–nondrinker differences associated with the transition rather than causing it. The question must remain and is unfortunate, given that so much of this cross-sectional work has been consistently replicated to a greater degree than is true in some of the other areas covered here.

The Columbia study (Margulies *et al.*, 1977) implicates parental alcohol use as a predictor of the transition to drinking by the adolescent. This drinking-specific factor has repeatedly turned up in old as well as recent studies of adolescent drinking (Maddox & McCall, 1964; Mandell, Cooper, Silberstein, Novick, & Koloski, 1962; Rachal *et al.*, 1975). It is by now well acknowledged that most adolescents have their first drinking experiences in the home and, at least to some degree, are modeling parental behaviors when they carry on these practices outside the home. The Margulies *et al.* data show that while both parents' drinking patterns predict the child's transition, the father's influences are more powerful than the mother's, but the details of why this might be remain puzzling.

Other cross-sectional data on the development of problem drinking in adolescence offer one reasonable place to look for explanations: in child-rearing practice interactions between sex of parent, sex of child, and child-rearing behavior (cf. Zucker & Barron, 1973; Zucker & DeVoe, 1975). These studies strongly suggest that there is a differential impact of the father's versus the mother's behavior on the child's drinking as a function of the sex of the child.

The remainder of studies that focus on the details of the parent's influence (nondrinking-specific elements) as they relate to drinking acquisition are quite sparse and not very fine-grained in focus, and all are cross-sectional. Nonetheless, they are consistent with each other. The Wechsler and Thum (1973a) data show a weak effect of greater perceived closeness to mother and father among nondrinkers and light drinkers (in terms of ability to talk about drugs) than is true of the heavier drinkers in their samples. Demone's (1973) large-scale, cross-community study sample reported that among nondrinking males there was parental confidence, discussion of issues between parent and child, and a sense on the part of the child of a strong obligation to the parents (all of these data were as reported by the adolescent). Nonetheless, within this group, there were two quite different parental positions about drinking: (a) the parent viewed the decision as ultimately up to the son; (b) the parent was unequivocally opposed to drinking under any circumstances. These findings fit rather well with those reported by Alexander (1967) bearing on the relationship of closeness to father, closeness to peers, and perception of peer and parent attitudes toward drinking. The Alexander (male-only) data indicate that basically positive family relationships tend to moderate child intake once drinking has started, even when parent attitudes are disapproving of alcohol use. Only when father–child relationships are distant is the paternal negative attitude about alcohol likely to precipitate the child into a rebellious, abusive kind of drinking.

One other point needs to be made about Demone's data as they bear on the move to drinking. It is clear from the cluster of findings that the family relationships of nondrinkers are in a very real sense atypical of the adolescent period. Families are closer, and there is more parent–child dialogue than exists among drinkers. In these respects, the nondrinker is what might be termed, from the standpoint of adult culture, a *positive deviant*. We will have more to say about this is Section 4.4., where other data on transitional phenomena are reviewed.

Turning now to Class IV influences during this developmental era, studies are largely confined to personality measures and a mixed assortment of behavioral variables differentiating drinkers and nondrinkers. The only two longitudinal studies that speak directly to the transition are those of the Jessors (Jessor & Jessor, 1977) and of the Columbia group (Margulies *et al.*, 1977). The former will be dealt with in considerable detail in our discussion of the phenomena of early adulthood. The Margulies *et al.* data underscore the the importance of the individual's ongoing *behavioral repertoire* as a predictor of later drinking. Prior involvement in minor delinquent activity; prior involvement with peers in dating, parties, and the like; prior political involvement—all have strong relationships to later drinking of distilled spirits. These behavioral relationships are stronger than the parallel ones involving *attitudes* about the same behaviors (i.e., drinking, politics).

We have noted earlier that the Columbia study transition data are not pure in the sense that some of their nondrinking subjects already had been drinking beer and wine. Nevertheless, their findings generally are consistent with Demone's (1973) cross-sectional data, which show lesser involvement in antisocial behavior and less dating among abstainers. In addition to the Demone data, other large-scale surveys of the 1960s and 1970s demonstrate fairly close agreement about a number of intraindividual-level differences between nondrinkers and drinkers. Better school performance, somewhat more religious involvement and/or church attendance, somewhat more "moral concern," a greater sense of personal happiness, and a less rebellious stance all characterize nondrinkers to a greater degree than drinkers (Davies & Stacey, 1972; Maddox & McCall, 1964; Rachal *et al.*, 1975; Wechsler & Thum, 1973a, 1973b). Despite the degree of overlap among these studies, at the most they can provide only indirect markers of the transition to alcohol use. Even the Columbia work, with its attention to the comparative power of classes of effect, is limited in the sense that it does not address the question of mechanisms for the multilevel transition. It would be useful for these workers to address this issue, particularly within a developmental context. The next section deals with one fairly extensive study of another type of intraindividual influence that does just this.

4.3.2. *Cognitive (Class IV) Developmental Issues Related to the Drinking Transition*

In all of the work discussed so far, developmental issues are brought in by the back door. The data points for assaying differences related to drinking and nondrinking have been selected to cover middle to late adolescence. In this respect, some attention is paid to the notion that chronological age, and presumed change related to it, makes some difference. Nevertheless, developmental processes within the individual are largely ignored in data sampling and are almost completely ignored in accounting for the results.

This is not the case in one very important study of cognitive factors related to the development of attitudes toward alcohol use. The work, done by Jahoda and Cramond (1972) in Glasgow, is part of a two-phase project concerning the development of attitudes about alcohol and of early drinking behavior; it was commissioned by the Scottish Home and Health Department. Its importance lies in the demonstration of interactions among intraindividual developmental factors (age, stage of cognitive development), parental influences, social structural influences, and the child's personality in determining attitudes about alcohol use.

Utilizing a Piagetian frame of reference in devising experimental tasks (e.g., sorting a variety of different containers into groupings and observing, when some of the containers are for alcoholic beverages, whether this is one of the category schemata the children use) and other age-appropriate eliciting stimuli, these investigators explored the development of conceptual structures (cognitive representations) and attitudes concerning alcohol in three age groups (6-, 8-, and 10-year-olds) and also collected some data on a small 4-year-old sample.

Of note is the authors' stress on the fact that any assessment of alcohol-related cognitions must be set within the framework of the child's more general capacity for cognitive processing. This is not the place for a thorough review of Piaget's stages of cognitive development. The interested reader is referred to works by Ginsburg and Opper (1969) and Flavell (1963) for a detailed summary of that evidence and related theory. For our purposes, it is sufficient to note that the Jahoda and Cramond sample began with the period of preoperational cognitive processing, where the child develops symbolic functions and is involved in intuitive problem solving but only begins to develop the ability to think in classes and about relationships, and continued through the stage of concrete operations, where there is an ability to assume a nonegocentric mode and where classification and seriation are possible. It is only in adolescence that there is the capability for true abstraction, flexibility, and mental-hypothesis testing, what Piaget calls "formal operations."

The study convincingly demonstrates the importance of using age-relevant dependent variables and highlights the importance of understanding developmental changes in the capacity to process information, as these relate to the responses that children give. For example, at age 4 only 14% of the children were able to recognize alcoholic drinks by smell. At ages 6, 8, and 10, the percentages of recognitions (of beer and whiskey) were 39%, 53%, and 61%, respectively. However, over this age span, the cognitive capacity to identify three smells of any kind changes markedly. When this fact was taken into account by excluding children who could identify fewer than three smells, the percentage of identification among 4-year-olds rose to 66%—not noticeably different than the parallel figure of approximately 70% recognition (among those who could identify at least three other smells) for all the other, older age groups. In short, where recognition of alcohol as a discrete type of beverage was developmentally possible at all, the data indicate very early exposure and no demonstrable learning over time.

Other findings of note were that only 42% of the 6-year-olds but 90% of the 8-year-olds and older children were able to differentiate alcoholic beverages from others (the bottle-sorting test). Nevertheless, even at age 10, only 31% of the sample used the generic term *alcohol* as a way of describing their groupings. As a side comment, I would point out that these findings have direct relevance for teachers. These data strongly suggest that any attempts at discussion of alcohol and its general effects, without first educating about what "alcohol" is, are likely to pass over the heads of somewhat more than half of a class of 10-year-olds (fourth-graders). They may be able to give back verbal information, but their personal utilization of the concept in their own activities is likely to be more limited.

Other results showed an age trend toward increasing unfavorability of attitudes toward alcohol with increasing age (41% of the oldest children said they would drink in the future, but 70% of the youngest did). Even so, approximately 40% of the children, across age groups, viewed drunkenness as a pleasurable state. In integrating these somewhat contradictory multilevel findings, the authors took note of the multiple types of influence that serve to create them, some of which are internal and to a considerable degree are a function of maturation (i.e., cognitive changes), and some of which are the direct result of age-specific environmental influences. The model they developed is quite close to the one I present here. It is reproduced in Table 1 (see p. 116–117) as an illustration of the complexity of developmental processes as they shift across classes of influence and ages.

A number of provocative conclusions can be drawn from the Jahoda and Cramond study. Some the authors make themselves. We offer a few others here. The interested reader would do well to consult this work and draw his or her own:

(a) Given both that early childhood impressions are favorable to alcohol and that the great preponderance of younger children anticipate drinking in the future, this earlier learning, when coupled with observations of peer drinking in adolescence, may very well be a part of the learning-to-drink process. One clear need is for studies to evaluate the relative potency of these two sources of effect. Heretofore most explanations of drinking acquisition have presumed it to be entirely a function of learning during adolescence, undoubtedly in part because the contribution of earlier attitudinal influences was both unknown and unassayable.

(b) Cognitive inputs after ages 8–10 probably do not have impact on earlier congitive structures; instead, what seems to happen is that a negative attitudinal structure is learned that is in accord with the somewhat negative institutional values implanted by both parents and teachers. Yet it can be argued that if core (earlier) attitudes about drinking are to be truly modified, new learning should build upon the more positively toned earlier attitudes.

(c) Education about alcohol by age 12–14, which is primarily oriented toward the modification of cognitions about alcohol, is being conducted at the developmentally most inappropriate time. There should be peak resistance to such inputs during this developmental era because negatively toned education is being offered at a time when there is maximum observational learning of an opposite message from peers: that learning to drink is fun and may also provide increasing affective involvement with those most important to the student, that is, his/her peers.

4.3.3. *The Development of Problem Drinking during Middle Childhood and Adolescence*

Since the bulk of the available data relating to this section focuses on familial (Class II) and intraindividual (Class IV) influences, our primary focus in this section will be devoted to these two sources of effect.[1] However, much of what is said in earlier sections—and in the next major section (4.4.)—would be equally applicable here, since there tends to be little developmental differentiation of findings contrasting early–middle adolescence versus late adolescence–early adulthood. In reviewing the evidence for this period, there is one major question that needs to be kept in mind: To what extent are the phenotypic manifestations of problem drinking at this time reflective of an underlying process (or processes) that will continue and eventually manifest itself as adult problem drinking or alcoholic disorder? In contrast, to what extent are these manifestations simply reflections of age- and stage-specific developmental process(es)? To distinguish between these two alternatives, at the very least one would look for (a) evidence of continuity versus subsidence of drinking problems over time, and (b) evidence for a single pattern versus more than one pattern or type of problem drinking even during adolescence.

Genuinely developmental data on family influences related to problem drinking during this time frame are quite limited. Only two studies

[1] The discussion of family influences here relies heavily on the author's earlier review in this area (Zucker, 1976).

Table 1. Jahoda and Cramond's Schema for Developmental Changes in Influencing Factors as They Relate to Drinking Attitudes and Behaviors[a]

		Ages			
		4	6	8	10	14
Cognitive		Learning about specific drinks.		Operational alcohol concept.	Beginnings of verbal concept.	Concept fully established.
Personal influences	Parents	Serve as models, but little if any specific teaching.		Provide some negative information (little factual) and exhortations, often contradicted by behavior; some children in extreme drinking or abstaining groups begin to react against parents.		Decline of parental influence.
	Peers	Negligible until adolescence.				Peers exert pressure toward alcohol; offer of first drink.
External social influences (presumably incl. school, church, mass media)		No discernible impact.		Learning of negative evaluations of alcohol and drinking on the part of authoritative persons and institutions; no trace of media effects.		Negative evaluations from authority sources discounted; mass media support for drink.

Resultants	Expressed attitude to drink	?	Neutral	Increasingly negative.	Positive, with residual guilt?
	Declared intention about drinking in future	?	High: will do as everybody does.	Substantially declining.	Majority drink.

[a] Reproduced from Jahoda and Cramond, 1972, p. 37.

concern themselves with the details of the parental influencing process, and both are cross-sectional. The first, a community study done in one of the Middle Atlantic states, investigated both parental influences and child characteristics as these related to child problem drinking in middle to late adolescence, among both boys and girls. The study utilized a delinquency theory of problem drinking, in the sense that problem behaviors while consuming alcohol were viewed as expressions of an impulsive and/or antisocial personality style. Family interactions that had previously been linked to such impulsive and antisocial activity—such as weak family affectional ties, inadequate limit setting and disciplinary practices, and low family solidarity—were hypothesized to predict drinking problems (Zucker & Fillmore, 1968; Zucker & Barron, 1973; Zucker & DeVoe, 1975).

Table 2 provides a summary of the basic study findings. Strong support for a delinquency formulation of problem drinking—in terms of child's behavior findings, family climate, and parental behavior and child-rearing practices—was found among both boys and girls. Qualitative differences between predictors of heavy drinking, problem drinking, and antisocial behavior measures indicated that the basic model was applicable to all three types of dependent variables. Within this framework, adolescent personality measures and parental data showed that a harsher, more negative familial environment and a more impulsive behavioral style were characteristic of antisocial behavior more than of problem drinking and were more characteristic of problem drinking than of heavy drinking.

The other socialization study (Jessor *et al.*, 1968) also involved both males and females in high school but only obtained information from mothers. According to the deviancing theory developed here, decreased access to and/or participation in the community opportunity structure should lead to an increased rate of personal deviancy. The family as the primary socialization unit clearly influences potential access to and acceptance of the dominant values within this structure. The influencing process itself is conceptualized as operating via three substructures: the parental reward structure, the parental belief structure, and the parental control (disciplinary) structure. All three of these structures are viewed as being intermediary between social class and ethnic group membership on the one hand, and the child's potential for deviant behavior (including problem drinking) on the other hand.

Findings were largely supportive of the theoretical network and the predictions generated from it. Lower socioeconomic status, as an index of low access to the societal opportunity structure, was associated with low maternal responsiveness, greater maternal alienation, and greater

Table 2. Summary of Rutgers Study Findings Relating to Family and Intraindividual Influences on Children's Problem Drinking in Adolescence

Male results	Female results
I. Family influences	
A. Family climate Greater parental defiance by children. Greater perceived family tension.	Same as findings for boys.
B. Parental behavior and personality High consumption of alcohol by father and mother.	No clear relationship of father's or mother's intake to girl's consumption.
Greater worrying by mother about her own alcohol consumption.	Mothers are aggressively sociable; this in turn relates to daughter's higher intake and greater antisocial activity.
C. Child rearing practices (1) As perceived by parents: Fathers show greater absence and greater deprivation of privileges and property	Father's perceived role not clear; some suggestion of sporadic and inconsistent involvement with daughter.
Mothers perceive themselves as more absent from home	Mothers show less affection, use more social isolation for discipline; are more likely to intercede in father–daughter conflicts.
(2) As perceived by the child: More failure of affective environmental supports by father (less nurturance, affection).	Same as for boys, but also perceived to be true of mothers.
General patterns of lack of involvement by both parents.	Lack of instrumental companionship by both parents.
II. Intraindividual influences	
More overt aggression. More delinquent role involvement. Earlier and more sexual activity. Greater distrust and cynicism.	Same as findings for boys.

[a] Data sources from Zucker and Barron (1973) and Zucker and DeVoe (1975).

exposure of the child to already deviant role models within the family. When family relationships were examined as they related to personal deviance and problem drinking among the adolescent children studied, the linkage of socialization practices to deviant child behavior also was established. Low alcohol consumption was related to high mother–child interaction, while high frequency of drunkenness was related to low interaction, less maternal responsiveness to the child's needs, more maternal alienation, greater intrafamily exposure to deviant role models, and more opportunity for deviant behavior.

The correspondences across these two studies are considerable and are discussed in detail in the author's prior review (Zucker, 1976). The family variables can be organized via three subcategories of influence: (a) parental characteristics that serve as modeling alternatives; (b) parent reward structures that are available to shape the child in ways that reflect family standards and values; and (c) quality of family affectional interaction. The latter category of behaviors has a direct impact on the group maintenance functions of the family; only by way of the affectional system does the group provide sufficient emotional connections to maintain itself as a discrete entity. Utilizing this schema, the Zucker and Jessor studies point to fairly major disturbances in all three areas in families where adolescents show problem-drinking signs. Parent characteristics are of deviant personal behavior and heavier drinking; in addition, cynicism and distrust are modeled. Reward structures are inadequate in the sense that there is maternal and paternal disinterest and lack of involvement. Family affectional interactions are infrequent; there is little interaction and little nurturance. Rejection is displayed more via absence of positive display than via outright punishment and abuse.

The behavioral and personality data from these studies are also consistent; deviant behavior of an antisocial cast (i.e., aggressively oriented) as well as asocial, impulse-related activities (e.g., earlier and more sexuality, faster driving, cursing) are related to drinking problems. The studies do not make it methodologically possible to establish what is cause and what is effect in these relationships, but they strongly suggest that these patterns—both personal and familial—have been going on for some time and are not simply phenomena of adolescence, even though that is the time frame within which drinking problems start.

In contrast to the cross-sectional work, where the concern has been about personal and familial influences on drinking behavior in adolescence, a number of longitudinal studies have examined the period of middle childhood through adolescence as being where later alcohol problems and alcoholism have their beginnings. Table 3 summarizes the findings on adolescent males who later became alcoholic or had serious alcohol-related difficulties. Female data from the Oakland Growth Study (Jones, 1971) and male longitudinal data on the transition to problem drinking during adolescence (Jessor & Jessor, 1973, 1977) are not included, because they are single studies and space limitations do not allow for their separate discussion here.

On the level of both interactional behaviors and individual characteristics, these data show a remarkable correspondence across studies and also a great deal of parallelism with the cross-sectional work summarized above that was oriented more specifically toward middle childhood and adolescence. On an interactional level, the across-study longitudinal findings show a move away from family influences toward interpersonal involvement with peers. At the very least, the data indicate that the quality of such interactions is more likely to be counterdependent and ascendant, rather than egalitarian and mutual. There is some intimation that in addition, these interactions may be set in a context of rebellion against family influences. At an individual level, there is also clear evidence for more impulsive and antisocial behavior, an undercontrol of aggression, and an active, rapid temperamental style.

Age of first contact for the different studies varies between 10 (Jones; McCord & McCord) and 13 years (Robins), yet the amount of across-study similarity is remarkable. It underscores in a concrete way that the personal and familial characteristics so often considered adolescent precursors of later alcohol problems in fact extend considerably further back into middle childhood.

The other characteristics found across studies indicate that the later-to-be alcoholic's functioning is not completely marked by impulsivity and aggression; to this extent, some differentiation is possible between the cross-sectional and the longitudinal work. Some of the traits have a neurotic quality (daydreaming, nail biting, rated as "less productive"). Conceivably, these may be earlier developmental markers of different types of alcoholism in adulthood (e.g., Barry's [1977] psychopathic versus neurotic types).

Considering the longitudinal and cross-sectional studies as a group linked by the common thread that all concern the production of problem alcohol use, we have already noted significant parallels. These parallels, including those on family influences discussed in the 1976 review, are qualitatively remarkably alike, but they are quantitatively distinct in the sense that later-to-be alcoholics show intraindividual and familial characteristics that are somewhat more pathological in adolescence. However, this greater extremity might be expected anyway, given that all but the Oakland Growth Study subjects were themselves initially selected on the basis of institutional contact. In other words, their behavior

Table 3. Characteristics in Childhood and Adolescence Related to Alcoholism

	McCord & McCord (1960)	Robins *et al.* (1962)
Subject characteristics and source	Predelinquent males, identified for a youth project preventive program, blue-collar	Males and females, childhood psychiatric clinic patients, primarily blue-collar, heavily court and social agency referred
Age at first contact	10	Median = 13
Time to follow-up	20+ years	30 years
Criterion for adult diagnosis	Public records (hospital, welfare, court)	Personal interview data and public records
Characteristics of control (comparison) samples	Predelinquents from same study with no public record of alcohol problems	1. Other clinic patients not diagnosed alcoholic 2. Elementary school pupils without school behavior problems—matched for residence, sex, and age
1. Background influences	Neural disorders	Disproportionately male, Irish, lower SES
2. Interpersonal behavior	Outwardly self-confident Disapproving of mothers Coolness–indifference to sibs	—
3. Impulsivity and management of aggression	More aggressive More sadistic	Antisocial

(Problem Drinking) in Later Life

Investigator		
Robins (1966)[a]	Jones (1968) Males	Berry (1967) Berry & Ricks (1970)
Same as Robins *et al.* (1962)	Males and females—Oakland Growth Study, primarily middle-class	Males, child guidance clinic patients, mixed social class
	10	11–16
	Extensive contact through adolescence; then three contacts at 23, 28, and 33 years	Adulthood
	Extensive interview data and medical exam	Hospital diagnostic record
	Growth Study subjects who were not diagnosed problem drinkers	1. Other clinic patients later diagnosed schizophrenic or impulsive character 2. Clinic patients later socially adequate
Adolescent characteristics		
Blue-collar background (M) Broken homes via divorce (M) Parental loss via death	—	—
Runaways	Jr. H.S. Talkative Assertive Less dependent Less accepting of dependency (also Sr. H.S.) Less considerate Other directed Negativistic Sr. H.S. Less aware of impression on others	Antisocial behavior with peer group ties and loyalties
Record of theft and other serious offenses (male)	—	—

(Continued)

	McCord & McCord (1960)	Robins *et al.* (1962)
4. Temperament	Undisturbed by abnormal fears Hyperactive	—
5. Other	Fewer abnormal fears	More often problem children (clinic-referred)

[a] The 1966 book represents a second set of analyses on the same longitudinal study population at a later point in time, with somewhat more complete subject location. However, the data breakdown and analyses in this latter report are more confusing from the standpoint of a simple interest in alcohol abuse. This is a function of Robins's use of a psychiatric diagnostic framework and her treatment of alcohol abuse as a specific disease entity ("alcoholism") rather than as a symptomatic

during adolescence was sufficiently extreme to get them attended to by social agencies. This was not the case with the cross-sectional community studies.

On all of these grounds, it seems reasonable to suggest that the problem drinkers of adolescence form the hard core of those moving on into adult alcohol abuse and at least some forms of adult alcoholism. Studies of pathological alcohol abuse among delinquent populations (e.g., MacKay, Phillips, & Bryce, 1967; Blacker, Demone, & Freeman, 1965) also point heavily in this direction, although controls for this research have been inadequate for firm conclusions to be drawn. Lastly, at least two reviews of these data have commented that there may be more than one prodromal pattern to later alcohol problems—involving delinquent signs as a primary indicator for one group, and involving alcohol abuse signs as a primary indicator for the other group (Barry, Barry, & Blane, 1969; Mandell & Ginzburg, 1976).

4.4. Into Young Adulthood and Beyond

4.4.1. *The Developmental Context*

In general, as we look to the long span of adulthood, including middle and old age, there is evidence from cross-sectional data of more moderate patterns of drinking and a greater proportion of abstainers at older ages (Cahalan, Cisin, & Crossley, 1969; U.S. Department of Health,

Table 3. *(Continued)*

Investigator		
Robins (1966)[a]	Jones (1968) Males	Berry (1967) Berry & Ricks (1970)
—	Jr. H.S. Expressive Sr. H.S. Rapid tempo	—
Out late School truancy (M) Eating problems or underweight Daydreaming and inattention Nail biting	Jr. H.S. Pushes limits Self-indulgent Sensuous Initiates humor Sr. H.S. Less productive	—

behavior that may cut across several nosological categories. Thus, persons diagnosed as sociopathic or schizophrenic are excluded from her category of alcoholic—even though they show signs of serious alcohol abuse—if the other diagnostic label was judged to make a better clinical fit. This defect is not present in her 1962 report. (See Cahalan, 1970, Chapter 1, for another, more general discussion of this issue.

Education, and Welfare, 1974). Evidence related to heavy consumption and drinking problems is much more equivocal, particularly when data bases are available to deal with the over-65 population, who no longer have work ties to stabilize their lives (USDHEW, 1974). These differences between patterns of drinking versus nondrinking as compared to alcohol abuse appear to hold cross-nationally, although clearly there are culture-specific effects that make each country somewhat different (Sadoun, Lolli, & Silverman, 1965; Mäkelä, 1971).

The pattern of heavy drinking and possible abusive drinking is far less clear. Among women, a parallel decline in proportion of heavy drinkers with increasing age past the middle 40s is observable, but with men, there is greater cross-sectional evidence of variability of high consumption rates. Clearly, before we can make maturational sense out of these findings, we need information that will allow us to separate generational effects from maturational effects. At the very least, as I have noted earlier, the culture in which each of these cohorts has matured has had a different social base and has consequently treated alcohol differently.

Despite these cultural, perhaps era-specific vicissitudes, an obverse pattern to that of old age can be observed in young adulthood. If we look at the issue of stability of the drinking population across age, proportions of drinkers *increase* steadily until the 21- to 24-year-old age group. At this point, the data shift, and increasing percentages of the population become nondrinkers (USDHEW, 1974). This pattern holds true, as does the age break-point of the curve, for both men and women and is illustrated in Figure 3. In short, from a drinker versus nondrinker standpoint, cross-sectional evidence indicates that old age (or a pattern similar to it) starts around age 22 and continues unabated from there on. Before that developmental point, a different process appears to be operative.

No such obverse, or even parallel, pattern is evident when we look at indices of problem drinking. Sex differences are there in the usual direction, but the peak developmental time for drinking problems is age 18–20. The implied developmental curve (implied, because of cross-sectional data) is a shallow U-shaped one, with another, less strong peak at age 35 to 39, followed by a gradual decline. This pattern is illustrated in Figure 4: "The 18- to 20-year old group has the largest proportion of persons who had experienced some problem in connection with drinking (27 percent) followed by those aged 21 to 24 (18 percent) and those 35 to 39 (15 percent)" (USDHEW, 1974, p. 25).

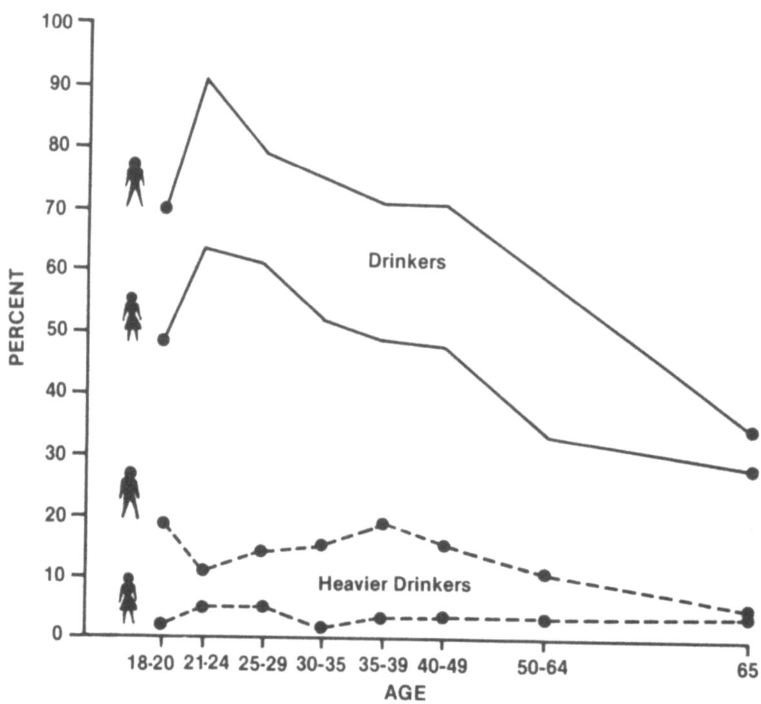

Figure 3. Percentage of drinkers and heavy drinkers among adults by sex and age, U.S.A., Fall 1972. (Reproduced from USDHEW, 1974, p. 14.)

One apparent difference between these two types of developmental phenomena is that drinking versus nondrinking has a smoother course of increase and decline. To fully explain it in adulthood, we simply need to explain the *process* of increase, the reasons for interruption of that process at the peak point of the curve, and the process of decrease. In contrast, problem drinking at the very least has more vicissitudes connected with it, and the shape of the developmental curve suggests far greater complexity among men. As far as process is concerned, after age 35–39, there is evidence for a "maturing out," via death as well as via a subsidence of problems leading to the drinking. In fact, the Cahalan and Room (1974) report on American males suggests two changes in rate (or maturing out), one after the early 20s, the other after about age 40. Among women, there are some data suggesting that problem drinking may actually increase in the older years (Rosin & Glatt, 1971). Thus, the explanations necessary to account for these variations may need to take cognizance of multiple processes, including those related to sex differences. The remainder of this section deals first

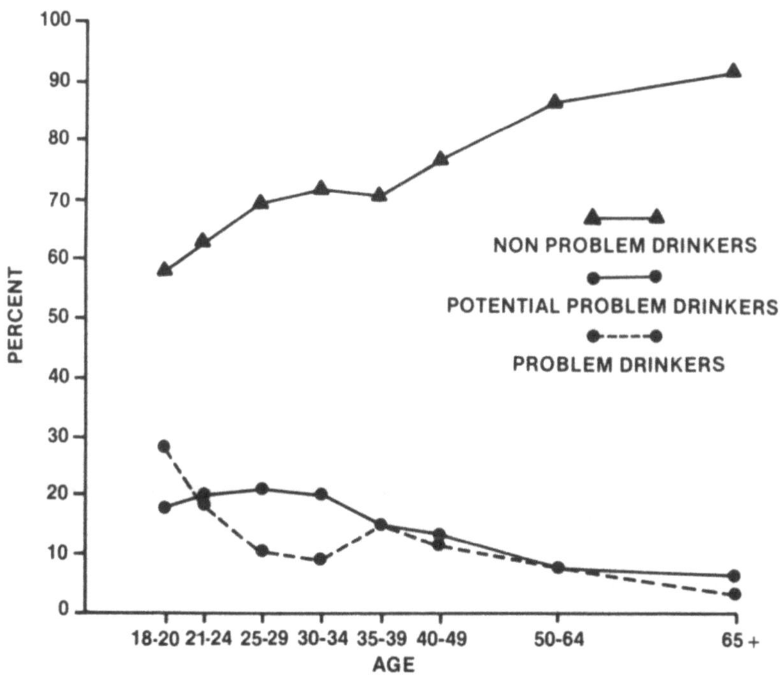

Figure 4. Percentage of problem drinkers among adults by age, U.S.A., Spring 1973. (Reproduced from USDHEW, 1974, p. 27.)

with changes in drinker–nondrinker status, then with changes related to rates of problem drinking.

4.4.2. *Increases and Decreases in Drinker Status in Young Adulthood and Thereafter*

As noted above, to explain the peak of population rates of drinking at age 21–24, all we need do is explain the process of rise in the curve, the process of decrease, and the rationale for why, developmentally, the break occurs when it does.

Referring back to our earlier discussion of drinking behavior in middle childhood and adolescence, it was noted that two main elements of the generic model account for most of the effect at this developmental period. These were peer influences and intraindividual factors. In elaborating these sets of influences as they relate to the developmental question of change in early adulthood, we draw heavily on the Jessors' Colorado study (Jessor & Jessor, 1977). The Jessors' major concern in their 1969–1972 longitudinal project was to account for developmental shifts in deviance. In their specialized report on drinking onset (Jessor & Jessor, 1975), as well as in the extended monograph, they traced out the way motivational and other personality structures and perceived environmental influences change ontogenetically, and how they may precede and ostensibly cause the transition to drinking to take place.

The Jessors found that a number of characteristics, including positive values on academic achievement, intolerance of deviance, perceived parental controls, and church activity, all decrease with increasing age through adolescence, particularly through ages 13–17. Some leveling out of the data on virtually all of these variables is evident as the student approaches the end of high school. (I will have reason to comment on this social–structural transition later.) Where developmental data are presented across the age span 13–22 on valuing academic achievement, there is evidence for a moderate rebound effect from the high school years, followed by a steady decline again, up through age 20. Thereafter, this variable stays steady through age 22 for boys and increases sharply to a level comparable with that found among 15-year-olds for the girls. In contrast, a number of variables increase with increasing age; these include valuing independence, a general measure of delinquent behavior (what the authors call "deviant behavior"), and the perception that friends are involved in drinking.

There are a number of levels of significance in these findings. First, their manner of shift illustrates that adolescence is a time of change and that concomitant with it, there is a general move toward lower levels of prosocial values and behavior in the individual, as well as perceptions of lesser values and amounts of such behavior in one's peers. Parallel with this decrease is an increase in what might be termed *asocial activity*, increasing valuation of independence, and the perception of increases in deviant behavior among one's peers. Second, the Jessors, and others before them (e.g., Zucker & Fillmore, 1968), have demonstrated a conclusive association among the acts of deviance measured; that is, having engaged in one type of asocial activity increases the probability that one will engage in others, at least of the sort assessed here (marijuana use, sexual activity, delinquent behavior, and drinking). Third, in general, the presence of these "transition-prone attributes" co-occurs for those making the transition to drinker status. Fourth, these behaviors not only predict who will become drinkers; they also are time-related. The shift to greater deviant behavior, or lesser valuing of achievment, etc., occurs chronologically in the same time span that the shift to drinker status occurs, irrespective of chronological age.

At a more general developmental level, the Jessors have made the case that adolescence is a time of transition-proneness, where such transitions have to do with the increasing probability of engaging in problem behaviors that depart from regulatory norms. From a theoretical standpoint, the Jessors have posited that adolescence is a time of transition away from conventionality and toward tolerance of and engagement in transgressive behavior. From this perspective, the rising curve of drinker status with age (through the early 20s) can be viewed as the result of an increasing awareness on the part of youth that this is a viable and survivable behavioral option. In addition it becomes one that is harder and harder to escape, insofar as one sees one's friends migrating in that direction.

There are, however, two problems in this conceptualization. First, the problem-behavior cast of the Jessors' choice of variables makes it difficult to evaluate fully whether it is the engagement in transgressive or antisocial behavior that is critical, or whether it is *the involvement in behaviors that are productive of independence from family and established institutions* (i.e., where the behaviors are more asocial and narcissistic). An equally strong case can be made for this latter conceptualization on the basis of shifts in valuing independence and in perceived lessening of controls by parents, in short, a recognition by the individual that greater freedom is possible. Second, there is the issue of what the primary social, attitudinal, and behavioral characteristics are that instigate this process. No direct answer is possible from the study's design, but variance indicators of clarity of effect suggest that a generalized behavioral propensity for deviance is central, as are personal belief structure and perceived environmental structure about drinking. In other words, a nondrinking-specific personality variable and several drinking-specific ones having to do with personal attitudes and (perceived) peer attitudes and behavior are the most powerful ones. It should be noted that neither of these criticisms obviates the reality of the Jessors' data. These observations are made in an effort to restructure the framework of their findings so as to include the possibility that transition-proneness involves moves toward independence, and in order to highlight the importance of within-individual behavioral and attitudinal characteristics.

What form might this restructuring take? The explanation I propose is that behavior stabilities and changes of both increase and decrease not only are a function of present interpersonal and personal influences and ongoing behaviors but also (a) have a time line built in and (b) are reactions as well to the individual's ongoing experience of his/her own behavior. The *time line* refers to the person's awareness of past experience, as a springboard to new experience and behavior, as well as to his/her anticipations and expectations about that which is likely (i.e., normatively prescribed and age-graded for the future) but has not yet occurred. The issue of anticipation of the future is most salient for the present discussion. The internal reactivity element we refer to here might also be termed *assimilation* within a Piagetian conceptual framework; in order to integrate what the individual has already encountered, she/he needs to react to it internally to the point of digestion (Piaget, 1952). From this perspective, awareness of anticipated transitions and the structure of relationships and behaviors following that transition should play an important role in pretransition behavior, insofar as the individual utilizes his/her expectations as an early attempt to accommodate to what he/she has not yet experienced. Additionally, once the actuality of the transition has taken place, further integrations are necessary to achieve a sense of internal balance about it, at which point the individual then becomes more open to the possibility of new experience (changes are possible again).

The point of this extensive discussion is that the data indicate that theoretical conceptualizations of behavior change that focus only on the behavioral realm (preexisting behavioral repertoires) and environmental press via peer influences are insufficient to account for the major predictive sources of variance. What I am proposing additionally, to account for all of the predictive elements, is a framework of expectations about the future and an internally organized schema that maintains or changes the individual's behavior on the basis of needs for continuity or change.

Once these latter two sources of influence are included, increasing valuation of independence, increasing deviant behavior, and increasing positive attitudes toward drinking can be seen as future-oriented activities related to the transition away from high school and away from the home environment. They co-occur presumably because all of these experiences are viewed by the individual as consistent ways of being, which in turn lead increasingly to his/her becoming a drinker.

Lloyd Johnston's (1973) study of changes in alcohol and other drug use patterns from the senior year in high school to the year following graduation, and of changes in alcohol use as a function of the type of environment the person then enters (e.g., work, college, the military), provides data that on a behavioral level are consistent with the second part of my theoretical position. In Johnston's study, alcohol use increased substantially in the year following graduation and seemed to do so differentially as a function of the context of later major activity. Britt and Campbell's (1977) data concerning shifts in peer involvement, drinking, and attitudinal patterns from high school to college provide evidence that is consistent with the first point of our theoretical reformulation; they found that the major source of variance across the transition from high school social structure to college is the personal belief system of the individual:

> If causal priority is to be assigned, it appears to be to the individual rather than the social environment since there appears to be more adjustment of the social environment to both normative structure and behavior than vice versa. Consonance among these elements, in short, appears to be attributable to the activity of the individual in adjusting his drinking behavior and norms to one another and selecting social environments that are supportive of this adjustment. (pp. 1645–1646)

Within this restructured context, how do we explain the peak and the dropoff in the drinker curve? Very briefly, we propose that the dropoff of the curve occurs somewhere in the early stages of another process, one that is separate from moves toward independence from the nuclear family, that commences around age 22–23 (see Figure 3), and that continues thereafter. The phenomenon that marks the break is marriage and its related values for increased interdependence, achievement, and prosocial activity (starting a family, holding down a steady job, etc.). I hypothesize that the presumed developmental transition away from drinking is related to this significant psychological and social-structural event. We can see that the median age of marriage at the time that the Harris data on drinking were collected (1972) coincides approximately with the break in the drinker curve (Harris and Associates, 1972–1975); that is, in 1972, the median age of marriage for males was 23.3 years, for females, 20.9 years (*Statistical Abstract of the United States*, 1977).

We are not aware of any data that directly test these propositions, both as to the underlying variables involved and as to the importance of increasing interpersonal intimacy in moderating drinking versus nondrinking activity. There is some evidence that marital disruption increases problem drinking (Cahalan, 1970), and some provocative cross-sectional data link decreases in impulse expression (preferring speed in cars, daredevil driving, driving for relief, etc.) and the expression of anger in young drivers to both increasing age and positive marital events (engagements, marriage) (Pelz & Schuman, 1971; Schuman, Pelz, Ehrlich, & Selzer, 1967) in an age sequence that fits fairly well with the break point in the drinker developmental curves. However, until there are more direct tests of these hypotheses, my revised conceptualization must be viewed as speculative.

4.4.3. *Problem Drinking in Young Adulthood and Thereafter*

Referring back to Figure 4, the reader will note that—at least, by way of the Harris study cross-sectional data, and utilizing this particular definition of problem drinking—the highest rates of problem drinkers occur at age 18–20, followed by notably lower rates thereafter. A secondary peak occurs toward the latter part of the early adult era (age 35–39; see Levinson, 1978). Although some across-study variations would be expected on the basis of cohort (generational), definitional formula, and methodology differences, a comparison with national survey data collected in 1967 and 1969 (Cahalan & Room, 1974) shows a basically parallel pattern. Insofar as we can assume that the data are representative of bona fide developmental changes—a matter that ultimately needs to be traced via longitudinal studies—of particular developmental interest are four aspects of this process: (a) What accounts for the highest rates of problem drinkers in the 18- to 20-year period, and why do rates drop off after this? (b) Assuming there is any relationship to the process of becoming a drinker, why is the peak of the problem-drinker curve at an earlier developmental point? (c) What can account for dropoffs in problem-drinker rate over time? Within this context how can the increase in the late 30s be explained? (d) What evidence, if any, is there for stability or shift in this population over time—that is, to what extent are these increases and decreases attributable to the same drinkers' entering, remaining in, or leaving the problem-drinker pool?

Before dealing with the substantive aspects of these questions, an important semantic distinction needs to be made. Earlier in this section, as well as in earlier parts of this chapter, I have treated the terms *problem drinker* and *problem drinking* equivalently. Such an equivalence presumes that those who have the characteristic (i.e., show problem drinking signs or symptoms) are by fiat also to be considered problem drinkers (i.e., the drinking problem is a personal characteristic). This framework implicitly suggests that there is within-individual consistency and stability over time (Allport, 1961; McClelland, 1951); otherwise, it is semantically more correct to refer to problem drinking as an attribute of situations, events, or even age (Mischel, 1968, 1969; Magnusson & Endler, 1977). With such semantic confusion, we run the risk of presuming what is verifiable only by way of data. This issue is of no special importance when our time-frame focus is short-term. It is of vital importance when we examine continuities and discontinuities over long spans. Hereafter, in this section, I use the term *problem drinker* when I deal with the issue of presumed within-person stability over time; otherwise, the less pejorative term *problem drinking* is used.

Turning now to our questions, what accounts for the peak rates of problem drinking observed in the 18–20 age group, and what factors or processes might account for the dropoff after that? In the review of middle childhood and adolescence (Section 4.3.), it was noted that by and large, the same variables that are identified with differences between drinking and nondrinking also are predictive of differences between problem and nonproblem drinking. The major difference is a qualitative one, of greater intensity and deviance of impulsive activity, a more rejecting child-rearing environment, and peer-group involvement with more of a rebellious cast, rather than one of independence from parents. Data on the process aspects of drinking after the high school years are sparse. The few studies concerned with this period (Kalin, McClelland, & Kahn, 1965; Williams, 1968, 1970; McClelland *et al.*, 1972; Jessor & Jessor, 1977) point to a continuity of processes from adolescence into early adulthood.

Age-related maturational data across this period are even more rare, but the Colorado longitudinal work and the Michigan Institute for Social Research studies of young drivers (Pelz & Schuman, 1971; Schuman *et al.*, 1967) point to a high point for deviant activity, impulsivity, and hostility reached sometime between ages 17 and 21, never later than that. Typical developmental shifts from adolescence through the college years indicate a gradually increasing level of impulse-related thought and activity through the high-point time, followed by a dropoff of varying slope (Jessor & Jessor, 1977; Schuman *et al.*, 1967; Schuman & Pelz, 1970; Pelz & Schuman, 1971). The one curve available on "countervailing" forces, in this case related to valuing academic achievement, shows an exact obverse pattern (Jessor & Jessor, 1977, p. 149).

These data, while suggestive rather than definitive, point to the operation of a maturational process of shifting toward more impulse undercontrol followed by a shift away from it. In the last section, I suggested some of the within-individual and environmental elements that might contribute to the process. Insofar as problem drinking is part of the impulse-undercontrol cluster (and a good deal of already reviewed evidence shows that it is), it should covary along with other elements in the cluster in the same age-related way.

Why, then, should the problem-drinking peak rate occur at an earlier age than the drinker peak, given that the same contributing elements are operating for both? Other evidence relating earlier first-drink experience to later greater problem-drinking patterns (Zucker & DeVoe, 1975; Ullman, 1962) points to one possible explanation. Insofar as earlier problem behavior is to some degree normative and transition-related, the earlier the start, the earlier the likelihood of moving on to other non-problem-related adaptations and transitions of adulthood. Secondarily, for those who start drinking later, drinking problems are less likely to be present at all. Both of these effects should add together to produce a problem-drinking developmental curve that shows an earlier peak.

The latter questions I posed concerned a possible developmental explanation for the slight rise in problem-drinking rates among males in the late 30s and the question of long-term, within-person stability–instability of problem-drinking behavior. Here also we find only the beginnings of a data base that will allow for a firm empirical and conceptual understanding of developmental effects. Follow-up of earlier national survey respondents (Cahalan, 1970), retrospective report data on stability versus change in drinking patterns over several years (Cahalan & Room, 1974), and one approximately 25-year follow-up on former college students (Fillmore, Bacon, & Hyman, 1977) all show some similar data trends: (a) While there is evidence for significant across-time stability in terms of who remains a problem drinker and who does not, there is also clear evidence for a substantial amount of shift into and out of this category of personal and social behavior pathology. (b) There is also an across-study parallel in the observation that problem drinking in young adulthood is a somewhat different phenomenon than is true as the drinker approaches middle age.

The former pattern is marked more by behavioral deviance and social consequences, the latter by the problem of problematic intake (high consumption, binges, and the like). The earliest of these reports (Cahalan, 1970) implicated not only one structural change (marital status) but also psychological characteristics such as increased alienation and impulsivity in the production of increased problem drinking in adulthood. No age differentiations were made. These variables should be familiar insofar as they are quite similar to the structural and personality variables predictive of transitions in drinking in earlier years. Whether they can also be specifically and causally linked to the developmental issues of early–middle adulthood remains to be seen.

One recent historical-developmental theory of age stages in adulthood (Levinson, 1978) suggests that the latter part of the 35- to 39-year-old period marks the beginning of another transition, that of middle adulthood. In this context, it is provocative to take note of the findings of differences between early and middle adulthood independently arrived at by the Rutgers study. Utilizing alcohol-related phenomena as their developmental marker, the Fillmore *et al.* study (1977) calls attention to the basic dissimilarity in patterns of use and abuse in these different developmental eras, as a function of the life issues confronting these different age groups. In other words, even when the primary focus is on drinking, developmental issues remain a vital part of the explanatory process. It is also of interest to note that the Rutgers investigators called attention to the need for different educational, prevention, and intervention approaches at later stages of the life cycle, as an outgrowth of the differing developmental context of drinking in that time frame. Independently, without awareness of the Jahoda and Cramond (1972) work and with a subject population who were approximately 35 years older than those studied in Britain, the need for developmentally tuned intervention techniques reemerged.

One final note: at least in their preliminary report, the Rutgers group emphasized patterns of change in alcohol problems across the span of early to middle adulthood, even though evidence was presented for both stability and change. This may very well be corrected in their later, more complete accounts of this time period. In contrast, the Social Research Group has moved from an initially more instability oriented, situation-specific position about problem drinking (Cahalan, 1970) to one calling attention to both enduring patterns of stability and situation-specific, hence varying, patterns of immediate context in the prediction of alcohol abuse (Cahalan & Room, 1974). Given the open advocacy in this review of a multiple influence theory of drinking problems, it is gratifying to note that when these investigators took care to include measures of personality, childhood history, adult social differentiation, and peer and social-context influences of both drinking and nondrinking specific types, these different areas of variance contribute importantly but differentially to abuse problems in adulthood. Some (the social differentiation variables) relate more to which individuals are at risk for drinking problems by way of their heavy drinking behavior; the personality variables are then the major determinants, among the at-risk group, of who will end up with drinking difficulties. On this basis,

Cahalan and Room posited a two-stage model for the etiology of drinking problems. The reader would do well to examine their 1974 volume in detail in order to do justice to the complexity of findings concerning this process.

5. Developmental Processes and Continuity–Discontinuity: Some Issues

5.1. Developmental Notions of Stages and Their Relevance to Continuity–Discontinuity Issues

Jane Loevinger (1966), in a review of her own theory of ego development, spent some time discussing two types of developmental models that are highly useful in resolving some of the conceptual misunderstandings about developmental processes in the alcohol field. One model she called "embryonic," the other "hierarchic."

The embryonic type of model is characterized by a notion of invariant stages of development. The organism is presumed to pass through all stages, in a fixed sequence, usually with a fixed or specified timetable attached. Implicit in this structure is the notion that critical periods exist. Once passed through successfully, they need not be of concern; once passed through unsuccessfully, their residues remain at later stages and can be found either in vestigial form or in dormant but potent form, ready to be reawakened by the appropriate environmental stimulus or stressor. Finally, there is no intrinsic, logical relationship between adjacent stages; they simply are time-bound to each other. Freud's theory of psychosexual development is one example of the embryonic model; Erikson's theory of psychosocial development is another.

In contrast, the hierarchic model also presumes an invariant sequence of stages, with an invariant order but not an invariant progression; all individuals do not necessarily progress through all stages. They may remain at early or middle developmental levels and never progress all the way up the line. No stage can be skipped, and each stage both is based upon the preceding one and prepares the person for the succeeding one. Although progression is not necessary, once one is within a stage earlier stage characteristics are reassimilated into a new, stage-specific context. In that sense, residues of earlier development are far less easy to identify. Piaget's theory of cognitive development is one example of the hierarchic model; Loevinger's theory of ego development is another; Jellinek's (1960) disease concept of alcoholism is a third. These two types of developmental model have a number of implications for the conceptualization of drinking behavior over fairly long time spans. For one, a hierarchic model presumes that developmental change is marked by comparative discontinuity of processes. On these grounds, once an individual has moved from one, developmentally related drinking stance (e.g., nondrinking) to another (e.g., drinking), there should be comparatively little predictability on the basis of earlier developmental attributes. In contrast, an embryonic formulation would imply that continuities still remain.

Another implication is that differing aspects of alcohol problems may developmentally behave according to one type of sequence or the other. There have been good and cogent reasons for criticizing the disease concept of alcoholism (Cahalan, 1970; Cahalan & Cisin, 1976). But the fact that not all elements of problem drinking empirically obey the requirements of a hierarchic developmental model is not the same thing as saying that no characteristics do. As has already been noted, some developmental evidence supports a discontinuity model and hence a hierarchic one; other evidence supports a continuity or embryonic model. One clear task for the future is to specify which attributes of drinking and drinking problems are best characterized by the one developmental framework and which by the other; such differentiation would ultimately allow for more accurate estimates of "risk" and "prognosis" as well as specify whether such concepts are meaningful at all for a particular kind of alcohol-related behavior.

5.2. Developmental and Nondevelopmental Typologies of Problem Drinking (Alcoholism) in Adulthood

At this juncture, it is appropriate to note that the alcohol field, in contrast to other areas of psychopathology, has been rather slow to make use of developmental typologies of the sort outlined above. Why this should be is something of a mystery, given that as far back as the late 1930s, Knight (1937) made an early distinction between essential and reactive alcoholism on the basis of premorbid etiology; in the language of this review, his differentiation of these two types of addictive drinking was made on the basis of developmental course. Others throughout the years since then have found this distinction to be a useful and differentiating one relating to premorbid history and level of social competence (Rudie & McGaughran, 1961; Sugerman, Reilly, & Albahary, 1965; Levine & Zigler, 1973; Wagener & Hartsough, 1974). Although this research is still in its infancy, it tends to be consistent with the literature on schizophrenia in demonstrating that that type of premorbid functioning, which is itself initially non-alcohol-related, is an important and discriminating etiological characteristic that ultimately relates to alcoholic symptomatology as well as to other attributes of social functioning in adulthood.

What is especially suggestive about this work is that if it should continue to parallel the findings from the schizophrenia literature, it will move researchers away from a preoccupation with classifications of symptomatic content (e.g., Schuckit, Pitts, Reich, King, & Winokur, 1969; Mandell & Ginzburg, 1976; Barry, 1977) and toward the structural issues of early developmental course. The interested reader would be advised to consult Garmezy's (1970) comprehensive review of the process-reactive dimension in schizophrenia research for the lessons that it has to offer.

5.3. Sex Differences and Developmental Course

Although sex differences have occasionally been alluded to in this review, the bulk of the evidence examined here has been confined to that concerning male drinking and male developmental issues. There have been two reasons for this lack of coverage: (a) the greater preponderance of drinking literature focuses more on male subjects, since they are the ones with greater frequency and intensity of alcohol problems; and (b) space limitations preclude a thorough coverage of female developmental issues as they relate to drinking. While some studies report an essentially parallel process in males and females (e.g., Jessor & Jessor, 1977), by far the larger number that focus on both sexes show some areas of similarity and important areas of difference (e.g., Fillmore *et al.*, 1977; Jones, 1971; Margulies *et al.*, 1977; Zucker & DeVoe, 1975). To do justice to these differences would require a considerably more detailed expository treatment of sex roles and differences as these relate to generic developmental issues; this is the context in which the drinking findings would need to be placed. Such an exposition, although clearly needed, was beyond the scope of the present review.

6. Summary

For a developmental model to be truly representative, it must relate processes to time and link both to ongoing events in the life of the organism and the life of the external environment. It must deal with unfolding and maturation, as well as with the influences of physiological, psychological, social, and sociocultural processes, as they affect the person and are affected by him or her. In these respects, we need to deal with a transactional model of mutual interplay among internal and external events, rather than with one concerning the action of one class of events on another.

Within this broad prescriptive framework, conceptual models of drinking and problem-drinking behavior that attempt to account for variations in these phenomena by means of single classes of influence—whether they be sociological, psychological, or physiological—are no longer appropriate. A multiple-influence framework is presented here that takes account of four levels of influence: (a) sociocultural and community influences; (b) primary-group (family) influences; (c) intimate secondary-group (peers and family of procreation) influences; and (d) intraindividual influences, including cognitive and personality variables and nonrepresentational elements such as genetic factors. By the use of this model both cross-sectionally and through organismic time, the evidence for each of these levels of influence is reviewed at three developmental periods from birth through adulthood. Within each period, evidence of the effects of drinking-specific factors as compared with non-drinking-specific factors is contrasted. An attempt is made to summarize and highlight both consistency and inconsistency in development over fairly long time spans as these relate to later drinking and problem drinking in adolescence and thereafter.

Some of the across-study, across–developmental-time-frame conclusions were:

1. There is evidence of the early childhood appearance of behavioral markers that show developmental stability into adulthood and that relate to the later emergence of problem drinking.
2. Mainstream educational efforts about alcohol directed at middle childhood and adolescence generally miss their focus because the cognitive capacity of children at these ages and their earlier learning are at odds with both the content and the timing of the educational messages offered.
3. Significant internal restructuring of peer and family influences goes on, to the extent that efforts to predict drinking behavior on the sole basis of environmental influences will lead to inadequate and statistically less substantial predictive models.
4. Conversely, attempts at predicting the developmental peak age for learning to drink and the peak age for problem-drinking behavior not only need to take account of individual, transition-related attitudes and behaviors but also need to focus on the social-structural demand characteristics of the normative structure into which the individual is moving in a developmentally appropriate way.
5. Multiple-level influence theories are best utilized not by contrasting which type of influence is most predictively powerful at any specific developmental time point (cross-sectional analysis) but rather by asking which influences are either directly or interac-

tively salient at specified developmental times, and in what way they contribute.

6. Theorizing about the development of drinking, drinking problems, and alcoholism has until now been artificially limited by the use of only one kind of developmental model at a time. Distinctions between two types of model were made, one being called *embryonic*, the other *hierarchic*. Some examples of the advantages of utilizing both types of developmental stage theory were given. With some drinking phenomena a discontinuity (hierarchic) model is more appropriate, for others a continuity (embryonic) model fits better. Investigators are encouraged to look for the presence of both types of phenomena in future studies of drinking, drinking problems, and alcoholism.

References

Ablon, J. Family structure and behavior in alcoholism: A review of the literature. In B. Kissin & H. Begleiter (Eds.), *The biology of alcoholism. Vol. 4: Social aspects of alcoholism*. New York: Plenum Press, 1976.

Alexander, C. N. Alcohol and adolescent rebellion. *Social Forces*, 1967, *45*, 542–550.

Alexander, C. N., & Campbell, E. Q. Peer influences on adolescent drinking. *Quarterly Journal of Studies on Alcohol*, 1967, *28*, 444–453.

Alexander, C. N., Jr., & Campbell, E. Q. Balance forces and environmental effects: Factors influencing the cohesiveness of adolescent drinking groups. *Social Forces*, 1968, *46*, 367–374.

Allport, G. W. The historical background of modern social psychology. In G. Lindzey (Ed.), *Handbook of Social Psychology* (Vol. 1). Reading, Mass.: Addison-Wesley, 1954.

Allport, G. W. *Pattern and growth in personality*. New York: Holt, Rinehart & Winston, 1961.

Bacon, M. K., Barry, H., & Child, I. L. A cross-cultural study of drinking. II: Relations to other features of culture. *Quarterly Journal of Studies on Alcohol*, Supplement 3, 1965, 29–48.

Bacon, S. D. Defining adolescent alcohol use: Implications for a definition of adolescent alcoholism. *Journal of Studies on Alcohol*, 1976, *37*, 1014–1019.

Bales, R. F. Attitudes toward drinking in the Irish culture. In D. J. Pittman & C. R. Snyder (Eds.), *Society, culture and drinking patterns*. New York: Wiley, 1962.

Baltes, P. B. Longitudinal and cross-sectional sequences in the study of age and generation effects. *Human Development*, 1968, *11*, 145–171.

Barry, H., III. The correlation between personality and the risk of alcoholism. In C. M. Idestrom (Ed.), *Recent advances in the study of alcoholism*. Amsterdam: Excerpta Medica, 1977.

Barry, H., Jr., Barry, H., III, & Blane, H. T. Birth order of delinquent boys with alcohol involvement. *Quarterly Journal of Studies on Alcohol*, 1969, *30*, 408–413.

Berry, J. C. Antecedents of schizophrenia, impulsive character, and alcoholism in males. *Dissertation Abstracts*, 1967, *28*, B-2134 (Columbia University).

Birch, H. G., & Gussow, J. D. *Disadvantaged children: Health, nutrition and school failure*. New York: Grune & Stratton, 1970.

Blacker, E., Demone, H. W., & Freeman, H. E. Drinking behavior of delinquent boys. *Quarterly Journal of Studies on Alcohol*, 1965, *26*, 223–237.

Blane, H. T., & Barry, H., III. Birth order and alcoholism: A review. *Quarterly Journal of Studies on Alcohol*, 1973, *34*, 837–952.

Blane, H. T., & Hewitt, L. E. *Alcohol and youth: An analysis of the literature, 1960–1975*. Springfield, Va.: National Technical Information Service, U.S. Department of Commerce, 1977.

Block, J. *Lives through time*. Berkeley, Calif.: Bancroft, 1971.

Britt, D. W., & Campbell, E. Q. A longitudinal analysis of alcohol use, environmental conduciveness and normative structure. *Journal of Studies on Alcohol*, 1977, *38*, 1640–1647.

Cadoret, R. J. Genetic determinants of alcoholism. In R. E. Tarter & A. A. Sugerman (Eds.), *Alcoholism*. Reading, Mass.: Addison-Wesley, 1976.

Cahalan, D. *Problem drinkers*. San Francisco: Jossey-Bass, 1970.

Cahalan, D., & Cisin, I. H. Drinking behavior and drinking problems in the United States. In B. Kissin & H. Begleiter (Eds.), *The biology of alcoholism. Vol. 4: Social aspects of alcoholism*. New York: Plenum, 1976.

Cahalan, D., & Room, R. *Problem drinking among American men*. New Brunswick, N.J.: Rutgers Center of Alcohol Studies, Publications Division, 1974.

Cahalan, D., Cisin, I. H., & Crossley, H. M. *American drinking practices: A national study of drinking behavior and attitudes*. New Brunswick, N.J.: Rutgers Center of Alcohol Studies, 1969.

Cantwell, D. P. Psychiatric illness in the families of hyperactive children. *Archives of General Psychiatry*, 1972, *27*, 414–417.

Carpenter, J. A., & Armenti, N. P. Some behavioral effects of alcohol on man. In B. Kissin & H. Begleiter (Eds.), *The biology of alcoholism. Vol. 2: Physiology and behavior*. New York: Plenum, 1972, pp. 509–543.

Clausen, J. A. Family structure, socialization, and personality In L. W. Hoffman & M. L. Hoffman (Eds.), *Review of child development research* (Vol. 2). New York: Russell Sage Foundation, 1966.

Davies, J., & Stacey, B. *Teenagers and alcohol: A developmental study in Glasgow*. London: Her Majesty's Stationery Office, 1972.

de Lint, J. E. E. Alcoholism, birth rank and parental deprivation. *American Journal of Psychiatry*, 1964, *120*, 1062–1065.

Demone, H. W. The nonuse and abuse of alcohol by the male adolescent. In M. E. Chafetz (Ed.), *Proceedings of the Second Annual Conference of the National Institute on Alcohol Abuse and Alcoholism*. Washington, D.C.: Department of Health, Education, and Welfare, 1973.

Field, P. B. A new cross-cultural study of drunkenness. In D. J. Pittman & C. R. Snyder (Eds.), *Society, culture and drinking patterns*. New York: Wiley, 1962.

Fillmore, K. M., Bacon, S. D., & Hyman, M. *Alcohol drinking behavior and attitudes: Rutgers panel study*. New Brunswick, N.J.: Unpublished final report to the National Institute on Alcohol Abuse and Alcoholism, June 1977.

Flavell, J. H. *The developmental psychology of Jean Piaget*. Princeton, N.J.: Van Nostrand, 1963.

Fox, R. The alcoholic spouse. In V. W. Eisenstein (Ed.), *Neurotic interaction in marriage*. New York: Basic Books, 1956.

Fox, R. Children in the alcoholic family. In W. C. Bier (Ed.), *Problems in addiction: Alcohol and drug addiction*. New York: Fordham University Press, 1962.

Garmezy, N. Process and reactive schizophrenia: Some conceptions and issues. *Schizophrenia Bulletin*, 1970, No. 2, 30–74.

Gil, D. G. Violence against children. *Journal of Marriage and the Family*, 1971, *33*, 637–648.

Ginsburg, H., & Opper, S. *Piaget's theory of intellectual development—An introduction*. Englewood Cliffs, N.J.: Prentice-Hall, 1969.

Globetti, G. *A survey of teenage drinking in two Mississippi communities*. Social Science Research Center Preliminary Report No. 3. State College, Mississippi: Mississippi State University, 1964.

Goodwin, D. W. Is alcoholism hereditary? *Archives of General Psychiatry*, 1971, *25*, 545–548.

Goodwin, D. W. The question of a genetic basis for alcoholism: A response. *Quarterly Journal of Studies on Alcohol*, 1973, *34*, 1345–1347.

Goodwin, D. W. Genetic and experiential antecedents of alcoholism: A prospective study. Unpublished manuscript, Department of Psychiatry, Washington University, St. Louis, 1976. (a)

Goodwin, D. W. *Is alcoholism hereditary?* New York: Oxford University Press, 1976. (b)

Goodwin, D. W., Schulsinger, F., Hermansen, L., Maxe, S. B., & Winokur, G. Alcohol problems in adoptees raised apart from alcoholic biological parents. *Archives of General Psychiatry*, 1973, *28*, 238–243.

Goodwin, D. W., Schulsinger, F., Moller, N., Hermansen, L., Winokur, G., & Guze, S. B. Drinking problems in adopted and non-adopted sons of alcoholics. *Archives of General Psychiatry*, 1974, *31*, 164–169.

Goodwin, D. W., Schulsinger, F., Hermansen, L., Guze, S., & Winokur, G. Alcoholism and the hyperactive child syndrome. *Journal of Nervous and Mental Disease*, 1975, *160*, 349–353.

Graham, P., Rutter, M., & George, S. Temperamental characteristics as predictive of behavior disorders in children. *American Journal of Orthopsychiatry*, 1973, *43*, 328–339.

Harris, L., and Associates, Inc. Public awareness of the National Institute on Alcohol Abuse and Alcoholism advertising campaign and public attitudes toward drinking and alcohol abuse. Phase One: Fall 1972. Study No. 2224; Phase Two: Spring 1973. Study No. 2318; Phase Three: Fall 1973. Study No. 2342; and Phase Four: Winter 1974 and Overall Summary. Study No. 2355. Reports prepared for the National Institute on Alcohol Abuse and Alcoholism. Cited in U. S. Department of Health Education and Welfare, *Second Special Report to the U. S. Congress on Alcohol and Health: New Knowledge*. Washington, D. C.: DHEW, June 1974.

Hetherington, E. M., & Parke, R. D. *Child psychology*. New York: McGraw-Hill, 1975.

Jackson, J. K. Alcoholism and the family. In D. J. Pittman & C. R. Snyder (Eds.), *Society, culture and drinking patterns*. New York: Wiley, 1962.

Jacob, T., Favorini, A., Meisel, S. S., & Anderson, C. M. The alcoholic's spouse, children and family interactions: Substantive findings and methodological issues. *Journal of Studies on Alcohol*, 1978, *39*, 1231–1251.

Jahoda, G., & Cramond, J. *Children and alcohol*. London: Her Majesty's Stationery Office, 1972.

Jellinek, E. M. *The disease concept of alcoholism*. Highland Park, N.J.: Hillhouse Press, 1960.

Jessor, R., & Jessor, S. L. Problem drinking in youth: Personality, social and behavioral antecedents and correlates. In Chafetz, M. E. (Ed.), *Proceedings of the Second Annual Alcoholism Conference of the NIAAA*. Washington, D. C.: U. S. Government Printing Office, DHEW Publication No. (NIH) 74-676; 1973, pp. 3–23.

Jessor, R., & Jessor, S. L. Adolescent development and the onset of drinking: A longitudinal study. *Journal of Studies on Alcohol*, 1975, *36*, 27–51.

Jessor, R., & Jessor, S. L. *Problem behavior and psychosocial development: A longitudinal study of youth*. New York: Academic Press, 1977.

Jessor, R., Graves, T. D., Hanson, R. C., & Jessor, S. L. *Society, personality and deviant behavior: A study of a tri-ethnic community*. New York: Holt, Rinehart, & Winston, 1968.

Johnston, L. *Drugs and American youth*. Ann Arbor: Institute for Social Research, University of Michigan, 1973.

Jones, M. C. Personality correlates and antecedents of drinking patterns in adult males. *Journal of Consulting and Clinical Psychology*, 1968, *32*, 2–12.

Jones, M. C. Personality antecedents and correlates of drinking patterns in women. *Journal of Consulting and Clinical Psychology*, 1971, *36*, 61–69.

Kaij, L. Studies on the etiology and sequels of abuse of alcohol. Lund, Department of Psychiatry, University of Lund, 1960 (cited in D. W. Goodwin, Is alcoholism hereditary? *Archives of General Psychiatry*, 1971, *25*, 545–549).

Kalin, R. *Alcohol, sentience and inhibition: An experimental study*. Unpublished doctoral dissertation, Department of Social Relations, Harvard University, 1964.

Kalin, R., McClelland, D. C., & Kahn, M. The effects of male social drinking on fantasy. *Journal of Personality and Social Psychology*, 1965, *1*, 441–452.

Kessen, W. Research design in the study of developmental problems. In P. Mussen (Ed.), *Handbook of research methods in child development*. New York: Wiley, 1960.

Kissin, B. Theory and practice in the treatment of alcoholism. In B. Kissin & H. Begleiter (Eds.), *The biology of alcoholism. Vol. 5: Treatment and rehabilitation of the chronic alcoholic*. New York: Plenum, 1977.

Knight, R. P. The dynamics and treatment of chronic alcohol addiction. *Bulletin of the Menninger Clinic*, 1937, *1*, 233–250.

Knoblock, H., & Pasamanick, B. Prospective studies on the epidemiology of reproductive casualty: Methods, findings and some implications. *Merrill-Palmer Quarterly of Behavior and Development*, 1966, *12*, 27–43.

Koller, K. M., & Castanos, J. N. Family background and life situation in alcoholics: A comparative study of parental deprivation and other features in Australians. *Archives of General Psychiatry*, 1969, *21*, 602–610.

Levine, J., & Zigler, E. The essential-reactive distinction in alcoholism: A developmental approach. *Journal of Abnormal Psychology*, 1973, *81*, 242–249.

Levinson, D. J. *The seasons of a man's life*. New York: Knopf, 1978.

Loevinger, J. The meaning and measurement of ego development. *American Psychologist*, 1966, *21*, 195–206.

MacKay, J. R., Phillips, D. L., & Bryce, F. O. Drinking behavior among teenagers: A comparison of institutionalized and non-institutionalized youth. *Journal of Health and Social Behavior*, 1967, *8*, 46–54.

Maddox, G. L. Adolescence and alcohol. In R. G. McCarthy (Ed.), *Alcohol education for classroom and community*. New York: McGraw-Hill, 1964.

Maddox, G. L., & McCall, B. C. *Drinking among teenagers*. New Brunswick, N.J.: Rutgers Center of Alcohol Studies, Publications Division, 1964.

Magnusson, D., & Endler, N. S. (Eds.). *Personality at the crossroads: Current issues in interactional psychology*. Hillsdale, N.J.: Erlbaum Associates, 1977.

Mäkelä, K. Consumption by Finnish problem users of alcohol: A preliminary report. *The Drinking and Drug Practices Surveyor*, 1971, No. 4, 1–5.

Mandell, W., & Ginsburg, H. M. Youthful alcohol use, abuse, and alcoholism. In B. Kissin & H. Begleiter (Eds.), *The biology of alcoholism. Vol. 4: Social aspects of alcoholism*. New York: Plenum, 1976.

Mandell, W., Cooper, A., Silberstein, R. M., Novick, J., & Koloski, E. *Youthful drinking, New York State, 1962*. Staten Island, N.Y.: Staten Island Mental Health Society, 1962.

Marden, P., Zylman, R., Fillmore, K. M., & Bacon, S. D. Comment on "A national study of adolescent drinking behavior, attitudes and correlates." *Journal of Studies on Alcohol*, 1976, *37*, 1346–1358.

Margulies, R. Z., Kessler, R. C., & Kandel, D. B. A longitudinal study of onset of drinking among high-school students. *Journal of Studies on Alcohol*, 1977, *38*, 897–912.

Mayer, J., & Black, R. Potential for child abuse by drinking parent cited. *National Institute of Alcohol Abuse and Alcoholism Information and Feature Service*. Oct. 6, 1976, p. 2.

McClelland, D. C. *Personality*. New York: Dryden, 1951.

McClelland, D. C., Davis, W. N., Kalin, R., & Wanner, E. *The drinking man: Alcohol and human motivation*. New York: Free Press, 1972.

McCord, W., & McCord, J. *Origins of alcoholism*. Stanford, Calif.: Stanford University Press, 1960.

Mendelson, J. H. Biochemical mechanisms of alcohol addiction, In B. Kissin & H. Begleiter (Eds.), *The biology of alcoholism. Vol. 1: Biochemistry*. New York: Plenum Press, 1971.

Mischel, W. *Personality and assessment*. New York: Wiley, 1968.

Mischel, W. Continuity and change in personality. *American Psychologist*, 1969, *24*, 1012–1018.

Morrison, J. R., & Stewart, M. A. A family study of the hyperactive child syndrome. *Biological Psychiatry*, 1971, *3*, 189–195.

Morrison, J. R., & Stewart, M. A. The psychiatric status of the legal families of adopted hyperactive children. *Archives of General Psychiatry*, 1973, *28*, 888–891.

Nathan, P. E., & Lansky, D. Common methodological problems in research on the addictions. *Journal of Consulting and Clinical Psychology*, 1978, *46*, 713–726.

National Council on Alcoholism, Criteria Committee. Criteria for the diagnosis of alcoholism. *American Journal of Psychiatry*, 1972, *129*, 127–135.

Partanen, J., Brunn, K., & Markkanen, T. *Inheritance of drinking behavior*. Helsinki: Finnish Foundation for Alcohol Studies, 1966.

Pasamanick, B., & Knoblock, H. Retrospective studies on the epidemiology of reproductive casualty: Old and new. *Merrill-Palmer Quarterly of Behavior and Development*, 1966, *12*, 7–26.

Pelz, D. C., & Schuman, S. H. Motivational factors in crashes and violations of young drivers. Mimeoed paper, Highway Safety Research Institute and Institute for Social Research, Ann Arbor, Mich. (Presented at the American Public Health Association Meetings, October, 1971).

Piaget, J. *The origins of intelligence in children* (2nd ed.). New York: International Universities Press, 1952.

Rachal, J. V., Williams, J. R., Brehm, M. L., Cavanaugh, B., Moore, R. P., & Eckerman, W. L. A national study of adolescent drinking behavior, attitudes and correlates. Springfield, Va.: National Technical Information Service, 1975.

Rachal, J. V., Hubbard, R. L., Williams, J. R., & Tuchfeld, B. S. Drinking levels and problem drinking among junior and senior high-school students. *Journal of Studies on Alcohol*, 1976, *37*, 1751–1761.

Ricks, D., & Berry, J. C. Family and symptom patterns that precede schizophrenia. In M. Roff & D. F. Ricks (Eds.), *Life history research in psychopathology*. Minneapolis: University of Minnesota Press, 1970.

Riester, A. E., & Zucker, R. A. Adolescent social-structure and drinking behavior. *Personnel and Guidance Journal*, 1968, *33*, 304–312.

Robins, L. N. *Deviant children grown up*. Baltimore: Williams & Wilkins, 1966.

Robins, L. N., Bates, W. M., & O'Neal, P. Adult drinking patterns of former problem children. In D. Pittman & C. R. Snyder (Eds.), *Society, culture and drinking patterns*. New York: Wiley, 1962.

Rosin, A. J., & Glatt, M. M. Alcohol excess in the elderly. *Quarterly Journal of Studies on Alcohol*, 1971, *32*, 53–59.

Rudie, R. R., & McGaughran, L. S. Differences in developmental experience, defensiveness, and personality organization between two classes of problem drinkers. *Journal of Abnormal and Social Psychology*, 1961, *62*, 659–665.

Sadoun, R., Lolli, G., & Silverman, M. *Drinking in French culture*. New Brunswick, N.J.: Monograph No. 5, Publications Division, Rutgers Center of Alcohol Studies, 1965.

Sameroff, A. Transactional models in early social relations. *Human Development*, 1975, *18*, 65–79.

Sameroff, A. J., & Chandler, M. J. Perinatal risk and the continuum of caretaking casualty. In F. D. Horowitz, M. Heatherington, S. Scarr-Salapatek, & G. Siegel (Eds.), *Review of child development research* (Vol. 4). Chicago: University of Chicago Press, 1975.

Schaie, K. W. A general model for the study of developmental problems. *Psychological Bulletin*, 1965, *64*, 92–107.

Scholom, A., Zucker, R. A., & Stollak, G. S. Predicting child adjustment from infant and parent temperament. *Journal of Abnormal Child Psychology*, in press.

Schuckit, M. A., Pitts, F. N., Jr., Reich, T., King, L. J., & Winokur, G. Alcoholism. I: Two types of alcoholism in women. *Archives of General Psychiatry*, 1969, *20*, 301–306.

Schuman, S. H., & Pelz, D. C. A field trial of young drivers. *Archives of Environmental Health*, 1970, *21*, 462–467.

Schuman, S. H., Pelz, D. C., Ehrlich, N. J., & Selzer, M. L. Young male drivers: Impulse expression, accidents and violations. *Journal of the American Medical Association*, 1967, *200*, 1026–1030.

Smart, R. G. Alcoholism, birth order, and family size. *Journal of Abnormal and Social Psychology*, 1963, *66*, 17–23.

Snow, R. W. *Spatial dimensions of drinking behavior: An application of symbolic interaction theory*. Unpublished doctoral dissertation, University of Illinois, 1975.

Snyder, C. R. Culture and Jewish sobriety: The ingroup–outgroup factor. In D. J. Pittman & C. R. Snyder (Eds.), *Society, culture and drinking patterns*. New York: Wiley, 1962.

Sommer, R. The isolated drinker in the Edmonton Beer Parlor. *Quarterly Journal of Studies on Alcohol*, 1965, *26*, 95–110.

Spieker, G., & Mouzakitis, C. M. Alcohol abuse and child abuse and neglect. Paper presented at the Annual Meeting of the Alcohol and Drug Problems Association of North America, New Orleans, Sept. 1976.

Statistical Abstract of the United States. Washington, D.C.: U.S. Government Printing Office, Bureau of the Census, 1977.

Sugerman, A. A., Reilly, D., & Albahary, R. S. Social competence and essential-reactive distinction in alcoholism. *Archives of General Psychiatry*, 1965, *12*, 552–556.

Thomas, A., & Chess, S. *Temperament and development*. New York: Brunner/Mazel, 1977.

Thomas, A., Chess, S., Birch, H. G., Hertzig, M. E., & Korn, S. *Behavioral individuality in early childhood*. New York: New York University Press, 1963.

Thomas, A., Chess, S., & Birch, H. G. *Temperament and behavior disorders in children*. New York: New York University Press, 1968.

Tolor, A., & Tamerin, J. S. The question of a genetic basis for alcoholism: Comment on the study by Goodwin *et al.* and a response. *Quarterly Journal of Studies on Alcohol*, 1973, *34*, 1341–1345.

Ullman, A. D. First drinking experience as related to age and sex. In D. J. Pittman & C. R. Snyder (Eds.), *Society, culture and drinking patterns*. New York: Wiley, 1962.

U.S. Department of Health, Education, and Welfare. *Second Special Report to the U.S. Congress on Alcohol and Health: New Knowledge*. Washington, D.C.: DHEW, June 1974.

Wagener, J. M., & Hartsough, D. M. Social competence as a process-reactive dimension with schizophrenics, alcoholics and normals. *Journal of Abnormal Psychology*, 1974, *83*, 112–116.

Wahl, C. W. Some antecedent factors in the family histories of 109 alcoholics. *Quarterly Journal of Studies on Alcohol*, 1956, *17*, 643–654.

Wechsler, H., & Thum, D. Alcohol and drug use among teenagers: A questionnaire study. In M. E. Chafetz (Ed.), *Proceedings of the Second Annual Alcoholism Conference of the National Institute on Alcohol Abuse and Alcoholism*. Washington, D.C.: Department of Health, Education and Welfare, 1973. (a)

Wechsler, H., & Thum, D. Teen-age drinking, drug use, and social correlates. *Quarterly Journal of Studies on Alcohol*, 1973, *34*, 1220–1227. (b)

White House Conference on Children. *Profiles of children*. Washington, D.C.: U.S. Government Printing Office, 1970.

Williams, A. F. Psychological needs and social drinking among college students. *Quarterly Journal of Studies on Alcohol*, 1968, *29*, 355–363.

Williams, A. F. College problem drinkers: A personality profile. In G.L. Maddox (Ed.), *The domesticated drug*. New Haven, Conn.: College and University Press, 1970, pp. 343–360.

Williams, A. F. The alcoholic personality. In B. Kissin & H. Begleiter (Eds.), *The biology of alcoholism. Vol. 4: Social aspects of alcoholism*. New York: Plenum, 1976.

Wilson, C., & Oxford, J. Children of alcoholics: Report of a preliminary study and comments on the literature. *Journal of Studies on Alcohol*, 1978, *39*, 121–142.

Zucker, R. A. Parental influences upon drinking patterns of their children. In M. Greenblatt & M. A. Schuckit (Eds.), *Alcoholism problems in women and children*. New York: Grune & Stratton, 1976.

Zucker, R. A., & Barron, F. H. Parental behaviors associated with problem drinking and antisocial behavior among adolescent males. In M. E. Chafetz (Ed.), *Research on Alcoholism I. Clinical Problems and Special Populations*. Washington, D. C.: U. S. Government Printing Office, 1973, [DHEW publication 74-675].

Zucker, R. A., & DeVoe, C. I. Life history characteristics associated with problem drinking and antisocial behavior in adolescent girls: A comparison with male findings. In R. D. Wirt, G. Winokur, & M. Roff (Eds.), *Life history research in psychopathology* (Vol. 4). Minneapolis: University of Minnesota Press, 1975.

Zucker, R. A., & Fillmore, K. M. Motivational factors and problem drinking among adolescents. Paper presented at the 28th International Congress on Alcohol and Alcoholism, Washington, D.C., Sept. 1968.

Zucker, R. A., & Van Horn, H. Sibling social structure and oral behavior: Drinking and smoking in adolescence. *Quarterly Journal of Studies on Alcohol*, 1972, *33*, 193–197.

5

Ecological Factors in Drinking

Thomas C. Harford

1. Introduction

Many would agree that the environment influences human behavior and development. This chapter examines the role of environmental factors in alcohol and drinking behavior among young adults from an ecological perspective.

Ecology is most commonly applied to the study of the natural environments of animals. Recent extensions of this discipline to the study of human behavior have suggested that such ecological factors as climate and geography exert strong influences on individual and group behavior (Moos, 1973). The study of ecological dimensions as applied to human behavior also includes aspects of the man-made environment (i.e., architecture) and the social milieu. The complexity and scope of this discipline are evident in the variety of ecological variables—noise level, temperature, physical design, crowding—that have been related to such behaviors as physical health, crime, suicide, intelligence, self-esteem, and other aspects of mental health. Insel and Moos (1974) subsumed these topics under the term *social ecology*, which is the study of the interaction of man with his physical and social environment. The underlying issue posed by these efforts is how the environment influences human behavior.

While the importance of the environment has been acknowledged in many formulations of human behavior, attempts to measure it are

Thomas C. Harford • Department of Health, Education and Welfare, National Institute of Alcohol Abuse and Alcoholism, Rockville, MD 20857.

not well developed. Part of the difficulty in measurement stems from the absence of a conceptually adequate definition of the environment. The traditional approach in ecology has been to define and measure the environment in purely physical and objective terms. Koffka (1935), however, argued that human behavior does not spring from the objective properties of the stimulus world but from the stimulus world transformed into a psychological environment. Social ecology must contend with both of these approaches to conceptualization.

Social ecology is akin to field theory, which views behavior as a function of the person and his environment. For Kurt Lewin, however, the immediate context of behavior is the perceived environment (Lewin, 1951). The selection of this unit as the interactive link between the environment and behavior is important in considering different ways of conceptualizing the environment. Lewin's preference for the perceived environment, rather than the objective environment, is based on his contention that behavior can be more fully understood if it is related to the personal environment. In contrast, Barker (1968) has proposed the term *behavior setting*, which is an ecological unit containing both an environmental and a behavioral component. It is in this manner that environmental and behavioral components are interrelated in defined contexts. The environment and behavior should be described and measured independently if one is to understand the nature of the relationship between them. The ecological environment comprises a different class of phenomena and cannot be described solely from the person's behavior. The study of the environment, or context, of a person cannot be described in terms of the point of contact with the person. This interaction examines only a part of the characteristics of the environment. The distinctions between the objective and the perceived environment are important in understanding the types of studies that have related ecology to behavior and, more specifically, to drinking.

Another issue that ecology in human environments must deal with is the distinction between physical and social objects. Environmental influences that emanate from a person or a group are quite different from those of physical objects. A person, unlike an object, has intentional control over the causal lines emanating from him or her (Heider, 1958). One can avoid a falling object by getting out of the way (the object has direction but not intent), while avoiding a blow to the head from another person may not be possible if the other is more powerful (the person has control over direction and intent).

Physical objects influence behavior by initiating, supporting, and setting limits on action. The physical ecology of a behavior setting such as a bar, for example, influences the types of behavior that can be engaged in (sitting, dancing, milling around, etc.) by the amount of space and the spatial properties in the setting (chairs, dance floor, music). A person in this setting, unlike a physical object, can influence behavior under a variety of circumstances. A female patron may avoid contact with a male stranger by glancing in another direction, engaging others in conversation, or changing her location. If the stranger is persistent, however, the female may be forced to leave the setting completely or seek intercession from others. Cavan (1966, pp. 88–111) has indicated that physical seating arrangements in bars (bar stools versus chairs and tables) differentially influence interaction patterns. The female patron, uncomfortable in the structure imposed by one seating arrangement, may move to another without thought of that structure, intentionally redirecting its field of influence.

To summarize, a comprehensive social-ecological view must include the objective environment and the psychological environment, the social and physical objects in the objective environment, and the way in which these properties in the objective environment are transformed into the psychological environment.

The present chapter has as its primary focus the relationship between ecology and drinking behavior among young adults. In view of the paucity of good empirical studies in this area, a literal treatment of this topic would yield much conjecture and little fact. The approach adopted is a conceptual examination of ecology and alcohol, a selective review from the broad literature relating ecology to alcohol and a speculative link between the two as they relate to the drinking behavior of adolescents and young adults. An appropriate place to begin is an examination of the drinking behavior of young adults as illustrated in a few case histories. The material for these case histories was taken from a survey of drinking contexts in metropolitan Boston for which information was obtained over a consecutive four-week period of time (Gerstel, Mason, Piserchia, & Kristiansen, 1975).

1.1. Case Histories

Sarah, a 25-year-old Roman Catholic, is married to a police officer. She is a high school graduate and is unemployed. She has lived at the present address for three years and expects to remain there for at least five more years. Less than half her relatives drink regularly, but more than half of her friends are regular drinkers.

The month's drinking started on *Saturday night* from 8 to 11 at a relative's house for a party. Sarah was with her husband and a large group of relatives. She had two mixed drinks. *Wednesday night* from 9 to 11 at home alone, she drank one beer with a snack. *Friday night* from 8:30 to 11:30, at home with her husband and 15 relatives, Sarah had two mixed drinks. The second week consisted of only one drinking event, which was on *Sunday night* from 7 to 10 at a friend's house for a cookout with her husband and a large group of friends. She drank three beers. The following week started on *Thursday night* from 6 to 8 at a restaurant with her husband and their two children. She had one mixed drink with dinner. *Saturday night* from 9:30 to 11, at a restaurant with her husband and another couple, she had two mixed drinks with dinner. *Later Saturday*, from 11:15 to midnight, at a bar with the same people, Sarah had one mixed drink. The last week began on *Tuesday afternoon* from 12 to 3, at her sister's house. She had four mixed drinks with lunch. *Wednesday night* from 8:30 to 9, at her mother's house, Sarah drank one beer. *Friday night* from 8:30 to 9, at her sister's house, Sarah drank a glass of wine. *Later Friday night*, from 9 to 1 A.M., at a restaurant, she had one mixed drink with dinner. *Still later that night*, from 2 A.M. to 3 A.M. at a cocktail lounge, Sarah drank coffee with rum. *Saturday night* from 10 to 11, at her mother's house with four family members, Sarah had one beer. *Sunday night* from 10 to midnight, at a private club, she drank two beers.

Jim, a 19-year-old high school graduate, is employed as a grocery clerk. He is single and is living with his parents. He is a Unitarian. More than half his relatives are regular drinkers and all his friends drink regularly.

The month's drinking started on *Sunday evening* from 6 to 6:30. Jim was at a restaurant with his parents. He drank a glass of wine with dinner. *Wednesday night* from 8 to 9:30, at an outdoor party with six friends, he drank four beers. The next week started on *Friday afternoon* from noon until 12:45. Jim was at a restaurant with a friend and drank a beer with lunch. *That night* from 8 to 10, at an outdoor party with 15 friends, Jim drank five beers. The third week started on *Wednesday night* from 8 to 10, at an outdoor party. With seven friends, Jim drank four beers. *Friday night*, from 8 to 10, at home with five friends, Jim drank four beers. *Saturday night* from 8 to 8:30, at home with a friend, Jim drank a beer with dinner. *Later that night*, from 8:30 to 10, at home alone, Jim drank two beers. *Sunday afternoon* from 2 to 2:30, at home with two friends, he drank a beer. The last week started on *Wednesday night* from 8 to 10. Jim was at an outdoor party with five friends. He drank six beers. *Friday night* from 10 to midnight, once again at an outdoor party, Jim drank four beers with six friends. *Saturday night* from 8 to 10, at home on his birthday, Jim drank five glasses of champagne. Nine of his friends were there to celebrate. *Sunday afternoon* from 3 to 3:30, at his relative's house, Jim drank a beer. *Monday night* from 9 to 9:30, at home alone, he had one mixed drink.

Michael, a 23-year-old Roman Catholic, is married and an officer in the U.S. Coast Guard attending graduate school. He plans to stay in the coast guard until retirement. He has lived at the present address for six months and expects to stay there for another year or two. Less than half his relatives are regular drinkers, while nearly all his friends drink regularly.

The first event reported for the month was *Saturday evening* from 7:30 to 9, at a restaurant with his wife. He had one mixed drink. *Monday afternoon* from 12 to 12:30, at the school pub with a male friend, Michael had two beers with lunch. *Later Monday evening,* from 6 to 6:30, at the school pub with a male friend, he had two beers with supper. *Tuesday afternoon* from 12 to 12:30, at the school pub with a friend, Michael had two beers with lunch. *Tuesday evening* from 6:30 to 7, at the school pub, he had two beers with dinner. *Later Tuesday evening,* from 7:15 to 9:30, at the officer's club, Michael drank eight beers. *Still later,* from 9:45 to midnight, at a bar with a male friend, he drank seven beers. *Thursday* from 9 A.M. to 3:30 P.M., at home by himself, Michael drank five beers. *That night* from 6:30 to midnight, on the beach with his wife and 14 friends, he drank 12 beers. *Friday* from 9 A.M. to 6 P.M., on the beach with his wife and 14 friends, Michael had two mixed drinks and 18 beers. The next week started on *Sunday* from 10 A.M. to 3 P.M. Michael was home with two friends. He drank two beers and 12 mixed drinks. *Later Sunday,* from 7:30 to 8:30, at home with 12 couples, Michael had six mixed drinks. *Tuesday night* from 8:30 to 9, at a bar alone, he had one beer. *Wednesday afternoon* from 12 to 12:30, at the school pub with two male friends, he had two beers with lunch. *Thursday evening* from 6:30 to 7, at the school pub with a friend, Michael drank two beers with dinner. *Later,* from 8 to 11, at a bar with a friend he had five beers. *Friday evening* from 4:45 to 5:15, while driving his car, Michael drank a beer. *Later Friday,* from 7 to midnight, at a friend's house with his wife and four other couples, Michael had 15 mixed drinks and 4 glasses of wine. The following week started on *Saturday*. His drinking was continuous from 10 A.M. until after midnight. Michael started the day off at home drinking with a male friend. He drank 6 beers and 16 mixed drinks from 10 A.M. to 6 P.M. At 6:30, his wife and five couples joined the group. He consumed four mixed drinks and a glass of wine with dinner. *Later that night,* from 7:30 to 12:30, Michael drank 18 mixed drinks with his wife and approximately 20 other couples. *Sunday* from 8 A.M. to 6 P.M., Michael drank six beers at a friend's house. *Tuesday afternoon* from 12:30 to 1, at the school pub, he had two beers with lunch. *Wednesday afternoon* from 12 to 1, at the school pub with a friend, Michael once again had two beers with lunch. *Later Wednesday,* from 6:30 to 7, at the school pub, Michael drank two beers with dinner. *Still later,* from 7 to 10, at the officer's club, Michael drank seven beers. The last week once again started with an all-day drinking event on *Saturday*. From 9 to noon, Michael was at home with a male friend. He drank four beers. Later that day, from 12:15 to 12:45, at a friend's house, he had a beer with lunch. From 6 to 8, on the beach with his wife and 20 other people, Michael had two mixed drinks with dinner. *Saturday night* from 9:30 to 11, at a friend's house, Michael drank two mixed drinks. *Sunday* from 11 A.M. to 5 P.M., at a relative's house, Michael had six beers with his cousin. *Wednesday evening* from 4 to 8:30, at the officer's club with nine friends, Michael drank five beers and two mixed drinks. *Thursday night* from 9 to midnight, Michael drank five beers while watching a football game. *Later on Thursday*, from midnight to 2 A.M., at a different bar, Michael drank two more beers. The last reported event for the month was *Friday* from 5 to 11 P.M. Michael was at a friend's house with his wife and 12 other couples. He drank six beers and six mixed drinks.

1.2. Synopsis

Sarah's use of alcohol, while frequent, rarely exceeds one or two drinks. Most of her drinking is with relatives and with her husband, though she does drink alone occasionally. Much of her drinking takes place outside of the home, visiting relatives, restaurants, cookouts, cocktail lounges, and at most times in the company of her husband.

Jim also represents a pattern of frequent drinking, though the amounts consumed are more varied than those of Sarah. He typically consumes four to five beers at parties with friends, and these occasions occur on a weekly basis. At other times, he usually has one or two beers. Much of his drinking takes place with friends as drinking companions, although he also drinks alone and on certain occasions with his parents.

Michael's use of alcohol is distinguished from Sarah's with respect to the amount consumed more than frequency. He presents a varied set of occasions of use, ranging from one or two beers with a classmate at school, which occurs on a weekly basis, to 15 or more mixed drinks with his wife and a large group of other married couples, which occurs with regularity on weekends. Weekend drinking is not confined to evening get-togethers but covers the entire day, with variations in location and the number and types of people present. Weekday drinking at the school pub is usually restricted to two or three beers unless it carries over into the evening hours at other bars or clubs. While Michael's use of alcohol may be indicative of potential problems, the presence of a large network of drinking companions must be viewed as contributory. His light and heavy use of alcohol is clearly demarcated by situational contexts.

Despite the short period of coverage—four weeks—discernible and idiosyncratic patterns of alcohol use emerge. At this level, the material underscores individual variability in alcohol use. This individual framework for organizing the drinking information is, in part, a consequence of the survey design, which sampled persons and not the drinking setting. Had the settings themselves been sampled, individual differences would be less pronounced. From an ecological perspective, the case histories are suggestive of environmental and situational determinants of alcohol consumption. Occupational and marital status clearly demarcate differences in opportunities to drink. The complexity and variety of social networks and drinking locations differentially shape expectations and behaviors. It is the task of this chapter to systematically examine these ecological factors and assess their influence on drinking behavior. The next section, by way of introduction, views drinking behavior in a more appropriate framework, one that includes both individual and environmental sources of variation.

1.3. Perspectives on Drinking

Recently, Straus (1977) has provided some clarity on the issues of alcoholism and problem drinking, particularly as they relate to youth, by distinguishing between drinkers who are responding to internal needs and drinkers who are responding to external needs. He noted that this distinction is important since the strategies for prevention and change are quite different, depending upon whether the primary processes are internal or external to the person. He further noted that much of the problem-drinking behavior among young people appears to be a response to perceived needs to meet the expectations and the requirements of social situations.

This conceptualization is extremely useful in separating the traditional concerns of psychology and sociology as they relate to behavior. It also implies that the study of alcohol and youth would benefit from an emphasis on ecological influences on drinking behavior. The conceptualization also conveys a developmental framework, namely, that the balance of internal and external forces tilts in the direction of environmental properties among youth and in the direction of internalized needs among adults. Straus (1977) was not suggesting that the disciplines of psychology and sociology should focus exclusively on youth and adults, respectively, but was, rather, directing attention to potentially important sources of influences on drinking behaviors for these two populations.

While it is important to take note of the source of major influence when examining individuals at different points on the developmental spectrum, it is also important to take note of the potential interaction of both of these processes at each point on the spectrum. Much of social behavior is often the consequence of situational factors interacting with individual attributes. While the topic of this chapter relates to environmental factors, it is important to retain the broader context of behavior.

Most comprehensive theories of behavior acknowledge the contribution of both the person and the situation. Murray (1938), for example, has provided an interactive model in which both the individual and the environment are classified along the same dimensions. The categorization of individual "needs" is matched with a classification of environmental "presses," which serve to facilitate need gratification or need frustration.

There are, however, more recent formulations of an interactive nature operationally specifying the conditions under which each component is most influential. Fishbein (1967), for example, has proposed two major factors that determine behavioral intention: a personal or "attitudinal factor" and a social or "normative" factor. Behavioral intentions are viewed as the best predictors of overt behaviors. A discussion of the conditions that affect the relationship between intention and behavior may be found in Fishbein and Ajzen (1975, Ch. 8). The attitudinal component relates to the person's evaluations of the perceived consequences of performing a particular behavior. The normative component deals with the influence of the social environment on behavior and refers to the person's perception of how significant others (reference groups) would react to that behavior. While normative factors could be considered as part of the attitude (consequences of behaving may be acceptable or unacceptable to significant others), Fishbein maintains the distinction for conceptual reasons. Different processes underlie attitude formation and normative belief.

The important point of the model, which bears on the present topic, is that behavioral intentions are a function of the weighted sum of these two variables, the relative contributions of which vary as a function of the kind of behavior being predicted, the conditions under which the behavior is to occur, and the type of person who is to perform the behavior.

This model has been used in research on such behaviors as cooperative competition, leisure activities, purchases of commercial products, and cheating on exams. The studies yield impressive predictions of behavioral intentions based on information on the attitudes and the normative components of the model. Empirical application of the model allows further specification of the differential weight afforded each component in the model. Fishbein and Ajzen (1975), for example, reported on intentions to engage in premarital sexual intercourse among undergraduates. The findings indicated that attitudinal components were more important than normative considerations for female students, while normative factors were the primary determinants of behavioral intentions among male students.

Recasting Straus's formulation into the present model, internal needs relate to the attitudinal factor and external needs relate to the normative factor. The point of all of this has been simply to clarify some basic propositions underlying behavior and to indicate possibilities of translating conceptual issues into scientific terms capable of empirical study and more precision. Unfortunately, studies of behavioral intention to drink with respect to attitudes and norms have not been conducted with different age groups. The general hypothesis that normative factors would outweigh attitudinal ones among youth has not been tested, nor have the conditions been specified. Thus, while normative factors may be more important generally for youth, the contributions may vary with respect to the conditions or context in which drinking is to occur. For example, the intent to drink at a party when adults are not present may be subject to normative influence, while the intent to drink at mealtimes is not.

Fishbein (1977) concluded from an analysis of the literature on smoking that normative factors may be more important in the initiation of smoking, while attitudinal factors may be more salient in the maintenance or cessation of smoking. The fact that the majority of youth are more involved with issues in terms of onset or initiation of drinking may be taken as support of Straus's basic proposition that a normative focus is of critical concern in studies of adolescent drinking.

2. The Objective Environment

2.1. Ecology and Alcohol

Studies relating ecological factors in the objective environment to alcohol may be grouped in two topic areas: (a) those dealing with the production and distribution of beverage alcohol, and (b) those concerned with alcohol consumption and drinking patterns. Each of these topics is reviewed here separately.

Climate and geography are of ecological significance to alcohol. Although the effects of seasonal variations on drinking patterns has not been systematically studied, logically it may be supposed that the winter months introduce drinking settings that are distinguished from those of the summer months. The case histories presented earlier provide several examples of out-of-doors contexts that would be unlikely in bad weather. A study by Irgens-Jensen (1970) on the use of alcohol in an isolated area of northern Norway indicated that the use of alcohol was less pronounced during the winter months than in the summer. Seasonal variation had the effect of influencing the degree of social contact that appeared to be the most influential factor in explaining drinking habits.

Sulkunen (1976) has noted the role of ecological factors in the physical availability of alcohol. The production of wine and distilled spirits, for example, depends upon the supply of raw materials. Leading wine-producing countries depend upon favorable geographic locations. Agricultural produce is generally abundant in countries that produce distilled spirits. Beer-producing countries are less dependent upon the supply of raw materials than they are upon the presence of a nonagricultural work force that makes up a large proportion of the labor force.

Several studies have examined the ecology of alcohol with respect to its distribution in the environment. Cavan (1966) noted that approximately one-third of the total number of public drinking places in San Francisco are located in two general areas of the city: the night-life section and the central-business and skid-row area. Generally, the ecological distribution is associated with the distribution of potential patrons. The majority of drinking places (70%) are located in census tracts that contain 52% of the single-male resident population. In this area, there is one drinking place for every 308 residents 21 years of age and over, whereas in areas that contain only 18% of the single-male population, there is only one public drinking place for every 1,952 residents of legal drinking age (Cavan, 1966, pp. 24–30).

Pfautz and Hyde (1960) have reported the distribution of the number and types of licensed outlets in a New England city and have examined their ecological relationship to other community institutions. The majority of these outlets in 1958 were licensed for on-premise consumption. Among the on-premise outlets, the "tavern–bar– cocktail lounge" (non-eating places) predominated (36%), followed by "restaurant– bar" (24%) and "private clubs" (7%).

The spatial distribution of all outlets included a heavy concentration in the downtown area of the city, including the business district. Despite a concentration of restaurant–bars in this area, the other types of licensed sources were dispersed throughout the city. A second characteristic of the distribution pattern was the tendency to follow the major traffic arteries on all sides of the city. The only exception was a section of upper- and upper-middle-class residential areas, where there was an absence of on-premise outlets.

The study also indicated similarities among the spatial distribution of outlets, population, schools, and churches. On-premise outlets such as bars and taverns departed somewhat from this ubiquitous pattern. The distribution of restaurant–bars was least similar to the distribution of the other social institutions studied. An inverse relationship between socioeconomic status and the ratio of alcohol outlets to population was reported and is suggestive of differences in drinking patterns among these population groups. The distance between residences and outlets is less (high physical availability) for all but the upper-class population of the city.

The ecological factors relating to the distribution of on-premise outlets would be expected to vary as a function of the type of setting. Cavan (1966) has developed a bar typology based on the primary function of these settings. "Convenience" bars provide easy access to patrons who wish to kill time in the course of other social activities (e.g., waiting for transportation, in a theatre). Many of these establishments are located in areas of a large influx of people. Their hours of operation may vary within those prescribed by law in order to adjust to the schedules of the population who dominate the area. "Home-territory" bars, on the other hand, function like neighborhood taverns, and though not limited to residential areas, they have a broader distribution network in the community than either "convenience" bars or "night spots." The "night-spot" bars generally concentrate in the entertainment section of the city or in adjacent locations easily accessible to the night life of the city.

The physical topography of the environment also provides natural places for drinking in other than enclosed premises (e.g., alleys, street corners, gutted buildings, parks, picnic areas). Rubington (1968) has noted several ecological factors that serve to structure the activities of *bottle gangs*. This term applies to the typical form of street drinking for indigent men. They meet on the street, pool funds, and share alcohol, usually in "open-air" settings. Skid-row areas provide more resources with respect to large numbers of indigent men, outlet stores, and established territory. The ecology of skid row yields low surveillance and low exposure to external controls, with relaxed and leisurely interactions in drinking settings. The absence of an established territory, or a skid-row area, requires greater mobility in areas where potential gangs are more dispersed, few in number, and highly visible to social response. Rubington noted that under these conditions, drinking is surreptitious, with weakened internal controls for deviancy and high levels of interpersonal tension.

These studies are suggestive of factors in the ecological environment that relate to the production and distribution of alcohol. They share a common conceptual framework that specifies the circumstances of drinking with respect to the physical availability of alcohol (e.g., restaurants, taverns, alleys). Caution should be exercised, however, in interpreting the strengths of the association or inferring any causal relationship between ecological features in the community and the physical availability of alcohol. While it is more likely that outlets locate in areas where patrons are accessible, rather than patrons' taking up residence where outlets are available, both the production and the distribution of alcohol are strongly influenced by factors other than ecology. A discussion of the legal restraints on the physical availability of alcohol, for example, may be found in Popham, Schmidt, and de Lint (1976). There is a need for more studies that examine the influence of ecology on the distribution of alcohol while controlling legal restriction for population, hours of sale, and other relevant variables.

2.2. Ecology and Drinking

The influence of the ecological environment on the physical availability of alcohol may be extended to drinking behaviors as well. Geographical variations in drinking patterns have been reported in several studies and provide a further source of information with respect to environmental factors and alcohol. Cahalan and Room (1974) have related ecological factors to drinking at several levels of analysis: census regions, urban and rural areas, neighborhoods, and census tracts.

When census regions were characterized with respect to temperance attitudes and drinking patterns (wet versus dry), Cahalan and Room (1974) noted differences in the drinking patterns among national samples of men aged 21–59. Drier regions have lower proportions of heavy drinkers and higher proportions of nondrinkers.

Comparisons by regional wetness and extent of urbanization indicated that a pattern of heavy but intermittent drinking was more common in urban areas of dry regions than in wet ones. They further noted that the prevalence of social consequences due to drinking (problems with family and job) in dry regions reverse those in wet regions (Cahalan & Room, 1974, p. 81).

Similar findings were obtained when the neighborhoods, or sampling clusters, from national surveys of men were characterized with respect to wetness based upon the proportion of drinkers sharing certain patterns of drinking (Cahalan & Room, 1974, pp. 161–179). These aggregate data provide independent measures of the ecological drinking climate, or social context, in which the men drank. The findings indicate that heavy drinking was more likely to result in severe social consequences in dry than in wet neighborhoods. They also showed that infrequent but heavy (binge) drinking formed a proportionally greater part of the heavy drinking in dry neighborhoods. The authors attributed the presence of social consequences to the combination of heavy drinking in a community context of disapproval.

Ecological correlates of problem drinking were further examined in a community survey in San Francisco (Cahalan & Room, 1974, pp.

193–202). These data allowed more specific delineation of ecological factors than was otherwise possible in the national surveys. The census tracts and the aggregation of these into 13 districts formed the ecological units for analysis. Ecological variables included social status (median income), segregation (proportion of nonminorities), and familiation (proportion of nonnuclear families). The results indicated relationships between drinking problems and residence in census tracts of low familiation or low social status. These two variables were interrelated and were clustered in particular city districts.

Sulkunen (1976) reported variations in drinking patterns associated with the physical availability of beverage-specific alcohol among the world's population. The relationship between ecology and drinking patterns is mediated by the physical availability of beverage-specific alcohol. National consumption relates to national production. In countries where per capita consumption of wine is heavy, the production of wine is large. In countries where substantial proportions of alcohol consumption are based on imports, per capita consumption is low. Sulkunen further demonstrated that national consumption of specific beverages is associated with differences in drinking patterns. In predominantly wine-drinking countries, alcohol is typically integrated with meals, while spirits-drinking cultures usually separate drinking from meals and other social activities. Beer-drinking countries typically integrate alcohol with social contacts and conviviality.

The relationship between these ecological variables and drinking is not a direct one. Ecological factors contribute to the physical availability of beverage-specific alcohol, which, in turn, is associated with variations in national drinking patterns.

A more direct association between ecology and drinking is present in the argument that alcohol consumption relates in some positive way to the number and type of licensed outlets where people drink. The relationship between the physical availability of alcohol and alcohol consumption is a complicated one, and a discussion of the basic issues may be found in Parker and Harman (1978) and Schmidt and Popham (1978). Studies that have examined the relationship between the distribution of alcohol and per capita consumption have failed to control for legal restrictions in the number of outlets per unit of population. Recently, Parker, Wolz, and Harford (1978) indicated a strong relationship between the number of outlets and per capita consumption while controlling for legal restrictions. There is need for more studies that examine the influence of ecology on the distribution of the number and types of outlets and its relationship to drinking practices in which other relevant factors are controlled.

3. The Perceived Environment

The work of Jessor and his colleagues in the study of problem behavior in youth is of direct relevance to the present topic for several reasons (Jessor, Graves, Hanson, & Jessor, 1968; Jessor & Jessor, 1977). First, they have developed a theoretically derived model of the social environment that provides a logical basis for linking the environment with behavior. Second, they have been concerned with studying problem behavior, including heavy alcohol use, among adolescents. Third, they have empirically examined several propositions from the model with data obtained from a four-year longitudinal study. And fourth, they have elaborated the context of the perceived environment into distal and proximal structures.

Variables in the distal structure of the perceived environment relate to general support and control from parents and friends. They include such items as "Would you say that your parents generally encourage you to do what you are interested in doing and show interest in those things themselves?" and "Do you feel free to talk to your friends about personal problems when you want to?" The distal variables of the perceived environment are relatively more remote from specific behaviors and relate these behaviors by mediating variables in the proximal structure. The theoretical linkage between the distal and the proximal structures has been developed by Jessor and his associates (Jessor *et al.*, 1968; Jessor & Jessor, 1977) and assists in the transformation of distal to proximal influences on specific behavior. The emphasis on the perceived environment, however, does not imply a rejection of the "objective" environment. Rather, its effects are mediated by the perceived environment. The relative location of the adolescent in the parental and peer substructures of the distal environment defines the proneness to problem behavior but is a less powerful prediction of specific behaviors. The conceptualization of a proximal structure provides a logical extension of the distal structure with a theoretical elaboration of the mediating variables relating to specific problem behavior.

The theoretical concern of the proximal environment is the degree to which the adolescent is located in a social context where problem behavior is prevalent and there is social support for its occurrence. Variables in the proximal structure include measures of parental and peer approval–disapproval of specific behavior and the presence–absence of friends as models for these behaviors. They include such items as "About how many kids your age do you know who drink fairly regularly?" and "Do you have any close friends who drink fairly regularly?"

To summarize a complex model very briefly, the likelihood of problem drinking in adolescence relates to the relative balance between perceived social controls against problem drinking and the perceived models of support for problem drinking. Social controls are more prominent in the distal environment, while models and support are more prominent in the proximal structure. While variables in the proximal structure exert more influence on specific behavior than those in the distal environment, the influences of the latter are mediated by the proximal environment. It is the relative balance of variables in both of these structures, as they unfold developmentally, that relates to shifts and transitions from nonproblem behavior to problem behavior.

Data relating the perceived environment to drinking behavior were obtained from a four-year longitudinal study of adolescents (Jessor & Jessor, 1977). Questionnaires were administered annually to cohorts in the seventh, eighth, and ninth grades. At the end of the four years of study (fourth testing), the students were divided into five groups: those who remained abstinent throughout the study; those who were drinkers throughout the study; and three groups of students who made the transition from abstainer to drinker at three different points in time: the second, third, and fourth years of testing. The results indicate a developmental relationship between the perceived environment during each year of testing and the transition with respect to drinking status. The extent of personal friends as models for drinking, a strong predictor of both drinking status and problem drinking within the proximal structure, was systematically related to the time of onset of drinking. Group 1 (abstainers) reported the lowest prevalence of models, while Group 5 (drinkers) reported the highest prevalence of models of all the groups. The three transition groups yielded orderly and consistent increases in prevalence of friends who were models in relation to the onset of drinking. Furthermore, the same set of theoretically derived measures relate to both nonproblem- and problem-drinking adolescents. With respect to the array of variables in the perceived environment, heavy and problem drinkers were characterized as having low parental support and controls, low peer controls, low compatibility between parent and peer expectations, and low parental influences relative to peers in the distal structure and, in the proximal structure, low parental disapproval of problem behavior and high friends as models and friends' approval for engaging in problem behavior. Abstaining adolescents and nonproblem drinkers were characterized by the same theoretical dimensions, with a patterning of scores favoring high parental support and controls and low friends as models and approval for engaging in problem drinking.

While the focus of the present review is on environment and behavior, it should be noted that personality structures occupy as prominent a role as does the perceived environment. Furthermore, excessive drinking is only one of a matrix of behaviors studied, and these behaviors are viewed as a product of the interaction of personality variables and variables in the perceived environment.

While generalization of these findings is curtailed because the group studied was not a random selection from the adolescent population, recent analyses of the national survey of junior and senior high school students (Rachal, Williams, Brehm, Cavanaugh, Moore, & Eckerman, 1975) have provided corroboration of many of the theoretical dimensions of the model (Donovan & Jessor, 1978; Jessor, 1978).

It has been noted earlier in this chapter that one of the difficulties in studying the perceived, or psychological, environment is that no provision is made theoretically to examine how features of the objective environment are transformed into psychological reality. A second problem encountered in using the respondent as informer is the relationship between the perceived and the objective environment. It was noted in the previous section that the prevalence of perceived friends as models for drinking was closely associated with drinking behavior. Is there an isomorphism between perceived and real prevalence? It is possible that the increase in perceived prevalence is a function of a new perceptual framework within which to perceive the objective environment, a framework that has as its source one's own behavior. There is much evidence in the literature on social perception to substantiate this argument. Does the adolescent who makes the transition from abstainer to drinker have a new perceptual framework for viewing the world? Does he now perceive a reality of drinking that already is historical fact? This argument is somewhat attenuated, but not completely demolished, in the work of Jessor and Jessor (1977), since the strongest predictor in the proximal environment was that of friends as drinking models. It is unlikely, though not impossible, that adolescents would be unfamiliar with the drinking behavior of their friends.

A third problem encountered in the perceived environment is the issue of disentangling the potential sources of influence on behavior. Assuming an isomorphism between the objective and the psychological environment, does the adolescent initiate drinking for personal reasons, rather than for situational press, and then seek out social support for behavior already initiated by befriending others who drink? Or does an increase in the actual prevalence of friends and peers as drinking models intrude on the psychological structure of the perceived environment of the adolescent and exert an influence on his own behavior?

While the reality of empirical research in social perception would make an affirmative nod at both of these sources of influence, the issue raised is that a focus on just the perceived environment fails to provide an opportunity for establishing the conditions under which the objective environment shapes psychological reality and behavior, the conditions under which the organism adapts to an objective reality, and the conditions under which the perceived environment effectively attenuates or distorts an environment different from or incompatible with behavior.

4. Behavior Settings

Barker (1968) has proposed the term *behavior setting* as an ecological unit that has both an environmental and a behavioral component. Behavior settings are standing patterns of behavior that occur over and over again in a given place at a given time (e.g., a football game, a grocery store, a doctor's office). Behavior settings are natural phenomena that have a spatiotemporal locus that is self-generating. The behavior setting exists regardless of whether or not people are there and, if they are there, regardless of the type of people present. The method is observational and allows for independent measurement of the environment and behavior. Once behavior settings are identified, behavioral data and descriptive aspects of the setting are obtained. The criteria for defining behavior settings and the scales for quantifying behavior are complex and difficult to learn. Few investigators, other than Barker and his colleagues, have applied this methodology, though the conceptualization of behavior settings as an ecological unit has been influential in environmental research (Bechtel, 1977).

This conceptualization is of obvious applicability to a variety of settings in which alcohol is consumed (e.g., a party, a wedding, mealtimes). The "cocktail party" is often cited as an occasion of heavy and unhealthy drinking and is illustrative of the interdependence of ecological factors (crowding, absence of food, noise level) and behavior (milling around, gulping drinks, smoking) (Lolli, 1963; Chafetz, 1970).

Cavan's (1966) study of San Francisco bars provides further examples of the relationship between ecology and behavior. She noted that lateral seating arrangements at the bar relate to fluidity of movement of patrons. Boundaries are less clear and easier to cross, with the result that patron contact is encouraged by these spatial arrangements. The absence of bar stools provides more structural support and encouragement for behavior mobility.

In contrast, seating arrangements at tables demarcate groups and foster face-to-face interactions and general insulation from bar activities. Settings that provide entertainment may vary the physical milieu for the purpose of controlling the audience. Cavan noted that in the night-spot bar, where highly programmed entertainment schedules start and stop, the arrangement of tables and chairs serves to demarcate small groups and couples and to inhibit table-hopping and standing or milling around. These structural features thereby diminish movement and contact among the unacquainted.

Kruse (1975) has observed Finnish youth, aged 16 years and over, in discos and restaurants in Helsinki. The physical milieu of these behavior settings provided a structure for the initiation of heterosexual contact between youth. Spatial arrangements of tables, dance space, and music were conducive to milling around and table-hopping. Kruse noted that seating patterns were critical for making contacts. The table provided structural support for the assimilation of a person into a group and was supportive in the development of group cohesion. Dancing provided further opportunity to screen contacts.

Kruse further noted that patterns of contact were sharply reduced in a nondancing milieu. Contact in restaurants was usually restricted to a single boy approaching all-female groups at tables and contrasted with the wider range of contact styles in discos.

Drinking behavior was interrelated with behavior and structure in a number of ways. Kruse observed that heterosexual contact was rarely initiated without the help of alcohol, with limits on the amount that was useful. Too much drinking by boys led to nonacceptance by girls. Contact had several effects on subsequent drinking as well. Once contact was made, maintaining the contact was more important than drinking. The failure to make contact, however, generally yielded two outcomes: boys would either have a few drinks and leave, or they would remain and drink a great deal. Group status also influenced the amount of consumption. The groups of boys who stayed for long periods of time consumed the most alcohol. Increased consumption was also observed among mixed groups, which became more cohesive over time. Group pressure to drink usually took the form of reciprocating purchases of drinks (standing rounds).

The relationship between group status and drinking has been the subject of a number of observational studies of public drinking. Sommer (1965) observed the drinking patterns of men in beer parlors in Edmonton, Canada. He observed that men drinking in groups consumed more beer than those who were drinking alone. When both types of drinkers were matched according to the amount of time spent in the beer parlor, group drinkers and isolates did not differ in overall amount of consumption. Group drinkers drank more than isolates, not because they drank faster, but because they remained for longer periods of time in the beer parlor. In an observational study of beer parlors in Vancouver, Cutler and Storm (1975) also reported that group status had less effect on tempo of drinking than on duration of stay. Harford, Feinhandler, and Dorman (1975) observed male patrons in different public drinking settings in Boston. They noted that while the duration of stay was longer for groups than for solitary drinkers, the effects of group status on drinking style varied by type of setting. In one bar, a middle-class pub, the amount of consumption was greater in groups, while drinking rates, estimated from the amount of time spent on the first drink, did not differ. In another bar, a quasi-neighborhood bar with a more varied clientele, the amount of consumption did not differ between group and solitary drinkers, but solitary drinkers consumed their first drink at a faster rate. The failure to introduce controls on such relevant variables as ecological location, patron characteristics, physical milieu, and behavior functions precludes a clear interpretation of observational findings in public drinking settings. The studies reviewed, however, do provide a logical basis for relating ecology to drinking in specific behavior settings, but one that needs more conceptual refinement and systematic and controlled study.

5. Ecological Indicators

Blane and Hewitt (1977) have provided a comprehensive analysis of the literature on alcohol and youth for the years 1960–1975. They noted that many of the questionnaires administered to school youth contain information on drinking location and presence of others. Barker's (1968) concept of behavior setting, as well as Heider's (1958) distinction between social and physical objects within these settings, provides a theoretical framework for examining the role of ecological variables in adolescent drinking. Behavior settings are ecological units, according to Barker, and variables of physical location and types of persons present may be viewed as indicators of the environmental component in this unit. Several aspects of this framework must be qualified. First, drinking settings are not solely ecological in nature and have as antecedents other environmental factors as well (e.g., control policies). Second, this conceptualization does not permit the identification of the determinants, both environmental and psychological, that influence differential accessibility of behavior settings among subpopulation groups (control policies legally proscribe access to public drinking establishments for minors). And third, most of the information on the circumstances, or contexts, of adolescent drinking are based on self-reports (the perceived environment) and relate to "average" or "typical" drinking occasions. Despite these limitations, a review of these variables allows a specification of the contexts in which youth drink, one that is useful in suggesting potential ecological contributions.

5.1. Adolescents

Information on the physical location or setting in which alcohol is consumed among adolescents provides a general framework in the approach to the role of ecological variables.

Harrison, Bennett, and Globetti (1970) surveyed factors related to alcohol use among a sample of 162 preadolescents (sixth grade) in Mississippi. The majority of these students reported that their current use of alcohol was confined to drinking at home in the presence of parents or adult relatives. Smaller proportions of these students reported other drinking settings, such as cars, parties, and the homes of friends. The distribution of drinking locations, however, does not necessarily imply information on the amounts of alcohol consumed and/or the occurrence of related activities. If the presence of parents or relatives may be presumed to have a controlling influence on the behavior of children in these settings, and there is some reason to justify this assumption, then it may be concluded from this study that (a) a majority of preadolescent users drink alcohol under relatively safe and controlled conditions and (b) only a small proportion drink in settings away from home with no adult supervision. The findings, however, must be qualified by such methodological limitations as geographic region (Mississippi) and nonrandom selection of respondents. The interpretation that the mere presence of adults has an inhibiting influence on drinking behavior also needs qualification. Swanson, Bratrude, and Brown (1971) observed a small group of American Indian drinkers over a 10-year period. These children drank regularly and became intoxicated at least four times a year. The authors reported that adult encouragement was a major factor contributing to the drinking behavior of these children.

Studies of adolescent samples also indicate that the majority of students drink at home. The proportion who report drinking outside of the home, however, is greater than that reported by preadolescents. Chappel and Goldberg (1953) indicated that while 66% of a sample of 1,000 students used alcohol at family occasions, 42% drank at friends' parties, 25% on dates, and 18% at postgame celebrations. Similarly, Mandell, Cooper, Silberstein, Novick, and Koloski (1963) in their survey of New York high school students, reported home to be the major context for the consumption of alcohol. Approximately 22% of the boys drank at a friend's home (21% of the girls), 17% at a bar (12% for girls), 16% at a "secluded spot" (4% for girls), and 8% in cars (3% for girls). These studies do not clarify the relationship between location and drinking behavior or location and other ecological variables. Some studies, however, have indicated that heavier or more frequent drinkers are more likely to report peer settings rather than family settings for alcohol use (Maddox & McCall, 1964; Rachal *et al.*, 1975).

A second ecological indicator of importance to drinking is the type of drinking companion and the number of persons present. As noted earlier in the review of location, the type of person present is not altogether independent of physical setting. Adolescents who drink at home are often in the company of parents, while settings away from home usually include peers.

Drawing upon a survey of teenage drinking in two Mississippi communities, Globetti (1964) reported that peers were the most frequent drinking companions among both frequent and occasional drinkers. Perhaps of greater interest is the study of 639 students by Globetti (1972), in which companion status was linked to problem drinking. Students who drank with friends, or alone, were more likely to be problem users, while those who drank with parents or relatives were more likely to be nonproblem users. Both of these studies are important in that they link companion status with drinking patterns. The findings, however, may not be generalizable to other geographic regions.

The only study that provides information on the number of drinking companions is by Kline (1972). Based on a survey of 567 junior high school students in California, he reported that adolescents more typically drink in the company of several other persons (62%) rather than alone (11%) or with one other person (27%).

The review by Blane and Hewitt (1977) indicates that adolescents are more likely to drink in the company of peers than with parents. While this finding may appear discrepant with previous discussions of the home as the major setting for drinking, the discrepancy is due, in part, to the types of questions asked of the respondents and to variation in survey methodology. Both of these variables are age-related, and discrepancies are partly due to the age of the samples selected. Both of these variables, location and companion status, may be viewed as ecological indicators in the drinking contexts of adolescents. Their utility is somewhat limited as isolated variables. There is need to study how, and if, unsupervised or peer-only settings relate to amount of consumption as well as to tangible consequences. Studies need to isolate specific ecological factors in the physical setting and the nature of the dynamics of companions.

Several of the surveys of adolescent drinking included questions on the perception of peer pressure. To what extent is adolescent drinking a function of perceived pressure from drinking companions to engage in drinking? Mandell *et al.* (1963) reported that peer pressure was an infrequently stated reason for drinking. Maddox and McCall (1964) found much less endorsement for drinking for the sake of conformity.

While peer pressure does not emerge from survey reports as a major factor in drinking, several studies have examined peer influence. Polk (1964) and Polk and Burkett (1972) indicated that peer involvement is a significant variable in the drinking behavior of adolescent boys. As time spent with friends increased, drinking also increased. The work of Jessor and Jessor (1977), previously reviewed, also indicated that adolescent drinking became more frequent and heavier as the extent of perceived drinking among peers increased. It has already been noted that the dynamics of this relationship remain unclear. Also needed are studies that independently assess the contribution of parents and peers to adolescent drinking.

As Blane and Hewitt (1977) have noted, the ecological findings reported in these surveys are largely of a descriptive nature and fail to provide any conceptual or theoretical framework. One consequence of the absence of a theoretical position is that the relevant variables are rarely controlled. Generalizability of the findings are further limited since most of the studies fail to draw random samples from the population.

5.2. A Developmental Perspective

Information on the circumstances of drinking among adolescents was included in the national survey of junior and senior high school students conducted by the Research Triangle Institute (Rachal *et al.*, 1975). Approximately 13,000 students in a stratified two-stage random sample of high schools in the United States were given a self-administered questionnaire in small school classrooms. The questionnaire included eight items dealing with the frequency of drinking in specific settings, for example, "at teenage parties where others are drinking and your parents or other adults are not present" and "at dinner at home with the family." Harford (1976) grouped these items into the following mutually exclusive categories: at home (parents present) *and* in peer settings (parents not present); at home exclusively; in peer settings exclusively. Peer settings included teenage parties, local hangouts, and school settings.

The majority of the adolescents in the survey reported that they drank both at home and in peer settings. For these students, more drinking took place outside of the home with less adult supervision. The proportion of students in this category increased with increasing age. The data further indicated that the trend toward increased drinking away from home was accompanied by increases in the reported frequency of drinking and increases in the amount of alcohol typically consumed per occasion.

Smaller proportions of students reported drinking exclusively at home, and these proportions tended to decrease with increasing age. In addition, there were no age-related trends in the frequency and the quantity of consumption among these students. That is, despite the decreased prevalence of exclusive home drinking with increasing age, older students who continued to drink exclusively in this setting did not exhibit increases in drinking frequency or amount consumed per typical occasion. Overall, the frequency and the quantity of drinking in this group were substantially lower than for the majority of students who drank in both types of setting.

Additional comparisons within the larger category of students permitted more specific contextual observations. Among students who drank both at home and with peers, a noticeable shift in the proportion of heavy drinkers occurred between the ages of 12–13 years (36%) and 14–15 years (57%). This shift coincided with an increase in the proportion who drank frequently in peer settings for these age groups (from 31% to 53%) and a decrease in the proportion who drank frequently in home settings for these age groups (from 34% to 23%). The data suggest an association between the amount of alcohol consumed and the drinking setting, although the effects of the physical location and the types of companion are confounded.

A small proportion of the students in the study (13%) reported that they drank exclusively in peer settings. A comparison of these students with the majority, who drank both at home and in peer settings, indicated that they drank on a less frequent basis but that the amounts consumed per typical occasion were similar to those for the majority of students. Further comparisons of these two groups yielded interesting differences (Harford & Mills, 1976). Students who drank exclusively in peer-only settings tended to be drawn from rural southern regions of the United States. Their perceived religious and parental sanctions against drinking were more prevalent. Larger proportions of their parents were abstainers, and they reported starting to drink alcohol at a later age than their peer counterparts. These variables serve to introduce differences in the access to alcohol among the two groups. Parental prohibitions against drinking limit access to alcohol and foster a dependence on others to obtain it. Support for this interpretation is provided by the survey conducted in Mississippi by Globetti (1964). He noted that the major source of alcohol among the high school students studied was bootleggers or merchants.

These national data are consistent with the review of the adolescent literature of Blane and Hewitt (1977) summarized earlier. Despite the cross-sectional design of the national study, the representativeness of the large sample at several consecutive grade levels and the age-related trends in setting impute a developmental course to adolescent drinking. With the exception of a small proportion of youth, adolescent drinking begins in the home, and during the course of development, it is characterized by more frequent exposure to away-from-home contexts and to contexts in which the peer group occupies a more important role. This transition, it was noted, is accompanied by increased levels of alcohol consumption. These data, then, expose a continuity of drinking among adolescents, one that takes us into the drinking patterns of young adulthood, the age group initially presented as case histories, to which we now turn for a more systematic examination.

5.3. Young Adults

Information for the case histories presented earlier was obtained from a survey in metropolitan Boston conducted by the Research Triangle Institute in the summer of 1974 (Gerstel *et al.*, 1975). Respondents were 18 years of age and over and were current drinkers (at least once a month or more). The data were collected on a drinking-event basis for a consecutive four-week period. A retrospective listing procedure, referred to as the chronological drinking record (CDR), was administered, by interview, for the entire week preceding the interview. Information for each reported drinking event during the week included amount and type of alcohol consumed, physical location, type and number of persons present, day of week, and duration of drinking event. In the three-week follow-up period, drinking information was obtained by the CDR for one-half of the sample. The other respondents provided identical information in a daily drinking record (DDR), which was completed daily by the respondent without interviewer assistance. Several analyses of this data have indicated that the two procedures yielded essentially comparable data (Gerstel *et al.*, 1975; Gerstel, Harford, & Pautler, 1977a,b; Harford & Gerstel, 1978).

Contextual drinking typologies were obtained by a cross-tabulation of five dichotomized contextual dimensions yielding 32 possible cells. The contextual dimensions were as follows: weekday–weekend; one-hour duration–more than one-hour duration; private setting–public setting; relative–friends present; two or fewer persons present–more than two persons present. Table 1 presents the distribution of the total drinking events for the four weeks of study, in percentages, by age group. The contrast between young adults, 18–25 years, and elderly adults, aged 63 and over, is illuminating. It is difficult to typologize young adults, since they drink in a variety of contextual settings. This was evident in the case histories presented earlier and is also revealed in a way representative of the larger sample. Elderly adults, by contrast, are easy to typologize. They drink in relatively few contexts (60% of their events are of short duration, in private settings, with family members, and with two or fewer persons present); 35% of these events occur on weekdays and 24% on weekends.

Table 1. Distribution of Contextual Typology of Drinking Events by Age, in Percentages

Day	Weekdays																Weekends																
Duration	1 Hour or less								More than 1 hour								1 Hour or less								More than 1 hour								
Location	Private				Public				Private				Public				Private				Public				Private				Public				Total Number of Events
Type[a] and	Rel		Frnd		Rel		Frnd		Rel		Frnd		Rel		Frnd		Rel		Frnd		Rel		Frnd		Rel		Frnd		Rel		Frnd		
Number of companions[b]	2	3	2	3	2	3	2	3	2	3	2	3	2	3	2	3	2	3	2	3	2	3	2	3	2	3	2	3	2	3	2	3	
Age Group																																	
18–25	6	2	4	3	1	—	4	3	2	1	3	4	1	—	5	4	5	2	4	4	1	1	4	4	2	2	3	9	1	1	5	9	2,107
26–35	10	3	3	2	2	1	3	3	3	1	3	4	1	—	3	4	7	5	2	5	3	1	2	3	4	2	2	7	2	1	3	5	2,172
36–48	13	7	1	2	2	—	3	3	6	2	1	2	1	—	1	3	10	6	1	3	2	—	2	3	6	3	1	5	2	1	3	5	2,513
49–62	23	3	1	2	5	—	2	2	6	1	—	2	1	—	—	1	18	5	2	3	4	—	1	2	4	2	1	3	1	1	1	2	1,414
63 & over	35	4	3	2	2	—	1	2	4	—	—	2	—	—	—	—	24	5	2	2	1	—	1	1	3	1	1	3	1	—	—	2	1,013

[a] Relatives, friends.
[b] Two or less, three or more persons present.

Young adults, on the other hand, display a wide range of contextual settings, the more prominent of which include the following:

1. Weekends, longer durations, in public settings, with three or more friends (9%)
2. Weekends, longer durations, in private settings, with three or more friends (9%)
3. Weekdays, shorter durations, in private settings, with two or less relatives (6%)
4. Weekends, shorter durations, in private settings, with two or less relatives (5%)
5. Weekends, longer durations, in public settings, with two or less friends (5%)
6. Weekdays, longer durations, in public settings, with two or less friends (5%)

Conspicuous among these patterns are drinking contexts in public settings with friends (20%). Two age trends with respect to contextual typologies are also apparent in Table 1. First, drinking in contexts of short duration, in private settings, with two or fewer relatives, on both weekdays and weekends increases with age. And second, the frequency of drinking in settings of long duration with three or more friends decreases with age.

These data expose the continuity of drinking between adolescence and young adulthood, a period in which alcohol consumption appears to peak. The trends toward increased frequency of away-from-home drinking and increased involvement with peers among adolescents culminate in a diversity of drinking contexts among young adults in which friends and public settings occupy significant roles. The Boston data, despite the limitation of the cross-sectional design, are suggestive of continuing trends in contextual drinking style with increasing age. The trends, however, reverse those of adolescents, with movement away from public settings and friends as drinking companions. They culminate, among the elderly, in private setting with one or two relatives as drinking companions. On a broad developmental level, the review of both adolescent and adult drinking patterns suggests a curvilinear relationship with age of physical setting (private to public to private) and types of companions (family to peers to family).

5.4. Ecology and Drinking

The review of ecological indicators among youth and adults suggests age-related trends with respect to these indicators and a general association between these indicators and alcohol consumption. While several observational studies have examined drinking behavior in specific settings, a number of surveys have attempted to make a specific link between the drinking setting and the amount of consumption using representative population samples.

Davies and Stacey (1972) examined alcohol use in a sample of 1,321 schoolchildren, 14–17 years of age, in Scotland. Included in the questionnaire were several items pertaining to recent drinking behavior in each of three types of settings: the home of a parent or an adult relative; the home of a friend; somewhere other than a home (a dance, in a hotel or pub, in the open air). Most of the teenagers drank at home (92%) and consumed relatively small amounts of alcohol. Fewer (71%) drank in the home of a friend and consumed more alcohol than when in the home setting. Fewer still (66%) drank outside the home and consumed more than in the home setting.

For younger boys, age 14, most drinking took place in the home, while for older boys, age 17, most drinking occurred away from home, although their home drinking was more frequent than was the case for younger boys. A similar, though less pronounced, pattern was present for girls.

For both sexes, the frequency of drinking in public houses increased with age, while "open-air" drinking in parks or streets decreased with age. The frequency of drinking at dances was highest for older girls, age 17.

In the home settings, parents were usually present (68%) and more likely to be serving drinks (45%) than not (23%). Teenage peers were present on these occasions (43%) but less likely to serve alcohol (17%). The amount of beer and whiskey consumed by boys increased with age. Age trends were less conspicuous for girls, though there was a slight increase in beer consumption with age and a slight decrease in the amount of cider and sherry with age.

In the home of a friend, parents were less likely to be present (15%), while other adults were more likely to be present (40%) and serving drinks (32%). The major contrast between this setting and the home was the presence of teenage peers, 47% of whom served drinks. Among boys, the quantity of beer and whiskey increased with age. For girls, there was some indication of heavier drinking of beer and spirits other than whiskey with age.

As noted earlier, there was a general tendency for boys and girls to consume more alcohol in this setting than in the home setting. These differences were somewhat attenuated for older boys and more striking for younger boys.

In settings other than the home, a pattern similar to the home of a friend was reported. Parents were least likely to be present (13%), whereas teenage peers predominated (67%). For boys, the amount of beer and whiskey increased with age, although whiskey consumption was highest for young boys, age 14. This finding coincided with higher frequencies of "open-air" drinking among this age group. For girls, there was a noticeable increase in the amount of spirits other than whiskey with age.

These data provide further support for the hypothesis that social controls for teenage drinking are more likely to be exercised in the home of parents, a setting where access to alcohol is generally under the supervision of parents or other adult relatives. As was the case in the review of other questionnaire surveys, the physical setting is confounded with types of persons present. It would be useful to know, for example, if the amount of consumption in the home of a friend varied with the presence and absence of parents and other adults. Also of interest is the influence of the physical setting on drinking when the composition of the teenage peer group is varied. The study of youth in peer contexts assumes further importance in view of the several studies of adolescents described as having problems with alcohol and with society in general. These studies indicate that patterns of early use of alcohol occur with peers without parental supervision and in such typical locations as alleys, playgrounds, cars, friends' homes and that these adolescents maintain current drinking patterns away from home and with peers. (Blacker, Demone, & Freeman, 1965; MacKay, Phillips, & Bryce, 1967; Pearce & Garrett, 1970; Widseth & Mayer, 1971).

Problems with the interdependence of location and types of persons are also encountered in adult studies. Average consumption was higher in public versus private settings among a sample of adults who reported drinking in both of these settings (Harford, 1975). Public drinking, however, was more likely to include friends as drinking companions. The presence of friends usually related to heavier amounts of alcohol consumption. The national survey of American drinking practices (Cahalan, Cisin, & Crossley, 1969), for example, indicated that Americans report drinking more than usual amounts with close friends and less than usual amounts with relatives and neighbors.

The observational studies of public drinking settings suggest that both the physical setting and the type of drinking companions are contributory factors. A more careful study is needed of the conditions relating to heavier consumption among adults, with friends as drinking companions. Presumably, among these adult interactions, the issue of social control does not assume the same level of intensity as it does among youth. There is a need, then, to extend these studies to teenage settings where parental and other adult social controls are absent. What factors initiate and sustain heavier drinking when adults are interacting with friends, and are these factors comparable to adolescent peer-group interactions?

Recently, Harford (1978) reported on the relationships among physical setting, the number and type of persons present, and the amount of alcohol consumed. These data served to clarify the interactions between physical setting and type of persons present in the drinking situation. Data on the most recent drinking event reported by the adults in the survey of metropolitan Boston (Gerstel *et al.*, 1975) were used. The findings indicated significant interactions between location and type of person present for both men and women. The amount of alcohol consumed in home settings was significantly higher with friends than with relatives. For men, the amount of alcohol consumed in bars was higher than in other settings, irrespective of who was present. For women, the amount of consumption in bars was greater with friends than with relatives. These findings help to assess the relationship between these two variables. Apparently, drinking amounts in home settings are influenced by the types of persons present. A similar conclusion is suggested in the study of Davies and Stacey (1972). For men, however, the physical setting of the bar was associated with heavier drinking, regardless of the types of people present.

The major problem with this analytic design is its failure to disentangle the influences of persons and settings. Rather, the results reveal an association between the amount of consumption by one group of drinkers in one setting and the amount of consumption by another group of drinkers in a different setting. Whether the present findings can be attributed to individual differences (e.g., heavy drinkers) or ecological factors in the drinking setting is an issue for further study.

The attempt to relate ecological variables to drinking behavior is not without difficulty when the data are based upon self-report, although some studies have attempted to adjust for this by comparing self-reports of drinking in different settings for the same drinker. Observational studies, it has been noted, also confound characteristics of the person and the setting.

This methodological shortcoming is partly resolved in experiments in which the random assignment of subjects to different conditions serves to reduce individual differences. The random assignment of individuals to experimental conditions that systematically vary, for example, the number of persons present and the type of setting allow for greater control of ecological factors, factors that vary independently of the subjects.

Although several experimental studies have examined the proximal antecedents of drinking, none have specifically focused on the influence of the setting and the types of drinking companions. It should be noted that human experiments do not control antecedent individual differences. This problem places some constraints on the extent to which relationship status can be manipulated. It is difficult to experimentally manipulate friendship and other dyadic relationships (e.g., spouse, other relatives). The solution, of course, is to conceptualize the processes underlying the relationship as they bear on drinking and to test functional hypotheses rather than purely structural variables (Higgins, 1976).

The results of several experiments are suggestive of the processes that mediate ecological factors and the amount of drinking in specific behavior settings. Caudill and Marlatt (1975) studied the effects of modeling on drinking. A sample of 48 male undergraduates who did heavy social drinking were randomly assigned to one of six cells in a 3 × 2 factorial design in which the subjects were paired with a confederate in a wine "taste-rating" task. The subjects were exposed to one of three conditions: a high-consumption model, a low-consumption model, and a no-model control. Subjects were also randomly assigned to one of two conditions designed to produce either a warm or a cold interaction with the confederate prior to the wine taste-rating task. The findings indicated that students exposed to a heavy-drinking model consumed significantly more wine than students exposed to either a light-drinking model or a no-model control. The interactions with warm or cold confederates did not influence drinking behavior.

Garlington and Dericco (1977) also studied the effects of modeling when three male college seniors were paired with a drinking confederate over time in several drinking sessions. The modeled drinking rates were shown to influence the subjects' rates of beer consumption. Despite the small sample size, the design allowed the full effect of the modeling process to appear, that is, increases and decreases in drinking rates.

Miller, Hersen, Eisler, Epstein, and Wooten (1974) examined the relationship of alcohol cues to drinking behavior. The subjects, 20 chronic alcoholic and 20 nonalcoholic male patients, received alcoholic beverages by manipulating an operant under cue and no-cue conditions. Pictures of alcoholic beverages were placed on the operant panel during cue conditions. An analysis of the mean number of operant responses yielded a significant interaction between alcohol cues and alcoholism. The nonalcoholic social drinkers responded significantly more than alcoholics under cue conditions.

Billings, Gomberg, Nash, Kessler, and Weiner (1978) examined the social cueing of drinking in samples of nine drinking married couples and nine alcoholics and their wives. Research groups consisted of three married couples who met as a group for two one-hour sessions in which alcohol was available. The groups were homogeneous in drinking status:

either social drinking couples or alcoholics and their wives. The number of "synchronous sips" of alcohol was used as the measure of social cueing. A sip was said to be synchronous when the subjects were in direct visual contact and both sips occurred within a 10-second interval. The findings indicated that social drinkers synchronized their drinking to a greater extent than did alcoholics.

These studies indicate that the drinking behavior of nonalcoholic social drinkers is influenced by both physical (Miller *et al.*, 1974) and interpersonal (Billings *et al.*, 1978) cues. The studies by Caudill and Marlatt (1975) and Garlington and Dericco (1977) draw particular attention to the pervasive influences of social encounters and the need to develop theoretical models that include both the objective and the perceived environment. Had these subjects been queried as to their drinking, it is unlikely that they would have reported this source of influence. Much more work is needed, however, before these findings can be utilized to account for the relationship between the number and type of drinking companions and the amount of alcohol consumption. Under what conditions and with whom is a drinker likely to match amount and rate of consumption with others? What factors relate to the selection of a model?

6. Ecology in Perspective

A comprehensive view of ecology and alcohol must include the objective and the psychological environment, the social and physical objects in the objective environment, and the way in which properties of the objective environment are transformed into the psychological environment. Aspects of the objective environment such as climate, geography, and the sociobehavioral characteristics of populations have been shown to relate to the physical availability of beverage alcohol and to drinking patterns. Interpretation of the impact of ecology on alcohol, when viewed in the domain of the objective environment, are curtailed by several issues. First, empirical studies have yet to demonstrate the impact of the ecological environment on drinking when other environmental factors, such as legal control policies, are taken into account. Second, interpretations of the relationships between ecological variables and alcohol require intervening variables that have yet to be integrated into a more comprehensive theoretical framework. And third, there is no general consensus on the strategies for conceptualizing the environment and for translating properties of the objective environment into psychological experience and action. These issues draw attention to the fact that human behavior occurs in a context of multiple levels of reality and meaning. As Jessor and Jessor (1973) have observed, "Recognition of such inherent multiplicity serves to remind us that the idea of an ultimate, univocal environment is a myth of concrete thinking" (p. 804).

A conceptual alternative to the studies of the objective environment may be found in the subjective approaches that address the phenomenology of the person. Research efforts in this area have been reviewed and yield several strong relationships between the perceived environment and drinking behavior. The extent of perceived friends as drinking models, for example, has been shown to be a strong predictor of both drinking status and problem drinking. But subjective approaches to the conceptualization of the environment, like objective strategies, are also constrained by several factors. Among other problems, it has been noted that the ecological environment comprises a different class of phenomena than the perceived environment and cannot be described solely from the perspective of the individual. The inherent difficulties and conceptual issues involved in relying upon respondents as observers or ethnographers of their environments have also been noted. Jessor and Jessor (1973) observed that techniques that cultivate ethnographic roles in respondents are differentially sensitive, depending upon which aspects of the environment are reported on. Salient aspects, such as drinking locations, may be less vulnerable than more subtle aspects, such as perceived pressure to drink. A more complete discussion of the issues involved in introspective and cognitive processes may be found in Nisbett and Wilson (1977).

It has been noted that a general theory of the environment must specify how properties of the objective environment are transformed into psychological reality and action. The elaboration of the perceived environment into distal and proximal structures by Jessor and Jessor (1977) is an initial approach to the process by which the distal components of the objective environment are transformed into the phenomenological world of the drinker.

Barker's (1968) concept of the behavior setting provides a logical unit for studying the relationship between ecology and behavior and is a promising approach through which to elucidate the conditions under which distal variables enter the perceived environment. This framework provides an opportunity for the introduction of multiple strategies for assessing the environment and ones that encompass both objective (observational techniques) and subjective (perceived environment) methodologies. Barker's (1968) approach emphasizes the development of observational techniques. The review of observational bar studies yielded several preliminary relationships that suggest the influence of ecological factors on drinking behavior. These efforts, however, in failing to control such relevant variables as ecological location, patron characteristics, and physical milieu, do not allow for clear interpretations of drinking behavior. Reliance on a strategy of observational techniques also fails to yield data that specify the mediating links between variables such as group status and drinking behavior (Kruse, 1975; Sommer, 1965). A comprehensive model must incorporate both independent measures of the setting and measures of the actors' perceptions in these settings. One of the major conceptual underpinnings in this approach is how the objective environment can be measured independently of the actor and yet be related to the actor's behavior.

The concept of the behavior setting needs to be extended to settings other than public drinking establishments in order to expose the dynamics of alcohol and human behavior. Of even greater importance is the pressing question of what aspects of the environment are relevant to drinking behavior. Barker's (1968) concept of behavior settings and Heider's (1958) distinction between social and physical objects within these settings provide a useful framework for examining the role of ecological variables and alcohol. Studies were reviewed here with respect to drinking location and drinking companions and indicated that these variables are aligned along an age continuum suggestive of a developmental paradigm of alcohol use. The review of both adolescent and adult drinking patterns also indicated a relationship between these ecological indicators, on the one hand, and drinking behavior, on the other. These variables, however, comprise only part of what appears to be a very elusive context of human behavior.

References

Barker, R. G. *Ecological psychology: Concepts and methods for studying the environment of human behavior*. Stanford, Calif.: Stanford University Press, 1968.

Bechtel, R. B. *Enclosing behavior*. Stroudsburg, Pa.: Dowden, Hutchinson & Ross, 1977.

Billings, A. G., Gomberg, C. A., Nash, B. H., Kessler, M., & Weiner, S. Synchronized sipping in alcoholics and social drinkers: A preliminary investigation. *Journal of Studies on Alcohol*, 1978, *39*, 554–559.

Blacker, E., Demone, H. W., Jr., & Freeman, H. E. Drinking behavior of delinquent boys. *Quarterly Journal of Studies on Alcohol*, 1965, *26*, 223–237.

Blane, H. T., & Hewitt, L. E. Alcohol and youth: Analysis of the literature 1960–75. Final report submitted to the National Institute on Alcohol Abuse and Alcoholism, Contract ADM-281-75-0026, 1977.

Cahalan, D., Cisin, I. H., & Crossley, H. M. *American drinking practices* (Monogr. No. 6). New Brunswick, N.J.: Rutgers Center of Alcohol Studies, 1969.

Cahalan, D., & Room, R. *Problem drinking among American men* (Monogr. No. 7). New Brunswick, N.J.: Rutgers Center of Alcohol Studies, 1974.

Caudill, B. D., & Marlatt, G. A. Modelling influences in social drinking: An experimental analogue. *Journal of Consulting and Clinical Psychology*, 1975, *43*, 405–415.

Cavan, S. *Liquor license: An ethnography of bar behavior*. Chicago: Aldine, 1966.

Chafetz, M. E. Clinical syndromes of liquor drinkers. In R. Popham (Ed.), *Alcohol and alcoholism*. Toronto: University of Toronto Press, 1970.

Chappel, M. N., & Goldberg, H. D. *Use of alcoholic beverages among high school students*. New York: Mrs. John S. Sheppard Foundation, 1953.

Cutler, R. E., & Storm, T. Observational study of alcohol consumption in natural settings: The Vancouver beer parlor. *Journal of Studies on Alcohol*, 1975, *36*, 1173–1183.

Davies, J., & Stacey, B. *Teenagers and alcohol* (Vol. 2). London: Her Majesty's Stationery Office, 1972.

Donovan, J. E., & Jessor, R. Adolescent problem drinking: Psychosocial correlates in a national sample study. *Journal of Studies on Alcohol*, 1978, *39*, 1506–1524.

Fishbein, M. Attitude and the prediciton of behavior. In M. Fishbein (Ed.), *Readings in attitude theory and measurement*. New York: Wiley, 1967.

Fishbein, M. Consumer beliefs and behavior with respect to cigarette smoking: A critical analysis of the public literature. A report prepared for the Staff of the Federal Trade Commission, May 1977.

Fishbein, M., & Ajzen, I. *Belief, attitude, intention and behavior: An introduction to theory and research*. Reading, Mass.: Addison-Wesley, 1975.

Garlington, W. K., & Dericco, D. A. The effect of modelling on drinking rate. *Journal of Applied Behavior Analysis*, 1977, *10*, 207–211.

Gerstel, E. K., Mason, R. E., Piserchia, P., & Kristiansen, P. L. A pilot study of the social contexts of drinking and correlates. Final report submitted by the Research Triangle Institute to the National Institute on Alcohol Abuse and Alcoholism, Contract HSM 42-83-110(NIA), 1975.

Gerstel, E. K., Harford, T. C., & Pautler, C. Relative validity of two drinking level estimates. Unpublished paper, 1977. (a)

Gerstel, E. K., Harford, T. C., & Pautler, C. The reliability of drinking level estimates obtained with two data collection methods. Unpublished paper, 1977. (b)

Globetti, G. *A survey of teenage drinking in two Mississippi communities: Preliminary Report No. 3*. State College: Mississippi State University, Social Science Research Center, 1964.

Globetti, G. Problem and non-problem drinking among high-school students in abstinence communities. *International Journal of the Addictions*, 1972, *7*, 511–523.

Harford, T. C. Policy implications of a contextual analysis of drinking. Paper presented at the 21st International Institute on the Prevention and Treatment of Alcoholism, Helsinki, Finland, 1975.

Harford, T. C. Drinking contexts: A developmental approach. Paper prepared for the 22nd International Institute on the Prevention and Treatment of Alcoholism, Vigo, Spain, 1976.

Harford, T. C. Contextual analyses of drinking events. Paper presented at the World Congress of Sociology, Uppsala, Sweden, 1978.

Harford, T. C., Feinhandler, S. J., & Dorman, N. Drinking in bars: An observational study. Unpublished paper, 1975.

Harford, T. C., & Gerstel, E. K. The consistency of weekly drinking cycles. *Drinking and Drug Practices Surveyor* (Berkeley, Calif.), 1979, *14*, 7–8.

Harford, T. C., & Mills, G. S. Adolescent drinking contexts. Unpublished paper, 1976.

Harrison, D. E., Bennett, W. H., & Globetti, G. Factors related to alcohol use among pre-adolescents. *Journal of Alcohol Education*, 1970, *15*, 3–10.

Heider, F. *The psychology of interpersonal relations*. New York: Wiley, 1958.

Higgins, R. L. Experimental investigations of tension reduction models of alcoholism. In G. Goldstein & C. Neuringer (Eds.), *Empirical studies of alcoholism*. Cambridge, Mass.: Ballinger, 1976.

Insel, P. M., & Moos, R. H. Psychological environments: Expanding the scope of human ecology. *American Psychologist*, 1974, *29*, 179–188.
Irgens-Jensen, O. The use of alcohol in an isolated area of northern Norway. *British Journal of Addictions*, 1970, *65*, 181–185.
Jessor, R. Drinking behavior and the social environment of youth. Paper presented at the World Congress of Sociology, Uppsala, Sweden, 1978.
Jessor, R., Graves, T. D., Hanson, R. C., & Jessor, S. L. *Society, personality and deviant behavior*. New York: Holt, Rinehart & Winston, 1968.
Jessor, R., & Jessor, S. L. The perceived environment in the behavioral science. *American Behavioral Scientist*, 1973, *16*, 801–828.
Jessor, R., & Jessor, S. L. *Problem behavior and psychosocial development: A longitudinal study of youth*. New York: Academic Press, 1977.
Kissin, B., & Begleiter, H. (Eds.). *The biology of alcoholism, Vol. 4: Social aspects of alcoholism*. New York: Plenum Press, 1976.
Kline, J. A. Evaluation of a multimedia drug education program. *Journal of Drug Education*, 1972, *2*, 229–239.
Koffka, K. *Principles of gestalt psychology*. New York: Harcourt, Brace, 1935.
Kruse, L. Teenage drinking and sociability. *Urban Life*, 1975, *4*, 54–78.
Lewin, K. *Field theory in social science*. New York: Harper, 1951.
Lolli, G. The cocktail hour: Physiological, psychological and social aspects. In S. P. Lucia (Ed.), *Alcohol and civilization*. New York: McGraw-Hill, 1963.
MacKay, J. R., Phillips, D. L., & Bryce, F. O. Drinking behavior among teenagers: A comparison of institutionalized and non-institutionalized youth. *Journal of Health and Social Behavior*, 1967, *8*, 46–54.
Maddox, G. L., & McCall, B. C. *Drinking among teen-agers: A sociological interpretation of alcohol use by high-school students* (Monogr. No. 4). New Brunswick, N.J.: Rutgers Center of Alcohol Studies, 1964.
Mandell, W., Cooper, A., Silberstein, R. M., Novick, J., & Koloski, E. *Youthful drinking, New York State, 1962*. Staten Island, N.Y.: Staten Island Mental Health Society, Wakoff Research Center, 1963.
Miller, P. M., Hersen, M., Eisler, R. M., Epstein, L. H., & Wooten, L. S. Relationship of alcohol cues to the drinking behavior of alcoholics and social drinkers: An analogue study. *The Psychological Record*, 1974, *24*, 61–66.
Moos, R. H. Conceptualization of human environments. *American Psychologist*, 1973, *28*, 652–665.
Moos, R. H. *Issues in social ecology: Human milieus*. Palo Alto, Calif.: National Press Books, 1974.
Murray, H. *Explorations in personality*. New York: Oxford University Press, 1938.
Nisbett, R. E., & Wilson, T. D. Telling more than we can know: Verbal reports on mental processes. *Psychological Review*, 1977, *84*, 231–259.
Parker, D. A., & Harman, M. S. The distribution of consumption model of prevention of alcohol problems. *Journal of Studies on Alcohol*, 1978, *39*, 377–399.
Parker, D. A., Wolz, M. W., & Harford, T. C., The prevention of alcoholism: An empirical report on the effects of outlet availability. *Alcoholism: Clinical and Experimental Research*, 1978, *2*, 339–343.
Pearce, J., & Garrett, H. D. Comparison of the drinking behavior of delinquent youth versus non-delinquent youth in the states of Idaho and Utah. *Journal of School Health*, 1970, *401*, 131–135.
Pfautz, H. W., & Hyde, R. W. The ecology of alcohol in the local community. *Quarterly Journal of Studies on Alcohol*, 1960, *21*, 447–456.
Polk, K. *Drinking and the adolescent culture*. Eugene, Ore.: Lane County Youth Project, 1964.

Polk, K., & Burkett, S. Drinking as rebellion: A study of adolescent drinking patterns. In K. Polk & W. Schafer (Eds.), *Schools and delinquency*. Englewood Cliffs, N.J.: Prentice-Hall, 1972.

Popham, R. E., Schmidt, W., & de Lint, J. The effects of legal restraint on drinking. In B. Kissin and H. Begleiter (Eds.), *The biology of alcoholism. Vol. 4: Social aspects of alcoholism*. New York: Plenum Press, 1976.

Rachal, J. V., Williams, J. R., Brehm, M. L., Cavanaugh, B., Moore, R. B., & Eckerman, W. C. *A national study of adolescent drinking behavior, attitudes and correlates*. Research Triangle Park, N.C.: Research Triangle Institute, 1975.

Rubington, E. The bottle gang. *Quarterly Journal of Studies on Alcohol*, 1968, *29*, 943–955.

Schmidt, W., & Popham, R. E. The single distribution theory of alcohol consumption. *Journal of Studies on Alcohol*, 1978, *39*, 400–419.

Sommer, R. The isolated drinker in the Edmonton beer parlor. *Quarterly Journal of Studies on Alcohol*, 1965, *26*, 95–110.

Straus, R. Conceptualizing alcoholism and problem drinking. In P. A. O'Gorman, S. Stringfield, & I. Smith (Eds.), *Defining adolescent alcohol use: Implications toward a definition of adolescent alcoholism*. New York: National Council on Alcoholism, 1977.

Sulkunen, P. Drinking patterns and the level of alcohol consumption: An international overview. In R. J. Gibbins, Y. Israel, H. Kalant, R. E. Popham, W. Schmidt, & R. G. Smart (Eds.), *Research advances in alcohol and drug abuse problems* (Vol. 3). New York: Wiley, 1976.

Swanson, D. W., Bratrude, A. P., & Brown, E. M. Alcohol abuse in a population of Indian children. *Diseases of the Nervous System*, 1971, *32*, 835–842.

Widseth, J. C., & Mayer, J. Drinking behavior and attitudes toward alcohol in delinquent girls. *International Journal of the Addictions*, 1971, *6*, 453–461.

6

Sex Roles and Adolescent Drinking

Sharon C. Wilsnack and Richard W. Wilsnack

1. Introduction

In the United States, as in most other societies, men and boys drink more alcohol more frequently than do women and girls (Cahalan, Cisin, & Crossley, 1969; Child, Barry, & Bacon, 1965; Johnson, 1978; Rachal, Williams, Brehm, Cavanaugh, Moore, & Eckerman, 1975). The sex differences occur across all age levels, ethnic groups, and socioeconomic levels. The consistency of sex differences in drinking behavior suggests that drinking may be associated with traditional sex roles, that is, with traditional ideas about what constitutes appropriate and distinctive behavior for men and for women.

One possible link between drinking and sex roles is that drinking may provide evidence or signals to other people about the kind of sex role one is trying to perform. In particular, drinking in male groups has been one way in which men and boys can show their manliness or *machismo*, by being able to consume large quantities of alcohol without losing the ability to behave competently, and by showing generosity and comradeship to other men through sharing drinks (Abad & Suarez, 1975; Jellinek, 1977; Kunitz & Levy, 1974; Madsen, 1961; Treviño, 1975). Zucker (1968), studying high school boys, concluded that "the major

---

Sharon C. Wilsnack • Division of Psychiatry and Behavioral Science, Department of Neuroscience, University of North Dakota School of Medicine, Grand Forks, ND 58202. **Richard W. Wilsnack** • Department of Sociology, University of North Dakota, Grand Forks, ND 58202. The research reported here was supported in part by Contracts No. PLD-0453-76 and PLD-04101-78 from the National Institute on Alcohol Abuse and Alcoholism.

characteristic differentiating heavier from lighter drinkers is one of sex-role facade. That is, the difference is in conscious self-representation, with heavier drinkers picturing themselves as more masculine" (p. 880).

Another reason to believe that sex roles are related to drinking is that during the present era of sex-role change and redefinition, there has also been an increase in drinking among women, particularly among younger women. Between 1964 and 1972, the proportion of American women in their 20s who drank at least once a month increased from 50% to more than 60% (USDHEW, 1971, 1974). The proportion of college women who drank at least occasionally increased from 61% in 1949–1952 (Straus & Bacon, 1953) to 73% in the early 1970s (Hanson, 1974). By 1974, 69% of junior high school and high school girls in a national sample reported drinking at least occasionally (Rachal *et al.*, 1975), a higher percentage than in any of the local and regional surveys of the 1950s and 1960s (Bacon & Jones, 1968). Other surveys of teenage drinking in the 1970s also show declining differences between boys and girls (Gold & Reimer, 1975; San Mateo County, 1973; Wechsler, 1978; Wechsler & McFadden, 1976).

The recent changes in young women's drinking patterns have led to speculation that increased drinking and drinking problems are a consequence or "price" of women's liberation. Dr. Ernest Noble, former director of the National Institute on Alcohol Abuse and Alcoholism, has suggested that "as women go out more into society, . . . they may be exposed to the same kinds of problems . . . that men have been exposed to earlier, and this may cause increased drinking" (U.S. Senate, 1976, p. 8). Rachal *et al.* (1975) raised the possibility that drinking is becoming more common among female adolescents because of the " 'new female's' . . . more liberated sharing of traditionally masculine attitudes and behaviors" (p. 41).

It is important to understand *how* traditional sex roles and drinking behavior may have become connected in ways that are now subject to social change. Scholars have suggested four possible connections. First, sex roles may determine people's *opportunities* to drink. Men and boys may drink more because traditionally they have had more legitimate opportunities to drink, and their drinking opportunities have been subject to less restrictive social control. A survey of drinking contexts for men and women in Boston (Harford, 1977) indicated that drinking was integrated into a broader range of activities and social settings for men than for women. Other studies have shown that women and girls have been more likely to drink in contexts where social restraints on drinking are stronger (e.g., at home, with family or parents present), while men and boys have been more likely to drink with peers in less restrictive settings (Clark, 1967, 1977; Maddox & McCall, 1964; Ullman, 1957).

Sex roles have also involved sex-typed *norms* about desirable or permissible drinking behavior for men and women. In effect, traditional sex roles have *obligated* men and women to behave differently toward alcohol. In the United States, both sexes have been less tolerant of women's drinking than of men's (Johnson & Garzon, 1977; Knupfer, 1964), although recent surveys (see Rachal *et al.*, 1975) indicate that attitudes toward female drinking are becoming more permissive. Attitudes toward drunkenness in women may also be changing. In a California survey in the 1960s (Knupfer, 1964), a majority of men and women respondents believed that it was worse for a woman to become intoxicated than for a man. In the 1970s, responses of a California college sample and a smaller nonstudent sample (Stafford & Petway, 1977) showed no significant differences between evaluative semantic differential ratings of "a drunk man" and "a drunk woman."

Sex roles may influence drinking behavior in a third way by affecting the *needs and motives* of the individual. Goals, aspirations, and conflicts related to sex-role performance may influence an individual's use of alcohol by creating demands that are easier to satisfy under the influence of alcohol, by producing stress and discomfort that alcohol seems to reduce, and by involving the individual in activities and situations where one is expected to drink. Since much of the research to date on sex roles and drinking has focused on motivational connections, this research is reviewed subsequently for each sex.

A fourth connection between sex roles and drinking is that drinking may be used *symbolically* to *communicate* to other people the kind of sex role one is trying to perform. We have referred previously to ways in which drinking has served traditionally as a way to display masculinity (Jellinek, 1977; Madsen, 1961; Treviño, 1975; Zucker, 1968). For girls and women, the association of drinking with traditional masculine role performance may make drinking useful as a way of symbolizing or expressing "liberation" or rejection of traditional feminine roles (Curlee, 1967).

To summarize, traditional masculine and feminine roles may influence drinking behavior in at least four ways: by creating opportunities to drink, by creating normative obligations to drink (or not to drink), by creating needs and desires to drink, and by creating symbolic uses for drinking. With a few exceptions, the relevant literature has not clearly distinguished among these four relationships. The sections that follow review that literature that seems most pertinent to relationships between sex roles and adolescent drinking. However, it must be emphasized at this point that sex-role influences are *not* the basis for a comprehensive explanation or "theory" of adolescent (or adult) drinking. Instead, sex roles appear to be only one part of a complex set of causes and conditions that determine adolescent drinking patterns. A necessary task for the future is to explore how sex roles fit together with personality variables, parental and peer influences, experience with deviant behavior, and other well-recognized influences on adolescent drinking.

2. Sex Roles and Male Adolescent Drinking

In the past, sex roles have affected drinking contexts and drinking norms in ways that made it easier for boys to drink than for girls, allowing boys more opportunities to drink, with fewer restrictions and with less normative disapproval. Maddox and McCall (1964), for example, reported that boys in a midwestern community were more likely than girls to drink in peer groups, where they would be relatively free of adult controls over their alcohol use, and that boys were more likely to work away from home, where they would have both opportunities for unsupervised drinking and the money to take advantage of such opportunities. Earlier, Ullman (1957) noted that boys were more likely than girls to have their first drinking experience with friends at an unusual location (not at home or at a bar or restaurant); this introduction to drinking in relatively uncontrolled settings may have contributed to the boys' tendency, after the first drinking experience, to drink again sooner than the girls.

In the 1970s, however, sex differences in opportunities and norms for adolescent drinking seem to have a declining influence. Gold and Reimer's (1975) national survey data show that between 1967 and 1972, male–female differences in the self-reported frequency of drinking without parents' permission were declining or disappearing for 13- to 16-year-olds, controlling for effects of ethnicity, age, parental socioeconomic status, and residential setting. Responses to the 1973–1974 NIAAA national survey (Rachal *et al.*, 1975) showed that only 26% of the girls and 30% of the boys felt that it was worse for a girl to drink than for a boy. From such findings, one might predict a gradual weakening of the *situational* effects of sex roles on drinking (i.e., the effects of drinking norms and opportunities) to the extent that traditional sex-role definitions are being blurred or abandoned.

Other possible influences of sex roles, on the motives for male adolescent drinking, may not be as quickly affected by recent social change. Two psychodynamic theories of drinking raise the possibility that the overall demands of performing masculine roles may create special needs that drinking can satisfy and special conflicts that drinking can reduce. One of the theories links excessive drinking to conflicts arising from dependency needs (Barry, 1976; Blane, 1968; McCord & McCord, 1960). According to this theory, drinking gratifies male dependency needs (e.g., by producing feelings of warmth, sentimentality, and closeness to others) but allows the drinker to maintain an outward appearance of independence and maturity, thus averting negative sanctions traditionally directed at overt dependent behavior in men. Evidence from both clinical studies (see Blane, 1968) and cross-cultural research (e.g., Bacon, 1974; Barry, 1976) indicates an association between dependency conflicts and drinking. In one of the few relevant studies of adolescent boys, Blane and Chafetz (1971) found that heavy-drinking delinquent boys were higher on covert dependency needs but lower on overt dependency needs than were lighter-drinking delinquent boys.

A question remaining open is how traditional masculinity affects dependency conflicts and how dependency conflicts in turn may affect desires for traditional masculinity. One possibility is that men and boys who are strongly committed to traditional masculine roles feel more conflict about their dependency needs and thus drink more heavily. A second possibility is that dependency conflicts and associated characteristics may defensively enhance the conscious desire for traditional masculinity. Taking the second view, Blane (1968) described the male problem drinker as having an unconscious "feminine identification" with the mothering figure who either overindulged or underindulged his early dependency needs. As a defense against both his suppressed dependency needs and his underlying feminine tendencies, the problem drinker presents a "hypermasculine" facade of assertive, impulsive activity, which often includes drinking (see also McCord & McCord, 1960).

The available data on young men support an association between drinking and overt "hypermasculine" traits but provide little evidence for the existence of unconscious feminine tendencies. Several studies of heavy-drinking adolescent boys, or boys who later became problem drinkers, report a cluster of traditionally masculine behavior patterns, including assertiveness, aggressiveness, rebelliousness, high activity levels, and impulsivity (Jones, 1968; Kammeier, Hoffman, & Loper, 1973; McCord & McCord, 1960; Robins, 1966). Zucker (1968) found that heavier-drinking adolescent boys scored as more masculine on a test of conscious self-image but did not differ from lighter-drinking boys on a measure of "unconscious masculinity–femininity." Blane and Chafetz (1971), using different measures of masculinity–femininity, could find no differences between heavy- and light-drinking delinquent boys on either overt or covert sex-role orientation. Taken together, these findings raise a question about how to distinguish drinking as psychological need gratification (e.g., as satisfaction of covert dependency needs or denial of covert "femininity") from drinking as simply a part of social role performance.

A second psychodynamic theory of male drinking suggests that traditional masculinity specifically arouses the need for feelings of personal power, a need that is gratified by drinking (McClelland *et al.*, 1972). Because men traditionally have been taught to be concerned about their personal power and are more likely than women to experience social demands to display their personal power, they are more likely than women to desire the feelings of enhanced power produced by alcohol (perhaps through reduced inhibitions, heightened autonomic arousal, lowered anxiety, etc.). Studies of college-aged male social drinkers showed that large amounts of drinking increased thoughts of personal power (i.e., power in the service of self-aggrandizement). Subsequent research showed that men who had strong needs for personal power, or who experienced demands that they assert themselves and take charge, were likely to drink more heavily (Davis, 1972; McClelland & Davis, 1972). General behavioral inhibition also affected male drinking, with the heaviest drinking occurring among men with both strong power needs and low levels of inhibition (see McClelland & Davis, 1972; McClelland & Wilsnack, 1972).

With regard to adolescent drinking, the power theory would predict the heaviest drinking among boys who want to be powerful and are relatively uninhibited—in effect, the type of impulsive, aggressive adolescent reported in previous studies of heavy and problem drinkers. The theory would predict more moderate drinking among boys who have strong needs for feelings of power but equally strong inhibitions or self-restraint. However, the utility of the power theory for explaining boys' drinking remains uncertain, because the theory as yet has been directly tested only on adults, and because the adolescent drinking behavior that seems to fit the theory may be consistent with other explanations as well.

In both the theories summarized above, traditional masculinity has only an indirect effect on drinking, increasing certain emotional needs that in turn increase the desirability of alcohol. However, traditional standards of masculinity may also *directly* encourage drinking if boys believe that drinking can be *used* to help display and prove their ability to behave in an adult masculine way. This use of drinking is consistent with Zucker's (1968) finding that heavier drinking among high school boys was associated with a hypermasculine "sex-role facade," and with Maddox and McCall's (1964) conclusion that

> The more closely the teen-ager is identified with adult status by age, by experience of personal autonomy and responsibility in decision making, and

> by the opportunity to play adult roles, the more likely he is to identify himself as a drinker and to use beverage alcohol. (p. 41)

The use of drinking behavior as public evidence of both manliness and maturation has been noted across several ethnic groups (Kunitz & Levy, 1974; Madsen, 1961; Sterne, 1967; Treviño, 1975). Alcohol consumption may also be used to aid other aspects of traditional masculine role performance, for instance, by reducing inhibitions and internal conflicts that might interfere with self-assertive and aggressive behavior (Boyatzis, 1975; Lang, Goeckner, Adesso, & Marlatt, 1975; Topper, 1974).

In sum, there are several ways in which traditional masculine roles may encourage boys to drink: by selectively exposing them to situations in which unrestricted drinking is normally expected, by making it useful to drink as a means of showing adult manliness, and by creating internal needs and conflicts that drinking can assuage. It seems likely that these inducements to drink can operate either separately or in combination. It is important to note also that traditional masculinity not only positively encourages drinking but, in contrast to traditional femininity, apparently does not impose any specific *inhibitions* on drinking behavior. How much current sex-role changes may diminish the association between masculinity and drinking is not yet clear.

3. Sex Roles and Female Adolescent Drinking

The idea that orientation toward traditional sex roles may influence women's drinking is not new. Most clinical reports on alcoholic women mention problems of adjustment to feminine roles; this literature contains numerous references to women problem drinkers' "masculine identification," "inadequate feminine identification," "masculine role playing," and "inadequate adjustment to adult female roles" (e.g., Berner & Solms, 1952; Driscoll & Barr, 1972; Kinsey, 1966; Massot, Hamel, & Deliry, 1956; Wall, 1937; Wood & Duffy, 1966).

The utility of terms such as *masculine role playing* and *inadequate femininity* is open to question, not only because the terms are difficult to conceptualize and measure (see, for example, Bem, 1974; Spence, Helmreich, & Stapp, 1975), but also because they may become less meaningful as popular ideas about appropriate sex roles change. It is obvious that drinking is not automatically incompatible with contemporary notions of femininity (see Gomberg, 1978). What remains uncertain is *to what extent* young women have abandoned beliefs that femininity necessarily restricts their drinking, and *to what extent* young women have increased their participation in situations where their drinking would be regarded as normal behavior. Schuckit and Morrissey (1976) believe that women who deviate from traditional feminine roles will drink more as the result of increased drinking opportunities and more permissive drinking norms. They note that alcoholic women, compared with women in the general population, are more likely to occupy traditional masculine roles: they are more likely to be employed outside the home, to pursue traditionally masculine occupations, and to have completed at least some college. Such data, of course, do not indicate how much drinking opportunities and norms contribute to these women's alcohol problems relative to psychological factors that may initially lead them to seek traditionally masculine roles.

Only in the last decade has empirical research begun to investigate the precise relationships of sex roles to drinking among women, and this research has focused more on the *psychological* than on the *social* impacts of sex roles. A prominent idea in the recent research literature is that women may use the effects of alcohol to relieve stress and conflict related to sex-role performance. Such stress may be either internal (i.e., arising from conflicting dispositions toward sex roles within the personality) or external (i.e., arising either from conflicts between a woman's personal sex-role orientation and the style of behavior demanded by her social environment, or from attempts to perform multiple roles that impose conflicting sex-related social demands). Results of a 1975 national survey may reflect all three types of sex-role conflict: married women who were also employed outside the home had higher rates of heavy and problem drinking than either unmarried working women or married women not employed outside the home (Johnson, 1978).

Some studies report that women with drinking problems are particularly likely to show a discrepancy between overtly valuing traditionally feminine roles and attributes and covertly showing traditionally masculine attributes. For example, Wilsnack (1973) found that a sample of alcoholic women in treatment were traditionally feminine on measures of sex-typed attitudes and interests but scored in the traditionally masculine direction on less overt measures of interpersonal and expressive style. Pattison (1975) reported a similar pattern. Beckman (1978) found that a sample of alcoholic women were more likely than a matched sample of nonpsychiatric controls to show a combination of "conscious femininity" on tests of sex-typed attitudes and interests and "unconscious masculinity" on a projective test of expressive style, with roughly one-fourth of the alcoholics showing this pattern. Similarly, Anderson (1976) found an alcoholic sample to be traditionally "feminine" on attitude and interest tests and traditionally "masculine" on less overt measures, when their scores were compared with female test norms; interestingly, nonalcoholic sister controls showed the same pattern of deviation from female norms and did not differ significantly from their alcoholic sisters. Finally, Scida and Vannicelli (1979) administered tests of real (perceived) and ideal (desired) self-image to samples of social-drinking, problem-drinking, and alcoholic women. In the problem-drinking and alcoholic groups, two types of discrepancy occurred: (1) between perceived "masculinity" and desired "femininity" (the predominant pattern in most earlier studies), and (2) between perceived "femininity" and desired "masculinity." Scida and Vannicelli suggested that the *presence* of conflict concerning sex roles may be a more important factor in women's drinking than the particular *form* the conflict takes.

In contrast to studies reporting overt "femininity" and covert "masculinity" in alcoholic women, a study by Parker (1972) showed that alcoholic women overtly *rejected* female roles on a test of conscious role preferences. The rejection was clearest among primary (early-onset) alcoholics, who may have been more heavily represented in Parker's sample than in other studies (see Wilsnack, 1976). A second study by Parker (1975) showed that heavy-drinking women in a college sample rejected traditional female role preferences. Parker's findings raise the possibility that the relationship between sex-role orientations and women's alcoholism depends in part on the age of onset: early-onset alcoholic women may drink in association with early rejection of traditional feminine roles, while late-onset alcoholic women may adhere to traditional feminine roles and begin drinking excessively only after some life crisis threatens their ability to perform these roles adequately.

The literature reviewed so far suggests that the links between feminine roles and drinking are indirect, in the sense that drinking is used to relieve feelings of stress and conflict created by problems of sex-role performance. There is also some evidence that for women, drinking can reduce the salience of traditional masculine motivations, such as concerns about personal power or self-assertion (see Durand, 1975; Wilsnack, 1974), thereby reducing any interference by these motives with traditional feminine role performance.

However, drinking can also be used *directly* to symbolize or express attitudes toward traditional femininity. To the extent that women and girls view drinking as inconsistent with traditional ideas of femininity, they may drink to show their rejection of traditional femininity, apart from any emotional relief or gratification that the effects of alcohol provide (see Curlee, 1967).

A problem with interpreting the literature relating women's drinking to sex roles is that the literature is more relevant to adult, experienced drinkers than to adolescents. Adolescent girls may differ from adult women drinkers by being less committed or more undecided about their sex roles, and by behaving toward alcohol in ways more strongly affected by social and environmental influences and early drinking experiences. Furthermore, most of the adult women studied thus far have been drinking long enough so that their drinking may be an important cause of sex-role stress and conflict, not simply an effect. Finally, most of the adult women drinkers grew up in a context of stable feminine roles, whereas adolescent girls today are learning to drink during a period of changing ideas about femininity and its importance.

Data relevant to the sex-role orientations of female adolescent drinkers are extremely scarce. Widseth and Mayer (1971) found that in a sample of delinquent girls, the heaviest drinkers had the least desire to grow up to be like their mothers. Zucker and Devoe (1975) found that problem drinking in a sample of adolescent girls was related to "aggressive sociability" displayed by both the drinkers and their mothers. Among high school girls in a northeastern community (Zucker, 1968), heavy drinkers were less feminine than nondrinkers in fantasy preferences and scores on the Gough femininity scale (Gough, 1956), but the differences were not statistically significant. Finally, there is the previously mentioned finding by Parker (1975) that in a sample of college women, heavy drinking was related to rejection of traditional feminine roles. Taken together, these results suggest that among adolescent girls, the sex-role orientation most likely to be associated with drinking is an overt rejection of traditional femininity.

To summarize, traditional femininity may be related to girls' drinking behavior in several ways: by limiting access to drinking opportunities, by setting norms against drinking, by creating tensions and conflicts that alcohol can soothe, and by giving drinking special significance as a symbol or expression of sex-role orientation. The limited information available about girls' drinking suggests that it is associated with rejection of traditional femininity. Such rejection could create opportunities to drink, could be expressed through drinking behavior, and could aggravate tensions that alcohol might seem to relieve. Unfortunately, it is still unknown how much girls' drinking is influenced by the several possible connections to femininity. It is also unknown how much girls' drinking involves attitudes not just toward traditional femininity but toward traditional masculinity as well.

4. Some Current Research on Sex Roles and Adolescent Drinking

Recently we have been engaged in research to clarify a few of the possible relationships between sex roles and adolescent drinking (Wilsnack & Wilsnack, 1978 a, b). Although the research focuses primarily on the motivational aspects of sex-role orientation, we have been able to carry out systematic analyses of relationships to drinking behavior in a large and recent national sample of adolescents. Because the findings may help to specify how sex-role data can increase our understanding of adolescent drinking, it is worthwhile to summarize the research here.

4.1. Methods

4.1.1. *Survey Design*

Our data came from a 1974 national survey on adolescent drinking conducted by the Research Triangle Institute for the National Institute on Alcohol Abuse and Alcoholism; a detailed description is given in Rachal *et al.* (1975). A two-stage stratified cluster sample included approximately 15,000 students in grades 7–12, in the contiguous 48 states plus the District of Columbia. Selection of 50 primary sampling units was stratified by census region, community size, and ethnic characteristics. Ethnic stratification allowed oversampling of localities with high concentrations of Oriental, American Indian, and Spanish-American residents to ensure that these minorities would be adequately represented. Within each primary sampling unit, approximately 15 school homerooms were selected, stratified by grade.

All students in each homeroom were asked to complete an anonymous, self-administered questionnaire, which included items on drinking behavior, contexts and consequences of drinking, deviant behavior, and selected demographic, attitudinal, and personality characteristics. The overall response rate was 72.2%.

4.1.2. *Measures*

The primary measure of drinking behavior was a modification of the quantity– frequency (Q–F) scales used by Mulford and Miller (1960), Maddox and Williams (1968), and Jessor *et al.* (1968). The Q–F items asked about the average frequency of drinking and the average amount consumed per drinking occasion, repeating the same questions for beer, wine, and liquor. Scores for the beverage that was the respondent's largest reported source of alcohol were used to assign the respondent to one of 10 drinking levels. Levels ranged from abstainers (who never drank or drank less than once a year) and minimal drinkers (who drank no more than one drink per occasion, no more than once a month) to heavy drinkers (who drank at least once a week and typically had five or more drinks on each occasion). One of our dependent variables was a 10-point scale based on the 10 drinking levels.

Two other dependent variables were measures of problems associated with drinking. A drinking-problems scale was based on five negative consequences of drinking: getting in trouble with teachers, with friends, with dating partners, and with the police, and driving after drinking (from Jessor & Jessor, 1977). The scale score summed the number of times these five problems were reported. The second measure, a symptomatic drinking scale, summed the reported frequencies of 15 behaviors considered symptoms of actual or potential alcohol dependence (e.g., gulping drinks, drinking in the morning, drinking alone, not remembering behavior while drinking; from Cahalan, 1970).

To measure the independent variables (sex-role orientations), four kinds of data were available. First, the students used 12 adjectival phrases to indicate the kind of person they would like to be. In previous cross-cultural research (see Block, 1973), 6 of the items were endorsed more frequently by men and the other 6 more often by women. Second, the students responded to 6 Likert items stating attitudes toward sex-role performance (from Kinsey, 1966; Wilsnack, 1973). Third, responses to two 5-item scales indicated how much the students valued academic achievement and personal independence (see Jessor & Jessor, 1977). Finally, respondents indicated how much they valued an accomplishment traditionally valued by men (being successful in a chosen job or career) and two accomplishments traditionally valued by women (getting married and having children).

From the data, we constructed a six-item scale of traditional femininity that was besed on face validity and maximizing interitem covariance in 14 subgroups of girls, divided by grade and ethnicity. Scale items asked the students how much they would like to be loving and affectionate, sympathetic, and generous; how much they agreed with the statement "It is important to me to look as attractive as I can to others"; and how strongly they would like to get married and have children. Factor analyses of the six items for the grade-by-ethnicity subgroups showed that the first principal component accounted for 57–76% of the common factor variance, with all six items showing high positive loadings (above .4 in 67 of 84 cases). Responses were summed, with high scores indicating endorsement of traditionally feminine attributes and values. Low scores indicated rejection of traditional femininity but did not necessarily imply endorsement of traditional masculinity. Because the scale items were stated in the first person and in idealistic or future-oriented terms, the scores probably should be interpreted motivationally: they reflect a desire to conform to or to reject traditional feminine behavior.[1]

To measure orientations toward traditional masculinity, we used two approaches. First, we constructed a scale to measure the positive

[1] To be sure that traditional femininity scores did not merely reflect a generalized attitude toward being unconventional, we correlated scores in the subgroups with an index of attitudes toward deviant behavior (theft, vandalism, assault, etc.) and a measure of how much personal independence was valued relative to academic achievement (see Jessor & Jessor, 1977). Traditional femininity had only low correlations with disapproval of deviant behavior ($< .25$ in 11 of 14 cases) and with not preferring independence ($< .20$ in 13 of 14 cases).

desire for traditional masculine attributes and accomplishments. Items were chosen on the basis of face validity and consistently high interitem covariance in 14 grade-by-ethnicity subgroups of boys. Scale items asked students how much they would like to be bold and confident, dominating, competitive, self-controlled, and ambitious; how strongly they would like to be successful at a job or career of their choice; and five questions about their desire for academic achievement, averaged to count as a single item. The scale appears to have a unifying theme of "seeking to be successful." Factor analysis of the seven items for all grade-by-ethnicity subgroups showed that the first principal component accounted for 60–100% of the common factor variance, with all seven items showing high positive loadings (above .3 in 83 of 98 cases).

The second approach was to look for a consistent pattern in boys' responses to potentially feminine items. Prior research has shown that men favoring traditional masculine stereotypes emphasize the contrast between masculine and feminine attributes (Ellis & Bentler, 1973; Spence *et al.*, 1975). It is possible that male adolescents define their own sex roles in part by establishing distance from traditional feminine roles and attributes (David & Brannon, 1976).

Inspection of interitem correlations revealed three correlated negative responses: not wanting to be a "generous" person, not wanting to be a "reasonable, rational" person, and disagreeing with the idea that a man should help his wife with work around the house (see also Tomeh, 1977). More than any other items, these three seemed to reflect a desire to reject or deny social obligations. The boys who did not want to be generous, sensible, or helpmates were saying in effect that they did not want anyone else to have a hold over them. Viewing denial of social obligations as a traditionally masculine or at least antifeminine characteristic is consistent with analyses of *machismo* (Abad & Suarez, 1975), socially *un*desirable masculine attributes (Ponzo & Strowig, 1973; Wiggins & Holzmuller, 1978), and the association of femininity with valuing or respecting social obligations (e.g., Bakan, 1966; Block, 1973; Broverman, Vogel, Broverman, Clarkson, & Rosenkrantz, 1972; Gaudreau, 1977; Spence *et al.*, 1975; Waters, Waters, & Pincus, 1977). Summed scores on the three items were used as a measure of denial of social obligations. In factor analyses of responses to the items in all subgroups, the first principal component accounted for 100% of the common factor variance.

Three other predesigned scales were available that were potentially relevant to both role orientations and drinking behavior: specific measures of desire for independence (in the sense of being capable of making one's own decisions), desire for academic achievement, and self-reported participation in deviant behavior other than alcohol or drug use (e.g., theft, vandalism, truancy, assault). To estimate and control for demographic influences on role orientation and drinking, we used data on the student's grade in school, self-reported ethnicity and religious affiliation, father's and mother's level of education, and father's and mother's occupation.

4.2. Results

To organize and interpret the data, we relied on three modes of data analysis. Mean scores for subgroups of the total sample ($N = 13{,}122$) helped to clarify sex, grade, and ethnic differences on measures of drinking behavior and role orientations. Multiple regression analyses showed the impact of multiple independent variables on drinking behavior among the boys ($N = 6{,}339$) and girls ($N = 6{,}783$), allowing us to control for demographic influences. Finally, correlation analyses for boys and girls in 14 subgroups, divided by grade (7–8, 9–10, 11–12) and ethnicity (white, black, Spanish-American, Oriental-American, and American Indian) indicated the consistency of bivariate relationships, for example, between drinking and role orientations.[2]

4.2.1. Subgroup Differences

To compare proportions of drinkers in different subgroups, we used drinking levels to distinguish drinkers from nondrinkers. Nondrinkers were individuals who said that they completely abstained from alcohol or drank no more than once a month and no more than one drink per occasion; drinkers reported drinking more often and/or in larger amounts.[3] Table 1 shows that there are still sex differences in drinking among American adolescents. In all subgroups, a larger percentage of boys drank than girls. The percentage of students who drank also increased with grade level (except among Oriental high school girls). Furthermore, in 4 of 6 comparisons among ethnic groups, white students were the most likely to be drinkers, and in 5 of 6 comparisons black students were the least likely to drink (cf. Higgins, Albrecht, & Albrecht, 1977). An analysis of variance in drinking versus nondrinking showed

[2] Even with oversampling, the number of Oriental students was so small (particularly the number who drank) that in some analyses we combined the 9th- through 12th-graders.

[3] We treated abstainers and minimal drinkers as nondrinkers for two reasons. First, it seemed wrong to categorize students as drinkers if their drinking consisted of one drink on a few special occasions (e.g., rituals, holidays, family celebrations). Second, students who drank no more than one drink a month would not consume enough alcohol to experience drinking problems or symptomatic drinking. Cahalan *et al.* (1969), Jessor and Jessor (1975), and O'Connor (1975) have used similar combinations.

significant main effects of sex ($F = 85.7, p < .001$), grade level ($F = 116.3, p < .001$), and ethnicity ($F = 33.9, p < .001$).

Among the boys and girls who were drinkers, sex differences in drinking behavior persisted. Table 2 shows mean scores for subgroups of drinkers on the indexes of (1) quantity and frequency of drinking (Q–F); (2) problem consequences of drinking, and (3) drinking patterns symptomatic of alcohol dependence. Boys drank larger amounts more frequently, got into more trouble related to drinking, and were more likely to drink in ways symptomatic of alcohol dependence; altogether, boys exceeded girls in 43 of 45 comparisons. Symptomatic drinking was most common among the American Indians (5 of 6 comparisons) and least common among the blacks (5 of 6 comparisons). The amount of drinking increased consistently with grade among the boys but not among the girls (perhaps because drinking is specifically a part of adult male role performance). Analysis of variance confirmed the main effects of sex on all three drinking indexes (all F's > 19, all p's $< .001$), a main effect of ethnicity on symptomatic drinking ($F = 16.4, p < .001$), and an interaction effect of sex × grade on quantity–frequency ($F = 6.8, p < .001$).

Boys' and girls' scores on the three indexes of sex-role orientation differed consistently in the expected directions (see Table 3). Girls showed more desire to be traditionally feminine in 14 of 15 comparisons (i.e., except among 7th- and 8th-grade blacks) ($F = 14.0, p < .001$). Boys had a slightly higher desire for traditional masculine success in 11 of 15 subgroups ($F = 10.0, p < .001$) but showed a clearly stronger distaste

Table 1. Drinking by Sex, Ethnicity, and Grade in School

	Grade					
	7–8		9–10		11–12	
	Percentage drinkers (N)					
Female						
White	37.3	(1,428)	57.4	(1,542)	67.7	(1,531)
Spanish-American	30.9	(282)	48.8	(207)	53.9	(204)
Black	19.7	(137)	37.2	(137)	44.2	(120)
American Indian	27.2	(191)	57.9	(145)	61.2	(121)
Oriental	26.4	(53)	44.0	(25)	43.3	(30)
Male						
White	50.3	(1,339)	69.7	(1,288)	80.4	(1,341)
Spanish-American	46.1	(258)	64.3	(171)	84.1	(164)
Black	32.3	(124)	45.0	(111)	63.3	(90)
American Indian	45.7	(197)	65.6	(154)	72.3	(101)
Oriental	32.7	(55)	54.2	(24)	89.5	(19)

Table 2. Drinkers' Mean Scores on Drinking Indexes, by Sex, Ethnicity, and Grade in School

	Female				Male			
	Q–F[a]	Problems[b]	Symptoms[c]	(*N*)	Q–F[a]	Problems[b]	Symptoms[c]	(*N*)
Grades 7–8								
White	4.90	5.86	26.23	(570)	5.26	6.35	27.37	(715)
Spanish-American	5.22	5.59	26.52	(97)	5.51	6.96	28.15	(133)
Black	5.53	7.72	25.45	(33)	5.40	8.61	27.32	(50)
American Indian	5.28	6.67	30.11	(55)	5.63	8.29	30.92	(100)
Oriental	5.07	5.33	25.27	(15)	4.53	7.11	27.74	(19)
Grades 9–10								
White	5.08	6.22	28.59	(906)	5.73	6.75	29.09	(943)
Spanish-American	4.83	5.70	27.42	(109)	5.78	6.94	28.63	(117)
Black	4.78	6.00	23.98	(57)	5.94	7.42	25.78	(54)
American Indian	5.42	6.80	29.02	(86)	5.70	7.79	29.69	(113)
Oriental	3.83	6.33	24.00	(11)	5.47	6.43	28.21	(14)
Grades 11–12								
White	5.30	6.64	27.91	(1,062)	6.33	8.00	29.63	(1,110)
Spanish-American	4.69	6.17	25.44	(115)	6.27	8.04	27.88	(145)
Black	4.84	5.97	24.56	(59)	5.61	6.75	25.31	(64)
American Indian	5.04	7.32	28.03	(77)	6.52	9.63	30.43	(77)
Oriental	4.38	5.69	25.00	(13)	6.45	10.50	30.47	(17)

[a] Q–F range = 2–9, $\overline{X} = 5.49$, $SD = 2.64$:
[b] Problems range = 5–30, $\overline{X} = 6.85$, $SD = 3.16$:
[c] Symptoms range = 15–60, $\overline{X} = 28.21$, $SD = 7.83$.

Table 3. Role Orientations: Mean Scores by Grade, Sex and Ethnicity

	Grade					
	7–8		9–10		11–12	
	Male	Female	Male	Female	Male	Female
White						
Traditional femininity[a]	23.05	25.23	23.22	26.07	24.12	26.41
Masculine success[b]	28.65	28.05	28.69	28.32	28.94	27.96
Denial of obligations[c]	6.63	5.74	6.66	5.58	6.12	5.18
(*N*)	(1,304)	(1,379)	(1,273)	(1,503)	(1,306)	(1,515)
Spanish-American						
Traditional femininity[a]	22.64	23.78	23.30	25.10	23.61	25.09
Masculine success[b]	27.77	26.17	27.73	27.45	28.02	27.18
Denial of obligations[c]	6.81	6.11	6.56	5.62	6.06	5.19
(*N*)	(250)	(269)	(169)	(198)	(157)	(201)
Black						
Traditional femininity[a]	23.39	23.28	23.01	25.04	23.58	24.86
Masculine success[b]	26.96	26.37	27.76	28.13	28.33	28.22
Denial of obligations[c]	6.45	5.97	6.57	5.67	6.48	5.45
(*N*)	(120)	(129)	(110)	(131)	(89)	(120)
American Indian						
Traditional femininity[a]	21.55	22.68	21.41	23.23	22.70	23.86
Masculine success[b]	26.03	26.46	26.71	26.78	27.72	27.25
Denial of obligations[c]	6.90	6.29	7.28	6.30	6.58	6.08
(*N*)	(193)	(174)	(148)	(134)	(99)	(118)
Oriental						
Traditional femininity[a]	22.31	24.06	23.04	24.40	23.63	25.33
Masculine success[b]	28.12	27.62	29.38	26.65	27.67	28.42
Denial of obligations[c]	6.05	5.80	6.74	5.92	6.55	4.73
(*N*)	(53)	(50)	(24)	(25)	(19)	(30)

[a] Traditional femininity range = 6–30, $\bar{X}$ = 24.4, *SD* = 3.71.
[b] Masculine success range = 7–35, $\bar{X}$ = 28.05, *SD* = 4.14.
[c] No-obligations range = 3–15, $\bar{X}$ = 6.05, *SD* = 2.12.

for social obligations in all 15 subgroups ($F = 97.1, p < .001$). Grade and ethnicity also had main effects on all three indexes (all F's > 3.9, all p's $< .05$), indicating that to evaluate any relationship between sex-role orientations and drinking, it is important to control for grade and ethnic influences.[4]

[4] Effects of grade and ethnicity on the index scores may reflect actual differences in role orientation. However, it is also possible that ethnicity and grade level may be associated with differences in how students react to the social desirability of questionnaire responses.

Other measures of role orientations (not included in Table 3) also showed sex differences. Boys were less eager for academic achievement than girls were (11 of 15 comparisons; $F = 11.0, p < .001$), although the differences in scores were small. Since previous research has associated the rejection of academic achievement with adolescent drinking and problem behavior (Jessor & Jessor, 1977), such rejection might be associated with differences between boys' and girls' drinking. On the measure of desire for independence (as a capability to make one's own decisions), an unexpected finding was that girls desired independence more than boys did (11 of 15 comparisons; $F = 7.9, p < .01$), although differences are again small. This finding contrasts with the literature identifying independence as a traditional masculine attribute (e.g., Broverman *et al.*, 1972; Ponzo & Strowig, 1973; Spence *et al.*, 1975; Waters *et al.*, 1977). As with the sex-role orientation measures, grade and ethnicity had significant effects on desire for achievement and for independence (F's > 13, p's $< .001$).

4.2.2. Differences between Drinkers and Nondrinkers

Among the boys, being a drinker rather than a nondrinker was weakly related to denying social obligations ($r = .066$), desiring independence ($r = .144$), and *not* desiring academic achievement ($r = -.141$) ($N = 6{,}339$; all p's $< .01$, one-tailed). Being a drinker or a nondrinker had *no* apparent relationship to boys' desire to seek traditional masculine success ($r = .0001$) or to their desire to behave in traditionally feminine ways ($r = .018$). Among the girls, the difference between drinkers and nondrinkers showed some relationship to a desire for independence ($r = .192$) and a lack of desire for academic achievement ($r = -.150$) ($N = 6{,}783$; p's $< .001$, one-tailed). Sex-role orientations such as desires for traditional femininity ($r = .037$), for masculine success ($r = -.023$) and to deny social obligations ($r = -.031$) seemed to have little to do with the distinction between girls who drank and girls who did not. However, relationships may have been obscured or distorted by the influence of demographic characteristics and the interrelationships of the role orientation measures.[5] Therefore, we used multiple regression analysis to

[5] In comparing the five measures of role orientation, it is important to keep in mind that they are closely related though not synonymous. In particular, there were high intercorrelations among the measures of sex-role orientation. Denial of social obligations had strong negative relationships with desire for traditional femininity ($r = -.612$ for all boys, $N = 6{,}339$; $r = -.502$ for all girls, $N = 6783$) and with desire for traditional masculine success (boys' $r = -.529$; girls' $r = -.432$). Desire for traditional femininity and desire for traditional masculine success positively correlated (boys' $r = .521$, girls' $r = .426$), indicating that the social desirability of the items in both indexes had a powerful effect, and that rejection of ideals traditionally appropriate to one's own sex did not imply

show the separate effects of demographic characteristics and role orientations on the distinction between drinkers and nondrinkers. Because the regression analysis involved a dummy dependent variable and pairwise deletion for missing data, we interpret the standardized beta coefficients only as indicators of the *relative* impact of different variables.[6]

The beta coefficients in Table 4 indicate that among both boys and girls, the difference between drinkers and nondrinkers reflected role orientations, religious affiliation, and grade in school. Desire for independence and lack of desire for academic achievement were associated with being a drinker for both sexes. Denial of obligations also increased the likelihood that a boy would drink and had a similar but smaller effect among girls; in this particular respect, rejection of traditionally feminine virtues was relevant to drinking by both sexes. However, the more inclusive measure of traditional femininity had nothing to do with the difference between drinkers and nondrinkers among girls, while boys who found the feminine attributes desirable were somewhat more likely to be drinkers. One possible interpretation of these results is that the feminine attributes measured by the traditional femininity scale (e.g., being affectionate, sympathetic, or generous) mainly aid affiliation; drinking is also an important aid to affiliative behavior among adolescent boys but is less so among adolescent girls. Furthermore, if one aspect of succeeding in masculine roles is becoming a convivial drinker in social groups, this would explain why the desire for masculine success had a small positive effect on the likelihood of drinking in both sexes. [7]

Consistent with the findings presented earlier (Table 1), students in the higher grades were much more likely to be drinkers, and drinking was a little more likely among whites. Drinkers were somewhat more common among Catholic and Jewish students and somewhat less com-

---

adoption of ideals traditionally appropriate to the other sex. Seeking academic achievement was related to the desire for traditional masculine success (boys' r = .428; girls' r = .487) and somewhat less related to the denial of social obligations (r's = −.22) and the desire for traditional femininity (r's = .25). Wanting to be independent had comparatively small relationships with all the indexes of sex-role orientation (all r's ≤ .20).

[6] Using a dummy dependent variable in regression analysis produces unbiased estimates of standardized beta coefficients (Ashenfelter, 1969) but biased estimates of standard errors because of heteroscedasticity (Goldberger, 1964); thus significance tests are misleading.

We used pairwise deletion for missing data (see Kim & Curry, 1977; Mackelprang, 1970), because listwise deletion would have eliminated more than one-fifth of the respondents from analyses that involved parental characteristics, and the respondents eliminated would have been disproportionately from minority ethnic groups.

[7] We caution against assuming that there is a causal sequence only from role orientations to drinking behavior. Certain role orientations may allow or encourage an adolescent to drink, but the effects of drinking experience may change an adolescent's ideas about the roles he or she is willing and able to perform.

Table 4. Regression of Drinking vs. Nondrinking on Demographic Characteristics and Role Orientations

	Standardized beta coefficients	
	Boys	Girls
Father's occupation[a]		
1. Manager, owner	.003	.020
2. Office and clerical	−.001	.004
3. Skilled worker	.023	.030
4. Farmer	.000	.021
5. Semiskilled worker	.008	.003
Mother's occupation[a]		
1. Manager, owner	−.001	.033[b]
2. Office and clerical	.018	.036[b]
3. Skilled worker	.017	.009
4. Farmer	−.013	.012
5. Semiskilled worker	.016	.016
Father's education	.001	.044[b]
Mother's education	−.005	.010
Ethnic category[a]		
White	.046	.067[b]
Spanish-American	.004	−.020
Black	−.035	−.018
American Indian	.025	.028
Grade in school	.251[c]	.211[c]
Religious affiliation[a]		
Protestant	−.036	−.098[c]
Catholic	.062[c]	.055[b]
Jewish	.077[c]	.053[c]
Other	−.035[b]	−.053[c]
Role orientation		
Traditional femininity	.054[b]	.017
Masculine success	.046[b]	.038[b]
Denial of obligations	.124[c]	.085[c]
Academic achievement	−.157[c]	−.175[c]
Independence	.145[c]	.183[c]
R^2	.146	.156

[a] Use of dummy variables precludes listing a sixth occupational category (Professional), the category for Oriental ethnicity, and the category for no religious affiliation.
[b] Unstandardized beta coefficient is > 2 times its standard error.
[c] Unstandardized beta coefficient is > 3 times its standard error.

mon among Protestant students and those with other religious affiliations. However, parental occupational status and education had remarkably little impact: they did not affect the probability of boys' drinking at all and girls were only slightly more likely to drink if their fathers were highly educated or their mothers had white-collar jobs.

4.2.3. *Differences in the Behavior of Drinkers*

It is important to ask not only *which* adolescents drink but also *how* they drink. Among the youths who drink at least occasionally, it is possible that the influences on how they behave when drinking are not the same as the influences that led them to become drinkers in the first place. Therefore, we wanted to know whether among the *drinkers* there were any relationships between sex-role orientations and the indexes of (1) quantity–frequency of drinking; (2) drinking problems; and (3) symptomatic drinking.

Among the boys who reported drinking more than one drink a month ($N = 4{,}019$; 63% of the boys surveyed), denial of social obligations was related to greater quantity and frequency of drinking ($r = .107$), more problem consequences of drinking ($r = .141$), and more symptomatic drinking ($r = .163$; all p's $< .001$, one-tailed). The drinking indexes showed smaller but statistically significant relationships with negative attitudes toward traditional masculine success and toward traditional femininity. Among the girls who reported drinking more than one drink a month ($N = 3{,}463$; 51% of the girls surveyed), rejection of traditional femininity and denial of social obligations had small relationships with drinking quantity–frequency (r's $= -.095, .078$), problem consequences (r's $= -.084, .085$), and symptomatic drinking (r's $= -.087, .097$; all p's $< .001$, one-tailed). Rejection of traditional masculine success by the girls had even smaller but still significant relationships with the drinking indexes. It appears that although traditional femininity does not distinguish girls who drink from girls who do not, rejection of traditional femininity may have something to do with *how* the girls drink once they start.

To analyze more thoroughly the relationships between role orientations and drinking, we used multiple regression analysis as well as correlational analyses within grade by ethnic subgroups. The regression analyses summarized in Table 5 suggest that the links between sex-role orientations and drinking were not spurious. With demographic influences controlled, denial of social obligations among the boys was relatively strongly associated with drinking more, drinking more symptomatically, and getting into more trouble related to drinking. The same drinking patterns had consistent but somewhat weaker associations

Table 5. Drinkers: Regression of Drinking Quantity-Frequency, Problem Consequences and Symptomatic Drinking on Demographic Characteristics and Role Orientation

	Drinking characteristics (standardized beta coefficients)					
	Quantity-frequency		Problem consequences		Symptomatic drinking	
	Male	Female	Male	Female	Male	Female
Father's occupation[a]						
1. Manager, owner	−.014	.003	−.028	−.017	.009	.002
2. Office and clerical	−.017	−.009	−.036	−.018	−.002	−.013
3. Skilled worker	−.026	−.024	−.045[b]	−.020	.000	−.006
4. Farmer	.019	.017	.017	.059[c]	.012	.034
5. Semiskilled worker	.000	.006	−.024	−.020	.039	−.009
Mother's occupation[a]						
1. Manager, owner	.015	−.002	.004	.030	−.010	.011
2. Office and clerical	−.022	−.006	−.009	.000	−.010	.009
3. Skilled worker	.007	−.018	.024	.044[b]	.025	.016
4. Farmer	.007	−.015	.014	.053[c]	.017	.008
5. Semiskilled worker	.042[b]	−.026	.039[b]	−.024	.025	−.029
Father's education	−.020	−.005	−.036	−.051[b]	−.040	−.045
Mother's education	.025	.045	.004	.025	.008	.037
Ethnic category[a]						
White	.044	.054	−.090[b]	−.055	−.018	.039
Spanish-American	.042	.000	−.035	−.100[c]	−.024	−.020
Black	.018	.027	−.025	−.025	−.083[c]	−.080[c]
American Indian	.038	.039	.039	.020	.025	.050
Grade in school	.156[d]	.029	.168[d]	.103[d]	.068[d]	.033
Religious affiliation[a]						
Protestant	−.015	−.059	−.015	−.065[b]	−.030	−.014
Catholic	.007	.013	−.039	−.074[b]	−.072[c]	−.048
Jewish	.024	.001	−.035	−.058[c]	−.096[d]	−.125[d]
Other	−.028	−.015	−.008	−.036	−.021	−.023
Role orientation						
Traditional femininity	.011	−.068[c]	.073[c]	−.040	.040	−.044
Masculine success	.019	.041	−.057[b]	.026	−.011	.002
Denial of obligations	.124[d]	.055[b]	.153[d]	.069[c]	.165[d]	.075[c]
Academic achievement	−.124[d]	−.158[d]	−.067[d]	−.105[d]	−.102[d]	−.098[d]
Independence	.078[d]	.099[d]	.057[c]	.033	.136[d]	.130[d]
R^2	.062	.046	.081	.059	.083	.070

[a] Use of dummy variables precludes listing the sixth occupational category (Professional), the category of Oriental ethnicity, and the category for no religious affiliation.
[b] $p \leq .05$, two-tailed.
[c] $p \leq .01$, two-tailed.
[d] $p \leq .001$, two-tailed.

with boys' desire for independence and lack of desire for academic achievement. Desires for masculine success or traditional feminine ideals affected only the problems boys got into over drinking: boys wanting traditional masculine success were *less* likely to get into trouble related to drinking, and boys seeking traditionally feminine ideals were *more* likely to get into trouble.[8] One way to interpret the findings is that boys' drinking tends to become part of a general defiance of social control, but that drinking leads to negative social consequences only when boys act in antisocial ways (as in denying obligations) *or* behave inappropriately in terms of traditional sex roles.

Like the boys, the girls who had negative feelings about academic achievement and social obligations, plus a positive desire for independence, were likely to drink more, in more symptomatic ways, and with more negative social consequences. However, denial of social obligations was not as strong an influence as it was among boys, and among the girls a more general rejection of traditional femininity was associated with the quantity and frequency of drinking. In other regression analyses using traditional femininity as the only role orientation measure (Wilsnack & Wilsnack, 1978b), rejection of traditional femininity had larger, significant beta coefficients indicating a greater effect on drinking quantity–frequency (−.104), problem consequences (−.084), and symptomatic drinking (−.087; all p's $< .001$, two-tailed). The beta coefficients in the analyses presented here are smaller because we have controlled for denial of social obligations and desire for academic achievement, both of which were correlated with drinking girls' desire for traditional femininity (r's of −.510 and .236, respectively). If one recalls that denial of social obligations is itself a measure of antifemininity, and that girls viewed academic achievement as more desirable than boys did, the data show a consistent pattern: girls were likely to drink more heavily, more symptomatically, and with more negative social consequences when they generally rejected standards of behavior traditionally regarded as appropriate for their sex.

Our interpretation of the data thus far has stressed the *rejection* of traditional femininity and traditional standards of social obligation, and the way in which this rejection may increase drinking opportunities and motivations. An alternative interpretation is that adolescents who have a greater desire to *fulfill* social obligations or to *be* traditionally feminine will exercise greater self-restraint in their drinking behavior. Further data analyses, however, do not support this interpretation (see Wilsnack & Wilsnack, 1978a, b). Among drinking boys, for example, regression

[8] Desire for academic achievement was one component of the larger index of desire for masculine success. Controlling for the desire for academic achievement by entering it separately in the regression analysis reduced the apparent impact of success seeking.

analyses showed that denial of obligations was significantly associated with the amount of drinking and with problem consequences only for those boys who were *above* the median in their dislike of social obligations; the beta coefficients for symptomatic drinking were also higher in this group (.141) than among the boys who scored low on denial of obligations (.078). Among drinking girls, only those who were unusually negative about traditional femininity (scoring below the median on the scale) showed significant relationships between *how much* they rejected traditional femininity and how much they drank, how symptomatically they drank, and how much they got into trouble because of drinking. These results favor the belief that adolescent drinking and its undesirable consequences are associated with a rejection of traditional femininity or a more specific rejection of obligations to other people.

The regression analyses in Table 5 indicate that demographic influences on adolescent drinking cannot be completely ignored. Boys in higher grades reported not only more drinking (cf. Table 2) but also more symptomatic drinking and more problems resulting from drinking. Girls were less likely to experience problem consequences of drinking if they had some religious affiliation, but they were more likely to experience problems if they came from farm families, possibly reflecting a more conservative rural attitude toward female drinking. Adolescents of both sexes were less likely to drink in ways symptomatic of alcohol dependence if they were black or if they were Jewish. However, all these relationships were small enough and scattered enough to weaken any belief in a powerful general impact of demographic variables on adolescent drinking.

There remained the possibility, however, that sex roles and drinking would have different relationships within different demographic groups. To assess this possibility, we computed correlations between sex-role orientations and the three drinking indexes for drinking boys and girls in 14 grade × ethnicity subgroups. For drinking boys, the results in Table 6 confirm the link between denial of social obligations and heavier, more problem-related drinking. Denial of social obligations was positively correlated ($p < .10$, one-tailed) with drinking quantity–frequency in 10 of 14 groups, with problem consequences of drinking in 11 of 14 groups, and with symptomatic drinking in 11 of 14 groups (all p's $< 10^{-7}$, binomial theorem). In some groups, the bivariate relationships were quite strong. For example, denial of social obligations explained more than 10% of the variance in measures of symptomatic drinking and problem consequences among blacks. In contrast, neither rejection of masculine success nor rejection of traditional femininity was significantly correlated with any drinking index in more than half of the

Table 6. Drinking Boys: Correlations of Sex-Role Orientations with Drinking Quantity–Frequency, Problem Consequences, and Symptomatic Drinking

	Grade								
	7–8			9–10			11–12		
	Quantity–frequency	Problem consequences	Symptomatic drinking	Quantity–frequency	Problem consequences	Symptomatic drinking	Quantity–frequency	Problem consequences	Symptomatic drinking
White									
Traditional femininity	−.042	−.077[a]	−.034	−.073[a]	−.060[a]	−.113[b]	−.075[c]	−.020	−.093[b]
Masculine success	−.124[b]	−.188[b]	−.136[b]	−.101[b]	−.115[b]	−.072[a]	−.033	−.069[a]	−.100[b]
Denial of obligations	.115[b]	.150[b]	.140[b]	.151[b]	.136[b]	.196[b]	.096[b]	.098[b]	.139[b]
Spanish-American									
Traditional femininity	−.032	−.061	−.026	−.258[c]	−.376[b]	−.076	−.131[d]	−.185[a]	−.142[a]
Masculine success	−.076	−.147[d]	−.162[a]	−.264[c]	−.381[b]	−.068	.007	.078	.055
Denial of obligations	.153[a]	.137[d]	.139[d]	.234[c]	.294[b]	.186[a]	.042	.065	.081
Black									
Traditional femininity	−.243[d]	−.204	−.091	−.265[a]	−.152	−.347[c]	−.160	−.234[a]	−.345[c]
Masculine success	−.205	−.408[c]	−.252[d]	−.347[c]	−.147	−.143	−.028	.167	−.093
Denial of obligations	.230[d]	.482[b]	.330[a]	.196[d]	.366[c]	.430[b]	.086	.416[b]	.406[b]
American Indian									
Traditional femininity	.049	−.154[d]	−.272[c]	.014	.104	.123	−.176[d]	−.143	−.286[c]
Masculine success	.040	−.310[c]	−.288[c]	.049	−.058	.084	.029	−.042	−.164[d]
Denial of obligations	.030	.306[b]	.286[c]	.136[d]	.059	−.028	.258[a]	.204[a]	.265[a]
				9–12					
Oriental[e]									
Traditional femininity	.168	.410	.009	−.205	−.018	.015			
Masculine success	.034	.206	−.093	−.011	−.159	−.168			
Denial of obligations	.291	.553[c]	.610[c]	.257[d]	−.173	−.043			

[a] $P \leq .05$, one-tailed.
[b] $P \leq .001$, one-tailed.
[c] $P \leq .01$, one-tailed.
[d] $P \leq .10$, one-tailed.
[e] Drinkers in grades 9–12 were combined because the total $N = 35$.

subgroups. While the bivariate relationships cannot show how drinking might be linked to a complex configuration of role orientations, they do demonstrate that boys' drinking behavior in all grades and ethnic groups was influenced by a specific antifeminine hostility toward social obligations.

The data presented in Table 7 indicate that among drinking girls, sex-role orientations were associated most clearly with the drinking behavior of white, Spanish-American, and black girls. In these three ethnic groups, 62% of the correlations between sex-role orientations and the drinking indexes were significant at least at the .10 level. Only 18% of the coefficients for American Indian and Oriental girls were similarly significant. Even if we eliminate the scale (traditional femininity) and the ethnic group (whites) that contribute most to the difference, the contrast is still strong: 53% of the coefficients for the two masculinity scales are significant among the Spanish-American and black girls, compared with 27% of the coefficients among the American Indian and Oriental girls.

For the white, Spanish-American, and black girls, a general rejection of traditional femininity was consistently associated with having more drinks more frequently and getting into more trouble as a result (at the .10 level of significance in 7 of 9 subgroups; $p < 10^{-5}$, binomial theorem). Specific rejection of social obligations was linked to symptomatic drinking and also to problems associated with drinking (at the .10 level of significance in 7 of 9 subgroups; $p < 10^{-5}$, binomial theorem). A *negative* attitude toward masculine success had a less consistent relationship with the three drinking indexes, and its coefficients were usually smaller than those for the indexes more relevant to femininity. Thus, for three ethnic groups, girls' drinking was connected to a rejection of traditional feminine ideals but was not connected as clearly to any attitude toward traditional masculinity.

4.2.4. *Sex-Role Orientations, Drinking, and Deviance*

In both sexes, drinking was heavier and resulted in more problem consequences among adolescents who seemed to adopt socially undesirable orientations toward sex roles. An important question is to what extent both drinking and such role orientations may be part of a broader pattern of deviant or antisocial behavior. Toward that end, for the subgroups of drinkers within both sexes, we computed correlations of the three drinking indexes and the three measures of sex-role orientations with an index of self-reported participation in deviant behavior other than alcohol and drug use (e.g., theft, vandalism, truancy, assault).

The results presented in Table 8 show that heavier drinking, more

Table 7. Drinking Girls: Correlations of Sex-Role Orientations with Drinking Quantity–Frequency, Problem Consequences, and Symptomatic Drinking

	Grade								
	7–8			9–10			11–12		
	Quantity–frequency	Problem consequences	Symptomatic drinking	Quantity–frequency	Problem consequences	Symptomatic drinking	Quantity–frequency	Problem consequences	Symptomatic drinking
White									
Traditional femininity	−.099[a]	−.066[b]	−.155[c]	−.154[c]	−.084[d]	−.122[c]	−.100[c]	−.119[c]	−.103[c]
Masculine success	−.079[a]	−.207[c]	−.163[c]	−.082[d]	−.048[b]	−.073[a]	−.029	.014	−.023
Denial of obligations	.040	.052	.105[d]	.121[c]	.055[a]	.093[d]	.078[d]	.085[d]	.092[c]
Spanish-American									
Traditional femininity	−.024	−.244[a]	−.136	−.216[a]	−.071	.050	−.213[a]	−.235[d]	−.097
Masculine success	−.168[b]	−.184[a]	−.097	−.270[d]	.022	−.070	.011	−.093	−.046
Denial of obligations	.026	.140[b]	.262[d]	.084	−.004	−.024	.135[b]	.192[a]	−.005
Black									
Traditional femininity	−.266[b]	−.436[a]	−.185	−.062	−.069	−.178	−.217[b]	−.310[a]	−.463[c]
Masculine success	−.069	−.039	−.173	−.216[b]	−.249[a]	−.035	−.064	−.460[c]	−.520[c]
Denial of obligations	.343[a]	.593[c]	.505[d]	−.200	.334[d]	.212[b]	.398[c]	.536[c]	.492[c]
American Indian									
Traditional femininity	−.122	−.055	.172	.168	.177	.130	.027	−.126	−.066
Masculine success	−.319[a]	−.344[d]	−.076	−.085	.162	−.073	−.237[a]	−.096	−.126
Denial of obligations	.157	.100	−.048	.010	−.142	−.022	.128	.144	.171[b]
				9–12					
Oriental[e]									
Traditional femininity	−.234	.122	−.156	.224	−.233	−.034			
Masculine success	−.435[b]	.159	−.050	.062	−.344[a]	.158			
Denial of obligations	.409[b]	−.021	.291	−.015	.094	.356[a]			

[a] $P \leq .05$, one-tailed.
[b] $P \leq .10$, one-tailed.
[c] $P \leq .001$, one-tailed.
[d] $P \leq .01$, one-tailed.
[e] Drinkers in grades 9–12 were combined because the total $N = 25$.

Table 8. Correlations of Drinkers' Deviant Behavior and Drinking Indexes

	Grade					
	7–8		9–10		11–12	
	Male	Female	Male	Female	Male	Female
White						
Quantity–frequency	.293[a]	.241[a]	.307[a]	.342[a]	.339[a]	.298[a]
Problem consequences	.455[a]	.419[a]	.335[a]	.391[a]	.454[a]	.445[a]
Symptomatic drinking	.616[a]	.622[a]	.556[a]	.499[a]	.506[a]	.481[a]
Spanish-American						
Quantity–frequency	.331[a]	.199[b]	.386[a]	.151[c]	.346[a]	.372[a]
Problem consequences	.549[a]	.411[a]	.565[a]	.341[a]	.355[a]	.480[a]
Symptomatic drinking	.629[a]	.672[a]	.506[a]	.267[d]	.360[a]	.471[a]
Black						
Quantity–frequency	.131	.203	.422[a]	.321[b]	−.122	.386[d]
Problem consequences	.500[a]	.482[d]	.490[a]	.341[d]	.239[b]	.800[a]
Symptomatic drinking	.486[a]	.631[a]	.718[a]	.628[a]	.423[a]	.691[a]
American Indian						
Quantity–frequency	.210[b]	.354[d]	.192[b]	.298[d]	.333[d]	.414[a]
Problem consequences	.491[a]	.311[b]	.179[b]	.388[a]	.422[a]	.356[a]
Symptomatic drinking	.351[a]	.346[d]	.411[a]	.504[a]	.361[a]	.413[a]
			9–12			
Oriental						
Quantity–frequency	.464[b]	.489[b]	.445[d]	−.066		
Problem consequences	.416[b]	.735[a]	.785[a]	.340[c]		
Symptomatic drinking	.823[a]	.876[a]	.829[a]	.226		

[a] $P \leq .001$, one-tailed.
[b] $P \leq .05$, one-tailed.
[c] $P \leq .10$, one-tailed.
[d] $P \leq .01$, one-tailed.
[d] Drinkers were combined for grades 9–12 because of small *N*s.

symptomatic drinking, and increased problems related to drinking were all strongly associated with participation in deviant behavior by both sexes, in all grades and ethnic groups. Deviant behavior was most closely associated with symptomatic drinking (coefficients largest in 10 of 14 groups of boys and 8 of 14 groups of girls) and least closely associated with quantity–frequency of drinking (coefficients smallest in 12 of 14 boys' groups and in 12 of 14 girls' groups). The only apparent sex difference in the correlations is that boys showed a stronger relationship than girls did between deviant behavior and problem consequences of drinking, in 9 of 14 subgroups; however, this could be an artifact of lower variance in girls' scores on problem consequences.

The correlations between deviant behavior and sex-role orientations, shown in Table 9, are smaller than the correlations between deviant behavior and drinking. Thus, sex-role orientations are neither a simple reflection of deviance, nor are they irrelevant to it. The deviant behavior of drinking boys appeared to be related most consistently to their denial of social obligations, particularly among whites, Spanish-Americans, and blacks (at the .10 level of significance in 8 of 9 subgroups; $p < 10^{-7}$, binomial theorem). Correlations were less consistent and generally smaller for the other two measures of sex-role orientations and were insignificant for all three measures among Oriental boys and

Table 9. Correlations of Drinkers' Deviant Behavior and Sex-Role Orientations

	Grade					
	7–8		9–10		11–12	
	Male	Female	Male	Female	Male	Female
White						
Traditional femininity	−.140[a]	−.222[a]	−.137[a]	−.144[a]	−.090[b]	−.119[a]
Masculine success	−.196[a]	−.238[a]	−.128[a]	−.159[a]	−.108[a]	−.123[a]
Denial of obligations	.207[a]	.176[a]	.232[a]	.141[a]	.115[a]	.128[a]
Spanish-American						
Traditional femininity	−.044	−.086	−.313[a]	−.024	−.117[c]	−.126[c]
Masculine success	−.058	−.052	−.343[a]	−.020	.028	.077
Denial of obligations	.153[d]	.192[d]	.334[a]	−.026	.121[c]	.174[d]
Black						
Traditional femininity	−.153	−.264[c]	−.130	−.215[c]	−.096	−.382[b]
Masculine success	−.388[d]	−.350[d]	−.079	−.021	.141	−.516[a]
Denial of obligations	.404[b]	.557[a]	.267[d]	.102	.097	.520[a]
American Indian						
Traditional femininity	−.286[b]	−.300[d]	−.018	.053	−.070	−.127
Masculine success	−.291[b]	−.384[b]	−.063	−.131	−.048	−.290[b]
Denial of obligations	.339[a]	.070	.119	−.071	.091	−.034
			9–12			
Oriental[e]						
Traditional femininity	−.019	−.624[b]	.141	−.476[b]		
Masculine success	−.185	−.471[c]	−.121	−.448[d]		
Denial of obligations	.294	.680[b]	−.142	.418[d]		

[a] $P \leq .001$, one-tailed.
[b] $P \leq .01$, one-tailed.
[c] $P \leq .10$, one-tailed.
[d] $P \leq .05$, one-tailed.
[e] Drinkers in grades 9–12 were combined because the boys' $N = 35$ and the girls' $N = 25$.

American Indian boys in high school. Thus, deviant behavior appears most closely linked to that aspect of traditional masculinity that involves rejection of other people's demands or expectations, but the link is important only in certain cultural contexts.

The drinking girls showed a very different pattern. Their deviant behavior was related to all the sex-role measures; it increased with rejection of social obligations, traditional femininity, and masculine success. Furthermore, these relationships occurred across all ethnic groups (for each measure, at the .10 level of significance in at least 9 of 14 subgroups; p's $< 10^{-5}$, binomial theorem). Drinking girls' deviance seemed to be associated not with culture-specific or sex-specific role standards but with a more general abandonment of socially desirable ideals. While deviant behavior may entail only a few culturally limited changes in boys' roles, it seems to involve a more wholesale change in attitudes and role orientations for girls of any ethnic background.

At this point, it is not possible to specify the causal relationships among drinking, deviant behavior, and sex-role orientations, because the causal influences may operate in more than one direction. For example, boys' denial of social obligations may facilitate drinking and deviant behavior, which in turn may need to be rationalized by further denial of obligations. Girls rejecting traditional femininity may express this rejection by drinking more freely and becoming involved in deviance, but negative social reactions to their drinking and misbehavior may provoke them to be even more hostile to traditional expectations about how they should properly behave. The relative impact of different causal influences may be impossible to determine until time-ordered data becomes available. In the meanwhile, a reasonably cautious view is that drinking, deviant behavior, and a rejection of traditionally feminine responsibilities and ideals are a mutually reinforcing configuration that may play a part in a boy's effort to establish his masculinity and in a girl's refusal to behave according to traditional ideas of femininity.

4.3. Discussion

The results of our analysis of national survey data make clear that sex differences in adolescent drinking were still present in the mid-1970s. Even when we controlled for effects of ethnic and grade differences, boys were consistently more likely to drink than girls, and among the adolescent drinkers, boys drank larger amounts more frequently, showed more signs of dependence on alcohol, and got into more problems as a result of drinking. While these sex differences were smaller than some previous community surveys had reported, they had clearly not disappeared.

The results also confirm that there are links between drinking behavior and more general role orientations. To understand adolescent drinking one must take into account the social roles that adolescents are trying to perform. Of most interest in the present research, drinking behavior is associated with sex-role orientations, in ways that are consistent but not identical for boys and girls.

4.3.1. *Interpreting Boys' and Girls' Drinking*

Boys in this national sample showed more of a tendency than girls to deny social obligations, perhaps asserting their masculinity by rejecting a concern traditionally defined as feminine. The more the boys denied obligations, the more likely they were to drink heavily and symptomatically and to get into problems over their drinking. Denial of obligations was also associated with participation in antisocial deviance, but only in certain ethnic groups (white, black, and Spanish-American boys).

These findings could be compatible with either of the psychodynamic perspectives summarized earlier. Dependency theorists might view the denial of social obligations as an attempt to suppress unacceptable feelings of interdependence with other people, while power theorists might interpret the denial as an attempt to be free of other people's control. However, such motives may not be necessary to cause an individual to deny social obligations or to connect that role orientation to drinking. We can suggest at least four other reasons why denial of social obligations might lead to increased drinking. First, by trying to deny obligations to other people, a boy may also insulate himself from any restraints that others might have imposed on his drinking behavior. Second, drinking may serve as a symbol by which a boy can show his rebellion against adults who want him to behave properly and not to have adult privileges. Third, a boy may find that the effects of alcohol help to reduce his feelings of anxiety or guilt about violating social obligations. And fourth, a boy may learn that being under the influence of alcohol gives him a socially accepted excuse for being irresponsible in his behavior toward other people.

Interpreting boys' drinking as part of a role of resisting social obligations fits well with two themes in the literature on male drinking. Several authors (Alexander, 1967; Madsen, 1961; Zucker & Barron, 1973) have presented data or hypotheses suggesting that drinking is a symbolic, and perhaps also a comforting, part of rebellion against authority, in particular against parental authority. The people that a boy most wants to deny obligations to are often his parents. Another theme, emphasized by MacAndrew and Edgerton (1969), is that the socially recognized and interpreted effects of drinking may provide an escape from responsibility. Boys who want to deny their responsibilities to other people may drink because they know they cannot and will not be held fully responsible for their behavior when intoxicated.

Girls' drinking appears to be associated with a broad rejection of traditional feminine ideals, including not only social responsibilities but also positive emotional ties with other people, physical attractiveness, and family life. The effect of this rejection is not so much to start a girl drinking but rather to influence *how* she drinks once she begins. Drinking girls who reject femininity in one way or another are likely to drink larger quantities of alcohol more often, to show more symptoms of alcohol dependence, and to get into more trouble because of drinking. These links between drinking behavior and distaste for traditional femininity occur only in certain ethnic groups (white, black, Spanish-American). However, rejection of traditional femininity is related to participation in deviant behavior by girls of all ethnic groups.

Increased drinking and drinking problems among girls who abandon traditional femininity seem consistent with the few published findings about young women with drinking problems (see page 192). Furthermore, the drinking may be used for purposes similar to those suggested for boys, as a symbolic rebellion against traditional expectations (here, expectations about femininity) and as insulation against the stressful consequences of that rebellion. However, the results here seem inconsistent with other research showing overt *femininity* among older female problem drinkers (see pages 190–191).

The patterns of femininity among younger and older female drinkers may not be contradictory if women develop drinking problems for different reasons at different ages. Some adolescent girls who reject traditional femininity and drink heavily for symbolic and stress-relieving purposes may progress relatively quickly from their first drinking experiences to dependence on alcohol. Girls who *adhere* to traditional femininity may be better protected from early drinking problems, but their commitment to femininity may expose some of them to role crises and conflicts later in life that they may cope with by drinking.

4.3.2. *Ethnic Differences*

Among both boys and girls, the relation of sex-role orientations to drinking and deviance is affected by ethnicity. Specifically, among Oriental and American Indian boys who drink, denial of social obligations is related to the indexes of drinking and drinking problems but not as clearly to the index of deviant behavior. Among Oriental and American Indian girls who drink, rejection of traditional femininity is related to deviance but not to drinking behavior.

There are several reasons that the behavioral implications of rejecting traditional femininity in general or social obligations in particular might be less consistent among Oriental and American Indian students than among the rest. Of the five ethnic groups studied, these two subcultures differ the most from the culture of the white majority. Furthermore, subcultural influences on these students may have been unusually strong because the stratified-cluster sampling procedure drew them from locales where their ethnic communities were likely to be large and concentrated. It is also possible that the categories "Oriental" and "American Indian" are more heterogeneous than other ethnic categories. Under each heading, several nationalities or tribes with different relationships between sex-role orientations and drinking or deviance may have combined in a way that obscured these relationships for the whole category of respondents.

But why would denial of social obligations be linked to boys' drinking in all ethnic groups, while in all ethnic groups of drinking girls, there is a link between rejection of traditional femininity and deviance? The answer may be that among boys, the antifeminine denial of social obligations is connected to assuming a masculine role, while among girls, rejection of traditional femininity involves abandoning one sex role without necessarily having an alternative to adopt. Thus, among drinking boys, denial of social obligations and drinking may both be universally associated with ideas about masculinity, but whether masculine role-playing of this kind directs a boy into antisocial deviance may depend on the nature of the ethnic community in which he lives. Among drinking girls, rejection of traditional femininity can leave girls from any cultural background roleless and relatively uninhibited about participation in antisocial deviance, but whether that deviance includes drinking or not may depend on cultural differences.

4.3.3. *The Size of Relationships*

To interpret relationships between sex-role orientations and adolescent drinking, we must also try to explain why the observed relationships are so small. It would be easy to blame the small size of coefficients on measurement problems. The scales of traditional femininity and denial of social obligations are short, were constructed *post hoc* from available items, and have only modest interitem covariance. Furthermore, the scales refer to ideals rather than to current self-perceptions or activities, and that may attenuate their relevance to current drinking and deviant behavior.

However, we believe that there may be more fundamental reasons that the links between sex-role orientations and drinking do not appear strong. First, it is becoming evident to many researchers that "masculinity" and "femininity" are multidimensional concepts (see, for example, Constantinople, 1973; Heilbrun, 1968). It may be that only a few configurations of "masculine" or "feminine" characteristics are associated with adolescent drinking; for example, the survey data seem to indicate that while denial of social obligations is important for boys' drinking, desire for traditional masculine success is not. Furthermore, the configurations of sex-role characteristics relevant to drinking might include socially *un*desirable aspects not adequately assessed in the present survey. A boy's desire to be physically aggressive or a girl's distaste for traditionally feminine passivity or submissiveness might combine with other role orientations to intensify drinking and its attendant problems.[9] To measure traditional femininity as a single scale of socially desirable ideals, and to measure a single aspect of male antifemininity, may mean a failure to detect complex relationships between how adolescents drink and how they orient themselves to traditional ideas about being masculine or feminine.

A second possibility is that recent changes in sex roles and drinking behavior have eroded the connections between them. While drinking may still be an important aspect of male social behavior, it may now be so commonplace among boys (79% of the 11th- and 12th-grade respondents drank, and even 48% of the 7th- and 8th-graders) that it is not particularly useful as a way of showing defiance of social obligations. Furthermore, since 51% of the girls in the survey drank and 72% did not believe "it is worse for a woman to drink than it is for a man," drinking may also be less useful than previously for showing a general rejection of traditional femininity. Finally, it may be that adolescents of both sexes are becoming less concerned in general with whether their personal desires fit masculine or feminine stereotypes, with the result that scales measuring adherence to the stereotypes become less reliable and more loosely associated with other behavior. Consistent with this interpretation, we found it impossible to devise scales of traditional femininity and masculinity simply by use of factor analysis or multiple discriminant analysis of socially desirable ideals.

A third explanation for small relationships between sex-role orientations and adolescent drinking behavior is that the relationships, however skillfully measured, are indeed small. Sex-role orientations are only one of many influences on drinking behavior. Other influences linked more closely and powerfully to adolescent drinking have been

[9] Alternatively, rejection of certain socially undesirable sex-role characteristics (e.g., traditionally feminine passivity, submissiveness, or emotionality) might imply a degree of psychological health that would be associated with *fewer* drinking problems.

identified elsewhere, such as relations with parents and peers and experiences with deviant behavior (Jessor & Jessor, 1977; Margulies *et al.*, 1977; Zucker, 1976). Sex-role orientations may affect drinking behavior indirectly by influencing these variables or directly under certain conditions specified by these variables and others, such as ethnicity and attitudes toward drinking. We find it easiest to believe that sex-role orientations, as personal ideals, are not the basis for a theory or a general interpretation of adolescent drinking but rather are an irreducible part of some much more complex explanation of how adolescents drink.

5. Conclusions

The persistent differences between boys' and girls' drinking attest to the influence of sex roles. One cannot ignore the evidence that boys are still more likely to drink than girls are, and that boys are likely to drink more heavily, more symptomatically, and with more problem consequences. One also cannot ignore the evidence that these differences are declining at a time when sex roles are changing.

However, it is much more difficult to say *how* sex roles are influencing adolescent drinking. There are at least four different ways that traditional ideas about sex roles might influence how young people drink: (1) by creating different opportunities for boys and girls to drink; (2) by affirming norms that obligate boys and girls to behave differently toward alcohol; (3) by arousing different needs and motives for using alcohol; and (4) by making drinking behavior a way to symbolize the sex roles that boys or girls try to perform. At present, it is hard to estimate the relative importance of these influences or the extent to which they may interact.

Furthermore, there is the possibility that the effects of traditional sex roles may not all operate consistently to make boys drink more and girls drink less. A boy who would drink to show an antifeminine disdain for social constraints on his behavior might also restrain his own drinking to protect his masculine success and leadership among his peers. We know from the national survey data that some girls drink as part of a declaration of independence from traditional femininity, but we wonder whether this finding may conceal other girls who drink to soothe the effects of failure in trying to be traditionally feminine (e.g., who find themselves unattractive or without someone to love). To understand how sex roles are linked to adolescent drinking, it is inadequate to look only for one-dimensional or one-directional relationships.

Finally, as ideas about sex roles change, the influence of sex roles on drinking may change also. As drinking becomes common among *both* boys and girls, it may seem less useful to boys as a symbol of masculinity; on the other hand, some boys may feel that they must resort to more extreme drinking behavior to demonstrate that they are masculine and not feminine. A decline of traditional stereotypes about femininity may increase girls' opportunities to drink; it may also reduce some girls' need to drink in response to uncomfortable social pressures to be "feminine," while increasing the utility of alcohol for girls who feel distress from trying to live by traditional standards of femininity that are no longer respected or supported by their peers. Given this diversity of possible consequences, one should not expect recent sex-role changes to have a simple, direct relationship to adolescent drinking behavior.

In short, the ways in which sex roles may influence adolescent drinking are complicated, subtle, and hard to disentangle. However, this complexity does not imply that there is no general pattern in the relationships between sex roles and drinking behavior. We believe that there *is* a general pattern, suggested by both the previous research literature and the survey data analyzed here, a pattern that distinguishes boys' drinking from girls' drinking. Among boys, drinking has tended to be part of performing a well-defined, well-recognized masculine role, separate from and opposed to traditional feminine roles. Among girls, drinking has tended to be *roleless*, associated with abandoning one set of traditional behavior standards but not with adopting some well-established alternative set of standards.

Previous ethnographic and psychological studies have pointed out how young men drink to show their ability to perform desired traditional masculine roles. The national survey data analyzed here show that growing up (as indicated by grade in school) increases boys' drinking more than girls', perhaps reflecting increasing attempts by boys to enact what they believe to be adult male roles. The data also show a specific positive association between boys' drinking and denial of social obligations, a style of behavior by which boys can claim to be masculine by rejecting a traditionally feminine sense of social responsibility. In many ways, drinking and denial of social obligations can be mutually supportive behavior. Thus, drinking may seem like a natural accompaniment to a boy's attempts to appear positively and traditionally masculine.

For girls, on the other hand, drinking is not an integral part of a social role traditionally available to them. Instead, it seems to accompany a rejection of traditionally assigned roles, involving not only a denial of social obligations but in several ethnic groups (white, Spanish-American, black) a generalized negative attitude toward traditional femininity. And for girls who abandon traditional femininity and drink, there is no well-defined, socially accepted alternative role ready and waiting. This conclusion is consistent with the data showing that rejection of traditional femininity is instead associated with participation in antisocial deviance, more consistently among drinking girls than among drinking boys. While drinking may be a symbol and a solace for girls who want to be untraditional, there is nothing to suggest that it is a well-integrated part of a socially supported new lifestyle. Perhaps a loose connection between girls' drinking and their behavior other than deviance explains why the variables in our data analysis were not quite as good for predicting how girls drank as they were for predicting how boys drank.

If our speculation about the sex difference in drinking behavior is accurate, it may have important implications for adolescent drinking problems. Boys may be propelled into excessive drinking partly by their attempts to live up to certain ideas about masculinity, but such drinking as role playing may be limited to those social occasions when boys perceive an opportunity to prove their manhood by use of alcohol. In contrast, girls may not experience specific role demands to drink; even as a symbol of defying tradition, alcohol may be convenient rather than necessary. However, if there is no appropriate setting or role in which a girl can normally drink more than a small amount, then any excessive drinking by a girl will run the risk of unrestricted negative sanctions, treating the girl as deviant, with consequences that may not help to bring the drinking under control.

The sex differences we have described and interpreted in this chapter are only one of many influences on adolescent drinking behavior. One cannot construct a theory of adolescent drinking, or a strategy for preventing adolescent drinking problems, based simply on sex roles. However, the available literature and our own research do suggest two ways that sex roles should be taken into account in framing policies concerning adolescent drinking behavior. First, it is important to understand the sex-role performance that is part of the context for drinking behavior, for example, a boy's attempts to display traditional masculinity or a girl's attempts to disregard traditional femininity. One approach to changing adolescent drinking behavior would be to change this role context. Education or social change that encourages flexible or "androgynous" sex-role orientations might reduce the importance of traditional roles that adolescents try to conform to or rebel against by drinking.

A second, related point is that it is important to accelerate the decline in the importance of drinking as a symbol of sex-role orientations. The less that drinking seems an effective way to symbolize a boy's masculinity or a girl's liberation from traditional femininity, the less likely adolescents will be to drink for these utilitarian purposes. However, it may be hard to convince adolescents that drinking says little about their sex roles unless there are changes in how alcohol is advertised and in how parents teach their children to drink.

Our policy suggestions should not obscure the fact that knowledge about sex roles is likely to make only a modest contribution to preventing adolescent drinking problems. There may be a lesson in the literature and in the research summarized in this chapter: the time for simple explanations or simple solutions for adolescent drinking problems is long since past. If we have succeeded here in making the explanations a little more complex, that may be accomplishment enough.

ACKNOWLEDGMENTS

We thank Peter Burke, Richard Jessor, John Scanzoni, and Sheldon Stryker for helpful comments on earlier analyses of the findings presented here. We are also grateful to Thomas C. Harford and Ann Miksovic for technical assistance.

References

Abad, V. & Suarez, J. Cross-cultural aspects of alcoholism among Puerto Ricans. *Proceedings of the 4th Annual Alcoholism Conference of the National Institute on Alcohol Abuse and Alcoholism.* Washington, D.C.: Department of Health, Education, and Welfare, 1975, pp. 282–294.

Alexander, C. N., Jr. Alcohol and adolescent rebellion. *Social Forces,* 1967, *45,* 542–550.

Anderson, S. C. Patterns of identification in alcoholic women. Unpublished doctoral dissertation, Graduate School of Social Work, Rutgers University, 1976.

Ashenfelter, O. Some statistical difficulties in using dummy dependent variables. In W. G. Bowen & T. A. Einegan (Eds.), *The economics of labor force participation.* Princeton: Princeton University Press, 1969, pp. 644–648.

Bacon, M. The dependency-conflict hypothesis and the frequency of drunkenness: Further evidence from a cross-cultural study. *Quarterly Journal of Studies on Alcohol,* 1974, *35,* 863–876.

Bacon, M., & Jones, M. B. *Teen-age drinking.* New York: Thomas Y. Crowell, 1968.

Bakan, D. *The quality of human existence.* Boston: Beacon Press, 1966.

Barry, H. Cross-cultural evidence that dependency conflict motivates drunkenness. In M. W. Everett, J. O. Waddell, & D. B. Heath (Eds.), *Cross-cultural approaches to the study of alcohol: An interdisciplinary perspective.* The Hague: Mouton, 1976, pp. 249–264.

Beckman, L. J. Sex-role conflict in alcoholic women: Myth or reality. *Journal of Abnormal Psychology,* 1978, *87,* 408–417.

Bem, S. L. The measurement of psychological androgyny. *Journal of Consulting and Clinical Psychology,* 1974, *42,* 155–162.

Berner, P., & Solms, W. Alkoholismus bei Frauen. *Wein Zeitschrift der Nervenheilklinik,* 1952, *7.* Abstracted in *Quarterly Journal of Studies on Alcohol,* 1954, *15,* 128.

Blane, H. T. *The personality of the alcoholic: Guises of dependency.* New York: Harper & Row, 1968.

Blane, H. T., & Chafetz, M. E. Dependency conflict and sex-role identity in drinking delinquents. *Quarterly Journal of Studies on Alcohol*, 1971, *32*, 1025–1039.
Block, J. H. Conceptions of sex role: Some cross-cultural and longitudinal perspectives. *American Psychologist*, 1973, *28*, 512–526.
Boyatzis, R. E. The effect of alcohol consumption on the aggressive behavior of men. *Quarterly Journal of Studies on Alcohol*, 1975, *35*, 959–972.
Broverman, I. K., Vogel, S. R., Broverman, D. M., Clarkson, F. E., & Rosenkrantz, P. S. Sex-role stereotypes: A current appraisal. *Journal of Social Issues*, 1972, *28*, 59–78.
Cahalan, D. *Problem drinkers: A national survey*. San Francisco: Jossey-Bass, 1970.
Cahalan, D., Cisin, I. H., & Crossley, H. M. *American drinking practices: A national study of drinking behavior and attitudes* (Monogr. No. 6). New Brunswick, N.J.: Rutgers Center of Alcohol Studies, 1969.
Child, I. L., Barry, H., & Bacon, M. K. A cross-cultural study of drinking. III: Sex differences. *Quarterly Journal of Studies on Alcohol*, Supplement No. 3, 1965, pp. 49–61.
Clark, W. B. Sex roles and alcoholic beverage usage. Working Paper No. 16, Social Research Group, School of Public Health, University of California at Berkeley, 1967.
Clark, W. B. Contextual and situational variables in drinking behavior. Draft report prepared for NIAAA under Contract ADM-281-76-0027. Berkeley, Calif.: Social Research Group, 1977.
Constantinople, A. Masculinity–femininity: An exception to a famous dictum? *Psychological Bulletin*, 1973, *80*, 389–407.
Curlee, J. Alcoholic women: Some considerations for further research. *Bulletin of the Menninger Clinic*, 1967, *31*, 154–163.
David, D. S., & Brannon, R. *The forty-nine percent majority: The male sex role*. Reading, Mass.: Addison-Wesley, 1976.
Davis, W. N. Drinking: A search for power or nurturance? In D. C. McClelland, W. N. Davis, R. Kalin, & E. Wanner (Eds.), *The drinking man: Alcohol and human motivation*. New York: Free Press, 1972, pp. 198–213.
Driscoll, G. Z., & Barr, H. L. Comparative study of drug dependent and alcoholic women at Eagleville Hospital and Rehabilitation Center. Paper presented at the Alcohol and Drug Problems Association of North America 23rd Annual Meeting, Atlanta, Georgia, September, 1972.
Durand, D. E. Effects of drinking on the power and affiliation needs of middle-aged females. *Journal of Clinical Psychology*, 1975, *3*, 549–553.
Ellis, L. J., & Bentler, P. M. Traditional sex-determined role standards and sex stereotypes. *Journal of Personality and Social Psychology*, 1973, *25*, 28–34.
Gaudreau, P. Factor analysis of the Bem Sex-Role Inventory. *Journal of Consulting and Clinical Psychology*, 1977, *45*, 299–302.
Gold, M., & Reimer, D. J. Changing patterns of delinquent behavior among Americans 13 through 16 years old: 1967–1972. *Crime and Delinquency Literature*, 1975, *7*, 483–517.
Goldberger, A. S. *Econometric theory*. New York: Wiley, 1964.
Gomberg, E. S. Risk factors related to alcohol problems among women: Proneness and vulnerability. Paper presented at the NIAAA Workshop on Alcoholism and Alcohol Abuse among Women, Jekyll Island, Georgia, April, 1978.
Gough, H. G. The California Psychological Inventory. Palo Alto, Calif.: Consulting Psychologists Press, 1956.
Hanson, D. J. Drinking attitudes and behaviors among college students. *Alcohol and Drug Education*, 1974, *19*, 6–14.
Harford, T. C. Contextual drinking patterns among men and women. Paper presented at the Eighth Annual Medical-Scientific Conference of the National Council on Alcoholism National Alcoholism Forum, San Diego, May 1977.

Heilbrun, A. B., Jr. Sex role, instrumental-expressive behavior, and psychopathology in females. *Journal of Abnormal Psychology*, 1968, *73*, 131–136.

Higgins, P. C., Albrecht, G. L., & Albrecht, M. H. Black–white adolescent drinking: The myth and the reality. *Social Problems*, 1977, *25*, 215–224.

Jellinek, E. M. The symbolism of drinking: A culture-historical approach. *Journal of Studies on Alcohol*, 1977, *38*, 849–865.

Jessor, R., & Jessor, S. L. Adolescent development and the onset of drinking: A longitudinal study. *Journal of Studies on Alcohol*, 1975, *36*, 27–51.

Jessor, R., & Jessor, S. L. *Problem behavior and psychosocial development: A longitudinal study of youth*. New York: Academic Press, 1977.

Jessor, R., Graves, T., Hanson, R. C., & Jessor, S. L. *Society, personality, and deviant behavior: A study of a tri-ethnic community*. New York: Holt, Rinehart & Winston, 1968.

Johnson, P. Sex differences in drinking practices. Working note prepared for the National Institute on Alcohol Abuse and Alcoholism. Santa Monica: The Rand Corporation, 1978.

Johnson, S., & Garzon, S. R. Women and alcoholism: Past imperfect and future indefinite. Paper presented at the Annual Conference of the Association for Women in Psychology, St. Louis, Missouri, February, 1977.

Jones, M. C. Personality correlates and antecedents of drinking patterns in adult males. *Journal of Consulting and Clinical Psychology*, 1968, *32*, 2–12.

Kammeier, M. L., Hoffman, H., & Loper, R. G. Personality characteristics of alcoholics as college freshman and at time of treatment. *Quarterly Journal of Studies on Alcohol*, 1973, *34*, 390–399.

Kim, J.-O., & Curry, J. The treatment of missing data in multivariate analysis. *Sociological Methods & Research*. 1977, *6*, 215–240.

Kinsey, B. A. *The female alcoholic: A social psychological study*. Springfield, Ill.: Charles C Thomas, 1966.

Knupfer, G. Female drinking patterns. Paper presented at the North American Association of Alcohol Programs 15th Annual Meeting, Washington, D.C., September, 1964.

Kunitz, S. J., & Levy, J. E. Changing ideas of alcohol use among Navajo Indians. *Quarterly Journal of Studies on Alcohol*, 1974, *35*, 243–259.

Lang, A. R., Goeckner, D. J., Adesso, V. J., & Marlatt, G. A. Effects of alcohol on aggression in male social drinkers. *Journal of Abnormal Psychology*, 1975, *84*, 508–518.

MacAndrew, C., & Edgerton, R. B. *Drunken comportment: A social explanation*. Chicago: Aldine, 1969.

Mackelprang, A. J. Missing data in factor analysis and multiple regression. *Midwest Journal of Political Science*, 1970, *14*, 493–505.

Maddox, G. L., & McCall, B. C. *Drinking among teenagers: A sociological interpretation of alcohol use by high-school students* (Monogr. No. 4). New Brunswick, N.J.: Rutgers Center of Alcohol Studies, 1964.

Maddox, G. L., & Williams, J. R. Drinking behavior of Negro collegians. *Quarterly Journal of Studies on Alcohol*, 1968, *29*, 117–129.

Madsen, W. The alcoholic agringado. *American Anthropologist*, 1961, *66*, 355–361.

Margulies, R. Z., Kessler, R. C., & Kandel, D. B. A longitudinal study of onset of drinking among high school students. *Journal of Studies on Alcohol*, 1977, *38*, 897–912.

Massot, Hammel, & Deliry, Alcoolisme féminin: Données statistiques et psychopathologiques. *Journal de Médecine de Lyon*, 1956, *37*, 265–269. Abstracted in *Quarterly Journal of Studies on Alcohol*, 1957, *18*, 144.

McClelland, D. C., & Davis, W. N. The influence of unrestrained power concerns on drinking in working-class men. In D. C. McClelland, W. N. Davis, R. Kalin, & E. Wanner (Eds.), *The drinking man: Alcohol and human motivation*. New York: Free Press, 1972, pp. 142–161.

McClelland, D. C., Davis, W. N., Kalin, R., & Wanner, E. *The drinking man: Alcohol and human motivation.* New York: Free Press, 1972.

McClelland, D. C., & Wilsnack, S. C. The effects of drinking on thoughts about power and restraint. In D. C. McClelland, W. N. Davis, R. Kalin, & E. Wanner (Eds.), *The drinking man: Alcohol and human motivation.* New York: Free Press, 1972, pp. 123–161.

McCord, W., & McCord, J. *Origins of alcoholism.* Stanford, Calif.: Stanford University Press, 1960.

Mulford, H. A., & Miller, D. E. Drinking in Iowa. II: The extent of drinking and selected sociocultural categories. *Quarterly Journal of Studies on Alcohol,* 1960, *21,* 26–39.

O'Connor, J. Cultural influences and drinking behavior: Drinking in Ireland and England: A tri-ethnic study of drinking among young people and their parents. *Journal of Alcoholism,* 1975, *10,* 94–121.

Parker, F. B. Sex role adjustment in women alcoholics. *Quarterly Journal of Studies on Alcohol,* 1972, *33,* 647–657.

Parker, F. B. Sex-role adjustment and drinking disposition of women college students. *Journal of Studies on Alcohol,* 1975, *36,* 1570–1573.

Pattison, E. M. Personality profiles of 50 alcoholic women. Summary of unpublished study. University of California, Irvine, 1975.

Ponzo, Z., & Strowig, R. W. Relations among sex-role identity and selected intellectual and non-intellectual factors for high school freshman and seniors. *Journal of Educational Research,* 1973, *67,* 137–141.

Rachal, J. V., Williams, J. R., Brehm, M. L., Cavanaugh, B., Moore, R. P., & Eckerman, W. C. A national study of adolescent drinking behavior, attitudes and correlates. Research Triangle Park, N.C.: Research Triangle Institute, 1975.

Robins, L. N. *Deviant children grown up: A sociological and psychiatric study of sociopathic personality.* Baltimore: Williams & Wilkins, 1966.

San Mateo County, Department of Public Health and Welfare. Surveillance of Drug Use Study. San Mateo, Calif., 1973.

Schuckit, M. A., & Morrissey, E. R. Alcoholism in women: Some clinical and social perspectives with an emphasis on possible subtypes. In M. Greenblatt & M. A. Schuckit (Eds.), *Alcoholism problems in women and children.* New York: Grune & Stratton, 1976, pp. 5–35.

Scida, J., & Vannicelli, M. Sex-role conflict and female drinking. *Journal of Studies on Alcohol,* 1979, *40,* 28–44.

Spence, J. T., Helmreich, R., & Stapp, J. Ratings of self and peers on sex role attributes and their relation to self-esteem and conceptions of masculinity and femininity. *Journal of Personality and Social Psychology,* 1975, *32,* 29–39.

Stafford, R. A., & Petway, J. M. Stigmatization of men and women problem drinkers and their spouses: Differential perception and leveling of sex differences. *Journal of Studies on Alcohol,* 1977, *38,* 2109–2121.

Sterne, M. W. Drinking patterns and alcoholism among American Negroes. In D. J. Pittman (Ed.), *Alcoholism.* New York: Harper & Row, 1967, pp. 66–99.

Straus, R., & Bacon, S. D. *Drinking in college.* New Haven: Yale University Press, 1953.

Tomeh, A. K. Sex role orientation and structural correlates. Paper presented at the Annual Meeting of the American Sociological Association, Chicago, August, 1977.

Topper, M. D. Drinking patterns, culture change, sociability, and Navajo "adolescents." *Addictive Diseases,* 1974, *1,* 97–116.

Treviño, M. E. Machismo alcoholism: Mexican-American machismo drinking. *Proceedings of the 4th Annual Alcoholism Conference of the National Institute on Alcohol Abuse and Alcoholism.* Washington, D.C.: Department of Health, Education, & Welfare, 1975, pp. 295–301.

Ullman, A. D. Sex differences in the first drinking experience. *Quarterly Journal of Studies on Alcohol*, 1957, *18*, 229–239.

U.S. Department of Health, Education and Welfare. *Alcohol and health*. First Special Report to the U.S. Congress. Washington, D.C.: Government Printing Office, 1971.

U.S. Department of Health, Education and Welfare. *Alcohol and health: New knowledge*. Second Special Report to the U.S. Congress. Washington, D.C.: Government Printing Office, 1974.

U.S. Senate, Committee on Labor and Public Welfare, Subcommittee on Alcoholism and Narcotics. Alcohol Abuse among Women: Special Problems and Unmet Needs. Hearings, September 29, 1976.

Wall, J. H. A study of alcoholism in women. *American Journal of Psychiatry*, 1937, *93*, 943–952.

Waters, C. W., Waters, L. K., & Pincus, S. Factor analysis of masculine and feminine sex-typed items from the Bem Sex-Role Inventory. *Psychological Reports*, 1977, *40*, 567–570.

Wechsler, H. Epidemiology of male/female drinking. Paper presented at the NIAAA Workshop on Alcoholism and Alcohol Abuse among Women, Jekyll Island, Georgia, April, 1978.

Wechsler, H., & McFadden, M. Sex differences in adolescent alcohol and drug use: A disappearing phenomenon. *Journal of Studies on Alcohol*, 1976, *37*, 1291–1301.

Widseth, J., & Mayer, J. Drinking behavior and attitudes toward alcohol in delinquent girls. *International Journal of the Addictions*, 1971, *6*, 453–461.

Wiggins, J. S., & Holzmuller, A. Psychological androgyny and interpersonal behavior. *Journal of Consulting and Clinical Psychology*, 1978, *46*, 40–52.

Wilsnack, R. W., & Wilsnack, S. C. Drinking and denial of social obligations among adolescent boys. Paper presented at the Annual Meeting of the Society for the Study of Social Problems, San Francisco, September, 1978. (a)

Wilsnack, R. W., & Wilsnack, S. C. Sex roles and drinking among adolescent girls. *Journal of Studies on Alcohol*, 1978, *39*, 1855–1874. (b)

Wilsnack, S. C. Sex-role identity in female alcoholism. *Journal of Abnormal Psychology*, 1973, *82*, 253–261.

Wilsnack, S. C. The effects of social drinking on women's fantasy. *Journal of Personality*, 1974, *42*, 43–61.

Wilsnack, S. C. The impact of sex roles on women's alcohol use and abuse. In M. Greenblatt & M. A. Schuckit (Eds.), *Alcoholism problems in women and children*. New York: Grune & Stratton, 1976, pp. 37–63.

Wood, H. P., & Duffy, E. L. Psychological factors in alcoholic women. *American Journal of Psychiatry*, 1966, *123*, 341–345.

Zucker, R. A. Sex-role identity patterns and drinking behavior of adolescents. *Quarterly Journal of Studies on Alcohol*, 1968, *29*, 868–884.

Zucker, R. A. Parental influences on the drinking patterns of their children. In M. Greenblatt & M. A. Schuckit (Eds.), *Alcoholism problems in women and children*. New York: Grune & Stratton, 1976, pp. 211–238.

Zucker, R. A., & Barron, F. H. Parental behaviors associated with problem drinking and antisocial behavior among adolescent males. *Proceedings of the First Annual Alcoholism Conference of the National Institute on Alcohol Abuse and Alcoholism*. Washington, D.C.: Department of Health, Education and Welfare, 1973, pp. 276–296.

Zucker, R. A., & Devoe, C. I. Life history characteristics associated with problem drinking and antisocial behavior in adolescent girls: A comparison with male findings. In R. D. Wirt, G. Winokur, & M. Roff (Eds.), *Life history research in psychopathology* (Vol. 4). Minneapolis: University of Minnesota Press, 1975.

III

Public Policy Implications of Drinking Problems among Youth

Policy concerning alcohol since Repeal in the 1930s has fit generally into a utilitarian model—the greatest good for the greatest number—with an added contradictory feature of requiring people to pay extra for their pleasure. The utilitarian aspect of the policy states that alcoholic beverages should be safe: hence, the regulations that guarantee purity of the product through controlling its production. Further, those for whom alcohol is thought to be particularly dangerous—for example, children—should be protected: hence, the development of a Byzantine set of rules governing labeling and advertising under federal law, and governing types of outlets, hours of sale, minimum legal age for sale and use, and so on, at state and local levels. The feature of paying for one's pleasure may be seen in federal and state taxes levied on alcoholic beverages to help fill the general revenue coffers. For the historically minded, R. Wilkinson, in his book *The Prevention of Drinking Problems: Alcohol Control and Cultural Influences* (New York: Oxford University Press, 1970), covers in detail the development of this policy from the time when Prohibition was repealed in 1933 through the late 1960s. Since 1970, a federal social-health component has been introduced into alcohol policy, namely, to reduce and treat the number of human casualties to alcohol problems; this policy has been generalized to the states as well.

This brief synopsis may suggest a coherence and consensus concerning policy that does not in fact exist, as Reginald Smart's admirable review of preventive strategies, with special emphasis on youth, attests. In the United States, at least, the regulatory aspect of alcohol policy has never been integrated with the public health aspect. Only in recent years have tentative steps been taken in this direction. The alcohol-beverage control commissions of the states have uniformly seen their role as enforcing regulations concerning the production, distribution, and sale of alcoholic beverages and, for the most part, continue to do so. Any public health consequences of this enforcement, and there appear to be few, are accidental rather than planned. That this situation may change in the next few years is suggested by the increasing frequency of occurrence of congressional hearings that are attempting to examine the gap between regulatory and health agencies and other aspects at the federal level of alcohol policy.

The political aspect of bridging this gap may be advantageous or disadvantageous to the common welfare, as Richard Horman's chapter, based largely on his experiences as executive director of the Governor's Council on Drug and Alcohol Abuse in the Commonwealth of Pennsylvania, graphically demonstrates. The competing demands involved in generating additional public revenues to be used for the common good—which may, at the same time, increase the level of alcohol problems—are more than difficult to resolve. They obviously involve differing values of what constitutes public health and form the very issues that often result in political polarity. In the state of Pennsylvania, it made good sense to consider abolishing the state liquor-store system and opening it to the private market. It was argued that this would not only benefit the state economically in terms of additional tax revenues but would result in a less costly, more consumer-oriented distribution system than under a state control policy. On the other hand, there was evidence that if price were reduced and more outlets were made available (which would presumably occur under a private marketing system), the level of alcohol problems in the commonwealth would thereby be increased. Horman gives us a fascinating case study of the political intricacies involved in the outcome of this issue in the Commonwealth of Pennsylvania.

Lack of awareness and problems in communicating are two elements that clearly underlie the formation of the isolated and often insulated islands of policy that currently characterize policy concerning alcohol. Education in the broadest sense, and health education in particular, is a necessary ingredient in any cohesive program efforts in alcohol policy. However, as Lawrence Green argues, policy issues within the field of health education itself must be settled before this discipline can make its most effective contribution to controlling social problems such as those stemming from the overuse of alcohol. Well-trained health education generalists, experts in theory and research, must be available before the health educators can compete equally in a limited market for health and welfare resources. Green provides an intellectually stimulating analysis of some of the problems, both at the federal level and within the field of health education, that are involved in policy formulation around any social problem.

Discussions of alcohol policy in recent years have tended to polarize around a few issues: distribution of consumption versus education approaches; locus of prevention specialists and their training; prevention versus treatment; fiscal support through general versus categorical public funds; effects of the mass media. Smart touches upon most of these issues and demonstrates that the apparent incompatibilities in many instances are more illusory than real. This is not to say that genuine differences and divergences of approach do not indeed continue to exist. For instance, the precedent of the fate of preventive efforts in the community-mental-health-centers movement indicates that without extraordinarily careful planning, preventive efforts can be gobbled up by the larger treatment-oriented community. It follows that prevention programs need to be institutionalized separately from treatment programs. Another example has to do with designated tax monies (i.e., taxing alcoholic beverages to support alcohol problem prevention and treatment efforts). Clearly, categorical public funds used to support alcohol programs run the danger of institutionalizing problems rather than eradicating them.

The chapters in Part III are exploratory, as befits our current state of knowledge concerning alcohol policy. They offer no prescriptions but instead thoughtfully examine and describe issues and policies. They are diagnostic in the best sense of the term: they begin to point the way to solutions by analyzing problems with care and subtlety.

7

Priorities in Minimizing Alcohol Problems among Young People

Reginald G. Smart

1. Introduction

Although an ounce of prevention may be worth a pound of cure, we have not been able to provide a gram of either for youthful drinking problems. Certainly, the past 10 years have seen a remarkable development of interest in youthful drinking problems. Ideally, we should be able to apply the solutions derived from solving adult drinking problems to those of young people. Unfortunately, our success with adults gives us almost nothing about which we can be certain. We do not have techniques tested and established for the prevention of adult drinking problems and hence cannot transfer anything of that type to the new problem of youthful drinking. Despite the lack of tested technology for prevention, we have at least a set of theories and approaches to prevention that can be examined for their relevance to youthful drinking problems. We need to consider which of those approaches will have the largest potential, but the decision is likely to be made with fragmentary empirical support. Another important task is to define problems among young people and to define what is to be prevented. It is known that young people's drinking problems are different than adults in that they are less numerous and less serious in terms of clinical damage and physical disease. The purpose of this review is to examine several of the

Reginald G. Smart • Program Development Research, Addiction Research Foundation, Toronto, Ontario, Canada.

approaches for reducing youthful drinking problems and to examine the theoretical structures underlying these approaches and their empirical support. Hopefully, a set of priorities for prevention and treatment will emerge. The major approaches involve such public policy considerations as are raised by the distribution and social science approaches to prevention (Popham, Schmidt, & deLint, 1976), restrictions on drinking-age laws, advertising of alcoholic beverages, and other restrictions on availability. However, other approaches involve alcohol education and treatment of young alcoholics or alcohol abusers. It is hoped that some sort of balance between approaches can be suggested and conclusions drawn about the best approaches to pursue.

Minimizing alcohol problems among young people will likely require consideration of primary, secondary, and tertiary intervention. Primary prevention is, of course, the prevention of new cases; it will involve such activities as government alcohol policy, public education, and changes in customs, values, or mores that promote more satisfactory drinking. Secondary prevention is the early identification of prodromal or developing cases and their treatment or rehabilitation so that they do not develop into more serious or long-term cases. Tertiary prevention involves the treatment of serious cases so that they will not continue to be cases and hence cannot develop new cases by infection (not likely with alcoholism), social influence, modeling, or setting bad examples. Tertiary prevention might include treating alcoholic parents because they are likely to promote or foster alcoholic drinking among their children, or alcoholic children because they might similarly affect their siblings.

The definition of what constitutes a *case* is problematic. Tertiary prevention presents relatively few problems. Alcoholics or alcohol abusers come for treatment and hence become "cases" or "patients." They are self-defined or are defined by someone experienced in dealing with serious alcohol problems—the treatment staff or a relative who has experienced some sort of damage or hardship at the hands of the "case." However, what is a "case" when we speak of primary or secondary prevention? There seems to be little agreement about what the goal of primary prevention is for most sociobehavioral or mental health problems. Values, judgments, and personal opinions largely determine the definition of problem drinking.

The ways in which youthful problem drinking have been defined are very numerous (Smart, 1976). Some parents would, of course, define any drinking on the part of young teenagers (especially girls) as a problem. Others would tolerate drinking but not drunkenness. However, we know that drunkenness is frequently the goal of youthful drinking. We also know that clinically definable "alcoholism" is rare among young people if it is made to include loss of control and physical damage such as liver cirrhosis, peripheral nervitis, and withdrawal symptoms. Becoming a drinker is essentially a part of growing up (Jessor & Jessor, 1975) in today's society.

Problems that are common among young drinkers include drunkenness, drinking–driving accidents, and alcohol-induced difficulties in school, family, or social relationships. Many of these problems are, of course, early signs of alcoholism in later life. For some young persons, the problems increase and result in adult alcoholism. For others, they are a reflection of inappropriate drinking habits that later disappear without much serious ill effect (Fillmore, 1974).

Studies done prior to 1968 (Bacon & Jones, 1968) in seven areas of the United States showed that only 11–17% of students had *ever* been drunk. Only 4% reported having been drunk in the past six months, and this is an almost insignificant proportion. However, a study by Cutler and Storm in 1973 showed that 40% had been drunk in the past four weeks. About 7.4% were getting drunk about once a week. A study by Smart, Gray, and Bennett (1978) in two Ontario high schools showed that 42% of students had been drunk at least once in the past month, with 5.8% being drunk five or more times, or about weekly. However, only 6.7% actually passed out, and 1.3% were made ill from drinking. It appears very likely that 5–10% of high school students are getting drunk once a week or more. Whether this is seen as a significant problem depends on the point of view taken. Is it mere recreation or is it harmful? A dependence on drunkenness for fun is likely to divert young people from other more nurturing pursuits and to expose them to alcohol dependency and to alcohol-related accidents, since many of them also drive cars.

Traffic accidents are a growing problem among young persons, particularly in jurisdictions that have lowered their drinking ages. It has been known for some time that young persons have accidents at lower blood alcohol levels than do adults (Borkenstein, Crowtha, Shumate, Ziel, & Zylman, 1964). Unfortunately, it is not known whether they have an especially low tolerance for alcohol because they are young or because they are inexperienced in drinking. Very likely, the combination of high risk-taking propensities and inexperience with drinking and with driving is most important.

Other kinds of social, interpersonal, and dependency problems have also been investigated among young people. Definitions of drinking problems and alcoholism are highly varied. Some definitions require the presence of a particular symptom, such as intolerable craving, physical dependence as shown by withdrawal symptoms, loss of control over drinking, or even all of them. An important definition has been proposed by Jellinek (1960), who proposed that *alcoholism* is "any use of alcohol that causes any damage to the individual or society or both." In this definition, no particular clinical psychological or psychiatric symptom is required. The problem word in the definition is *damage,* which has many meanings. Surely damage would have to include physical damage and damage to social or family relationships, to work potential, to school performance, and the like.

Most of the studies of alcoholism and problems among young people have taken this "damage" approach rather than a clinical symptoms approach. The earliest scale used to assess drinking problems among youth was developed by Straus and Bacon (1953) for their studies among college students. They developed three scales: one each for social complications, warning signs of problem drinking, and anxiety about drinking. The social complications scale includes questions on social damage, for example, failure to meet obligations (missed appointments, school work), accidents or injury, formal discipline for overdrinking, losing friends, and the like. The warning signs involved problem-drinking signs such as blackouts, becoming drunk alone, drinking before or instead of breakfast, and participating in aggressive or destructive behavior when drunk. In the early 1950s, only 6% of male and 1% of female college students had drinking problems involving all of the categories.

In 1966, Globetti and Chamblin (1966) used a nine-point scale based on the Straus and Bacon scale. They found that 38% of high school drinkers were "problem drinkers" with scores of three points or more. A Canadian study using a five-point scale found that in 1972 about 12% of the high school population or 15% of the drinkers exhibited one or more of the "problem-drinking" signs.

One of the most recent studies using a modification of the Straus and Bacon scale was done in Ontario in 1975 (Smart & Gray, 1978). Some 1,171 students in grades 9–13 completed the questionnaire dealing with drinking and problem drinking. About 42% of the students reported no problem at all. About 14% reported three or more problems, and only 2.1% reported six or more problems. This latter category should include students with very serious drinking problems, although those in other categories also have problems that are far from trivial.

Another study conducted in Ontario in 1977 used a four-point scale (Smart, 1977b). It emphasized reactions to problems and included items on whether the student wishes to drink less, whether his parents felt he drank too much, if he had been arrested or warned by police or treated by a doctor or counselor. By far the most common symptom was being arrested or warned by the police. Very few had been treated or seen by any sort of counselor. This suggests that a large proportion of youthful problem drinkers get no treatment. In all, 11.7% reported one or more problems, but only 2.7% reported two or more. As predicted, problems were most common among older students, males, those in the higher grades of school but with a low level of success in school, and those living in the northern areas of the province. The north is an area that is isolated and thinly populated. Traditionally, it has had a frontier sort of culture with strong social support for heavy drinking among men. This study, together with the earlier ones, suggests that in Ontario about 2–3% of high school students have significant alcohol problems, probably requiring some sort of treatment or amelioration. Of course, there is a much larger proportion of students with less serious problems—probably 8–10% of students would be in this category.

In general, we need to develop methods of preventing drinking with damage whether it be social, familial, educational, or physical. Chiefly, this damage will be shown in young people by chronic drunkenness, involvement in alcohol-related traffic accidents, and disruption of family, school, and social life. Far more young persons are likely to show the clinical symptomatology of older alcoholics. Such cases exist, but they are likely to be rare compared to problems of a less serious type.

2. Public Policy Considerations

2.1. Models of Prevention

It is argued here that no proven method of preventing alcohol problems has been found that can actually be utilized by governments. The largest reductions in both drinking and drinking problems seem to have been achieved in wartime or in times of total prohibition (Bruun, Edwards, Lumio, Mäkelä, Pan, Popham, Room, Schmidt, Skög, Sulkunen, & Oesterberg, 1975). No government is likely to start a war merely to deal with its alcohol problems, and few seem likely to introduce total prohibition. We are therefore left with certain largely untried models of prevention. Although several have considerable bodies of empirical data supporting their arguments, they have not been tested in large-scale social experiments. They are all models that require government intervention on different scales if they are to have any impact, and some require almost no intervention.

The three most popular models are the "distribution" or "single distribution" model, the "integration" or "social-cultural" model, and the "bimodal" model. Only the first two have any degree of empirical support and are worthy of further study.

The bimodal model seems rarely to be taken seriously. It argues that the distribution of consumption is bimodal in character with normal drinkers and abnormal or alcoholic drinkers (Popham *et al.*,1976). The problems of alcoholics are seen to have little to do with drinking but to be symptomatic of psychiatric or physical disorders of unknown origin. Proponents stress that normal drinking is not problematic and hence should be free of government interference while alcoholics are treated and the etiology of their disease investigated. This view is regularly taken by manufacturers of alcoholic beverages. However, as pointed out by Popham *et al.* (1976), such scholars as Bales (1946) and Ullman (1958) have "denied that the level of alcohol consumption in a group has anything to do with the rate of alcoholism or insobriety." In the "distribution" model discussed below, it can be seen that much evidence exists to refute the idea that the distribution is bimodal and to support the idea that alcohol consumption and certain types of problems are related. The bimodal model is particularly inappropriate for dealing with youthful problems, since so few of them are symptomatic of any "underlying" disorder. Clinical as opposed to sociobehavioral problems among young people are rare, and it has been shown that the frequency of such problems decreases with severity and that bimodality is not evident (Smart & Gray, 1978).

2.2. The Distribution Model: Reducing Per Capita Consumption

The "distribution" model of prevention was developed largely by the efforts of researchers at the Addiction Research Foundation in Toronto and the Finnish Foundation for Alcohol Studies in Helsinki (Popham *et al.*, 1976; Bruun *et al.*, 1975; Mäkelä, 1978; Skög, 1977). It is based in part upon the earlier work of Sully Ledermann (1956), who unfortunately died prematurely and hence could not carry the work to its fully developed state. As pointed out by Room (1978), various aspects of the theory have developed and changed over time. The best current expressions of the approach are probably those in the review by Popham *et al.* (1976) and the book by Bruun *et al.* (1975). Although the theory began essentially as a French and Canadian effort, it has now been accepted in a variety of countries and is now the subject of a book supported by the World Health Organization and authored by persons from a variety of countries.

It is beyond the scope of this review to examine the development of the model, all of its various tenets, and the empirical support for them. This sort of review has been well done in the publications noted above. Nor is it part of the work of this paper to review all of the various critiques and rejoinders made to presentations of the theory. It can be said that the model has had its critics, particularly in the United States (Room, 1971; O'Neill & Wells, 1971; Miller & Agnew, 1974; Parker & Harman, 1977). It is proposed here to set out only the main tenets of the theory and the main areas of criticism. The major purpose here is not the validity of the model in general but its applicability to minimizing youthful drinking problems, and it has already been argued that they are somewhat different (at least in rates) than those of adults.

The main tenets of the distribution model are:

1. "The general level of consumption in a population is closely related to the prevalence of heavy use: the larger the amount of alcohol consumed by a population the higher will be the number of heavy consumers" (Bruun *et al.*, 1975).
2. "A lowering of the total consumption of alcohol is likely to be accompanied by a reduction in the prevalence of heavy users" (Bruun *et al.*, 1975).
3. "The degree of overall availability of alcohol seems to have an independent effect on the general level of alcohol consumption in a society" (Bruun *et al.*, 1975).
4. "Governments should make efforts to stabilize or reduce per capita or total consumption of alcohol chiefly by increasing prices and by reducing availability of alcoholic beverages. These methods will eventually reduce the total proportion of heavy users (or alcoholics) in the population" (Addiction Research Foundation, 1978).

The main elements of criticism that are relevant here (Parker & Harman, 1977) include:

1. A denial that the available data consistently show a close enough correlation between the general level of consumption and heavy use to be practically useful.
2. Arguments that lowering total consumption could reduce "normal" drinking and leave heavy users unaffected.
3. Pointing out that the data in support of the theory are correlational and spatial in nature, that is, that propositions about social change are derived from static data.
4. Pointing out that the distribution model relies too heavily on liver cirrhosis data to the exclusion of other types of data.

All of these criticisms have been answered to some extent by Schmidt and Popham (1978). In all probability, the model will remain a controversial one until some country or state decides to follow the practical suggestions for policy. In general, it appears to be the model with the largest amount of empirical support, but that support will always be incomplete until some major social experiment is made.

The distribution model was developed essentially without reference to youthful drinking problems. The theory applies to drinking in the general population and takes little cognizance of different drinking patterns or motivations. However, proponents of the theory have argued (Addiction Research Foundation, 1978) that restrictions on availability should include raising the drinking age in Ontario from 18 to 19.

To what extent the distribution model is applicable to minimizing youthful drinking problems is unknown at present. The actual distribution of total consumption in the youthful population seems to be unknown, as is the relation between mean consumption and problems. Also no information exists on how the number of youthful heavy users are affected by drastic changes in price or decreases in availability. It is not clear that it should be assumed that youthful drinking will be as responsive as adult drinking to price changes. Although most young people have lower overall incomes than adults, almost all of their income is disposable and available for leisure pursuits such as drinking. Whether they would respond more or less carefully to alcohol price changes than adults is debatable.

Another possible problem with the distribution model as applied to youth is that the criterion for "damage" or alcoholism has so often been liver cirrhosis. Of course, this is an inadequate criterion for damage among young people, who rarely develop physical symptoms such as cirrhosis. The relationship between the level of alcohol consumption and the social consequences of drinking is not very close.

Mäkelä (1978) has recently reviewed research in this area, and the data are complex. For example, Schmidt and Smart (1963) found a nonsignificant correlation between per capita consumption and proportion of fatally injured drivers in the United States. Room (1974a) reported negative correlations between per capita consumption and drunk driving in various states. Also, Bunce (1976) analyzed data from regions of California and found no correlations between indices of various problems, for example, arrests for drunkenness, drunk driving, and social problems due to alcohol.

Another problem is that young people are overrepresented among persons reporting drinking problems in surveys. However, it is also known that they drink far less than middle-aged persons. It could be that the actual level of consumption is less important in creating problems for young people than the actual methods of drinking. For example, they are more likely than adults to get drunk on a given occasion, to drink heavily, and to drink quickly. Fillmore's longitudinal study (1974) has also pointed out that the occurrence of problems is less adequately explained by the frequency and the amount of drinking among younger people than among older persons. She found that such variables predicted problems significantly for young and middle-aged drinkers. However, less variance was explained by these variables at the younger age levels. Mäkelä (1978) has concluded that "there is a consistent positive relationship between overall intake and consequences of drinking. Much of the variation in consequences remains, however, unexplained even if we have full knowledge of the frequency and amount of intake." For young people, the consistency is lower and the explanatory value of level of consumption poorer. This finding must lead to some doubt about the impact of price and availability controls on youthful drinking problems. It is possible that substantial reductions in youthful per capita consumption could occur without changing the frequency of their alcohol-related social problems. It is necessary, however, to return to the need for an experiment based on the distribution approach. In all likelihood, price and availability controls, if they affected per capita youthful consumption, would also reduce problems. The extent of the reduction *might* be less than for adults and of a disappointing magnitude.

2.3. Sociocultural Approaches: Modifying Drinking Norms

A set of approaches to prevention has been loosely defined as *sociocultural* or *normative*. Often these approaches are seen as totally opposed in their implications to those of the "distribution" model. The approaches termed *sociocultural* are varied, and a complete expression of the theory is difficult to find. Contributions to the theory have been made by Wilkinson (1970), Bales (1946), Ullman (1958), and Room (1974). Good reviews of the approach have been presented by Popham *et al.* (1976), Whitehad (1977), and Wilkinson (1970). As with the distribution approach, it is not proposed to review here all of the possible variations in the sociocultural approach but only the major ones.

The major tenet of the sociocultural approach is that the eradication of drinking problems requires changes in the social norms around drinking. Usually it is believed (e.g., Ullman, 1958) that per capita alcohol consumption is irrelevant to rates of alcoholism. It is believed that problems result from the lack of norms in society for "safe" drinking as well as from guilt about drinking. It is contended, as for example in some of the Co-operative Commission reports (Wilkinson, 1970), that certain patterns of drinking are associated with a low level of problems from drinking. The approaches to drinking suggested to be not associated with drinking and recommended for the American people include:

1. Reducing emotionalism about drinking and ambivalence about drinking norms.
2. Making a clear distinction between drinking *per se* and drunkenness.
3. Drinking in situations of restraint, that is, where drunkenness is out of the question.
4. Drinking when drinking itself was not the focus of the group's activities.
5. Drinking with food, both to integrate drinking with other activities and to reduce alcohol levels.

For the most part, the sociocultural model eschews strong government interventions that limit availability or increase the prices of alcohol, chiefly because they are seen to be irrelevant to the pattern of drinking.

The sociocultural approach depends greatly upon analyses of drinking among Jews and Italians. They were seen to embody the accepted drinking practices in their cultures and to have both a low rate of alcohol problems and a high rate of consumption. This analysis has been shown to be false (Popham *et al.*, 1976). In fact, Jews have a low rate of per capita alcohol consumption, although most are drinkers. They have low rates of alcoholism—in part, because they have low rates of overall consumption. Italians have been shown to have a high rate of liver cirrhosis (de Lint & Schmidt, 1971).

Sociocultural approaches have led to the expectation that safe or responsible drinking should be the goal of alcohol policy. The model taken has been drinking practices in certain continental countries, such as France and Italy. Of course, the high rate of alcoholism and alcohol-related problems in Italy is well known (Ledermann, 1956). If safe drinking practices could be taught, they would lead to increased per capita consumption, and the conclusion seems inescapable that more, not fewer, problems would result (Bruun *et al.*, 1975). Another difficulty is that there is no evidence that persons without alcohol problems have a skill that those with problems lack. Beauchamp (1976) has pointed out that the drinking population cannot be divided into people with and without problems. This is particularly true with young drinkers, whose problems may be few or many and may be distributed according to frequency, not either "a problem" or "no problem."

Reference has also been made in some National Institute on Alcohol and Alcohol Abuse (NIAAA) literature to responsible drinking to Anstie's limit—which amounts to about two drinks for a adult. This so-called limit is based on a very old and inadequate paper that specified a supposedly safe limit for drinkers. Most drinkers do not drink this much now. If they were to be encouraged not to exceed it but to think that it was safe, it would greatly increase per capita consumption and hence physical problems in the society as a whole. The idea of a safe or responsible level of drinking was based partly on a level that would prevent the occurrence of drunkenness. It has been obvious to many observers that sociocultural theorists tend to be concerned with preventing drunkenness and distribution theorists with preventing physical damage, such as liver cirrhosis.

With regard to youth and drinking, the best exposition of the sociocultural approach seems to be that of Wilkinson (1970). He recommended that:

1. The minimum age for drinking be 18 not 21 and that those under 18 be allowed to buy drinks with their parents.
2. Drinking at home be subject to no legal age limit.
3. Mild alcoholic beverages be served at "teenage dances and parties" without being the prime means of entertainment.
4. There be more alcohol education for responsible drinking.
5. Colleges provide supervised drinking places for students.
6. Alcohol-related offenses for young people be decriminalized.

The underlying rationale was that most people should learn to drink at an early age and with their families. A real trial for these suggestions could have been made in a single city or town, with careful monitoring of changes, and in a comparable area used as a control. We are short of information on what effects the total package might have. It will be argued in a later section that reducing the drinking age has increased both drinking and drinking problems. Knowledge of the effects of the other changes is apparently lacking, but most of them would increase availability and hence, probably, overall consumption.

The value of the sociocultural approach is that it recognizes differences among drinking patterns and emphasizes controls on drunkenness. In all probability, the major problems for young people come from drinking too much on a single occasion rather than from constant long-term drinking. Physical damage and dependence on alcohol are rare among young people, although still worth considering. The most frequent difficulties, however, are drunkenness and alcohol-related traffic accidents, with disruptions of school and family life close behind. What is lacking so far is some proven method of teaching responsible drinking that will not increase per capita consumption. Whether special education courses can be developed that do this successfully is unknown. However, a major effort should be developed to experiment with such courses. Although the distribution approach is a compelling one for society as a whole, it is not clear that it is well adapted to the problem of young people.

As stated earlier, amount and frequency of drinking explain a small amount of the variance in drinking problems for young people. This leaves a large amount of unexplained variance, which could be explained by patterns of and motivation for drinking. Also, the correlation among various sorts of problems—for example, drunkenness, alcohol-related accidents, and clinical problems—is significant but far from perfect, especially with young people. Given these findings, it is probably too early to give up on approaches to prevention that involve sensible drinking and do not contribute to increasing the level of consumption. Very likely, their greatest effect will be in combination with measures to stablize or reduce per capita consumption.

2.4. Drinking-Age Laws

Probably no area of alcohol policy has generated the same level of public interest and debate as the drinking age. The issue has been debated in Canada, the United States, Britain, and several Scandinavian countries. Interest in it derives mainly from the high degree of public concern with everything to do with young people and from the realization that drinking among young people has been increasing in many areas. As stated earlier, the distribution theorists generally favor high age limits and sociocultural theorists do not.

During the late 1960s and early 1970s, there was an emphasis on the development of a single age of majority—usually 18. It was argued that if young people can pay taxes, join the military, vote, and get married at 18, they should also be able to drink. Part of the explanation in Ontario also involved the concept of responsible drinking. It was felt by politicians and others that young people should develop the ability to drink carefully, without excessive government restrictions. Some also argued the "forbidden fruit" theory (Wilkinson, 1970) that is, that alcohol was attractive to young people because of its illegality and that if it were legal they would drink less. In Canada, all 10 provinces lowered their drinking ages to 18 from 19, 20, or 21. In addition, 26 of the 50 United States also made age reductions. Whether these changes were wise or not is still being debated, and at least some jurisdictions have increased age levels again.

Many studies have examined some of the consequences of the changes made between 1970 and 1975. Many were conducted without adequate comparison or control groups against which the effects of the legal changes could be tested. Some studies were, of necessity, conducted in haste because of lack of warning about forthcoming changes in the law (e.g., in Ontario). Several studies were obliged to rely on *post hoc* analyses with or *without* the advantages of data extending over a long time period *prior to* and *following* changes in the law. The area is a controversial one, and not nearly enough research has been done, considering that the age change has been one of the largest and most common alcohol policy changes in North America.

Most of the available studies of changing the drinking age have been reviewed by Smart and Goodstadt (1977). They reached the conclusion that few studies had been done except for alcohol-related accidents, but that the available studies showed some consistent and possibly reliable effects. Their major conclusions were as follows:

1. Both self-report and sales studies indicate that substantial increases in youthful drinking occurred in Canada after the legal age for purchasing alcoholic beverages was reduced—probably, but not certainly, because of the change. Relevant data for the United States seem not to be available.
2. The largest changes in drinking probably involved on-premise consumption rather than sales in liquor stores or drinking with families.
3. The effects of the age change on per capita beer consumption varied from province to province in Canada.
4. There are usually greater increases in alcohol-related automobile accidents in areas where the purchasing age has been reduced than in comparison areas. These increases do not occur in all states (e.g., Vermont), but the reasons for the inconsistency are uncertain.
5. Changes in the alcohol-purchasing age probably affect the automobile crash experience of those aged 15–17 as well as those aged 18–20.
6. No information is available that shows conclusively (e.g., pre–post study with appropriate comparisons) that reducing the purchasing age has caused increases in educational, family, or public order problems. The data indicating increased admissions of young persons for alcoholism treatment are subject to a variety of interpretations.
7. The evidence, chiefly from studies of traffic accidents and inferentially from studies of changes in drinking patterns, suggests that there are public health reasons for not introducing changes in jurisdictions that have not yet reduced purchasing ages. Whether the arguments based on human rights or age of majority are superior depends on political, social, and cultural values too numerous to discuss here.

Since that study was published, several further studies have appeared.

There has been a study made of changes in the American states

(Smart, 1977a). This is a useful addition to the literature, most of which originated in one Canadian province. Per capita consumption figures were compared for 25 of the 26 changed states, separately for beer, wine, and spirits. This study compared each changed state with the geographically closest state that did not change, for the year before, the year of the change, and the year after. Large differences were found for the states: some states showed no effect of the change, when compared with controls, and some showed large changes. Overall, beer per capita comsumption increased more in the changed states, wine showed no change, and liquor increased in the year after compared with the year before. The increases were 5.7% for beer and 4.9% for liquor. Of course, we need far more study and analysis of these results, but they do lead us to expect small, inconsistent effects of the new age laws.

All of the studies reported by Smart and Goodstadt (1977) were done shortly after the laws were changed. In general, it can be expected that when a new law is introduced, the effect will be a short-term one. This has been seen with the introduction of the .08 law in Britain, which created a large reduction in drinking accidents for a short period of time. Also, when seat belts are made mandatory, it is often found that people wear them for a while and that then many stop wearing them after a few months.

Several new studies of the age laws have appeared relatively recently. Both of these studies cover a longer period of time than do the earlier ones; they are long-term trend studies. On of these studies was done in Michigan (Douglass & Freedman, 1977). The earlier study examined only 18 months of data after the law was changed in 1974. The latter study examined data for 10 years, that is for the years 1968–1973 (before the new law) and for 1974–1977 (after the new law). This later study showed that the increases in drinking accidents among young people were part of an overall, long-term trend. Young people were drinking more before the new law, increasing their total accidents and their drinking accidents as well. It appears in this study that the effect of the lower drinking age on accidents will decrease and become less significant. The long-term trend will continue. Probably, we should worry far more about the long-term trend and attempt to develop solutions and countermeasures to reduce youthful drinking and driving.

Two rather recent studies in Canada by Warren, Simpson, Collard, and Page Valin (1977) and Whitehead (1977) have reached similar conclusions. Warren *et al.* pointed out that when we examine a four-year trend, a very large impact on youthful fatalities is seen from the new age laws. However, the impact appears much smaller when we examine a 10-year trend. Warren *et al.* have also pointed out that it is very difficult to assess the effects of the new drinking law because a .08

law was passed just prior to it in many provinces. In those provinces in Canada where the .08 law and the drinking-age law were far apart in time (e.g., two years), the effects are easier to see. Where they appeared close together, they are difficult to see. This discrepancy points out a common problem in assessing the effects of legal changes on driving. Very often, legal changes are not made in a way that can be easily studied, and often we have to assess the effects of several changes at the same time. The conclusion seems warranted that in Canada the effect of the new drinking-age laws was to increase alcohol-related accidents at a time when they were already increasing for other reasons. In general, the newer studies do not invalidate the conclusions of the Smart and Goodstadt (1977) review but tend to support them.

The studies done so far do not make it clear whether jurisdictions that lowered drinking ages should increase them again to reduce drinking problems. In fact, several have increased them, including Saskatchewan, Maine, and Minnesota. To date, no analyses have been seen of the effects in these areas. The Ontario government has decided to increase the drinking age in Ontario as of December 31, 1978. It will be raised to 19, having been 18 between 1971 and that date. Whether a change of one year can make a noticeable difference in drinking is debatable. However, the change will remove drinking almost entirely from the high schools, as only about 5% of students are 19 or more. Also the change is to be introduced along with several others. These include restrictions on lifestyle advertising, stricter penalties for drinking and driving, higher penalties for licensees who serve minors, more enforcement of underage drinking laws by licensees (requiring age-of-majority cards with pictures), and more alcohol education. Probably, increasing drinking ages is most sensible when combined with other measures. Small changes in availability are known (Bruun *et al.*, 1975) to have small or insignificant effects on consumption. It does seem clear that for reasons of health, jurisdictions that have not reduced drinking ages should not do so. Those who wish to increase them should combine the change with others likely also to reduce the availability of alcoholic beverages.

3. Alcohol Education in the Mass Media and Schools

Both distribution and sociocultural proponents advocate that alcohol education be developed. The approaches taken would vary, of course, with distribution theorists requesting education oriented toward reducing per capita consumption and socioculturalists arguing for "responsible drinking." An example of the sociocultural approach might be the

"Dialogue on Drinking" sponsored by the Canadian federal government. It attempts to get people to talk about their drinking with friends and relatives, to explore their motives for drinking, and to develop drinking norms. The various drinking–driving programs that emphasize responsible drinking or a one-drink-an-hour limit are also examples. Education programs directly based on distribution concepts have not been attempted yet. The Ontario government program is close to what might be expected, and it emphasizes one's being one's "own liquor control board" as well as some of the hazards of drinking. Alcohol education could involve both the mass media and the school-based approaches.

A major problem with alcohol education has been a lack of consensus on its aims. Is the goal to reduce per capita consumption or only heavy drinking? Is the aim to reduce drunkenness among people or only harmful drunkenness, such as drinking and driving? Do we want to prevent current drinking problems among young people or future ones or both? Do we want only to give people the facts about alcohol and have them make up their own minds, or are we attempting to push them in one direction or another? To what extent do we want to give people information, change their attitudes, or modify their behavior around drinking? Frequently, these various questions are not answerable for educational campaigns. Most tend to be very general in their aims and hence are difficult to evaluate. Many schools and mass media programs of alcohol education do not state aims and objectives clearly enough to frame methods of evaluation.

3.1. Mass Media Programs

Numerous media programs concerning drinking and drinking–driving have been mounted in the past 10 years. Prior to World War II, virtually all alcohol education had a temperance rather than a health or safety orientation. With the decline of the temperance movement in North America, such programs have almost completely disappeared, to be replaced with more sophisticated attempts based more on scientific facts and having no religious basis. The content in many of these, along with many of the evaluations, has been revised by Blane and Hewitt (1976).

Many reviews have been made of the literature on public education and mass media campaigns. The best of these in the drinking–driving area are probably those of Driessen and Bryk (1973) and Wilde (1975) and in the alcohol area generally, the one by Blane and Hewitt (1977). The general conclusions from these reviews are not at all positive. Almost all of the reviews evaluate the effects of the mass media with other factors, such as a change in the law. No evaluations, according to

Bryk and Driessen, show that alcohol-related accidents have been reduced solely because of a campaign. Many have been ineffective. Public education seems to educate in terms of providing information to people about alcohol and other matters. However, people do not necessarily change their behavior as a result. Many studies of alcohol education have not employed adequate designs, for example, before-and-after measurement and untreated controls (Blane & Hewitt, 1977), but it does seem clear that the effects of mass persuasion campaigns have not been encouraging. It seems most likely that public education about alcohol or about drinking and driving would be most effective if it immediately followed a change in the law or its enforcement. For example, a mass media campaign around youthful drinking problems would be far more effective when combined with a change in the drinking age than if presented independent of such changes. The same might be said of measures to enforce underage drinking laws. Mass persuasion about this would be more effective if it could be shown that enforcement of current laws was to be increased. This expectation is in keeping with the findings of Pierce, Hieatt, Goodstadt, Lonera, Cunliffe, and Pang (1975) that a media campaign about drinking and driving at Christmas reduced reported drinking and driving. Police enforcement of drinking–driving laws is, of course, greater at Christmas than at other times because of random checks. Similar findings occurred in the Vermont project (Worden, Waller, & Riley, 1975), which used mass media and increased enforcement to reduce drinking and driving. The conclusion of this study was that the campaign was effective when combined with countermeasures, although the campaign alone was better than no campaign. Greater efforts should be made to integrate mass persuasion with increased enforcement or the requirements of new laws.

A problem with mass education is, of course, its "mass" nature. It is designed for everyone and hence is expected to appeal to everyone in the population. Very few programs have been specifically developed for the high-risk groups, that is, young males who are heavy drinkers. Much better results might be obtained by tailoring persuasion programs to special groupings.

3.2. School-Related Alcohol Education

As with mass education, school programs about alcohol have been temperance-oriented. Before World War II, much of the school time devoted to alcohol in Ontario was actually taken up by temperance organizations, whose staffs gave the lectures or demonstrations. Most of this temperance orientation has disappeared throughout North America now, but the temperance aura still surrounds alcohol education, particularly in education based on distribution concepts. At first glance, it looks much like the temperance approach of the past. Of course, it is based not on religious or moral principles but on a commitment to the health and safety of the population. Whether alcohol education can overcome this past history depends on its being shown to be highly effective and objective in content.

A major problem with alcohol education in schools has always been its low exposure level. Apparently, no schools accept alcohol education as an academic subject deserving the same attention as more basic subjects. The same problem occurs with sex education, driver or safety education, and other special interest or health areas. Usually, they are a small part of a large curriculum in health or physical education. The situation in Toronto is probably typical of that in many other areas. Fieldstone (1974) found that alcohol education was part of the official curriculum in all six areas of Toronto. However, drugs and alcohol are only 2 of 19 topics suggested—but not required—in the health curriculum. Health is an optional subject in high school and not all students elect to take it, but probably a majority do. Only about 30 hours of class time are allotted to these 19 topics, and hence drug and alcohol education are usually not given more than 2 or 3 hours per year. Some teachers would give more, but many who have no special interest or training in this area would give less. In fact, in an unpublished study conducted in 1977, it was found that about 36% of the students reported spending no class hours on alcohol education at all, and 34% reported having had only one or two classes. No matter what the value of the alcohol education given, it seems unrealistic to expect that two or three hours a year can have a major impact.

The whole topic of alcohol education in schools seems underserved and understudied. Only two adequate evaluation studies have been made. The first of these, published by Williams, DiCicco, and Unterberger (1968), involved a controlled study of small-group discussions about alcohol. There were five class periods. The main aim was to "prevent excessive drinking by encouraging the development of attitudes found in moderate drinking groups with low rates of alcoholism." The course had a positive impact on attitudes that lasted until the one-month posttest, but not so long as the one-year follow-up. Frequency of drinking occasions did not differ in the experimental and the control groups, but the former reported fewer occasions when they were intoxicated. It may be that the positive effects of the program would have been maintained if some follow-up discussions or other educational inputs had been given later in the year.

A more extensive study of an alcohol education program has been recently reported by Goodstadt, Sheppard, and Crawford (1978). In this program, a group of researchers and teachers developed two series of lesson plans for alcohol education. The plans were made for teachers to use with students in grades 7 or 8 and grades 9 or 10. In all, there were 10 topics in each series, including alcohol and myths, drinking and driving, media portrayal of alcohol, alcohol and the family, and alcohol and sports. The lesson plans were developed in final form to be useful to teachers and to require almost no other material. They were designed as separate units that could be taught independently, but they made an integrated whole. The plans were revised in collaboration with teachers before being put in final form. They were tested with teachers and students in 16 Toronto schools. Control classes were used where no alcohol education was given. In all, 1,351 students were involved in the study, with different numbers receiving different combinations. The results were complex but have been summarized as follows (paraphrased from Goodstadt *et al.*, 1978):

1. The lessons were well received by students and teachers.
2. The lessons led to increased levels of knowledge and mixed effects on attitudes.
3. There were positive changes in reported alcohol use and expectations about future use.

This evaluation is the largest and most comprehensive of any yet reported. It gives overall positive results and leads to the expectation that sophisticated alcohol education can have a major impact on alcohol problems. At present, the lessons prepared for this study are being made available to all schools in Ontario for further study and trial. Lessons for the lower grades are also being developed. It may be possible to examine the effect on students of an integrated approach to alcohol education over a number of years.

It appears very likely that alcohol education can be effective and that further efforts to develop and experiment with extensive exposure to it will be beneficial.

4. Advertising

The past few years have seen frequent public debates about how the advertising of alcoholic beverages affects consumption, particularly among young people. Various legislatures in Canada, the United States, and Britain have debated the advisability of limiting or banning alcohol advertising altogether. A particular dislike is often expressed for lifestyle advertisements. These attempt to associate the use of a particular beverage with having fun, sexual attractiveness, status, and all types of enjoyable activity. They tend not to emphasize the beverage's own characteristics, such as its taste and quality. Often such advertisements on television and radio depict young people having fun, for example, sailing, camping, or bowling and drinking beer during or right after the event. It is often argued that young people grow up in an atmosphere where alcoholic beverages are associated with fun and growing up in general. Young people are led to believe through advertisements that life will be fuller if they drink. Among the 100 leading advertisers in the United States are Heublein, Seagrams, National Distillers, and Hiram Walker (Clark & Mitchell, 1976). It has been recognized by the liquor industry that young people, along with women and blacks, represent the best growth areas for sales. It is known that young people are heavily exposed to television and hence to many alcohol advertisements. On the other hand, manufacturers of alcoholic beverages claim that advertisements do not contribute to the total amount of drinking. They advertise only particular brands, help consumers to make a choice among brands, and make them aware of new brands. Despite these arguments, several legislatures have banned "lifestyle" advertisements. For example, they have been recently banned in Ontario and are to be phased out gradually.

Unfortunately, not much research has been done on alcohol advertising that would allow us to decide whether it affects youthful drinking. Several studies have been made of advertising in general, and they are only marginally relevant.

The question "Would restrictions on alcohol advertising affect alcohol consumption?" has been approached in several ways. One of the earliest studies was done by Simon (1969), who examined the sales of certain brands of liquor in 17 government monopoly states. Advertising revenue was used along with the sales data of other brands and along with prices to predict the sales of individual brands. Simon concluded that retention rate or brand loyalty was very high (.75) from year to year. It was not a function of price range, sales volume, or advertising volume. He also found that there are diminishing returns from advertising beyond a certain point and that lesser-known brands profit most from advertising.

Reference is often made to advertising bans in Communist countries. Probably the best studied is Russia, where Treml (1975) has shown that per capita sales of alcohol have risen steadily since 1957, although alcoholic beverages are not advertised in any way. Similar increases are believed to have occurred in other Communist countries.

Several temporary alcohol bans have also been investigated, although they are far from ideal. Alcohol advertising was banned in

British Columbia, a province of Canada, for 14 months in the early 1970s. Smart and Cutler (1976) studied the effects of this ban. Unfortunately, it was incomplete and existed for a short period of time. The ban had no measurable effect on beer, wine, or spirit sales. However, the ban was not a popular one with the public, and it grew more unpopular as time passed. Also, advertisements originating in British Columbia were effectively banned, but not those from outside the province. What the "ban" did was to reduce markedly the amount of alcohol advertising, especially that in newspapers and on local radio and television.

A rather different partial ban was introduced into Manitoba, another Canadian province. This ban affected only broadcast media and beer advertisements. The idea was that young people are heavily exposed to television, particularly in relation to sporting events. Hockey games on television in Canada are sponsored by breweries. Young people also tend to prefer beer to other beverages. Analyses of per capita consumption data showed no effect of the beer advertising ban. The picture is complicated by the institution of another ban at about the same time on fortified wines. This caused a shift to table wines and may also have affected beer sales in some unknown way. Nevertheless, the conclusion is the same as for the British Columbia ban: essentially no effect.

We are now completing a study of the contribution of advertising restrictions to sales in the various states. The liberality of advertising codes for alcoholic beverages varies greatly from one state to another, as do other aspects of availability. We have used an availability scale developed by Matlins (1976) for each American state. It gives each state a score based on the restrictiveness of its alcohol control laws. Regression analyses have been made using these scores, advertising restrictions, income, and other economic variables to predict per capita consumption. The analyses to date show no contribution of advertising restrictions to the consumption of beer, wine, or spirits.

The available data on advertising generate no confidence that restrictions on alcohol advertising would prevent drinking and drinking problems. None of the studies reviewed so far is ideal in content or methodology, but they all arrive at the same conclusion: no measurable effect on drinking. Unfortunately, the existing studies are not directly relevant to young people. It could be that young people are especially susceptible to alcohol advertising because of their media exposure and the way advertisements are presented, for example, with the use of young actors. Perhaps advertisements are an important element in seducing young people away from their abstention into drinking. The available "ban studies" have not been organized to evaluate the effects on youthful drinking, and hence little information exists to support any certain conclusions. The major priority for alcohol advertising research would be to investigate how it affects young people. Until further information is available on the topic, it is impossible on empirical grounds to recommend government action against alcohol advertising. On the grounds of taste, good sense, and public support, we could recommend reductions in advertising directed at young people, but the longterm effects may not be measurable.

5. Other Policy Activities Related to Youthful Drinking

The major policy initiatives concerning youthful drinking have already been discussed, but a few remain that are outside the main stream of interest. Chiefly these related to (a) better enforcement of current laws or general permissiveness concerning drinkers, and (b) manipulations concerned with drinking and driving problems. Generally, these policy initiatives are not associated with either of the major preventive models concerning youthful drinking.

It is clear from many studies (e.g., Smart & Goodstadt, 1977; Bruun & Hauge, 1963; Maddox & McCall, 1964) that many students start to drink before they are legally entitled to do so. People often argue that this is because of a "permissive" society or the lax enforcement of current laws about drinking. Straus and Bacon's study (1953), however, suggested that there were more drinking problems in colleges that were intolerant of drinking. Also, some studies show that in families where the parents are abstainers, the children are more likely to have problems if they drink (Skolnick, 1958; Globetti & Chamblin, 1966).

It may be that where restrictions on youthful drinking are strict, different problems arise than where they are lax. For example, Bruun and Hauge (1963) found in the Scandinavian countries that where young people's legal drinking was strictly controlled, they tended to drink out of doors. There was also more illicit drinking by underage drinkers in places where restrictions were in force. Stacey and Davies (1970) summarized evidence showing that in communities that were permissive about youthful drinking, young people got alcohol illegally but from a legal seller. Where there was less permissiveness, they obtained alcohol from bootleggers or other illegal sources. It may be that whether restrictions should be rigidly enforced or not depends upon the problems we are willing to tolerate. Such restrictions may reduce amounts of drinking but create other problems, such as surreptitious drinking (in parks, etc.) and contacts with illegal agents, such as bootleggers.

These considerations are important when it is realized that calls for stricter enforcement of drinking laws are not uncommon. As an example, there is the report on "Youth and Alcohol" (Jones, 1976) prepared for the Cabinet of Ontario. This report was written by a team supervised by Terry Jones, a member of the Provincial Parliament, and more than any other single event, it probably convinced the government to raise the drinking age in Ontario. Among its recommendations are that the age be increased, that prices be raised, and that more alcohol education be given in schools and in the mass media. However, other recommendations were also that (a) there be stricter enforcement of underage drinking laws; (b) penalties for underage drinking and purchasing be raised; and (c) penalties be raised for liquor-license holders who serve minors. If successful, such measures would, of course, lead to more criminalization of young drinkers. These measures could also lead to a different type of drinking problem, for example, surreptitious drinking with little adult supervision. If strictly enforced, however, they could reduce the total consumption of alcohol among young people. Unfortunately, we do not have any empirical study of the actual effects of these changes, although most of the enforcement suggestions in the Jones report have been acted upon.

The problems of drinking and driving among young people are difficult to solve. Young people seem to have alcohol-related accidents at lower levels than do adults (Borkenstein *et al.*, 1964). It is usually claimed that the reason is that they are novices at both drinking and driving. In North America, young people learn to drink and to drive at about the age of 16 or 17, although they probably have their very first drink a little earlier. The Jones report recommended more driver education and also probationary licenses that would be immediately withdrawn on any alcohol and driving offense. Other suggestions have been that the first driving and drinking be separated in time. This could best be done by leaving the drinking age at 18 or 19 but allowing drivers' licenses only to those aged 21 or over. Again, the idea seems a good one, but there is no real evidence to predict the effects of such a change. Would it result in more driving without a license, or would it really limit young people's exposure to drinking and driving? It might be worth an experiment, but it is likely to be so unpopular that few democratic governments would try it.

6. Treatment of Youthful Alcohol Problems: Secondary and Tertiary Prevention

It is recognized that some youthful drinking problems require treatment, whether it be hospitalization for alcoholism, outpatient care, or merely a few counseling sessions. The best-described types of treatment are those designed for adult alcoholics that are given to young people merely because they happened to be part of the patient population. Efforts to develop specialized treatments for youthful drinking problems have rarely been evaluated so far. Also, studies of early case finding and treatment have scarcely been attempted.

The precise rate of alcoholism among young people is difficult to determine, but cases do certainly exist. In Ontario, we found that about 4% of all admissions of alcoholics to treatment were aged 21 or under. The study by Goby (1977) in Chicago showed that 25% of all patients admitted to an alcoholism treatment center were aged 23 or less.

Although it is recognized that alcoholics can be very young, surprisingly few studies have been made of treatments for them. Only a few studies of young persons give an indication of the problems of treatment or overall recovery rates. Currently, many clinicians believe that young alcoholics are very difficult to treat, have more symptoms, and have lower recovery rates than do older alcoholics. Numerous studies have indicated clinical impressions supporting this view. For example, Rosenberg (1969) found that young alcoholics had a history of antisocial behavior, neuroticism, and anxiety and became dependent on alcohol at earlier ages than did older alcoholics. Gwinner (1977), who examined young alcoholics being treated in facilities for British Navy personnel also found that they developed symptoms earlier than older alcoholics.

Only a few studies of young alcoholics in treatment have used follow-up methods with a consistent time period after treatment. Tuchmann (1965) reported that alcoholics treated in the Kalksburg Centre in Austria required aftercare less often if they were under 30. Unfortunately, he did not do a structured follow-up. Rathod *et al.* (1966), in England, compared follow-up results for older and younger alcoholics, but this study included only eight alcoholics under 30 years of age. Of these, seven relapsed. Similar, rather depressing, results were reported by Goby (1977), with a follow-up varying from 11 to 25 months. Only 5 of 41 young persons in Goby's study reported sobriety, with the remainder mostly using alcohol excessively.

In a recent study by Smart (1979), he examined the propositions that young alcoholics had more problems at intake and were more difficult to treat than older alcoholics. In this study, 40 alcoholics aged 24 or under were compared with 40 randomly selected older alcoholics of an average age of 45.1 years. The study examined drinking symptoms and demographic characteristics at intake, the type and length of treatment and overall recovery rates in terms of drinking symptoms evaluated according to the Alcoholic Involvement Scale. The results showed that compared with older alcoholics, the younger ones entered treatment with fewer resources in terms of interests and people to help them, lower social stability, poorer attitudes toward abstinence, and lower motivation for treatment. However, the young people did not have more alcoholic problems or symptoms or a higher level of alcohol consumption. The main differences seemed related to age; that is, young alcoholics began their drinking careers earlier and had fewer social supports when they came into treatment. However, they had been treated less often in the past and had been in the "alcoholic game" for a far shorter period of time. The differences at intake should have made young people more difficult to treat. However, there was no difference in recovery rates or in the type or amount of treatment received. A number of questions remain. Is it likely that young alcoholics retain a resiliency because of their age, which allows them to overcome their problems of low motivation for treatment? Are young people less deteriorated physically than older alcoholics? In any case, there is no good evidence for expecting that young alcoholics will not do as well as older alcoholics in treatment. It seems that the pessimism about treating young alcoholics may be unjustified, and efforts to get young alcoholics into treatment are likely to be productive.

Efforts to develop early case findings and treatment for young alcoholics or problem drinkers are just beginning. It is known that certain types of young people represent greater risks of developing problems than others. Problem drinking is most common (Smart, 1976; Stacey & Davies, 1970) among:

1. Males
2. Heavy, frequent drinkers, especially those who drink beverages with high alcoholic content
3. Persons defined as big drinkers or problem drinkers by others.
4. Those who drank before the age of 12
5. Effect drinkers, that is, those who drink to improve their performance
6. Those who have alcoholic parents
7. Those who have personality traits such as dependency –independency conflicts, low endurance, and poor perseverance in tasks undertaken. Delinquents, especially those convicted of underage drinking

Knowledge of these characteristics would allow the development of special interventions for problem drinkers. The interventions could involve the assessment of problems, referral to treatment, and some sort of follow-up. Mere presentations of educational material might also be attempted. The "treatment" could range from full-scale clinical or hospital care for the worst cases to informal counseling sessions for the least damaged. Such activities could be mounted in schools with health or counseling services or in juvenile courts.

Only a few early intervention efforts seem to have been evaluated. McElfresh (1970) described a four-week "educational-supportive" program for teenaged children of hospitalized alcoholics. They would be at high risk for developing alcohol problems and in addition would have emotional problems connected with their parents' drinking. Unfortunately, the course proved to be unpopular with the teenagers. Only about half completed the 20 sessions. However, perhaps the course could be improved and made more attractive.

Similar, less formal activities for teenagers who have alcohol problems themselves or in their families are provided by Alcoholics Anonymous. The groups for young alcoholics are called Alateen. For those with alcoholic parent or spouse, Al-Anon groups have been formed. It is usually said that Alcoholics Anonymous cannot be evaluated. Certainly, there are limits on evaluations of AA, but a number of interesting studies have been made (Baekeland, Lundwall, & Kissing, 1975). More information on the utility of Alateen for young problem drinkers would be of help in understanding who goes to such groups and to what extent they respond.

Some evaluations of impaired-driver programs have been made, but they are usually not specifically for young people. The evaluations of the Alcohol Safety Action Programs for court-referred impaired drivers have essentially shown no effect (Zador, 1975). A recently devised program called the "NASAP" represents a more intensive program for navy personnel, most of whom are young. It involves a 36-hour education program for early problem drinkers and comprehensive treatment for alcoholics. A complete evaluation has not been published, but there is a claim of "dramatic decreases in re-arrests for DWI offenders" (Naval Training Center, 1977). It may be that military situations allow for much closer control over deviant behavior, once it is identified, than do civilian ones.

In summary, treatment for youthful alcoholics seems to be as successful as for older alcoholics. However, there is a large group of young problem drinkers who are probably not receiving any treatment, however minimal. Some case-finding studies of high-risk groups should be done to identify this group and to determine how many require treatment. High-risk groups can be easily identified with current knowledge, and efforts at intervention with this group should be attempted. The best sort of intervention would probably be far short of the routine clinical treatment given alcoholics. It could be counseling or didactic in nature. More information should be available on how many young problem drinkers want and need such intervention.

7. The Balance between Treatment and Preventive Priorities

Most observers would agree that the dominant priority in the alcohol field has been the treatment of alcoholics. Prevention and education have typically not been important in many programs. It is difficult to determine the precise ratio of spending on treatment and prevention for any given country. However, it is clear that most cities do not have extensive preventive or educational services. Few states and provinces have large-scale alcohol education programs in schools or mass media programs concerning drinking problems. However, almost all have treatment services for alcoholics, including clinics, hospitals, detoxification centers, halfway houses, and the like. Within Ontario, several hundred professionals and nonprofessionals are engaged full time in treating alcoholics, plus many part-time persons. However, not more than a handful of people are doing full-time prevention, and not many more do it part time except for classroom teachers.

Many people have pointed out the folly of spending so many of our health dollars on treatment. Among them is the head of the World Health Organization, Dr. Halfdan Mahler (1976) who has stated that "in far too many countries a privileged few are provided with health care of a highly sophisticated nature, leaving meagre or no health resources for the rest of the population." His remarks apply particularly to the developing countries, but they are also relevant to North America. In North America, hospital treatment for a few alcoholics is provided at a cost of $200 per day, while preventive programs for young people and others are rarely attempted.

Another reason for arguing for a shift of resources from treatment to prevention is the dismal success rate of treatment programs. For example, Emerick's review (1975) of alcoholism treatment shows that no treatment is probably just as good as sophisticated treatment in terms of overall recovery rates. The Edwards, Orford, Egert, Guthrie, Hawker, Hensman, Mitcheson, Oppenheimer, and Taylor (1977) study has shown that clinical treatment for alcoholics is no better than merely giving occasional advice of an unsophisticated sort. Annis, Giesbrecht, Ogborne, and Smart (1976) found that detoxification centers for alcoholics are not coming close to achieving their objectives. Probably, treatment for alcoholics must continue in order to provide training opportunities and clinical material for study. However, the myth that treatment of alcoholics is a successful venture must soon cease to engage our thoughts.

At present, there is promising data that show that alcohol education can be successful, as can some target media programs. We need a reorientation toward prevention and away from expensive treatment. It is also time to argue for a major trial of the preventive concepts that derive from the distribution approach.

8. Summary and Conclusions

Minimizing alcohol problems among young people will require primary, secondary, and tertiary approaches. Youthful problem drinking has been defined in various ways, and the number of problems found depends on the definitions employed. Clinically definable alcoholism is far less frequent than drunkenness, traffic accidents, and social or family problems. The most common approaches to prevention have involved the distribution model and the sociocultural model. Alcohol education can be a part of either model. The distribution approach chiefly emphasizes reductions in per capita consumption and stricter government controls, such as strict age laws, while the sociocultural model emphasizes responsible or safe drinking practices. Treatment or tertiary prevention for alcoholic young people has been attempted in a variety of settings.

Given the various approaches to prevention and education attempted so far, the following tentative conclusions can be made about the ways in which problems can be minimized:

1. It seems likely that a large number—perhaps half—of young people's drinking problems will disappear with time. They are associated more with youthful drinking patterns than with lifelong styles. This is not to say that youthful drinking problems are unimportant, only that many are not permanent.

2. The distribution model of prevention is currently the most compelling. It has the largest amount of empirical data supporting it. Unfortunately, it can never be tested in the laboratory. To confirm or deny its major implications requires a major social experiment, the main elements of which include drastic increases in prices of alcoholic beverages and reductions in availability. Governments should be encouraged to make the requisite social experiments.

3. In general, the sociocultural approach, which promotes "safe or responsible" drinking, is less adequately supported by empirical data than the distribution approach. A safe level of drinking and the necessity

of teaching it to people have not been established. Also, the approach tends to minimize the need for government intervention through price or availability changes. Teaching responsible drinking is also likely to increase per capita consumption.

4. The distribution model is acknowledged to have problems explaining youthful drinking, as it was devised as an explanation of drinking in society as a whole. Young people's drinking problems are apparently less adequately explained by the frequency and amount of drinking than are those of older people. This probability strongly suggests that factors related to the pattern of drinking or the motivations for drinking are also important. Therefore, it is essential that studies of such phenomena continue in relation to the prevention of youthful drinking.

5. The evidence from a variety of studies of the reduction in the drinking age suggests that it increased the extent of drinking and certain kinds of drinking problems, for example, traffic accidents. These data suggest that jurisdictions that have not lowered drinking ages should avoid doing so, on health and safety grounds.

6. It is uncertain whether raising drinking ages alone in areas where they have been lowered would be beneficial. Probably, the best approach would be a combination of the enforcement of underage drinking laws, penalties for those who serve minors, and age-of-majority cards with the bearer's picture.

7. Alcohol education, after an undistinguished temperance past, shows signs of being an important part of preventive programs. Several recent experimental studies have shown beneficial effects over short periods of time. Alcohol education should be expanded to cover more children, and long-term studies of its effectiveness should be planned.

8. Mass media and mass persuasion alcohol programs are mostly disappointing in their outcomes. Those that are most effective are associated with some increased enforcement or a new law. Such programs should be expanded for young people.

9. More mass media programs should be created that are designed for high-risk groups and specifically targeted for them. One of the high-risk groups is young males who are heavy drinkers.

10. The evidence suggests that restrictions on advertising have little effect on drinking or drinking problems of young people or the general population.

11. Stricter enforcement of drinking-age and other laws has an unknown effect on young people's drinking. It is likely that such laws may merely change the type of problem experienced; that is, they may lead to more drinking in parks and purchases from illegal rather than legal sources.

12. An experiment that separated the drinking age in time from the driving age would be of interest. This would, in practice, mean postponing the giving of driving licenses until age 20 or 21.

13. Treatment of young alcoholics seems as successful as for older alcoholics despite the greater problems in treating young alcoholics.

14. Case-finding studies of young alcoholics with serious drinking problems should be combined with assessment and a variety of interventions. More attention should be paid to assessments of how many young problem drinkers in schools need various types of treatment or advice.

15. The current balance between spending on treatment and spending on prevention in the alcohol field is not correct. Many treatment studies have shown negative results, whereas alcohol education and government intervention have shown considerable promise. A shift in resources away from treatment and toward prevention is strongly recommended in the area of alcohol policy.

References

Addiction Research Foundation. *A strategy for the prevention of alcohol problems.* Toronto: Addiction Research Foundation, 1978.

Annis, H., Giesbrecht, N., Ogborne, O., & Smart, R. G. *The Ontario Detoxication System: Task Force II Report on the Operation and Effectiveness.* Toronto: Addiction Research Foundation, 1976.

Bacon, M., & Jones, M. B. *Teenage drinking.* New York: Crowell, 1968.

Baekeland, F., Lundwall, L., & Kissin, B. Methods for treatment of chronic alcoholism: A critical appraisal. In R. Gibbins, Y. Israel, H. Kalant, R. E. Popham, W. Schmidt, & R. G. Smart (Eds.), *Research advances in alcohol and drug problems.* New York: Wiley, 1975.

Bales, R. F. Cultural differences in rates of alcoholism. *Quarterly Journal of Studies on Alcohol,* 1946, *6,* 480–499.

Beauchamp, D. E. Exploring new ethics for public health: Developing a fair alcohol policy. *Journal of Health Policy and Law,* 1976, *1,* 338–354.

Blane, H. T., & Hewitt, L. E. *Mass media, public education and alcohol: A state-of-the art review* (Final report, Purchase Order NIA-76-12). Pittsburgh: University of Pittsburgh, 1977.

Borkenstein, R. F., Crowther, R. F., Shumate, R. P., Ziel, W. B., & Zylman, R. The role of the drinking driver in traffic accidents. Bloomington, Indiana, Indiana University, Department of Police Administration, 1964.

Bruun, K., Edwards, G., Lumio, M., Mäkelä, K., Pan, L., Popham, R. E., Room, R., Schmidt, W., Skög, O. J., Sulkunen, P., & Oesterberg, E. *Alcohol control policies in public health perspective.* Finnish Foundation for Alcohol Studies, Helsinki, 1975.

Bruun, K., & Hauge, R. *Drinking habits among northern youth.* Helsinki: Finnish Foundation for Alcohol Studies, 1963.

Bunce, R. *Alcohol indicators in California.* Social Research Group, School of Public Health, Report No. 1. Berkeley: University of California, 1976.

Clark, W. B., & Mitchell, A. The advertising of alcoholic beverages. Paper prepared for Office of Alcoholism, State of California, 1976.

Cutler, R. E., & Storm, T. Drinking practices in three British Columbia cities. II: Student survey. Vancouver: Alcoholism Foundation of British Columbia, 1973.

de Lint, J., & Schmidt, W. Consumption averages and alcoholism prevalence: A brief review of epidemiological investigations. *British Journal of Addictions*, 1971, *66*, 97–107.

Douglass, R. L., & Freedman, J. A. A study of alcohol-related casualties and alcohol beverage market response to alcohol availability policies in Michigan. Highway Safety Research Institute, Ann Arbor, 1977.

Driessen, G. J., & Bryk, J. A. Alcohol countermeasures: Solid rock and shifting sands. *Journal of Safety Research*, 1973, *5*, 108–129.

Edwards, G., Orford, J., Egert, S., Guthrie, A., Hawker, A., Hensman, C., Mitcheson, M., Oppenheimer, E., & Taylor, C. Alcoholism: A controlled trial of "treatment" and "advice". *Journal of Studies on Alcohol*, 1977, *38*, 1004–1031.

Emrick, C. M. A review of psychologically oriented treatment of alcoholism: The relative effectiveness of treatment versus no treatment. *Journal of Studies on Alcohol*, 1975, *36*, 88–108.

Fieldstone, M. A preliminary report of a review of alcohol and drug programs found in the Metro Toronto educational system. Addiction Research Foundation, 1974.

Fillmore, K. M. Drinking and problem drinking in early adulthood and middle age: An exploratory 20 year follow-up study. *Quarterly Journal of Studies on Alcohol*, 1974, *35*, 819–840.

Globetti, G., & Chamblin, F. Problem drinking among high school students in a Mississippi community. Department of Sociology and Anthropology, Mississippi State University, 1966.

Goby, M. J. Follow-up study: Young adult patients, 1975. Alcoholism Treatment Center, Lutheran General Hospital, Park Ridge, Ill., 1977.

Goodstadt, M. S., Sheppard, M. A., & Crawford, S. H. Development and evaluation of two alcohol education programs for the Toronto Board of Education. Addiction Research Foundation, Toronto, Substudy No. 941, 1978.

Gwinner, P. D. The young alcoholic: Approaches to treatment. In J. S. Madden, R. Walker, & W. H. Kenyon (Eds.), *Alcoholism and drug dependence: A multidisciplinary approach*. New York: Plenum Press, 1977.

Jellinek, E. M. *The disease concept of alcoholism*. New Brunswick, N.J.: College and University Press, 1960.

Jessor, R., & Jessor, S. L. Adolescent development and the onset of drinking. *Journal of Studies on Alcohol*, 1975, *36*, 27–51.

Jones, T. Youth and alcohol. A study prepared for the Cabinet of Ontario by the Ontario Youth Secretariat, Toronto, 1976.

Ledermann, S. C. Alcool, alcoolism, alcoolisation. Données Scientifiques de Caractère Physiologique, Economique et Social, Inst. Nat. Études Demogr. Trav. et Doc., Cah. No. 29, 1956.

Maddox, G. L., & McCall, B. C. *Drinking among teen-agers*. New Brunswick, N.J.: Rutgers Center of Alcohol Studies, 1964.

Mahler, H. A social revolution in public health. *W.H.O. Chronicle*, 1976, *30*, 475–480.

Mäkelä, K. Levels of consumption and social consequences of drinking. In Y. Israel, F. Glaser, H. Kalant, R. E. Popham, W. Schmidt, & R. G. Smart (Eds.), *Research advances in alcohol and drug problems* (Vol. 4). New York: Plenum Press, 1978.

Matlins, S. A study in the actual effects of alcoholic beverage control laws. Medicine in the Public Interest, Washington, 1976.

McElfresh, O. Supportive groups for teenagers of the alcoholic parent: A preliminary report. *Medical Ecology and Clinical Research*, 1970, *3*, 26–29.

Miller, G. H., & Agnew, N. The Ledermann models of alcohol consumption. *Quarterly Journal of Studies on Alcohol*, 1974, *35*, 877–898.

Naval Training Center. Alcohol safety action program. Orlando, Fla., 1977.

O'Neill, B., & Wells, W. T. Blood alcohol levels in drivers not involved in accidents and the lognormal distribution. *Quarterly Journal of Studies on Alcohol*, 1971, *32*, 798–803.

Parker, D. A., & Harman, M. S. The distribution of consumption model of prevention: A critical assessment. Paper prepared for the NIAAA Symposium on Normative Approaches to Prevention, Coronado, Calif., 1977.

Pierce, J., Hieatt, D., Goodstadt, M., Lonero, L., Cunliffe, A., & Pang, H. Experimental evaluation of a community-based program against drinking–driving. In S. Israelstam & S. Lambert (Eds.), *Alcohol, drugs and traffic safety*. Toronto: Addiction Research Foundation, 1975.

Popham, R. E., Schmidt, W., & de Lint, J. The effects of legal restraint on drinking. In B. Kissin & H. Begleiter, (Eds.), *The biology of alcoholism* (Vol. 4). New York: Plenum Press, 1976.

Rathod, N. H., Gregory, E., Blows, D., & Thomas, G. H. A two-year follow-up study of alcoholic patients. *British Journal of Psychiatry*, 1966, *112*, 683–692.

Room, R. The effects of drinking laws on drinking behavior. Paper presented at Annual Meeting of Society for Study of Social Problems, Denver, 1971.

Room, R. Interrelations of alcohol policies, consumption, and problems in the U.S. states. *Drinking and Drug Practices Surveyor*, 1974, *9*, 21–31. (a)

Room, R. Minimizing alcohol problems. Paper presented at 4th Annual Alcoholism Conference of N.I.A.A.A., Washington, 1974. (b)

Room, R. Social science research and alcohol policy making. Paper given at Conference on the Utilization of Research in Drug Policy Making. Washington, 1978.

Rosenberg, C. M. Young alcoholics. *British Journal of Psychiatry*, 1969, *115*, 181–188.

Schmidt, W., & Popham, R. E. The single distribution theory of alcohol consumption. *Journal of Studies on Alcohol*, 1978, *39*, 400–419.

Schmidt, W., & Smart, R. G. Drinking–driving mortality and morbidity statistics. In B. H. Fox & J. H. Fox (Eds.), *Alcohol and traffic safety*. Publication No. 1043, Public Health Service, Washington, 1963.

Simon, J. L. The effect of advertising on liquor brand sales. *Journal of Marketing Research*, 1969, *6*, 301–313.

Skög, O. J. On the distribution of alcohol consumption. Paper given at Symposium on the Epidemiological Approach to the Prevention of Alcoholism, London, 1977.

Skolnick, J. H. Religious affiliation and drinking behavior. *Quarterly Journal of Studies on Alcohol*, 1958, *19*, 452–470.

Smart, R. G. *The new drinkers: Drinking and drinking problems among young people*. Toronto: Addiction Research Foundation, 1976.

Smart, R. G. Changes in alcoholic beverage sales after reductions in the legal drinking age. *American Journal of Drug and Alcohol Abuse*, 1977, *4*, 101–108. (a)

Smart, R. G. Problem drinking among high school students in Ontario. Addiction Research Foundation, Substudy No. 859, 1977. (b)

Smart, R. G. Young alcoholics in treatment: Their characteristics and recovery rates at follow-up. *Alcoholism: Clinical and Experimental Aspects*, 1979, *3*, 19–23.

Smart, R. G., & Cutler, R. The alcohol advertising ban in British Columbia: Problems and effects on beverage consumption. *British Journal of Addiction*, 1976, *71*, 13–21.

Smart, R. G., & Goodstadt, M. Alcohol and drug use among Ontario students in 1977: Preliminary findings. Addiction Research Foundation, Substudy No. 889, 1977.

Smart, R. G., & Gray, G. Parental and peer influences as correlates of problem drinking among high school students. *International Journal of Studies on Addictions*, 1979.

Smart, R. G., Gray, G., & Bennett, C. Predictors of drinking and signs of heavy drinking. *International Journal of Studies on Addictions*, 1979, *13*, 1079–1094.

Stacey, B., & Davies, J. Drinking behaviour in childhood and adolescence: An evaluative review. *British Journal of Addiction*, 1970, *65*, 203–210.

Straus, R., & Bacon, S. D. *Drinking in college*. New Haven, Conn.: Yale University Press, 1953.

Treml, V. G. Production and consumption of alcoholic beverages in the U.S.S.R.: A statistical study. *Journal of Studies on Alcohol*, 1975, *36*, 285–320.

Tuchmann, E. Rehabilitation of alcoholics at Kalksberg (Austria). *British Journal of Addictions*, 1965, *61*, 59–70.

Ullman, A. D. Sociocultural backgrounds of alcoholism. *Annals of the American Academy of Political and Social Science*, 1958, *315*, 48–54.

Warren, R. A., Simpson, H. M., Collard, D., & Page Valin, L. Point zero eight and change in the drinking age: One step forward and two steps backwards. Traffic Injury Research Foundation Reports, Ottawa, 1977.

Whitehead, P. C. Alcohol and young drivers: Impact and implications of lowering the drinking age. Department of National Health and Welfare, Monograph Series No. 1, Ottawa, 1977.

Wilde, G. J. S. Evaluation of effectiveness of public education and information programs related to alcohol, drugs and traffic safety. In S. Israelstam & S. Lambert (Eds.), *Alcohol, drugs and traffic safety*. Toronto: Addiction Research Foundation, 1975.

Wilkinson, R. *The prevention of drinking problems: Alcohol control and cultural influences*. New York: Oxford University Press, 1970.

Williams, A. F., DiCicco, L. M., & Unterberger, H. Philosophy and evaluation of alcohol education program. *Quarterly Journal of Studies on Alcohol*, 1968, *29*, 685–702.

Worden, J., Waller, J., & Riley, T. *The Vermont Public Education Campaign in Alcohol and Highway Safety: A Final Review and Evaluation*. CRASH Report 1–5, Vermont, 1975.

Zador, P. Statistical evaluation of the effectiveness of "alcohol safety action programs." Washington, Insurance Institute for Highway Safety, 1975.

8

The Impact of Sociopolitical Systems on Teenage Alcohol Abuse

Richard E. Horman

1. Introduction

If one assumes the "disease model" for alcoholism, there is no reason to discuss the impact of sociopolitical systems on teenage alcoholism. The disease model would define the etiology of the problem as being biologically based. As a result, sociological and political phenomena would not have any significant impact on the problem. For the purpose of this discussion, however, I submit that the disease model is invalid and that the problem of alcoholism can be defined only as a highly complex political and behavioral problem. I believe further that alcoholism is in and of itself symptomatic of deep and significant societal and psychological problems. Unfortunately, we have come to label alcoholism as a disease when it is merely a symptom of underlying diseases. Because we have decided to classify alcoholism as a disease, we have decided that the appropriate treatment objective for this disease is abstinence. It is unfortunate that we have given this complicated problem an easy label and an easy cure.

During the last ten years, I have had the rare opportunity of being a clinician, a public policymaker, and now a provider of services. I have specialized in the area of adolescent problems, and I have developed some ideas and thoughts about the problems of youth and alcoholism that may tend to be inconsistent with the general thinking in the field.

Richard E. Horman • National Psychiatric Institutes, Washington, DC 20036.

Alcoholism is first a sociological phenomenon that is reinforced or possibly encouraged by the actions of public policymakers. Alcoholism, for me, is secondarily a psychological and medical problem. Most people choose to define first of all the problem as being medical, for in this way, they can reduce their own anxieties about the complexity of the problem and simultaneously place the problem in the hands of the physician.

We tend to do this frequently with problems of an extraordinary nature. As an example, we are aware that certain cancers are caused by environmental problems. Yet we still look to the physician to deal with the prevention of cancer. In reality, only extraordinary changes in our materialistic values will result in prevention of this disease. These value changes will be necessary if we are to live in ways that that are less damaging to our environment and ourselves.

And so it is with the prevention of alcoholism; rather than being a problem for physicians, methods for its prevention will have to be undertaken by sociologists and public policymakers.

I doubt that few would argue that during the last 8 to 10 years, there has been a marked increase in the use of alcoholic beverages among young people. This increase in use comes directly after the major epidemic of psychoactive drug abuse among young people that began in the early 1960s. No one who has been involved in the treatment or the study of these problems should be surprised that this marked increase in alcohol consumption among young people followed the drug abuse epidemic. Alcohol is by all definitions a highly potent psychoactive drug. Moreover, as compared to street psychoactive drugs, it is readily available, and its purity is guaranteed by the federal government through its licensing and regulatory mechanisms. Unfortunately, the same government and its leaders, who guarantee the purity of this dangerous drug, simultaneously carry out actions that significantly affect the rates of of alcoholism.

This discussion attempts to focus on three areas that are sociologically and politically significant as they relate to this increase in alcohol consumption. The areas of interest are the continuing problem of the alienation of young people in this culture, the impact of our pricing structures on per capita consumption, and lastly, the effect of changing the legal age at which alcoholic beverages can be purchased by young people.

2. Alienation

The basic components of alienation are generally viewed as being feelings of powerlessness, normlessness, meaninglessness, isolation, and self-estrangement from the overall society. The concept of powerlessness has its historical orgins in the work of Marx. He saw the worker as separated from control of the economic system that determined the worker's destiny (Marx, 1932). As a result, Marx saw the worker as a helpless being whose destiny was determined by persons and things of whom he had no knowledge and over whom he had no control. Marx believed that the division of labor from management in a capitalistic society would inevitably lead the worker to feel powerless to effect any social change. Man then would even lose the ability to control his own actions.

The second major component of alienation is normlessness. This is most often thought of as what Durkheim (1960) called *anomie*. In looking at the economic system, he suggested that with continual economic gains and losses, man finds himself constantly in situations where there is little or no opportunity to set norms. Durkheim suggested that normlessness implies being without values to structure one's behavior. According to McGee (1962), "the anomic individual is thus in a situation in which norms that usually regulate behavior, and thereby describe the expectations made upon one for his behavior, are entirely absent or have become ineffective." Consequently, the anomic individual would be very predictable. The anomic person finds it necessary to isolate himself from group memberships. McGee suggested that the isolation occurs for two basic reasons:

> The anomic personality does not know how to behave or what to to do with himself because no one cares how he behaves or expects him to behave in any particular way; the anomic personality is unable, largely for lack of social reinforcement and support, to regulate and organize his own behavior for himself.

Merton (1964) used the term *anomie* to indicate certain components of a social system. He used *anomie* to describe the kinds of attitudes and behavior that would be found in people who reside in a normless society. In more specific terms, Merton saw anomie developing in situations where the individual finds an irreconcilable conflict in the socially accepted goals and the means to these goals. Because the person cannot deal with the conflict, he rejects the norms.

Isolation as a part of alienation can be tracked back to Durkheim's conception of anomie. If a person perceives that he cannot share the norms of the overall group, he may tend to remove himself from the group. Hajda (1961) found that alienated students are most likely to belong to few or no "collectivities." He saw the alienated student as one who involves himself exclusively with one "collectivity" that has a consistent ideology. These kinds of groups are not of the type to integrate themselves into the overall society.

Research by Gould (1969), defined *alienation* as a "general or core syndrome consisting of feelings of pessimism, cynicism, distrust, apathy, and emotional distance." A 20-item Manifest Alienation Measure was used to evaluate this syndrome. Gould found that those students studied (only males) who were high in alienation were more likely to be firstborn or only children as compared to those low in alienation. He suggested that the reason for this is that a firstborn or only child is more dependent than later-born children.

As indicated by Gould's work on alienation, the professional community in the last few decades has been looking more at the phenomenon as psychological rather than purely sociological. A study of alienation by Nettler (1957), indicated that alienation and anomie are highly correlated. She stated that it is "difficult to conceive of any notable degree of anomie that would not result in alienation." However, Nettler felt that the two should not be confused, although it is virtually impossible to discuss one without the other. This is suggested because normlessness (anomie) is part of the definition of alienation. Nettler's work on alienation involved studying 37 subjects who fit her definition of alienation: those who had "the feeling of estrangement from society." After conducting in-depth interviews and administering a behavior self-report scale, she arrived at the following conclusions:

1. That alienation is related to creativity.
2. That alienation is related to mental–emotional disorder.
3. That alienation is related to altruism.
4. That the alienated suffer a proclivity to suicide.
5. That they are prone to chemical addictions.
6. That they are poor marriage risks.
7. That their estrangement leads to criminal behavior.

This research defines the alienated individual as an isolated, unhappy, emotionally disturbed person. He does not view the society as causing the alienation but manifests alienation as a particular form of psychopathology.

Dean (1961) defined alienation in a similar manner to Seeman (1959), by listing the major components of the phenomenon as powerlessness, normlessness, and social isolation. Thus, he focused on alienation as a sociological construct. Through the use of attitude scales, he found that the three components are intercorrelated from .41 to .67. Because of the intercorrelations, he concluded that they are all a part of alienation. He defined the three components using the classical sociological definitions of Durkheim, Hegel, etc. Dean stated "that alienation is not a personality trait, but a *situation-relevant variable.*" It appears that Dean's and Marx's views agree on the origin of the phenomenon.

In Hajda's (1961) study of alienation and student intellectuals, he stated that "alienation of intellectuals is primarily a consequence of their intense attachment to and elaboration of abstract values." He indicated that the alienation of intellectuals "is very frequent and striking." He found that self-emancipation from the popular demands of society leads to the self-isolation of the intellectual. Hajda suggested that alienation is psychopathological, because among the students studied, there was "a high number of anxiety symptoms: headaches, insomnia, periods of feeling blue, periods when they cannot force themselves to work, worries about their school work, loss of appetite, and confusion about their goals." Hajda mentioned that he did not know if the anxiety leads to the alienation or the alienation causes anxiety. He concluded that academic institutions create for the intellectual student a rather paradoxical situation: a situation in which the student should be both like and unlike "everybody else." From Hajda's work, it can be stated that he sees alienation as a function of the individual and the overall society.

Struening and Richardson (1965) found cynicism and distrust, bordering on suspicion, to be strongly related to alienation. They concluded by indicating that they found that cynicism, pessimism, and distrust formed "a positively related syndrome of traits."

Taviss (1969) postulated two forms of alienation: social alienation and self-alienation. By analyzing popular magazine fiction from the 1900s versus the 1950s, she concluded that there was considerably greater self-alienation in the 1950s than in the 1900s and somewhat less social alienation in the 1950s. She stated that "alienation results from disjunctions between social demands and values-and-individual needs and inclinations." She defined social alienation as a situation in which the individual finds the society in which he lives too oppressive or imcompatible with his own desires, thus leading to feelings of estrangement. She defined self-alienation as a situation

> in which individual selves may lose contact with any inclinations or desires that are not in agreement with prevailing social patterns, manipulate their selves in accordance with apparent apparent social demands and/or feel incapable of controlling their own actions.

Taviss concluded from her study of magazines that the reason for the shift in alienation is that society no longer makes such harsh demands on the individual as it previously did. Consequently, the individual is not able to "blame" society for his situation.

Keniston (1960) stated that alienation is "estrangement, disaffection, anomie, withdrawal, disengagement, separation, non-involvement, apathy, indifference, and neutralism." He believed that alienation was at one time forced upon man as a result of an "unjust" economic system, which is similar to Marx's view. Keniston has suggested that now alienation is "chosen by men as their basic stance toward society." He termed this "new alienation, an an explicit rejection of what is seen as the dominant values of American culture" (1966). This conception of alienation reflects a composite of most theories concerning this topic. Keniston's definition is very global. His thoughts on the "new alienation" are very consistent with the findings of Taviss. Both suggest that there is now more self-alienation than in previous times.

In Keniston's (1966b) earliest empirical research, he developed a series of highly intercorrelated attitude scales: "These attitudes constitute a kind of empirical cluster or alienation syndrome." The scales are Distrust, Pessimism, Avowed Hostility, Interpersonal Alienation, Social Alienation, Cultural Alienation, Self-Contempt, Vacillation, Subspection, Outsider, and Unstructured Universe.

Distrust is viewed as the primary variable in the "alienation syndrome." In referring to the students studied, Keniston (1966a) remarked that they "believe that intimacy ends in disillusion, that attachment to groups entails the loss of individuality, and that all appearances are untrustworthy."

The major themes to be found in Keniston's work are that the alienated are very distrustful and pessimistic and that their unconscious desires are to return to times of greater security. In Keniston's view, alienation is a result of family situations and conflict-laden development. This conceptualization is markedly different from many of the views expressed earlier in his work.

My review of the literature has uncovered little research that deals specifically with alienation and alcoholism. Some researchers, in studying alienation, have suggested that the alienated are more prone to chemical use than the nonalienated (Keniston, 1966a; Nettler, 1957). Keniston (1966a), suggested that the reason is that drugs and alcohol provide the promise to the user of finding meaning in his existence and calming his intense anxieties. Considering the high degree of psychic discomfort of the alienated, this promise of drugs and alcohol is very enticing.

Irrespective of which of these many theories about alienation one accepts, one is impressed that four concepts appear throughout all the sociological and psychological literature on the topic. These concepts are that the alienated young person feels powerlessness and normlessness, as well as feeling distrustful and pessimistic about his culture and the institutions that provide for his enculturation: the family, his peer group, the church, and the schools.

American culture is only beginning to settle down after what could perhaps be described as the "cultural revolution" of the 1960s and the early 1970s. Whether this cultural revolution was a direct result of the conflict of values that surrounded American participation in the Vietnam War or was a result of some other basic cultural changes that occurred simultaneously with that war is probably irrelevant. What is relevant is that those institutions that we expect to provide for the enculturation of young people went through extraordinary changes during those years. Even today, it is very difficult to predict what the results of the continuing changes in the family structure, the schools, the churches, and the peer groups will be. The lack of stability of these institutions continues to reinforce the feelings of powerlessness, normlessness, distrust, and pessimism that we see in young people.

While the sociologists and psychologists have defined these phenomena well, the public policymakers and the formal leaders of this culture have done little or nothing to exert the kind of leadership that is truly necessary to bring this culture back together. The current President of the United States, Mr. Carter, talks continually of morality and honesty. Yet when faced with the realities of the political process, one finds nothing to distinguish him as a leader in promoting morality and honesty in government. During his campaign, Mr. Carter pledged that his administration would be dedicated to resurrecting the family unit as the primary unit of American society. But after two years, his administration provided nothing more than rhetoric in this area. In order to show his faith in his plan for the rebirth of public education in the United States, the President placed his young daughter in a typical Washington, D.C., public school. Within a year, he transferred her to another public school in Washington that happens to be located in one of the most affluent and culturally rich communities in the United States.

While it is true that Gerald Ford brought the United States out of an extraordinary political crisis, it is also true that his short administration did virtually nothing to pull together the basic institutions in our culture that have so badly deteriorated since the 1960s. He did not provide "cultural–societal leadership".

Obviously, Richard Nixon, by his proven actions and deeds, was morally incapable of providing the leadership necessary to bring the United States out of the cultural revolution of the 1960s. Moreover, he provided what can only be described as a very negative role model for the children of this country. His obsession to lead in foreign affairs only underscored and magnified his lack of willingness to deal with cultural–societal problems at home. Most of the positive events that occurred during his administration were probably wiped out in the minds of American citizens by the lying and deceit that exemplified his reelection and then the end of his administration.

Lyndon Johnson's orientation to public policy initiatives were quite the reverse of Richard Nixon's. Johnson will probably go down in history as the the man who initiated more social programs than any other single president. Unfortunately, that leadership was negated by his actions and decisions related to the Vietnam War. Moreover, as a moral leader, it is difficult to perceive Lyndon Johnson as providing the kind of leadership that would cause young people to idolize him and desire to follow the moral and social courses that he had established.

To a psychologist and politician, it is difficult to know or understand the implications of John Kennedy's presidency. The period of increased alienation and drug abuse by young people began shortly after his assassination. Whether it was the assassination of a youthful, energetic, and positively thinking president that precipitated the the social revolution of the 1960s or if in reality it was the decisions of our leaders to get into Vietnam that caused the fabric of American culture to disintegrate so badly will probably always be an open question. One must speculate that at least the public knowledge of John Kennedy was always positive in the areas of family, religious, and educational institutions. Had he lived and had the Vietnam War not become such an American tragedy, perhaps the alienation that has been so pervasive in the last 15 years might have been avoided.

The presidents of the United States should be the ultimate leaders, not only politically but morally and socially. It would be an understatement to say that the last 15 years of presidential leadership have done nothing significant to weave together our deteriorated American culture. It is no longer possible to pick up a newspaper and not read about the corruption at every level of government. While it is true that this corruption probably involves a relatively small number of people, it is also true that the elected leaders of the country, the states, and the cities are now subject to great cynicism by the taxpayers. Warranted or not, our expectations of leadership and the role models to be found from the elected political process have not been fullfilled for too long in this country.

Not only have our elected leaders shown themselves to be ineffective in providing the moral and social leadership that the culture requires, they have shown themselves to be frequently powerless in effecting significant change. Nothing is more symbolic of their failure than the fact that government bureaucracy at every level has become a self-sustaining, self-feeding machine of human beings who no longer seem to be subject to the controls of our elected leaders. Probably, the single person in the United States most powerless to deal with the bureaucracy is the president. No matter what has been tried during the last 15 years, most presidents have had to concede publicly that they are not able to control and administer the federal bureaucracy effectively.

If alienation means powerlessness, normlessness, distrustfulness, and pessimism, our elected leaders are truly the great symbols of these problems. They frequently show themselves to be powerless in carrying out much of the chief executive officer's responsibilities. Discussions of norms and values for so many of these people have turned out to be empty rhetoric. More and more of our public leaders have shown themselves to be tremendously distrustful of everyone but their closest personal staff. Richard Nixon was not the only politician who taped conversations and had notes taken of everthing that transpired in his office. That is a frequent occurrence with politicians. The tape recorder attached to the telephone was not invented in Washington during the Nixon administration. I must submit that as a consequence of all of this, pessimism and distrust have become the norm and not the exception in in this culture.

If we assume the validity of Nettler's (1957) work and the observations of Keniston (1960, 1966a,b), as well as Horman (1973), we should not be surprised that because of this creeping and insidious problem of alienation in the culture, we have a general increase in chemical abuse.

A review of the literature clearly establishes that availability is one of the key determinants of what substances are abused. The easy availability of alcohol and its ability to suppress the pain and anxiety experienced by alienated young people have made it the number one drug of abuse. It should be no surprise that the rates of alcoholism in the United States among teenagers continue to rise and that there is no expectation that the rate of the rise will change. The culture remains very unstable.

3. Availability of Alcoholic Beverages

Public policymakers could affect the per capita consumption of alcohol. They do not, however, choose to do so. Instead, they tend to bow to the political process rather than addressing the important issues and the real needs of the people who elect them. One of the issues that needs to be addressed is the increased availability of alcoholic beverages.

It is a well established fact that the per capita consumption of alcohol correlates positively with its availability. State government is directly responsible for controlling the availability of alcohol. There is nothing in the literature to indicate that this unit of government has attempted to change public policy in order to reduce the availability of alcohol since Prohibition. Moreover, in the last six years, during which increasing amounts of research have been generated on the topic of government control of alcoholic beverages, nothing of significance has been been done to affect availability.

The reason for this inactivity is not that government officials do not know what to do or how to do it. Rather, they choose not to act because of their fear of the reactions of special-interest groups.

In 1972, I was appointed the executive director of the Commonwealth of Pennsylvania's Governor's Council on Drug and Alcohol Abuse. Because of events that I will discuss, it became increasingly clear to me during my four-year term that the process of making public policy in Pennsylvania, and in most other states, was skewed against taking forceful actions that would affect consumption patterns. Most public policymakers would still prefer to spend millions of dollars on media campaigns about the evils of alcohol rather than deal concretely with the issues of alcohol availability and consumption.

The Commonwealth of Pennsylvania was the first state in the United States to enact a monopoly system of state-owned stores that sold distilled spirits and wine. This was done during the term of Governor Pinchot in 1933, shortly after the repeal of Prohibition. Although Pennsylvania was the first state to set up a monopoly for alcoholic beverages, 15 other states followed. Pennsylvania was and is the largest single purchaser of distilled spirits and wine in the United States; beer was never a part of the monopoly system in Pennsylvania.

While Governor Pinchot was clearly the architect of the legislation establishing the state control of distilled spirits and wine, he was also an avowed dry who campaigned for governor on a "bone-dry platform." Also, for 10 years before, he had sat on the State Board of Trustees of the Anti-Saloon League. Consequently, it is not surprising that Pennsylvania opted for a monopoly system rather than merely the licensing of businesses to sell liquor. The monopoly in Pennsylvania was not set up for the purpose of *controlling alcoholism;* it was an attempt to *regulate the morals* of the citizens. Governor Pinchot saw the state stores as a way of protecting the citizens of the state from moral decadence. A classic statement from Governor Pinchot's program that dealt with the end of Prohibition was "The saloon must not come back."

In 1970, Milton Shapp, who was running for election as governor of Pennsylvania, proposed that the state should dispose of its ownership of what have become known as the state stores. He suggested instead that the state license the sellers of distilled spirits and wine as it does the sellers of beer. He made this proposal for several reasons:

1. His general faith in the free enterprise system caused him to believe that the free enterprise system would do a better job selling the liquor than would the state.
2. There had been widespread allegations of corruption in the state liquor monopoly.

3. The fees from the initial sale of the state stores licenses were estimated to be between $150,000,000 and $300,000,000, exclusive of the sale of the real estate. Additionally, the state would be able to liquidate large numbers of buildings and leases for facilities that they were currently using to operate the state stores.
4. This proposal would result in a marked decrease in the number of state employees.

Shortly after he was was elected, Governor Shapp contracted with the accounting firm of Laventhol, Krekstein, Horwath, and Horwath to analyze the financial implications of the sale of the state stores. The consultants prepared a rather lengthy financial analysis of the proposal based on a number of computer models that they developed as well as on surveys that they conducted. The key points of that study that are relevant here are:

1. The state would realize between $150,000,000 and $300,000,000 in revenues from the sale of the licenses of the existing state stores.
2. Ongoing licensing fees would be significant.
3. Although the state would no longer have the "profit" from the sales, the tax revenues that would be generated would be significant. Sales would increase because in a free marketplace, there would be discounting. Also, it appeared that the consumer was price sensitive.
4. In general, the consultants felt that it would be an excellent financial opportunity for the state.

At no time did the consultants evaluate the social and medical implications of this major change in public policy in Pennsylvania.

Governor Shapp had also campaigned for the establishment of a comprehensive state drug abuse and alcoholism treatment and prevention program. He had a very strong personal commitment to the establishment of this program since Pennsylvania, which is the third largest state in the country, had few drug and alcohol treatment or prevention programs throughout many parts of the state.

For over a year after I assumed my position, legislation was being debated in the State General Assembly that would result in the disposal of the state stores. Interestingly enough, I was not asked to participate in the discussions surrounding the legislation, nor did I interject myself into the discussions. Somewhat naively, I did not feel that the way the substance was being dispensed would affect the rates of alcoholism in the state. As a matter of fact, it always seemed paradoxical to me that the state was dispenser of such a dangerous drug, when the real commitment of the administration was to establish alcohol treatment and rehabilitative services for its citizens.

By the winter of 1973, it became apparent that the legislation would be short a number of votes for passage. At the same time, the Retail Clerks International Union began an aggressive campaign to defeat the legislation. In Pennsylvania, most of the public employees, in addition to being civil servants are unionized. Moreover, as union members, these employees have the right to strike. The Retail Clerks International Union was the group representing the several thousand people who worked for the Pennsylvania Liquor Control Board, which administered the monopoly system. They were obviously afraid that if the monopoly was broken up and sold to individual owners, they would no longer be able to have unionization of all liquor outlets in the state.

It became clear to the governor in late 1973 that his proposal to sell the liquor stores was in jeopardy. While the polls indicated that more than a majority of the citizens of the state would prefer independent retail outlets, the depth of support was not there. Approximately 50% of Pennsylvania's population lives in rural areas, which tend to be rather conservative and very vocal on issues of morality; the population that wanted the state stores sold, however, tended to be liberal, lived in the urban areas, and were less vocal. Added to this problem were the unions, which were beginning to raise loud voices about the proposal.

Milton Shapp is a Democrat with strong labor backing. Consequently, the union support was critical to him. He had decided to run for office in 1974, and he and/or his political advisers wanted a way to get out of dealing with the state store legislation in a way that would not be politically embarrassing. In September 1973, I was called into the governor's office to discuss how we were going to extricate him from this problematic legislation with minimal political damage.

The thesis at the time was that perhaps the sale of the state stores would be detrimental to the problem of alcoholism and that I should use my researchers to find out if that was true. I remember saying at that time that I thought the idea absurd because an alcoholic is going to drink no matter what; who owns the stores is irrelevant. When someone wants to be an alcoholic, I thought, nothing is going to affect his behavior other than absolute isolation from the substance.

In the fall of 1973, I requested that Dr. Frederick Glaser, chief of the the Section on Drug and Alcohol Abuse at the Medical College of Pennsylvania, undertake a study for me to determine whether the sale of the state liquor stores would have any negative effects on public health. As I noted earlier, I did not expect the study to support the hypothesis that the sale would have any negative effect. The research was a review of the literature, all done on a retrospective basis. Any literature on the topic or related topics was of a correlational nature and consequently established relationships rather than cause and effect. There has never been any experimental research concerning what happens when a monopoly system is changed to a licensing system. However, in the making of public policy, we do not normally concern ourselves with the standards of research excellence that we require in academic settings.

The research was very interesting, and it included information obtained primarily from sources outside of the United States as well as from sources from within. It is worth noting that little research has actually been done in the United States concerning public policy and liquor consumption, particularly in the area of monopoly control sales and distribution. Again, it is important to note that I had been working at that time on the premise that the "disease model" was the appropriate model for defining the nature of alcoholism. The research prepared by Dr. Glaser and his staff was long and rather detailed. In summary, the research findings were the following.

1. There is no significant difference in the rate of alcoholism of those states or countries where the government operates the liquor stores and those states or countries that merely license the sellers of alcohol.
2. There is no significant difference in the per capita consumption of alcohol in states or countries that license liquor stores as compared to those states or countries where the government is the actual seller.
3. There is no relationship between the increase in the number of sales outlets and the prevalence of alcoholism (assuming that one is not discussing absolutes).

These findings were easily construed as supportive of the state administration's position on wanting to move forward with the liquidation of the state stores. However, a further review of the research shed important light on other issues that should be taken into consideration. The researchers continued by reporting the following.

1. A decrease in the price of liquor is directly and significantly related to an increase in per capita consumption. The Laventhol, Krekstein, Horwath, and Horwath Report and the Glaser Report were in agreement that prices would drop from the disposal of the state stores.

2. There is a significant and direct relationship between per capita consumption and the prevalence of alcoholism. As consumption increases, the number of alcoholics also increases.
3. There is a significant and inverse relationship between the cost of alcohol and the rate of alcoholism. As the price drops, the prevalence of alcoholism increases. In his report, Dr. Glaser noted, "the greater the percentage of his available income that a man must spend to purchase a given amount of alcohol the less likely he is to become alcoholic."
4. The disposal of the state stores would also result in the development of a powerful vested interest group. This group would have, as one primary goal, keeping prices and taxes down, thus creating an environment that would result in increased alcoholism.

After reviewing the research, it occurred to me, "why not sell the state stores, but have the commonwealth control the prices." However, at that point there were enough liquor, beer, and wine lobbyists in the capitol; the sale of the state stores would have resulted in a potential of 700 to 1,500 new lobbying groups throughout the state. This increase in the lobbying effort would make any attempt to control prices in the licensing system little more than a charade.

At that point, I also told the governor that a drop in the price of beer or wine is as dangerous as a price drop in liquor. The form that the alcohol is in is irrelevant to the problem of alcoholism. Much of the research cited in the Glaser Report reminded the reader that large numbers of alcoholics are strictly wine and beer drinkers.

It is also worth noting that during this time, great pressure was being brought to increase the number of "pop" wines that were on the lists to be sold in the state stores. If an alcoholic beverage was not "listed," it could not be sold in the state. The pressure to list these inexpensive sweet wines was enormous. Marketing studies indicated that these wines were consumed by "young people" and that these wines would be readily purchased and would thus generate increasing revenues. Pop wines were listed, and letters and calls indicated that empty bottles were to be found thoughout the school campuses and playgrounds of the commonwealth of Pennsylvania.

It was clear that the low prices of these wines appealed to young people. The disposal of the state stores would only have lowered the prices.

Because the research report had suggested the relationship between price and consumption, Dr. Glaser and his colleagues recommended that we consider legislating additional taxes on the sale of alcoholic beverages in order to effect some decrease in consumption. Needless to say, that proposal was immediately rejected as being politically unwise, even though the revenues from the additional taxes would be dedicated to a fund earmarked for the treatment and prevention of alcoholism problems.

The weight of the report and the 80 research studies reviewed in preparation of the report were sufficient for the governor to drop the proposal. Interestingly enough, complete copies of the study were never released to the press. Although we were satisfied that the research went to the heart of the matter, the commitment of a liberal Democratic administration to attempting to regulate alcoholism through public policy initiatives, other than standard treatment and prevention efforts, was nonexistent. Perhaps the concept of the government's regulating people's drinking behavior is too Orwellian for 1970 middle-class American culture. For some reason, we are willing to do anything and everything to regulate the control, use, and abuse of psychoactive substances other than alcohol. When we get to alcohol consumption, we become very reluctant to use many of the tools at hand to deal with the problem.

Pennsylvania did not dispose of its state stores. And no one who subsequently campaigned for governor has even raised the proposal again. The last time there was an attempt to pass the legislation (which was prior to publication of the research), it was defeated. Since then, no legislator has proposed to pass such a bill again.

As the debate on this public policy initiative died, it was followed by a call to reduce the legal age of alcohol consumption from 21 years to 18 years. Pennsylvania was only one of two dozen states to be forced to address the age debate during the 1970s.

4. The Drinking-Age Debate

The passage of the Federal Voting Rights Act of 1970, which gave 18-year-olds the right to vote in federal elections, was probably the single most catalytic public policy act that has resulted in dropping the drinking age from 21 to 18 or 19 years old. Since the passage of that act, 26 states have lowered their legal drinking age. The argument for this public policy change was that if an 18-year-old was old enough to vote, then the same person should be wise enough to choose whether to drink or not to drink and to to control his drinking behavior. The thesis is interesting and basically unsupportable: while choosing a political candidate is essentially an intellectual exercise, using and abusing alcohol is generally not shown to correlate significantly with intelligence.

Pennsylvania was not one of the states that chose to lower the legal drinking age to 18 or 19. From 1973 to 1975, four different bills were introduced into the State's General Assembly that would have lowered the drinking age to 18 or 19 years. The last legislation dealing with this issue to be proposed was defeated by only one vote. The then governor supported the proposed lowering of the drinking age; his council on Drug and Alcohol Abuse did not. The governor supported the lowering of the drinking age solely on the basis of its civil libertarian aspects. He supported the belief that since an 18- or 19-year-old now was generally viewed as having reached the age of majority, the 18-year-old should receive all the rights and privileges associated with adulthood.

Several years prior to the time Pennsylvania was considering the passage of a law to lower the legal drinking age, the drinking age was lowered in Ontario. Because of the work of the Addiction Research Foundation, some important studies were made available to us showing the effects of lowering the minimun age law in Ontario. The research indicated (Schmidt,1973) that after the drinking age was lowered, the overall consumption rate of alcohol rose. What was startling was that the on-premises purchases by those persons 18- to 21-years-old exceeded the purchases of all other persons over the age of 21. In his study, Schmidt also noted that these estimates "represent consumption in addition to the level of alcohol use that prevailed prior to the lowering of the legal drinking age." This research was related to an earlier study done in Ontario in 1968 (see Schmidt, 1973), which showed that 68% of the respondents in the 18–21 age group reported using alcoholic beverages and that their consumption was about half of the average for Ontario drinkers as a whole. Because of this finding, Schmidt concluded that the new law "not only legalized the status quo, but it also resulted in a considerable increase in consumption amongst those affected."

The other study of significance that was used to defeat the legislation to lower the minimum drinking age in Pennsylvania was again undertaken by the the Addiction Research Foundation. This research, conducted by Schmidt and Kornaczewski (1973), showed that lowering the minimum age in the province in Ontario from 21 to 18 years resulted in an increase in the number of youths involved in automobile accidents. The authors reported as follows:

> Through the study of statistical trends over time it could be demonstrated that, in the twelve month period after the reduction of the legal drinking age, the proportion of young drivers among drivers in all accidents increased significantly. This trend towards larger proportions of young drivers among

> accident drivers which was absent prior to the inception of the new law has continued. While it is not possible to attribute the increases observed entirely to the changes in the law, it is certain that a considerable part of it constitutes an addition to the total accident involvement of the age group that would not have occurred were it not for the lowering of the legal drinking age.[1]

In 1976, a private foundation, Medicine in the Public Interest, undertook a research project for the National Institute on Alcohol Abuse and Alcoholism. The report is entitled "An Examination of Proposed Changes in Minimum Age ABC Laws in Massachusetts and Minnesota" Matlins, 1976). This study was prepared for the NIAAA to help clarify its role and to provide guidance to the states as they considered changes in the legal drinking age. The study focused on the debates that were held in Massachusetts and Minnesota during 1976. This focus developed because both states were considering revisions of their drinking-age laws, which had been lowered two years earlier. The current debate had resulted in pressure to raise the drinking age. This study involved surveys of attitudes among key public policymakers in both states, as well as a careful analysis of the literature and an analysis of the documentation available in the specific states. The study concluded:

1. The question of raising the legal drinking age is being handled in the legislatures as an emotional and political issue.
2. Most state officials and community leaders appear indifferent both to the debate and the law itself.
3. A unique opportunity to study the effects of the lower minimum age law has been lost by the failure to track the experience adequately.
4. The absence of information and the presence of emotion make it likely that the changes now contemplated will not be permanent.

In summary, this study indicated that public policy as it related to the important issue of lowering the drinking age was not a result of a rational and logical process but was a result of an emotional process. Public policy-makers were not focusing on the substantive issue of health. They were not looking at and evaluating the research trends in the field even when faced with an increase in auto accidents and consumption. Even with the decision to reevaluate the laws on a "second

[1] However, for a more recent assessment of the complexities involved in evaluating the lowering of the drinking age in Ontario, see Smart's analysis in the preceding chapter—The Editors.

pass," the debate remained emotional and political rather than rational.It is of interest to note that this study received little distribution by the NIAAA, probably because it was perceived that it would be best for the federal government to avoid taking a leadership role in what had become a growing political debate. It would appear that some government agencies do not wish to take a role in addressing the public policy change of lowering the drinking age. Perhaps the reason is that the public policymakers are afraid that the only position they can take, based on the limited research available, is that "we must stop our children from killing themselves." In these days of great concern about civil liberties, more and more government officials do not see themselves as having a significant role in protecting the taxpayer from doing further damage to his or her physical and mental health.

5. Conclusion

This chapter has focused on the effects of sociopolitical systems on teenage alcohol abuse. It has addressed the problem with both theoretical constructs and a look at some directly observable actions that have occurred that affect teenage alcohol abuse.

The problem of alienation is certainly not new to this culture or to previous cultures. It is, however, an insidious problem. For the individual, it manifests itself as depression, nonspecific anxiety, and rebellion. For the community as a whole, it is a problem that has the potential of severely affecting not only current but future generations. During the 1960s, the alienated were using illicit drugs to medicate themselves. I submit that in the 1970s, they have turned to alcohol as a way to suppress the intense feelings of anxiety and depression associated with their feelings of powerlessness, normlessness, and meaninglessness. No significant actions appear to be occurring within the sociopolitical system that will have a positive impact on the problems.

Actions of public policymakers that can be seen, measured, and felt appear to be negative in consequences. My own personal opportunities to share in the making of public policy made it clear to me that there will not be any significant actions on government's part to affect the availability of alcoholic beverages. This lack of action results even when public policymakers are confronted with research findings that seem to indicate that positive actions on their part could have positive effects. However, since the failure of the "great experiment," Prohibition, it would appear that our elected and appointed government leaders see their responsibilities as ensuring purity, providing for taxation, and funding rehabilitation services for the casualties.

Because of these problems, our children are, in increasing numbers, joining the adults as participating members in this alcoholic culture.

References

Dean, D. Alienation: Its meaning and measurement. *American Sociological Review,* 1961, *26,* 753–758.

Durkheim, E. On anomie. In C. W. Mills (Ed.), *Images of man.* New York: Braziller, 1960.

Gould, L. Conformity and marginality: Two faces of alienation. *Journal of Social Issues,* 1969, *25,* 39–62.

Hajda, J. Alienation and integration of student intellectuals. *American Sociological Review,* 1961, *26,* 758–777.

Horman, R. Alienation and student drug use. *International Journal of the Addictions,* 1973, *8,* 325–331.

Keniston, K. *The uncommitted.* New York: Harcourt, Brace & World, 1960.

Keniston, K. Drug use and student values. Paper presented at the National Association of Student Personnel Administrators Drug Education Conference, Washington, D.C., Nov. 1966.(a)

Keniston, K. The psychology of the alienated student. Paper presented at the American Psychological Association, New York, Sept. 1966.(b)

Marx, K. *Capital, the communist manifesto and other writings.* Max Eastman (Ed.), New York: Modern Library, 1932.

Marx, K. On alienation. In C. W. Mills (Ed.), *Images of man.* New York: Braziller, 1960.

Matlins, S. An examination of proposed changes in minimum age ABC laws in Massachuetts and Minnesota, Washington, 1976.

Mc Gee, R. Social disorganization in America. San Francisco: Chandler, 1962.

Merton, R. Anomie, anomia, and social interaction. In M. B. Clinard (Ed.), *Anomie and deviant behavior.* Glencoe, Ill.: Free Press, 1964.

Nettler, G. A measure of alienation. *American Sociological Review,* 1957, *22,* 670–677.

Schmidt, W., & Kornaczewski, A. A further note on the effect of lowering the drinking age on alcohol related motor vehicle accidents (Substudy #558). Toronto: Addiction Research Foundation, 1973.

Seeman, M. On the meaning of alienation. *American Sociological Review,* 1959, *24,* 783–791.

Struening, E., & Richardson, A. A factor analytic exploration of alienation, anomia, and authoritarianism domain. *American Sociological Review,* 1965, *30,* 768–776.

Taviss, I. Changes in the form of alienation: The 1900's vs. the 1950's. *American Sociological Review,* 1969, *34,* 46–57.

9

Toward National Policy for Health Education

Lawrence W. Green

1. Introduction

Policy has been to health education as oil is to troubled waters: a slick, shining, and shifting layer over depths of unknown quality and quantity. Health education has been pumped or sprayed from a variety of sources into every problem of society related to health, usually with mixed, inconsistent, and submerged policies at first. As the initial flush or mist of health education activity begins to settle, the beads of policy emerge and congeal as a gloss, giving activities and programs the appearance of having a smooth, integrated consistency. Beneath that thin gloss of policy, typically, is a turbulent center of disintegrative or disconnected activity, like a whirlpool, and all around the edges are stagnant pockets where the only movement is Brownian.

The function of policy, under these metaphorical circumstances, has been to rationalize existing activity rather than to shape and to support new programs. It serves to give the appearance of a cohesive program when in fact it is camouflaging an incoherent mix of strong and weak solutions poorly distributed over the problems they were intended to extinguish.

The purpose of this paper is to review the ways that policy gets promoted and developed, the current issues bearing on policy in health

Lawrence W. Green • School of Hygiene and Public Health, The Johns Hopkins University, Baltimore, MD 21205.

education, and the priorities for development of health education so that it can provide the future resource needed to address chronic behavioral and social problems such as alcoholism. The formal review and recommendations for federal policy have been presented recently (Green, 1978). This presentation represents more of a defense and a postmortem, reflecting on the rationale, the emphasis, and the disposition of the federal policy paper. The recommendations of the previous paper converged on issues related to national health insurance. This paper relates more to issues of lifestyle, youth, and chronic conditions that will persist regardless of the passage or defeat of national health insurance legislation.

This paper does not attempt to improve upon the excellent review of education in the prevention of alcoholism by Blane (1976) nor the more general questions of educational and behavioral aspects of prevention (Berkanovic, 1976; Preventive Medicine USA, 1976; Shapiro, 1977; Wang, 1977) nor the broader issues of policy related to alcohol (Berry, 1976; Berry & Boland, 1977; Mäkelä & Vükari, 1977). Somewhere between these three bodies of literature floats a layer of policy issues bearing on health education in more generic and fundamental ways. Their outcomes will determine the potential for health education to contribute effectively to the prevention of problems such as alcoholism in the future.

2. The Empirical Approach to Policy

The perspective of this analysis of policy issues in health education attempts to separate matters of fact from matters of preference or principle. The approach is self-consciously, if not rigorously, empirical. The presentation is not numerical or encyclopedic, but the strategy proposed for movement toward a national policy for health education emphasizes the need for data, documentation, and evidence.

The use of the term *empirical* is from William James, one of the last of the great psychologists out of the philosophy tradition and one of the first of the modern psychologists in the empirical tradition. James (1914) distinguished the temperament of the "Empiricist meaning your lover of facts in all their crude variety" from that of the "Rationalist meaning your devotee to abstract and eternal principles. No one can live an hour without both facts and principles. So it is a difference rather of emphasis, yet it breeds antipathies of the most pungent character between those who lay the emphasis differently." In that brief statement, William James described not only the psychology but also the social structure of health education, a process, a profession, and a realm of social policy in which empiricists and rationalists lay their emphases differently on facts and principles.

Policy, whether it is being decided in a local school board meeting or in the congressional corridors of power, has both empiricist and rationalist temperaments at work. Principles are the stuff of constitutional law, theology, ideology, political persuasion, and the wisdom of experience. When policymakers want to be advised along these lines, they consult their constituencies; their lawyers; their priests, rabbis, ministers, or gurus; and their consciences. They do not need to consult health professionals.

When policymakers turn to health professionals to advise on policy, they are looking for facts. When the American Medical Association testifies on national health insurance from a political stance from which it derives principles of medical practice, Congressmen are skeptical, indeed incredulous. Such lobbying masqueraded as expert testimony from professional groups in the health field has put such testimony in disrepute to the point today that whenever congressional staff see testimony from a health professional, they expect first that it will be self-serving for that profession and, second, that any facts presented in that testimony must be carefully sifted and placed agianst the corresponding facts presented by other health professional groups who are competing for the same resources.

3. Policy Issue No. 1: The Level of Investment

This issue picks up where the President's Committee on Health Education (1974) left off, which was with "health education as social policy," as Simonds (1974) put it. The President's Committee made the most thorough investigation of the levels and location of health education expenditures that is available in the United States to this date. They found that less than one-half of one percent of the then $75-billion expenditures for medical, hospital and health care was expended for health education purposes. Less than one-fifth of one percent of the Department of Health, Education, and Welfare budget of $44 million for health was being expended on health education. Less than one percent of state and territorial health budgets was devoted to health education.

There has been little financial progress since then. Some of the total budgets have nearly doubled, whereas the expenditures on health education, except in a few areas, have remained rather stable. Hence, the proportionate investment in health education has declined. On the basis of the simple principle of the matter, that seems a rather hypocritical level of investment relative to the professed commitment of the government to health education as national policy or social policy. After the agonizing and the rhetoric, however, we are still hard put to answer the question, "How much is enough? How much do you need for health education?" That question sends us back from principles to facts, hoping that there are some facts available and that they will uphold the principle that health education should have more than just one-half of one percent of health expenditures.

Everything is, of course, relative, so one factual or empirical approach to this question is a comparison with the levels of expenditure for mass media advertising of unhealthful products, especially as represented by television and other mass media advertising of junk foods, cigarettes, alcohol, and other forms of fun. We argue from principle that health education should have at least as much money as is being expended by these "manufactures of illness," as McKinley (1975) called them. Empirical evidence is available not only on the amounts they are spending to advertise these forms of self-destruction but also on the levels of investment they make in sophisticated technology and research to improve upon their insidious effectiveness. The advocates for health education are tempted to argue on principle that if only they had the funds for more television time, they could win the hearts and minds of the American public.

Those who have argued in this way have won a certain hearing in policymaking circles, sometimes for the wrong reasons. Some agencies have decided to invest more heavily in mass media, not so much because they are convinced that it will make a difference in health behavior but more because they believe that it will give them or their cause visibility and public attention. Hence, by arguing on principle without sufficient empirical data to inform the policymakers properly, we end up having public relations rather than health education supported for the wrong reasons, and usually at the expense of the kind of health education that could hope to achieve changes in health-related behavior.

The other form that policy decisions take, when they are based on the principle of "the more the better," is that we sometimes get too much of a good thing. There is a point of diminishing returns in much of what we do in health education. If we request and spend twice as much as we need to achieve a specific result, we are subject to a judgment of being inefficient and wasteful (Green, 1977).

The third type of policy decision that may be misguided by professional advice based on the zealous application of principles rather than empirical data is the flooding of a resource at one point in time rather than a proper developmental allocation spread over a sufficient duration to fit the natural history of the health problem or behavior in question. This has happened in smoking education and drug education programs when policy has overreacted to press accounts of a crisis (Green & Green, 1977).

Three types of misallocation of the scarce resources for health education can occur. The first type of misallocation is the result of assuming that "something is better than nothing." The threshold level is the level below which the investment in health education will be insufficient to achieve the desired effect. The second type of misallocation is overexpenditure in time or space, exceeding the point of diminishing returns beyond which additional investments in health education do not receive proportionate increases in the behavioral changes intended. A third type of misallocation is that which causes a backlash effect because it is misdirected or poorly timed relative to public concern with the problem (Green, 1978). When a population has not been prepared appropriately for some messages, additional investments in communicating those messages result in negative reactions to the program (USDHEW, 1976).

Finally, there is a point beyond which a revision in the nature or the intensity of the effort in health education might yield incremental effects. Unfortunately, we do not have the kinds of data available to enable us to say with much confidence what these levels are for different behavioral changes, but this analysis at least points more concretely and empirically toward policy issues that demand health education research. In the meantime, health education must avoid overdrawing on its empirical accounts in advising policy where the data are inadequate to identify the threshold level and the point of diminishing returns for investments in health education.

4. Policy Issue No. 2: How Should the Investment in Health Education Be Channeled?

The question here is one that truly brings out what William James (1914) would have called the pungent character of the antipathies between those who argue on principle and those who argue on fact. The answer to the question of how much is needed for health education is followed by the question, "To whom should it be given?" There are those who argue on principle that it should be given entirely to government agencies because they are the only ones truly accountable to the taxpayers who contributed the resources. There are other rationalists who argue that it should be channeled through private agencies because they will use it more creatively (Victor, 1974) or efficiently

(Pearson, 1974), or to nonprofit agencies because they will use it more flexibly or objectively (Kent, 1974), or to some specially created consortium such as a National Center for Health Education because they might combine the several virtues of nongovernmental agencies utilizing governmental funds (Weingarten, 1974).

The empirical perspective on these issues would bring to bear data concerning the track record of these agencies in health education, the public perception of these different channels of communication, and data on some of the current problems of these agencies or channels that might predict their ability to utilize the health education resources effectively.

One perspective, for example, might examine the declining confidence in the ability of government agencies to serve the public. The Institute for Social Research at the University of Michigan (1974) has noted the statistics on public confidence in government in successive surveys between 1957 and 1973; the results show an increasing rate of decline in public confidence, with the most rapid drop to an all-time low in the Watergate years. The correlation between this trend and public reactions to government-sponsored health programs is not entirely incidental.

The empirical perspective would also tend to yield data suggesting the bureaucratic difficulties that might be expected if government agencies were to assume responsibility for health education to the same degree that they have assumed responsibility, for example, for social security and other health care programs. In these programs, the attempts to achieve equity in health care have contributed to rampant inflation of the medical care dollar, much of that dollar somehow going to people other than the intended recipients (Somers, 1977).

If we should conclude from these kinds of data that the investment in health education should be channeled as much as possible through nonfederal if not nongovernmental channels, then how do we achieve this allocation? This might appear on the surface to be an administrative rather than a policy issue. But it becomes a matter of policy when we recognize that the mechanisms that have traditionally been used in public health for the channeling of federal funds by their very character create policy for the utilization of those funds. I am referring particularly to the distinctions that the government makes between research and demonstrations, between grants and contracts as ways of supporting both research and demonstrations, and between categorical and block mechanisms for making grants and contracts.

If we acknowledge from the analysis on the first issue that we cannot justify large investments, except under sufficiently controlled circumstances to assure that we are not exceeding the point of diminishing returns (meaning that we must insist on evaluation as a condition of investments in health education for the time being), then we have ruled out most kinds of service budgets with fixed allocations. This leaves us with demonstrations and research projects as the initial mechanisms for the channeling of new resources into health education. This excludes, of course, those areas of health education effort where there is a well-established track record of success, such as immunization campaigns and family planning programs. For most other areas, a decision must be made as to the adequacy of the research base to justify demonstrations and the priorities among those problem areas where the research base is inadequate to justify large-scale demonstrations and, therefore, the need of further research.

The second subissue concerning mechanisms for channeling governmental funds in health education has to do with the distinction between grants and contracts. While it may be true that the government no longer has the credibility or the efficiency to conduct effective health education from the national level, that is not to say that the federal government should not maintain a degree of control over how governmental resources are used at the local level and through nongovernmental channels. If the government wants to maximize its control by defining the problem as well as the procedures and the timetable for health education, then it will use its contract mechanisms. If, on the other hand, the government does not perceive itself to be so certain of the right approach, the right priorities, and the right procedures for health education in regional and local areas, then the granting mechanism is to be advised as policy.

Finally, there is the subissue of categorical or block grants. If government policy is to "let a thousand lotus blossoms bloom," then block grants are necessary to give the regional and local agencies an opportunity to set priorities locally for the utilization of health education resources, or at least to compete nationally on the strength of their ability to justify the approach they want to take. If, alternatively, the government is quite certain about the categories of disease or health problems that must be given priority, then categorical grants for health education efforts must become the mechanism of choice.

That leads us to the third broad issue of health education policy, which is the purposes to which health education should be put.

5. Policy Issue No. 3: For What Purposes Should Health Education Be Given Priority?

On this policy issue, we have been historically at the mercy of every breeze that blows from Washington. We have seen the disease-of-the-year syndrome that somehow relates to what Congressmen are most afraid of dying from. We have then been subjected to the cost containment obsession, which would have us justify health education as well as other health expenditures in terms of the dollars saved in medical care. This obsession led in health education first to a preoccupation with the utilization of health services as the primary goal of health education efforts, and more recently to a concern with self-care, although both of these movements have had other sources of support besides cost containment.

The empirical look at this policy issue warns us that even if we left it up to professionals to decide rather than being subjected to the whims of Congress and presidents, we would still have difficulty in maintaining a single set of priorities over any duration. Empirical data show the complete reversal within a recent period of 10 years in the priorities for physical education as stated by physical educators at two different points in time. The nature of their physical education programs had not changed significantly, but the reasons they gave for doing them had fully reversed themselves in the stated order of importance. So much for the rationalist approach to policy. The rationalist becomes little more than a rationalizer when principles are based on the status quo or on opportunistic attachment to trends in public opinion or executive opinion.

6. Policy Issue No. 4: By What Means of Influence?

The fourth and final policy issue, before one steps down from the policy level to the administrative or managerial level, is the question of selecting the right technology or the acceptable approaches to health education. Clearly, most of the strategic decisions or at least the tactical decisions should be left up to the professional health educator at the site of practice. But there are some broad strategic questions that must be dealt with at a policy level because somebody has to set the limits on how coercive the practitioners may be allowed to be in their approach to health education; or in some circumstances, the policy question may be how noncoercive we can afford to let health educators be.

This kind of debate is epitomized by the carrot and the stick controversy as it has been played out in the Indian family-planning program with the change in prime ministers. When Indira Ghandi stepped up the family-planning effort, she went beyond family planning to a wide variety of sanctions and powerfully compelling strategies that would increase the rates of sterilization. Her successor has decreased some of those efforts but has nevertheles intensified the family-planning effort with more incentives and opportunities as the carrot for the practice of contraception.

The issues in health education in this country are perhaps less dramatic, though no less difficult, in the areas of smoking, seat belt usage, and other accident prevention strategies and areas of self-destruction, such as drug abuse, alcoholism, and suicide. We have particular problems with these policy questions on the continuum from incentives to regulatory to coercive methods when the practices or behaviors to be modified are ones that may harm not only the self but others as well. In one sense, this is true of all destructive behaviors because all of us bear the cost of medical care, rehabilitation, and long-term care for those whose negligence or self-destructive behavior leaves them a burden on society at some point in their lives. But there are some problems that may have a more immediate impact on the health of others, such as drunkenness by the alcoholic, violence by the drug addict, and environmental pollution by the industrialist.

Principles and empirical data concerning passive restraints for injury control present a clear-cut case of a policy issue at the level of strategy. Shall we make it unnecessary, indeed even impossible, for people to have to decide whether to buckle themselves in when they go driving in their cars, or should we continue through health education to leave the option open to people whether they should or should not use seat belts, thereby enhancing the principle of self-determination? The health educators of empirical temperament will come up with a different answer than those of the principled or rationalist temperament because the evidence clearly shows that a great many more lives could be saved and many times more injuries could be controlled through the regulatory process of requiring manufacturers to install passive restraints and safety devices in cars. But the aesthetic objections of individuals to some of these devices and the additional costs that must be passed on to the consumer for these devices cause some health educators to argue on principle that this should remain a strictly voluntary action on the part of individuals. In so doing, they play into the hands of the manufacturers, who are resisting the additional expense and regulation of installing these devices. Furthermore, the rationalist in this case comes off appearing to be more concerned with full employment for health educators than with saving lives or preventing injuries.

Let me take a somewhat less dramatic case study in health education policy that quickly devolves to the strategic level and evokes similar kinds of ethical versus practical and empirical considerations. Recent policy debates and deliberations on the question of patient-package inserts for prescription and nonprescription drugs revealed that the stakes are high, especially for the drug industry. Consumers are increasingly faced with complex drug interactions as we treat more and more chronic diseases and multiple co-morbidities in individuals with whole batteries of drugs. The first strategic issue is agreement on objectives for the patient-package insert, because there are many things that it could attempt to do but probably should not do because this is not the best vehicle for doing it. The second policy issue is what legal sanction or legal context to cast the regulation of patient-package inserts into. The Food and Drug Administration, the American Medical Association, and the drug industry have had different things to say on this issue. We end up with a patient-package insert that from the standpoint of health education policy becomes an educational nightmare. Everybody is pressing into the patient-package insert their own messages and concerns. Doctors, lawyers, consumer advocacy groups, and the women's movement all have different messages they want to squeeze into the patient-package insert. From an educational standpoint, we are clearly beyond the point of diminishing returns for this communication device, both in terms of its motivational impact and in terms of its cognitive impact. Together, the overload of frightening messages and technical detail results in no behavior change or in a negative response that is not altogether in the patient's best interest.

In the broader context of health education for drug utilization, the patient-package insert can be a specific communication device that will better serve each of a number of purposes if it is cast into the context of patient education, on the one hand, and extended community health education programming, on the other. We have offered a variety of ways in which this can be done and a variety of expected benefits if it is accomplished (Green & Faden, 1977).

These, then, are the main issues in health education that can properly be called policy issues. An empirical approach to these issues can save health education from some of the traps into which a strictly rationalist approach can lead it. In everyday health education practice, the problem is one of balance between the rationalist and the empirical temperaments. Clearly, one cannot practice health education on an empirical basis alone because the empirical base is too weak. We have not had enough of the kind of basic and applied research and certainly too little of the evaluative research that other health professions have to build upon in their practice (Somers, 1976). Therefore, we extrapolate from research in other areas, such as group dynamics and community organization as practiced in other fields, and from these extrapolations, we derive principles that guide us in practice. But at the policy level, that kind of balance is built into the policymaking process whereby principles take the form of politics (Somers & Somers, 1977). Principles are derived from constitutional law, religious convictions, moral persuasions, political alliances, and personal conscience. What the policymakers want from health professionals are facts, and they expect us to deliver these facts in an objective way. Otherwise, they would have no reason to call upon the professional associations as professional associations but could just as well call upon them as interest groups in the same way that they call upon trade unions. It requires no particular insights or perspective to realize that as an interest group, we are too small to warrant much attention from Congress or from most policy-making bodies.

There are many reasons, enumerated elsewhere, that we should bend ourselves to the tasks of documentation, data collection, and evaluation in health education. One excuse for not doing these things has been that we have been too busy trying to bring about changes in policy to gain support for health education. As it turns out, the most serious impediment to policy change relative to health education is precisely the paucity of persuasive evidence of effectiveness in the form of data. We must at least make use of what exists. This brings us to the questions of training and professional development.

7. Toward a More Empirical Health Education

Historical baselines for an assessment of training needs for the development of health education are provided by two observations of Mustard (1945):

> A new "profession," known as "health educators," is arising. Too often these workers are without the restraint that comes from scientific training and are not well grounded in factual material relating to health and disease. They do, however, possess a stimulating enthusiasm and, in varying degrees, competence in catching the public interest. (p. 176)

Although Mustard's characterization of the rising health educators was not flattering, he did acknowledge the difficulties in a scientific approach to health education: "Health education is an undertaking that produces its results slowly and these results are difficult to measure" (p. 175). This is even more true today. The question now is whether health educators have any greater claim to scientific training than Mustard thought they had in 1945.

The remainder of this paper examines the character of current needs for research in health education; reviews the capacity of health education specialists (as they are currently trained) and various other behavioral or biomedical scientists to evaluate and conduct research on health education that responds to these needs; and suggests policy guidelines for improving the training for a more empirical health education enterprise.

8. The Needs for Research in Health Education

In a background study for a World Health Organization (WHO) Task Force on Research in Health Education, Roberts and Green (1968) surveyed training institutions and ministries of health around the world to determine the status of research efforts at that time. Our results can be summarized as follows: (1) Virtually all of the research in 1968 was being carried out by health educators trained in the United States. Indeed, the majority of formal research projects in health education were being conducted in the United States. Those in Europe and Oceania were being conducted by Europeans, but most of those in the developing countries were being conducted by U.S. investigators in collaboration with U.S.-trained nationals. (2) Most of the research in the developing countries was descriptive rather than experimental, using survey methods, especially surveys of knowledge, attitudes, and practice (KAP) based on verbal reports from interviews with married people about family planning. (3) There had been little experimental evaluation except in a few isolated projects in which the object of evaluation was more likely to be a technique than a program. Young's (1967, 1968, 1973) reviews of the literature of the 1960s for the WHO yielded similar finding (*Research in Health Education*, 1969).

By the early 1970s, a turning point seemed to be developing, both in the nature of the research and evaluation being conducted in health education and in the training of health education specialists with greater skill in the use if not the conduct of research. There was also a growing number of behavioral scientists with greater skill in the evaluation of human service programs in collaboration with practitioners (Mico & Ross, 1975; Steuart, 1969).

The shift in emphasis from communicable diseases to chronic diseases was marked by a corresponding swing from nonexperimental survey approaches in the evaluation of immunization programs and family-planning programs in the late 1960s to experimental and quasi-experimental evaluations of health education in clinical settings, where the long-term management of chronic diseases was provided. These clinical settings provided opportunities for greater experimental control and randomized assignment of patients to experimental and control groups (Green & Figá-Talamanca, 1974). This shift has brought many health education practices under much closer scrutiny than they had been subjected to in the past. It also provided health education with opportunities to gain scientific credibility with the medical profession, which had always regarded health education as a humanistic but nonscientific enterprise, and with health administrators, whose attitudes toward health education had not changed much since Mustard's statement in 1945.

These changes in the early 1970s were also accompanied by a growing awareness of the allocation of increasing societal resources to human service programs and a concomitant demand for accountability in many countries. This led to increasing requirements for evaluation in cost–benefit and cost–effectiveness terms (Aujoulet, 1973; Green, 1974).

Despite all of these trends, which have brought the need for research and evaluation in health education more forcefully to the consciousness of the profession and of governments and health institutions, the usual practice of health education remains ideological, intuitive, idioscyncratic, and inductive. It tends to be *ideological* in the sense that many practitioners hold certain beliefs about the correct way to practice health education, beliefs that are based more on philosophy and the ideology of the institution where they work or where they were trained than on a careful assessment of the educational needs in the population or the situation in which they are working.

Practice tends to be *intuitive* in the sense that many health education programs are conducted without formal planning, or with plans that are based on implicit assumptions rather than on knowledge of the problem and the distribution of the problem and its causes in a population. Assumptions and intuition will always be necessary to some degree, but they need to be made more explicit so that they can be questioned.

Health education practice tends to be *idiosyncratic* in the sense that many practitioners believe themselves and their situations to be unique and without precedent. This attitude leads them to deny the relevance of experience elsewhere and to reject the utility of research and evaluation conducted elsewhere.

Finally, practice continues to be, as a result of the foregoing traits, more *inductive* than deductive. Many practitioners branch from their own peculiar experiences to generalizations about what works and what does not work in health education at large. This inductive tendency will always have a proper and major role in good health education practice, but it need not be a substitute for the deductive selection of methods or strategies where validated experimental evidence exists for their appropriate application.

These four characteristics of health education practice today must be acknowledged if research in health education is to be more than an academic exercise. The question, given these characteristics of practice, is whether the findings from research and evaluation in health education can ever hope to permeate the ideological, intuitive, idiosyncratic, and inductive practitioner or whether, on the other hand, it will be necessary to change these characteristics of practitioners in order to stimulate a more basic level of research and evaluation relevant to problems in practice.

9. The Policy Issues for Research Training

Society is faced, then, with several issues or policy questions for the development of manpower for research in health education.

1. Should the emphasis be on training more practitioners who know more about research or on more researchers who know more about practice? This is not a true dilemma because the answer clearly is that both are needed. But it is an apparent dilemma insofar as limited resources mean that one type of training can be done only at the expense of the other. If governments and training institutions must choose where to lay the greater emphasis, the foregoing analysis of the current status of health education practice would seem to argue for better training of practitioners who know more about the principles and methods of research applicable to practice. An approach toward training health education practitioners as experimenting practitioners would seem to be in order. Such an approach would emphasize the attitude of testing one's methods, rather than piously promoting them, and it would emphasize the development of skills in evaluation. At the same time, there will be a continuing need for more fully qualified research specialists, but it is clear from experience with behavioral scientists who have not had any experience in program planning or administration that highly sophisticated research can be done on trivial problems.

2. How much research training can be tolerated and absorbed in the professional preparation of practitioners? The complaint of most professors who accept the preceding response to the first dilemma is that there is already too much knowledge and skill to be crammed into the one- or two-year curriculum for most health education specialists. This cramming leaves little time for the additional training in research skills that would overcome the problems in practice identified earlier. One reason that this dilemma appears insurmountable to some is the tendency to proliferate formal courses in postgraduate programs for the professional preparation of health education specialists, in which didactic course work is expected to impart professional skills. It is generally accepted that didactic course work can be more effective in the transmission of foundation knowledge and skills, such as behavioral theory and research and statistical methods, than in teaching the more complex skills required in the planning and administration of health education programs. If this principle of learning were applied to the organization

of curricula in health education, the formal and didactic component of such curricula should consist a great deal more of foundation knowledge and skills in behavioral theory and analytic skills. Such curricula would then be supplemented by extended preceptorships or internships for the development of the more complex skills of practice.

3. Which of the behavioral or biomedical models of research should be emphasized? The dilemma here is that different problems of research and health education call for different research designs, data collection methods, measurement techniques, and analytic strategies. Should the designs to be emphasized be mainly experimental or mainly survey methods? Should the approach to data collection be largely sociological or primarily anthropological? Should the methods of measurement be primarily psychometric or applied behavioral analysis? The decisions on these choices will have to be left to the regional and the historical circumstances surrounding health education in those parts of the world where the training is being conducted.

4. How can we hope to build a cumulative scientific base with such divergent research methodologies? This dilemma goes to the core of the long-term issues in development of health education as a scientific practice. If the meager and dispersed research in this field is further splintered by the inconsistent methods applied by the investigators, the prospects of achieving that essential characteristic of a profession—namely, the cumulative nature of its literature—are slim. The answers to this dilemma seem to lie partly in the development of more robust theoretical models that will synthesize and organize diverse findings; partly in broader research training rather than in increased depth in narrow fields of methodological training; and partly in the development and use of information retrieval systems for health education's professional and scientific literature.

10. Recommendations

These dilemmas force choices that will have costs associated with any benefits to be derived from manpower development for research in health education. To add more research to existing curricula, for example, will cost the elimination of something else or an extension of the time required to complete degree programs. Indeed, any new emphasis on health education research in training or in practice will be at the expense of something currently included in the pool of resources or effort in health education, or else it will require societies to make new, additional investments in health education. The safest approach to formulating policy, then, would appear to be recommending innovations in training and practice that will hold the greatest promise for adding new resources while conserving and utilizing existing resources to their maximum potential.

The strategy for policy most likely to accomplish these ends will be one that improves and builds on the existing structure of research, training, and practice in health education, strengthening the weak links, filling the gaps, and extending the centers of excellence, rather than one that proposes the addition of new structures or new layers within the existing structure. Such a policy need not be a patchwork of *ad hoc*, disconnected activities throughout the world. It could be a comprehensive, integrated effort, with some degree of consensus among the concerned professions and governmental agencies.

10.1. Strengthening the Weak Links

In the chain of linkages between theory, policy, practice, training, and research, the weaknesses in health education are most notable between training and research and between practice and research (see Figure 1). Policy, in most countries, has caught up with theory (*arrow 1*), in the sense that most governments are now convinced of the need for greater emphasis on prevention and health education, and are now awaiting clarification of which strategies of health education are to be supported, which await better research (*arrow 4*), which awaits better training for research (*arrow 8*) and guidance of research by problems identified in practice (*arrow 3*).

The order of priority for strengthening the linkages should be to strengthen the research aspects of training and practice simultaneously (*arrows 3* and *8*), so that research in health education begins soon to benefit both from academic discipline and from practical experience. The need for such balance between rigor and reality is evident from the reviews of earlier research that revealed studies by practitioners on one side that had little credibility because of their weaknesses of internal validity, and studies by behavioral scientists on the other that had little

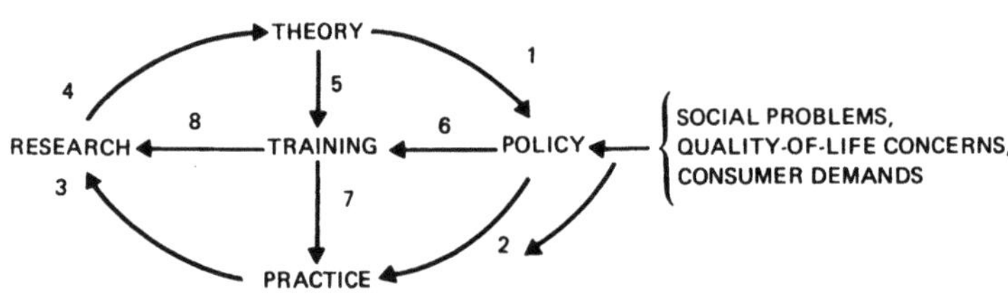

Figure 1. The cycle of professional development in health education.

credibility or influence with practitioners, administrators, and policy makers because they had severe limitations of specificity, external validity, or generalizability (Green, 1977, 1978; Hochbaum, 1960; Rosenstock, 1960).

10.2. Filling the Gaps

The three points of intervention implied by the foregoing analysis are (1) the need for practitioners who are better trained in the application and interpretation of research; (2) the need for a larger cadre of research specialists who have a balance of competence and experience in behavioral research methods and health education practice; and (3) the more effective translation of research and evaluation results into theory and policy to guide future training and practice in health education. This paper is concerned primarily with the first two, but the third must be addressed if the results of improved research and theory are to yield the benefits depicted in Figure 1.

The hope that practitioners will play a larger and more effective role in research is regarded by many as impracticable, unreasonable, or unnecessary.

Its *practicality* is assailed on the grounds that research is too complex to be mastered at anything but the most rudimentary level within the framework of baccalaureate or even postgraduate training programs for health education. Some of those who argue against training practitioners in research methods on the grounds of practicability go further in warning that a little knowledge is a dangerous thing and that the literature is already full of poor research. This case against the practitioner's being trained to carry out research in health education may go so far as to actively discourage practitioners from participation in research for fear that they will make things worse, casting health education into disrepute with research of poor quality.

These arguments fail to recognize or allow for a range of research applications in practice other than the ideal of randomized experimental trials published in refereed journals to provide definitive tests of the efficacy of a method, technique, or program. Practitioners can be made aware of this ideal but can benefit more from the application of subexperimental research methods in the everyday diagnosis, monitoring, and surveillance of their problems, activities, and programs. A variety of applications of the scientific method could make the routine practice of health education more systematic, better documented, and subject to more critical self-evaluation, peer review, and quality control. To deny these uses of research methods to practitioners on the grounds that "a little knowledge is a dangerous thing" is contrary to the very rationale for health education itself, which is to transfer scientific knowledge and self-help skills from the experts to the people who stand to benefit the most from their use.

The second argument against the training of practitioners in research methods is that it is *unreasonable* to expect them to fit research into their limited budgets, their mandate to provide services above all, or their work settings, which conspire against systematic data collection and objective reporting. This argument accepts the need for research in health education but also accepts the adverse circumstances of health education practice as a fact of professional life that precludes the practitioner from using or participating in such research. It may go so far as to argue for the protection of practitioners from the demands of zealous academics who fail to appreciate these "real-world" considerations.

This line of thinking leads to the "town-and-gown" split, causing some practitioners to view themselves as the "grassroots" workers in the trenches, toiling alone in the "real world" on behalf of the oppressed. They perceive themselves as beleaguered and harrassed by elitist, "ivory tower" academics who demean their work because it is unscientific. Such attitudes have been seen to turn from defensive to offensive anti-intellectualism, stereotyping all academics and researchers as out of touch with reality and uncaring about "the people." Some postgraduate training programs for health education specialists have played up this attitude by minimizing and even disdaining most theory and research in favor of "experiential learning," which they equate with their own ideological principles of group work, communications, or community organization. Their graduates leave training with a specific, though narrow, range of educational skills and with the conviction that these skills are the "correct" practice of health education regardless of the problem or the situation.

In the extreme, these attitudes lead to the argument that research and evaluation are *unnecessary*. If a practitioner is properly trained and properly supervised in the "correct" application of "correct" principles, then who needs research? Such hubris is most strident among some of the most ardent promoters and advocates of health education, so convinced are they of the correctness of their methods. It is difficult to argue with them without appearing to be an enemy of the cause or an educational heretic.

The only answer to those who believe that research is unreasonable or unnecessary in health education practice is to warn of the overselling of health education. The evangelical spirit from which their resistance to research springs also causes them to expect more and to claim more results than the field can guarantee. Their faith and enthusiasm is the very source of much of their effectiveness. Consequently, they create unrealistic expectations in the sponsors, the collaborators, and the consumers of their programs, leading to disappointment, disillusionment, disenchantment, and ultimately, if they persist, disrepute.

Failing this logical argument for a more cautious, experimenting approach to practice, the remaining hope of convincing these antiresearch practitioners of the need at least for more scientific training of future generations of practitioners is an appeal to authority. Most Expert Committees and blue ribbon committees or commissions on health education research or training have recommended it in one form or another. The Health Education Steering Committee of the Association of Schools of Public Health, for example, included as one of 11 recommendations in 1965 (Boatman, Levin, Roberts, & Rugen, 1966):

> that Schools of Public Health give more attention and support to research in health education through adjustment in teaching and administrative loads of faculty, through the inclusion of the elements of scientific investigation in the master's program, and through the development of advanced graduate level programs for the preparation of research workers. (p. 25)

The Society for Public Health Education has adopted or endorsed guidelines on the functions and the professional preparation of health education specialists, prepared in collaboration with committees of the American Public Health Association and the Professional Examination Service in 1967 and 1977, with detailed functions outlined under "research and evaluation."

The latest guidelines emphasize that (Society for Public Health Education, Ad Hoc Task Force, 1977a):

> there are increasing opportunities for professional health educators to perform at more advanced levels of administration, supervision, consultation, organization development, policy development, evaluative research, and cost benefit analysis. . . . This creates increasing pressure to upgrade the curricula for the preparation of the master's degree person in order to provide these more advanced functions and therefore creates pressure to upgrade the preparation of the baccalaureate for entry-level health education practice. (p. 81)

The Guidelines for Baccalaureate Programs in Community Health Education, published simultaneously, obliged with inclusion in the list of competencies under professional preparation (Society for Public Health Education, Committee on Professional Preparation and Practice, 1977):

> Knowledge of and skill in the use of the problem-solving approach and scientific method; knowledge and skill in basic data collection methods; knowledge and skill in using some commonly applied statistical methods; the nature of statistics and how to conduct small-scale studies. (p. 96)

These and the WHO (Postgraduate Preparation of Health Workers in Health Education, 1964; Research in Health Education: Report of a WHO Scientific Group, 1969) recommendations for research training in professional preparation for health education leave only one gap in the existing structure of research and practice. The group most unlikely to be touched by most of these recommended developments in training will be the current practitioners who received their professional training before the recommended curriculum changes were implemented or who entered the practice of health education through other disciplines or channels. Such practitioners, ironically, are still the most pervasive form of health educator. A program of extended research training for these practitioners must be included in a comprehensive approach to strengthening the scientific base of health education practice.

10.3. Extending the Centers of Excellence

The total structure of health education can be viewed as a pyramid, with a broad base of practitioners who have little formal training in health education, much less in research; a sizable but thinly dispersed middle range of professionally qualified health education specialists; and a narrow band of highly trained or experienced scientists and professionals who have a combination of skills in research and practice. The latter tend to be concentrated in universities, institutes, or centers of innovative practice or program development. The current system depends on a trickle-down process of influence on the broad base of practitioners.

An alternative process for reaching the base of this pyramid has been developed by the National Center for Health Education in cooperation with the American Cancer Society in California and is commended to governmental agencies for broader application. Practitioners in local units of the American Cancer Society are asked to identify the educational program, project, or activity that they would most like to have evaluated in their unit. They are brought together then in regional workshops to develop their objectives and evaluative research designs in consultation with a state-level expert. With the exception of being brought together again a year later to share results, they proceed with their respective evaluation efforts with continuing consultation available from the National Center for Health Education.

This is not a unique training design, but it has not been applied to research training. It appears to have resulted in considerable professional growth and improvement in local health education practices, even though the evaluative research findings are not expected to be of publishable quality or broad generalizability.

This case illustrates the main themes of this paper:

1. The limited pool of highly trained manpower for research in health education can be extended in its utility and effectiveness through the multiplier principle of transferring fundamental skills to practitioners in the field, so long as the expertise offered is focused on problems identified by the practitioners themselves.
2. Practitioners can benefit from the application of research methods to their practice.
3. Practitioners without prior research training can integrate new research training into their practice.
4. With small successes even at this rudimentary level of research, practitioners may be expected to be more receptive to and more appreciative of the research literature and the further development of their own skills in research and evaluation.

This experience and others like it in continuing education in educational diagnosis and evaluation for practitioners lead to the conclusion that the answer to the first dilemma posed in Section 9 is in favor of more research training for practitioners. There will continue to be a growing demand for research specialists in health education, trained at the doctoral level, but they can never hope to catch up with the needs for research in health education without enlisting and developing the talents and the cooperation of practitioners.

11. Summary and Conclusions

Policy in health education has been characterized as a thin veneer covering a multitude of sins and virtues, strong and weak programs, dedicated and lazy practitioners, good and poor training. Of the several points in the cycle of theory, research, policy, training, and practice where intervention might strengthen health education, priority should be given to the strengthening of training, both in professional preparation and in continuing education. Emphasis should be placed on training practitioners in a greater appreciation and aptitude for evaluation methods and procedures as integral components of health education programs.

This emphasis on evaluation could have the effect of upgrading the quality and the accountability of existing health education activities. More profoundly, it could be expected to strengthen the empirical base from which future training, planning, and practice will derive. Ultimately, these benefits of a more empirical health education could contribute more substantive guidance to policy than is now possible in the conflicted ideological and political ambience of health education.

References

Aujoulet, L. P. L'éducation pour la santé: Peut-on en évaluer la rentabilité. *International Journal of Health Education*, 1973, *16*, 21–27.

Berkanovic, R. Behavioral science and prevention. *Preventive Medicine*, 1976, *5*, 92–105.

Berry, R. E., Jr. Estimating the economic costs of alcohol abuse. *New England Journal of Medicine*, 1976, *295*, 620–621.

Berry, R. E., Jr., & Boland, J. P. *The economic costs of alcohol abuse*. New York: Free Press, 1977.

Blane, H. T. Education and the prevention of alcoholism. In B. Kissin & H. Begleiter (Eds.), *The biology of alcoholism. Vol. 4: The social aspects of alcoholism*. New York: Plenum Press, 1976, pp. 519–578.

Boatman, R. H., Levin, L. S., Roberts, B. J., & Rugen, M. E. Professional preparation in health education in schools of public health (United States and Canada): A report prepared for the 1965 annual meeting of the Association of Schools of Public Health. *Health Education Monographs*, 1966, *1*, (No. 21) 1–35.

Green, L. W. Toward cost–benefit evaluations of health education: Some concepts, methods, and examples. *Health Education Monographs*, 1974, *2*, (Suppl., 1), 34–64.

Green, L. W. Evaluation and measurement: Some dilemmas for health education. *American Journal of Public Health*, 1977, *67*, 155–161.

Green, L. W. Determining the impact and effectiveness of health education as it relates to federal policy. *Health Education Monographs*, 1978, *6* (Suppl. 1), 28–66.

Green, L. W., & Faden, R. Potential effects of patient package inserts on patients and drug consumers. *Drug Information Journal*, 1977, *11* (Suppl.), 64s–70s.

Green, L. W., & Figá-Talamanca, I. Suggested designs for evaluation of patient education programs. *Health Education Monographs*, 1974, *2*, 54–71.

Green, L. W., & Green, P. F. Intervention in social systems to make smoking education more effective. In J. Steinfeld, W. Griffiths, K. Ball, & R. M. Taylor (Eds.), *Smoking and health: Health consequences, education, cessation activities, and government action*. Proceedings of the Third World Conference on Smoking and Health. (NIH 77-1413). Washington, D.C.: Government Printing Office, 1977.

Hochbaum, G. M. Research relating to health education. *Health Education Monographs*, 1960, *1*, (No. 8), 10–20.

Institute for Social Research. Public asked to rank country's major institutions. *ISR Newsletter*, 1974, *8*.

James, W. *Pragmatism*. London: Longmans Green, 1914.

Kent, D. C. The role of the voluntary health agency in professional and public education. *Health Education Monographs*, 1974, 2 (Suppl. 1), 73–77.

Mäkelä, K., & Vükari, M. Notes on alcohol and the state. *Acta Sociologica*, 1977, *20*, 155–179.

McKinley, J. B. A case for refocusing upstream—The political economy of illness. In A. J. Enelow & J. B. Henderson (Eds.), *Applying behavioral sciences to cardiovascular risk*. New York: American Heart Association, 1975.

Mico, P. R., & Ross, H. S. *Health education and behavioral science*. Oakland, Calif.: Third Party Associates, Inc., 1975.

Mustard, H. S. *Government in public health.* New York: The Commonwealth Fund, 1945.
Pearson, D. E. An historical case for the role of the insurance industry in patient education. *Health Education Monographs,* 1974, *2,* 39–43.
Postgraduate preparation of health workers in health education (Technical Report, Series No. 278). Geneva: World Health Organization, 1964.
President's Committee on Health Education. *Report of the President's Committee on Health Education.* New York: Institute of Public Affairs, 1974.
Preventive Medicine USA. New York, Prodist, 1976.
Research in health education: Report of a WHO scientific group (Technical Report, Series No. 432). Geneva: World Health Organization, 1969.
Roberts, B. J., & Green, L. W. *International Survey of Research and Studies in Health Education by Ministries of Health and Universities.* Background paper for World Health Organization Study Group. Berkeley: University of California School of Public Health, 1968.
Rosenstock, I. M. Gaps and potentials in health education research. *Health Education Monographs,* 1960, *1* (No. 8), 21–27.
Shapiro, S. Measuring the effectiveness of prevention. *Milbank Memorial Fund Quarterly: Health and Society,* 1977, *55,* 291–306.
Simonds, S. Health education as social policy. *Health Education Monographs,* 1974, *2* (Suppl. 1), 1–10.
Society for Public Health Education, Inc., Ad Hoc Task Force. Guidelines for the preparation and practice of professional health educators. *Health Education Monographs,* 1977, *5,* 75–89. (a)
Society for Public Health Education, Inc., Committee on Professional Preparation and Practice. Criteria and guidelines for baccalaureate programs in community health education. *Health Education Monographs,* 1977, *5,* 90–98. (b)
Somers, A. R. (Ed.). *Promoting health: Consumer interest and national policy.* Germantown, Md.: Aspen Systems, 1976.
Somers, A. R. Consumer health education: Where are we? Where are we going? *Canadian Journal of Public Health,* 1977, *68,* 362–368.
Somers, A. R., & Somers, H. M. *Health and health care: Policies in perspective.* Germantown, Md.: Aspen Systems, 1977.
Steuart, G. W. Scientist and professional: The relations between research and action. *Health Education Monographs,* 1969 (No. 29).
U.S. Department of Health, Education, and Welfare. (OS77-50039). *National immunization conference: Policy perspectives.* Washington, D.C.: Government Printing Office, 1976.
Victor, D. The role of television drama in national health education. *Health Education Monographs,* 1974, *2* (Suppl. 1), 78–83.
Wang, V. L. Social goals, health policy and the dynamics of development as bases for health education. *International Journal of Health Education,* 1977, *20,* 13–18.
Weingarten, V. Report of findings and recommendations of the President's Committee on Health Education. *Health Education Monographs,* 1974, *2* (Suppl. 1), 11–19.
Young, M. A. C. Review of research and studies related to health education practice (1961–66). *Health Education Monographs,* 1967 and 1968 (Numbers 23–28).
Young, M. A. C. Review of research and studies related to the health education aspects of family planning (1967–1971). *Health Education Monographs,* 1973 (Numbers 33–35).

IV

Strategies for Reducing Drinking Problems among Youth

In an ideal world, strategies and programs would flow easily from a coherent statement of policy. As with many aspects of a democratic society, such an ideal is rarely reached. As a matter of fact, attainment of the ideal would begin to make the democratic process of negotiation and compromise suspect and might well be a political danger signal. In any event, the ideal is in no way reached in the area of alcohol problems. As we have indicated earlier, this is not surprising, since policy formulation concerning alcohol has never been strong, and it is only in relatively recent times that we have begun to witness the steps that must be taken to develop a coherent policy about alcohol in the United States. Programs and techniques for combating alcohol problems, while not necessarily entirely *ad hoc*, have a fortuitous quality about them. Often, programs are mounted simply out of a feeling on the part of a community that they are necessary; typically, little attention is given to the goals and objectives the programs are supposed to achieve and even less to how program content articulates these goals. Even more rarely are attempts made to measure the extent to which the program attains its objectives.

In Part IV, we have attempted to take the best strategies directed toward youthful alcohol problems. We deliberately chose those programs that pay considerable attention to goals and objectives, and the articulation of program components to meet goals and objectives, and we have included an evaluation to determine program effectiveness in reducing alcohol problems. The programs selected include a number of exciting strategies and techniques that have high potential for modifying alcohol-related problems among youth.

David Kraft, discussing programs directed toward college students, outlines a strategy based on theoretical analyses made by Robin Room of the Social Research Group at the School of Public Health at the University of California (Berkeley) and by Joseph Gusfield of the Department of Sociology at the University of California (La Jolla). Kraft has selected principles advanced by Room and Gusfield and creatively applied these at the college level in a program being conducted at the University of Massachusetts—Amherst. While the strategy discusses goals relative to changing drinking behavior so that the risk of inviting the adverse consequences attendant upon intoxication is reduced, it also focuses on such factors as the *insulation* of behaviors and a *redefinition* of problems. Insulation refers to restructuring the environment so as to insulate the heavy drinker from the negative consequences of drinking. An example from the University of Notre Dame is the provision of a bus service to bring students back to campus after a bout of drinking in distant off-campus pubs. Redefinition of drinking problems is adopted from the notion of redefining victimless crimes so that they are no longer in the criminal code; applied to drinking, behaviors associated with intoxication that are not harmful to others can be redefined as nonproblem behaviors. For example, if public drunkenness is removed as an offense in the criminal code, it implies other means for dealing with public drunkenness will be instituted that don't have the negative consequences associated with public drunkenness as criminal behavior.

Kraft, in the course of his discussion, also presents a comprehensive review of prevention tactics for young people, with a particular focus on college-aged students. Although Kraft draws many examples from his own program at the University of Massachusetts, he discusses prevention strategies that may be used in college settings in a generalized fashion. His work, therefore, not only is useful as a model of what can be done at one particular university but also outlines general principles that may be applicable in any college setting.

We have noted that the highest incidence of alcohol problems among young people occurs in the military services, largely because the majority of service persons are young, unmarried males. It is particularly appropriate that John Killeen, who is now director of Alcohol and Drug Abuse Programs for the Department of Defense, should present the department's strategy regarding alcohol problems. Killeen discusses the structure and organization of the Department of Defense policy and how the policy has been adapted in each branch of the service. Killeen places particular emphasis on the U.S. Air Force program, which he directed until recently. Included among the prevention strategies are such things as the reduction of "happy hours" and other mechanisms for changing the availability of alcohol in the military services, the mounting of alternatives to alcohol use, and the strengthening of the family, which is a conserving influence relative to alcohol consumption. Regarding the latter, provisions are made for family members to live on or adjacent to the base. Management structure, which is strongly emphasized in military programs, is of particular interest because of its potential transferability to the civilian scene. Nonmilitary programs are not always characterized by the managerial efficiency typical of military programs. Another aspect of military programs emphasizes evaluation and documentation of the extent to which program objectives are attained.

Many young people who like to drink nevertheless drink in ways that they don't like. For example, many young people do one or more of the following: drink more than they had planned to on a given occasion; spend more money than they had budgeted for on alcohol; are concerned over memory lapses when they have had too much to drink the night before; feel guilty or embarrassed over behavior they engaged in while drinking; and don't like the physical consequences, the hangover, the next day. While such young people may be frequent heavy drinkers and may suffer the negative consequences of heavy alcohol use, they are not candidates for treatment or psychotherapeutic intervention. Nor are they prepared to see themselves in that light. The notion of going to a traditional treatment resource, with its connotations of labeling them as alcoholic, and the still widespread public prejudice against those identified as alcoholic are factors that militate against young people's going to such facilities. Nevertheless, young adults who are in conflict about their drinking are interested in changing their behavior but simply do not know how to do it.

Peter Miller outlines techniques and programs based on social learning principles that he extends to drinking patterns and habits. The success of other programs based on these principles in achieving weight reduction, controlling smoking behavior, and promoting healthy lifestyle behaviors is well known. Miller discusses specific strategies and techniques that may be used to modify drinking practices among young adult social drinkers. These techniques hold great promise for enabling people to continue to enjoy drinking without suffering its negative consequences. Techniques such as monitoring sip size and size of drinks, knowing the relationship between the mix of alcoholic and nonalcoholic beverages in relation to body weight, and so on are discussed in detail in Miller's chapter. The possibilities that Miller outlines have not been attempted in any programmatic fashion but form a major strategy for future consideration.

An area not covered in any detail in Part IV or in other parts of this volume is the relationship between drinking and driving and accident behavior. The drinking–driving area has received more careful research than other alcohol-related problems. However, programs for reducing alcohol-related accidents have not been effective. Nevertheless, all the ingredients for an effective reduction program are in place, and it appears that in the present state of public opinion, major advances can be made. Required are a community approach that stresses the integration and coordination of public information and education campaigns, consistent enforcement by police and the courts of driving-while-intoxicated laws, and random roadside Breathalyzer surveys to detect the incidence of drivers drinking over the legal limit. Prior research indicates that communities in which public sentiment strongly favors the reduction of drinking–driving accidents and supports consistent enforcement measures can reduce accident behavior significantly.

10

Strategies for Reducing Drinking Problems among Youth: College Programs

David P. Kraft

1. Introduction

Drinking by college students in the United States has received increased attention from society over the past decade. The focus has become especially strong since the publication of the *Second Special Report to the U.S. Congress on Alcohol and Health* (U.S. Department of Health, Education and Welfare, 1974), in which the increasing prevalence of drinking by junior-high- and high-school-aged youth and the high rate of drinking problems among college-aged youth were highlighted. The National Institute on Alcohol Abuse and Alcoholism responded by designing and implementing a series of activities called "The University '50 + 12' Project" (Kraft, 1976, 1977). At the same time, many colleges and universities began their own programs to study the drinking practices and problems of students and to intervene effectively. As a result, many college and university campuses in the United States now have alcohol program activities designed to provide treatment for problem-drinking students, and some also seek to educate students about how to use alcoholic beverages in a safe manner.

While attention to college drinking practices and programs to reduce

David P. Kraft • Mental Health Division, University Health Services, University of Massachusetts, Amherst, MA 01003.

problem drinking by college students has increased, the effectiveness of campus efforts is poorly documented. A confusing array of activities have been devised and implemented, based on the different viewpoints that now exist in the field of alcohol abuse and alcoholism.

In order to describe the various strategies to reduce drinking problems now in use at colleges and universities, the present paper briefly reviews both the perceived needs of various campuses and the viewpoints and assumptions underlying many of the programs. The paper then outlines some of the methods and techniques employed and gives specific examples of those programs that currently exist.

2. The Need for College Programs

Numerous surveys conducted by various colleges and universities report that anywhere from 71 to 96% of students drink to some extent. Most schools report that between 87 and 93% of students drink at least once a year (Engs, 1977; Girdano & Girdano, 1976; Hanson, 1974, 1977; Kopplin, Greenfield, & Wong, 1977; Kraft, 1976; Kuder & Madson, 1976; Lester & Perez, 1977; Looney, 1976; Penn, 1974; Rouse & Ewing, 1974). According to a recent review of the literature by Blane (1978), the high prevalence of drinking among college students remained relatively stable over the decade from 1966 to 1975: 87% of students reported drinking to some extent, including 90% of men and 87% of women. Blane's review also showed that the frequency of drinking occasions for college students during the same 10 years was relatively constant: about 25% of college students reported drinking two or more times per week, with no changes in the amount consumed per occasion; and over 55% of students (twice as many men as women) reported having been drunk at least once in their lives. While the extent and the average consumption of alcoholic beverages by college students seem to have been stable since the mid-1960s, the levels have increased over those reported in Straus and Bacon's (1953) survey conducted between 1949 and 1952. A more detailed review of high school and college drinking practices is contained in Chapter 2.

If the prevalence of college drinking has remained fairly stable since 1966, why has so much concern been expressed about student drinking? The answer seems to be fourfold:

1. The reduced concern over the past decade regarding the use of illicit drugs, including marijuana, has brought an increased awareness of the prevalence of alcohol use by college youth.
2. The shift of attention in the alcohol field from a sole focus on

alcoholism to the broad array of problems related to excessive drinking, especially the acute problems most commonly experienced by youth (Cahalan, 1970; Cahalan & Cisin, 1976; USDHEW, 1974), has increased the sensitivity of alcohol experts to problems encountered by college-age youth.

3. Campus surveys have recorded an increased incidence in alcohol-related problems among college youth over the past 20 years (Blane, 1978; Kraft, 1976), although it is unclear whether the increase is actual or merely due to the change in focus of the alcohol field and subsequent survey approaches.
4. The increased emphasis on preventive health care and consumerism has fostered research and education efforts designed to help people take better care of themselves, including "responsible alcohol use."

The reported extent of alcohol-related problems among college students has varied from one survey to another. Single-problem rates given in Blane's review (1978) included: 30% of students reported driving while intoxicated at least once; 9% reported involvement in fights; 9% reported damaging property; and 4% reported receiving lower grades at least once because of excessive drinking. Recent surveys conducted at one large state university during 1976 and 1977 showed similar single yearly problem rates: 29% of students reported driving while intoxicated; 16% reported becoming abusive after drinking; 8% reported having destroyed property after drinking; 15% reported having sustained a minor physical injury after drinking; and 1% reported having been threatened with the breakup of a relationship due to his/her drinking (Kraft, Duston & Mellor, 1978a). The proportion of students between 1966 and 1975 who presented a constellation of problems, defined as "potential problem drinkers" by the method of Straus and Bacon (1953), involved from 8 to 23% of men and 5 to 6% of women (Blane, 1978). Surveyors who have attempted to determine the number of chronic problem drinkers or "alcoholics" have generally found a relatively small number at any given time. For example, one campus that conducted surveys in 1975, 1976, and 1977 showed that 0.1 to 0.2% of students considered themselves "alcoholics" (Kraft, 1979). Medical-clinic outpatient visits at the same campus revealed only 0.02% of medical visits involved chronic alcohol problems, including about 0.1% of the student body (Kraft, Duston, & Mellor, 1977).

In general, more college and university students are drinking than was true between 1949 and 1952, although the prevalence of drinking seems to have remained relatively constant since 1966. In addition, almost as many female as male college students now drink to some extent. Problems related to drinking do seem to have increased over the past 25 years, although it is not clear how much of the increase is due to a shift in awareness about acute drinking problems among youth rather than to an *actual* increase in incidence. A large number of college programs have been started over the past five years to help deal with the increase in alcohol problems on campus, although the approaches have varied according to the ways such problems are viewed.

3. The Goals of Various Programs

The explicit goals of a program reflect assumptions about alcohol use, the resources available, and decisions about which interventions are most useful. Strategies that are currently employed to reduce alcohol problems among college students are generally based on a number of more-or-less defined assumptions about alcohol and its use. Depending on the assumptions, program aims and methods have varied.

3.1. Assumptions

The assumptions underlying various programs follow the fairly standard viewpoints that currently exist toward alcohol. These viewpoints have been described in some detail by previous authors (Blane, 1976; Cahalan & Room, 1974). The viewpoints can be expressed in terms of the way alcoholic beverages are treated: alcohol is viewed as either a poison, an allergenic substance, a drug, or a food.

3.1.1. Drinking as a Vice

The events that culminated in Prohibition in the United States were largely based on beliefs that the use of alcoholic beverages was "bad" and that ideally alcohol use should be banned. Drinking was a moral issue, in which alcohol was treated as though it were an "irresistible force" that could poison the will and the mind if used at all. The view has been labeled the *vice, moral,* or *proscriptive model.* Although this view of alcohol may seem extreme and largely outdated to many contemporary Americans, the view persists in more subtle forms, such as the opinion that the only reason people drink is to "escape" or to "forget problems."

Many religious groups still view the use of any alcoholic beverage as morally wrong—in the tenets of certain Fundamentalist Protestant Christian church groups, drinking "defiles" the body, which is viewed as the "temple of the Holy Spirit" and should be kept as pure as possible. One result is that many colleges and universities, especially with strict religious views, prohibit the use of alcoholic beverages by their students as well as by faculty and staff. Abstinence is the ideal for everyone.

Little recent research validates the concept of drinking as a vice. Since the viewpoint is seen as a primarily moral rather than a scientific model, research validation should probably not be expected. However, certain advocates of the moral position are beginning to use scientific findings to bolster their beliefs. Research that indicates that even small amounts of alcohol may be detrimental have been used by certain temperance groups to persuade people of the dangers of *any* alcohol use. In addition, certain educational advocates continue to contend that drinking *should* be a moral issue, although not necessarily with abstinence as the only "right" outcome (Blane, 1976).

3.1.2. *Alcoholism as a Disease*

A widely held view, called the *disease model of alcoholism,* treats alcohol as though it were an allergic substance, analogous to an infectious agent or bacterium. Certain people are susceptible to the substance when exposed to it and develop the disease called *alcoholism.* People may be susceptible because of either a hereditary predisposition carried in the genes or poor early environmental training, often by one or both parents who themselves are alcoholic. Prevention and treatment measures are aimed at keeping alcoholic beverages away from such susceptible individuals, either through generalized control measures that make it harder for anyone to drink or through mechanisms designed to identify susceptible or "high-risk" individuals and help them stay away from alcohol. Any problem drinking or excessive drinking episodes are often treated as "prealcoholic" signs and symptoms, and individuals are warned of the consequences of continued excessive drinking. Although it is argued that some people have a natural "immunity" to the substance and that others gradually build up such immunity, the term is generally used as an analogue for enculturation processes rather than actual immunological processes.

Research does indicate a much higher rate of alcoholism in certain families. Some authors contend that certain nutritional factors account for the differences, such as varying requirements for vitamins. Other studies seem to show that alcoholics come from families that also have strong tendencies toward bipolar affective illness known as *manic-depressive illness* or *disease* (Johnson & Leeman, 1977, Winokur, Reich, Rimmer, & Pitts, 1970). This evidence suggests a common genetic defect for both disorders, although further research is needed to verify the initial findings. It appears that *some* persons now considered alcoholics may have an inherited predisposition to develop alcoholism and/or some type of manic-depressive psychosis, although many other chronic alcohol abusers have no such family history. Some advocates of the disease model believe that eventually it will be possible to find a "vaccine" that would effectively immunize (more appropriately, desensitize) susceptible individuals from the offending agent, alcohol.

There has been much criticism of the disease model of alcoholism. Although the concept did have the important effect of shifting the treatment of alcoholics out of the legal system and into the medical system, it also created a dichotomous type of thinking that looked at alcoholism as though "either you have it or you don't." Although there is no question that chronic alcohol abuse can either lead to or greatly contribute to certain diseases, such as cirrhosis of the liver and some forms of cancer, there has been little confirmation of a progression from early stages of the disease to later stages, as is true of most other disease entities. In fact, current evidence suggests that chronic alcohol abuse is more consistently viewed as a maladaptive or behavioral problem, with certain individuals falling into and out of alcohol problems during certain stages of life without any necessary progression (Cahalan & Cisin, 1976). While some persons with chronic alcohol problems may have a strong hereditary predisposition to alcoholism, many other persons with problems of alcohol abuse or alcoholism show no such background.

3.1.3. Alcohol as a Drug

Most contemporary alcohol experts view alcohol as a drug that can be used safely by most people within certain limits. However, it can also be used in a harmful fashion, as can any drug where overdosage is possible. This viewpoint is predominantly sociocultural and asserts that almost anyone *could* abuse alcohol, given the right (or wrong) set of circumstances, including personal and social factors. Drinking behavior is viewed within a larger set of behaviors, more or less integrated with other aspects of a person's personal and social life. The focus is on various *alcohol problems* that may ensue from overdrinking by anyone, dependent not only on the individual's tolerance for drug effects but also on the setting of the drinking, the reactions of others to the overdrinking, and the adverse consequences that result. Although the model can permit a view of alcohol as potentially beneficial, most of the focus is on problematic behaviors and habits and how to deal with them.

Research into various sociocultural factors related to alcohol use and abuse is abundant and popular. Much of the research has highlighted the lack of an integrated attitude toward drinking in American society, which proscribes overdrinking but alows moderate use of alcohol, especially as part of social activities or situations where drinking is not the major focus. The model views the family and the schools as major agents of socialization and tends to downplay or ignore biological factors as important (Blane, 1976). Corrective education of all people, drinkers and nondrinkers alike, is viewed as the main tool for correcting non-healthy views about the drug, alcohol, and its use. Regulatory measures are also viewed by some sociocultural adherents as necessary to help "shape" desired behaviors.

Most criticisms of models that view alcohol as a drug center on the broadness of its conceptualizations and the difficulties of proving or disproving its tenets or of generalizing research results. For example, the number of adverse consequences related to overdrinking are many and varied, each requiring a somewhat different approach and potentially affecting a somewhat different population. The desire to create more integrated and beneficial drinking norms in American society requires drastic changes in the society that are hard to implement, especially in a culture that so highly values individualism and individual freedom. Proponents of the disease model of alcoholism also fear that the broader sociocultural models will shift attention and resources away from continued research and treatment efforts with the small but significant proportion of people with chronic alcohol problems.

Most college and university programs eagerly embrace the "alcohol as a drug" viewpoint. The view fits well into the educational mission of the institution without requiring that the institution seek to ban the widespread use of alcohol by students, as suggested by the two previous models.

3.1.4. *Alcohol as a Food or Beverage*

Probably the most widely held view places alcohol in the category of pleasurable foods and beverages. Although some alcohol experts consider this model the same as the alcohol-as-a-drug model, it is separated here to underscore the essentially negative connotations of the first three models. Most people think of the positive effects of alcohol use (whether actual or perceived) and rarely think about its other potential effects, unless faced directly with some negative consequence of their own or others' drinking. The view of alcohol as a food or a pleasurable beverage is rarely discussed in the scientific alcohol literature but is extremely prevalent in nonscientific literature (novels, short stories, and cooking guides) and in advertisements for alcoholic beverages as well as in the beverage industry literature. The main focus is on the association between drinking (alcoholic beverages, of course) and enjoying oneself. The relative merits of one beer or wine over another, ways to fix cocktails, and which drinks to serve for which occasions are discussed. Efforts to use such a view and such vehicles on college campuses are viewed ambivalently by alcohol program staff: "We don't want people to think that we are advocating drinking." Criticisms of this model focus on the ways it plays down adverse consequences related to alcohol abuse and often ignores the potential harmful effects of strong social pressures to drink in order to have fun. The model seems to overlook the fact that alcohol is a psychoactive drug that requires special attention regarding potential abuses. The view also does not present positions that can generate funding and research into unhealthy practices.

Most campuses have many avenues open that portray alcohol as a food or a beverage. However, whether strategies designed to reduce alcohol problems can use these avenues successfully awaits further testing.

3.2. Aims

College and university programs may have general aims or purposes. For the present discussion, the so-called public health model of primary, secondary, and tertiary prevention is employed. Although there has been valid criticism of the model when applied to the field of alcohol abuse and alcoholism (Blane, 1976), it is widely used in the health field and has been adapted successfully to more sociocultural problem areas, as compared with the infectious disease paradigm (Caplan, 1964). An alternative but similar model has been developed by Morrill, Oetting, and Hurst (1972).

3.2.1. *Prevention of Alcohol Problems (Primary Prevention)*

The purpose of prevention programs is to intervene with individuals and/or groups before any problem is evident in order to avert the need for treatment or rehabilitation efforts. For programs that view "drinking as a vice," prevention measures would ban all on- and off-campus alcohol use by students and ensure compliance in whatever way is necessary; persuasive educational efforts would portray the use of any alcoholic beverage as bad and undesirable. For programs that subscribe to the "alcoholism-as-a-disease" model, prevention measures would seek to identify persons from high-risk families (e.g., one or both parents alcoholic, history of manic-depressive disorders, parents strongly abstinent but student no longer subscribing to the same belief system) and to inform them of their risks for developing the disease, alcoholism; the efforts would be attempted before the high-risk individuals developed problem-drinking behaviors. For programs that view "alcohol as a drug," prevention measures might include educating all students about the drug, alcohol, its properties, and ways of using it safely, as well as regulating the ways that alcohol is consumed at social events on campus; the efforts would focus on the variety of social influences on drinking behavior. For programs that view "alcohol as a food," almost all efforts would be preventive and developmental in nature (Morreill *et al.*, 1972), focusing on ways to use alcohol to enhance socialization and parties, ways to make attractive punches and foods, ways to distinguish wines from one another using real "wine-tasting" techniques, and ways to plan parties where alcohol is an enhancement, not the main attraction.

3.2.2. *Early Intervention with Persons with Alcohol Problems (Secondary Prevention)*

Early intervention programs would aim to identify as early as possible individuals or groups beginning to develop alcohol problems and to help them overcome the probems. For programs that view "drinking as a vice," early intervention might mean expulsion of an individual or group who will not adhere to the rules, or at least requiring some probationary period with corrective or punitive action. For programs that view "alcoholism" as a disease, traditional early intervention, through the use of lists of "warning signs" of alcohol abuse and alcoholism, might be used to identify problem drinkers. The individuals would then be guided into treatment programs, such as Alcoholics Anonymous groups or similar programs, where abstinence is viewed as necessary for the successful resolution of alcohol problems. For programs that view "alcohol as a drug," early intervention activities might include the use of a broad array of criteria in order to identify individuals and groups with various alcohol problems, including not only chronic alcohol abuse (alcoholism) but also occasional episodes of drunken driving, belligerence after drinking, accidental injuries, property destruction, impaired academic or work performance, and disrupted interpersonal relationships after drinking. Individuals so identified would be assisted to get help with the problem(s) as early as possible. Abstinence might be only one treatment approach, in addition to controlling drinking, arranging alternate forms of transportation, choosing a different set of friends, and so on. For programs where "alcohol as a food" is the view, some emphasis put on recognizing persons who might be having difficulties and where to refer them for help, similar to the "alcohol-as-a-drug" model, although much less attention is paid to early intervention.

3.2.3. *Rehabilitation of Persons with Alcohol Problems (Tertiary Prevention)*

The rehabilitation of persons with documented chronic alcohol problems is generally beyond the scope of most college programs, except with help from off-campus resources. Few students who require concentrated rehabilitative efforts can survive very long academically in most schools. Irrespective of the view about alcohol, most rehabilitative programs require abstinence in order to help the individual begin to function adequately in society.

3.3. Approaches

The remainder of the chapter focuses on the prevention and early intervention strategies (so-called primary and secondary prevention) employed by various colleges and universities. Various combinations of approaches are used in actual programs, depending on the level of intervention, the type of intervention, and the content of the intervention.

3.3.1. *Level of Intervention*

The level of intervention can involve one or more of the following four categories: (1) the individual student and his/her knowledge, attitudes, and behaviors; (2) primary affiliative groups of students, and their shared knowledge, attitudes, and behaviors; (3) campus organizations, groups, and agencies that deal with student life issues; and (4) key student and staff leaders of the college or university as an institution, who help set and enforce norms, procedures, and expectations of its members.

3.2.2. *Type of Intervention*

The type of intervention can usually be categorized as either (1) informational, educational, or persuasive in nature or (2) regulatory or manipulative in nature.

3.3.3. *Content of Intervention*

The content of the intervention can vary according to whether or not it is alcohol-specific and whether the intervention is aimed directly at the drinking itself, at reactions to the drinking-related behaviors, or at the precipitating factors leading to inappropriate behaviors. In general, one of three types of approaches may be used:

1. Change the drinking or related behavior either through alcohol-specific methods or through nonspecific methods. For example, the frequency of student drunkenness can be reduced either directly through education of students or limiting the amount of alcohol available, or indirectly through providing non-alcohol-focused alternative activities or ways to deal with stress.
2. Change the reaction to or consequences of drinking behavior. For example, people could be convinced to overlook student drunkenness as a natural part of student life, which students will "grow out of," or conversely they could be convinced not to tolerate abusive behavior from drunken students.
3. Insulate the behavior from the potential problem situation or reaction without modifying either the drinking behavior or the reaction. For example, students who drink off-campus can be provided bus service back to campus to reduce drunken-driving situations.

Any of these three basic approaches can be the aim of prevention efforts.

3.4. Illustrative Examples

The various program approaches might become clarified with examples of each model (see Table 1). One example might use a basic "drinking-as-a-vice" *assumption*, with the *aim* of prevention and early intervention. The *approach* to effect such a program might include the following. The individual student and student groups might be asked to agree, or pledge, not to drink alcoholic beverages at all while enrolled at the institution (a strategy that is *regulatory* in nature, whose content is directed at *changing the drinking behavior* through an *alcohol-specific* means). During enrollment, persuasive material would be presented about the evil nature of alcoholic beverages (an *educational* approach, with *alcohol-specific* content related directly to *changing the drinking behavior*), at the same time that a variety of social events and activities are planned that involve no alcoholic beverages (a *regulatory* type of intervention, whose content involves a *specific* approach to *changing the drinking behavior*). In addition, faculty, staff, and student leaders would be encouraged to enforce the strict prohibition against drinking "for the good of the community" (an *educational* intervention aimed at the *institutional regulators*, which seeks to *change the reaction to drinking behavior* by increasing negative sanctions for drinking). Anyone caught

Table 1. Examples of Possible Program Activities Based on Descriptive Factors

Activity description	Program assumption: Drinking as a vice	Alcoholism as a disease	Alcohol as a drug	Alcohol as food/beverage
Aim:				
Prevention and early intervention	Ban drinking.	Identify high-risk groups.	Educate regarding safe and unsafe use.	Enhance integration of drinking with social customs.
Approach:				
Individual level				
Change behavior	Students pledge to refrain from drinking.	Refrain from drinking if at high risk.	Learn to drink sensibly and to refrain from unsafe practices.	Learn to enjoy some drinking with meals.
Change reaction	Increase negative sanctions against any drinking.	Confront peers who drink excessively.	Decrease acceptance of drunken behavior by peers.	Increase desire to drink wine slowly to enhance taste.
Insulate	Refuse to permit students who drink to enroll.	At-risk students live separately from other drinking students.	Drive drunken friends home.	Plan parties away from residential areas.
Institutional level				
Change behavior	Ban drinking both on and off-campus. Alternative activities.	Educate about warning signs. Alternative activities.	Limit amounts of drinking at parties. Alternative activities.	Restrict drinking to beer and wine with food. Alternative activities.
Change reaction	Severe punishment for infraction.	Staff alert to decreased performance of students.	Overdrinking discouraged, other focus encouraged.	Create norms for sensible drinking.
Insulate	Expel students who drink.	Reduce general level of alcohol use by entire campus.	Provide transportation for potentially drunken students.	Locate parties away from town residents.

drinking would be immediately suspended (an *early-intervention* approach of a *regulatory* nature).

Another example might use the *assumption* of "alcoholism as a disease," with the *aim* of prevention and early intervention. The *approach* might include the following specifics. Individual students and student groups would receive information about alcoholism and its warning signs from either standard lists or specially designed lists of signs and symptoms of alcoholism (an *educational* strategy directed at *changing drinking behavior* through *alcohol-specific* means). Special speakers might be employed, including well-known "nondrinking alcoholics," to attract students and warn them of the devastating effects of alcoholism, of the groups at risk for developing such problems, and of the various stages leading up to alcoholism (an *educational* strategy aimed at *changing alcohol-specific drinking behavior*). At the same time, a variety of attractive activities would be planned not involving alcohol (a *regulatory* approach, involving an *alcohol-specific* strategy to *change the drinking behavior*). Individual students, student groups, and key staff would be trained in recognition of the early warning signs of alcoholism, places to refer persons showing such signs, and ways to "confront" problem drinkers about their behaviors and to urge them to get help either through local counseling services or through self-help groups like Alcoholics Anonymous (an *educational approach*, aimed at *changing the reaction to drinking behavior*). Some campuses might also train faculty and staff to recognize decreased performance due to drinking and to require the person to get treatment or else to face possible expulsion (a *regulatory* approach, aimed at *early intervention*).

A third example might use the *assumption* of "alcohol as a drug," again with the *aim* of prevention and early intervention. The *approach* might include the following features. The individual students and student groups would receive information about alcohol, its potential for abuse, and ways to avoid overdrinking (an *educational* approach, aimed at *changing alcohol-specific drinking behavior*). At the same time, students would be encouraged to help prevent friends who are intoxicated from driving home, from walking home through poorly lighted paths (to avoid accidental injuries), or from unnecessary acts of property destruction (an *educational* approach, aimed at *changing the reaction to or consequences of drinking behavior*). Students would also be alerted to campus regulations governing parties held on-campus that restrict large-scale events to certain locations away from town residential areas (a *regulatory* approach, designed to *insulate the behavior* from the potential reaction) and require that the focus of such parties involve some other activity besides drinking (a *regulatory* approach, using a *nonspecific* means to *change the drinking behavior*). Key student and staff leaders of the college or university would be trained to consistently enforce the university policies, which emphasize the safe planning and execution of parties where alcohol is not the major focus (an *educational* approach involving both *alcohol-specific* and *nonspecific regulatory* measures to *changing the drinking and related behaviors*). Students, staff, and faculty would all be exposed to information concerning various types of drinking problems and where to get help, either through the student health service or through the employee assistance program (an *early-intervention, educational* approach aimed at the *university community*). Health service and counseling staff would receive inservice training and supervision about how to help persons with various types of drinking problems (an *early-intervention* aim, involving the *education* of *key personnel* at the campus, designed to *change the drinking behavior* through therapeutic techniques).

A fourth program example might use the *assumption* of "alcohol as a food or beverage," with the *aim* of prevention in its broadest sense. The *approach* might include a number of features. Individual students and student groups would receive information about how to use alcohol as part of social activities in a creative manner, such as serving attractive alcoholic and nonalcoholic punches and mixed drinks, conducting wine-tasting parties, and making guests comfortable through various means, in order to maximize comfortable social interactions and minimize continuous drinking (*educational* approaches, using *alcohol-specific* and *nonspecific* means to *change drinking behaviors*). A discussion group on sexuality would consider sex-role issues and the use of alcohol that promotes or inhibits open communication (an *educational* approach, aimed at *changing drinking behaviors* through both *specific* and *nonspecific* means).

Various activities would also be encouraged where drinking is not a major focus (an *educational* approach, aimed at *changing drinking behavior* through *nonspecific* means). Individuals and groups would be assisted to establish norms that comfortably support moderate drinking behaviors but discourage drunkenness (an *educational* approach, aimed at *changing the reactions to drinking*). Staff and faculty would receive information to support student reactions that integrate sensible drinking with social activities and discourage overdrinking (an *educational* approach aimed at *changing the reactions to drinking*). Institutional regulations might also be used to support social events that model sensible, integrated drinking but severely restrict overdrinking (a *regulatory* approach to *change drinking behavior* and to *change reactions to drinking*). The emphasis would be much less problem-focused than the other three approaches.

4. The Educational Models and Techniques Employed

Most of the college programs to be described depend heavily on educational strategies and techniques. Although few program descriptions refer directly to a particular educational philosophy or rationale underlying their efforts, most programs attempt to change knowledge and attitudes or beliefs in order to change behavior. Relatively few programs rely on a behaviorist model, in which the focus is on molding or changing behaviors without regard for a person's attitudes or beliefs.

4.1. Theoretical Models

The most prevalent educational model that attempts to change behavior through knowledge and attitudes is the Rogers diffusion model (Lippitt, Watson, & Westley, 1958). The model outlines five discrete steps involved in behavior change:

1. Becoming aware of new information
2. Becoming interested and seeking further information
3. Examining current attitudes and beliefs in light of the new information
4. Testing new beliefs and/or practices consistent with the new information
5. Adopting new beliefs and/or practices

The strength of the model lies in its indication that more is involved in changing behavior than merely providing accurate information. The use of affective education techniques over the past decade is one attempt to help individuals not only receive new knowledge but also to examine current attitudes and beliefs and test out new attitudes and beliefs. Unfortunately, use of this and similar models has demonstrated that knowledge and attitudes can be changed fairly readily without leading to measurable behavior changes.

A somewhat more expanded model has been proposed by Fishbein (1967) in which beliefs and intentions to act are distinguished from attitudes. In particular, educational approaches that maximize the intention to act, through attitudes and/or normative beliefs, are more likely to produce behavior changes (Ajzen & Fishbein, 1974). Approaches that only influence attitudes without producing intentions to act generally fail. The model also recognizes the importance of normative beliefs (for example, peer-group influences) on subsequent behavior. Initial tests of this model seem much more encouraging concerning its predictive ability than tests of the Rogers model, although it has not yet been tested with alcohol education approaches and requires the ability to recognize intentions to act so that they can be measured.

The main behaviorist model focuses the attention of individuals on their alcohol beverage consumption and seeks to modify the rate and quantity of consumption through practice (Miller & Muñoz, 1976). The training often utilizes a Breathalyzer to assist persons in discriminating the behavioral effects of various blood alcohol levels (Marlatt, 1977). The rationale and techniques of a social learning approach are more fully described in Chapter 12.

4.2. Educational Techniques

In most programs, fairly standard educational techniques are employed either singly or collectively, in order to accomplish program goals. Some of the more common techniques follow, including the steps in the Rogers diffusion model where they seem best suited.

4.2.1. *Media and Materials*

Media and materials techniques encompass an assortment of ways to educate through written, spoken, and visual messages. They include, for example, posters, pamphlets, newspaper advertisements, newspaper articles, and radio or TV interviews, shows, or "public service announcements." The products of such techniques are less personal and more portable than other educational methods. They can be used in a variety of ways to aid any of the steps in the educational process, although they are especially well suited to promoting awareness, creating interest, or reinforcing an existing attitude or motivation. Once developed, media and materials can reach a large audience with relatively little energy expended by the educator, except for adequate distribution of the materials.

4.2.2. *Special Displays*

Special displays utilize various media and materials, with personal contacts, and are located in highly visible and accessible places. For example, a display on the student union concourse might highlight a short film about basic drinking facts and have literature available and a health educator present to answer questions; and a display in the evening outside a campus pub might feature posters about blood alcohol content (BAC) and driving, with a Breathalyzer present for students to test their BAC and an educator and an off-duty policeman present to answer questions. The technique is well suited to students' becoming aware and becoming interested in new information and to reinforcing social influences that foster self-assessment and self-care. This technique can reach a relatively high volume of people with a minimal time commitment by the educator.

4.2.3. *Speeches, Lectures, and Panel Presentations*

These techniques rely primarily on one-way verbal presentations from "experts" to a relatively passive audience. The methods are especially well suited to students becoming aware, becoming interested in new information, and, to some extent, examining their current beliefs and practices. The techniques can reach a comparatively large number of people with a limited expenditure of the educator's energy.

4.2.4. *Discussion Groups (Workshops)*

Ideally, these approaches involve active interchange between the discussion leader(s) and the attendees, and they sometimes involve selected exercises or "games" and role plays of specific situations to aid the verbal discussions. The techniques are well suited to students' becoming aware, becoming interested in new information, examining current beliefs and practices, and testing out new beliefs and/or practices, such as learning to say no when an alcoholic beverage is offered but not desired. The method works best with a relatively small number of participants, say, up to 20 people for each discussion leader, and with targeted but flexible goals. It requires a higher level of skills and staff energy than the above methods.

4.2.5. *Community Development*

Community development is both a set of techniques and a process. When it is a set of techniques the educator seeks out individuals or groups, helps them become aware of their needs and priorities, assists them in finding solutions to meet their needs, and helps them design and implement targeted strategies. As a process, community development encompasses every level of true education, so that the community or the individual becomes the active agent in creating and maintaining any changes that might be necessary. When the techniques are skillfully used, the results can be both dramatic and lasting. However, the amount of energy expended and the skill needed by the educator are high.

In general, the techniques that require the highest amount of staff effort (community development and discussion groups) have the highest potential for producing changes, but they may deal with only a relatively few people at any one time. Quite often such intensive techniques are focused on "key" individuals who are in a position to influence other persons around them, giving a so-called ripple effect to produce a desired result. Those techniques requiring relatively less staff effort (media and materials, special display and speeches, lectures, and panel presentations) have a lower potential for creating lasting changes but can reach more people at a given sitting with a given amount of staff energy. Successful programs seek to use a combination of approaches in order to achieve a critical level of effort with the available resources.

5. Examples of Various College Programs

The various assumptions, aims, approaches, and educational methods described above have been utilized in various programs. In fact, many programs described in literature have involved more than one assumption and approach (USDHEW, 1976; Goodale & Hewitt, 1978). Some programs combine features that warn people about the risks of "alcoholism as a disease," treat "alcohol as a drug" for most students, and try to help to change norms in the direction of treating "alcohol as a food or beverage"; a variety of activities are used to implement such programs.

This section describes various programs that are being used by colleges and universities to prevent or reduce alcohol problems. Most of the programs are described in either *The Whole College Catalog about Drinking* (USDHEW, 1976) or *A Monograph on Alcohol Education and Alcohol Abuse Prevention Programs at Selected American Colleges* (Goodale & Hewitt, 1978). Methods used mainly to influence individuals and primary affiliative groups are covered first. Methods aimed at organizational and institutional levels are then described.

5.1. Methods Focused on Individuals and Groups

5.1.1. Changing the Drinking and Related Behavior of Individuals and Groups

Most programs concentrate on methods that seek to *change the drinking behaviors* of individuals and groups of students. Whether the aim is prevention or early intervention, the same general activities and techniques are employed.

5.1.1.1. Surveys. Most college and university campuses with alcohol programs have conducted one or more surveys of student drinking practices. Although such surveys are used to demonstrate needs for programs or to test the effectiveness of interventions, they can also be used to *raise awareness* about alcohol-related issues and can even be used to give information, such as is done by Michigan State University (Oliaro, Heckler, & Olson, 1978). Many alcohol-use survey examples exist (see California Polytechnic State University and Indiana University examples, USDHEW, 1976), although one must be careful in choosing a survey, since some widely used instruments are based solely on an "alcoholism-as-a-disease" model and were standardized on older-aged clinical populations (Favazza & Cannell, 1977).

5.1.1.2. Posters. Attractive posters have been used in many programs to advertise various events, such as a symposium (Florida Technological University, USDHEW, 1976) or special "Alcohol Awareness Week" events. Many schools have also used posters to give specific alcohol-related information of either a primarily factual nature, such as the alcohol content of various beverages (Kraft, 1978b), or of a combined factual–emotional nature, such as a poster warning of risks of cirrhosis of the liver from excessive alcohol use (North Philadelphia Student Demonstration Project, USDHEW, 1976).

Posters are ideal for raising awareness and giving straightforward information. They can be used as a primary strategy or as part of the other activities, such as special displays, small discussion groups, or media contests. They can be posted on walls and bulletin boards around campus and in offices and rooms, as well as on campus buses and billboards.

5.1.1.3. Pamphlets and Manuals. Pamphlets, brochures, and booklets are used in a number of ways to raise awareness, give information, and at times suggest changes that can be made. Most college programs have developed booklets describing their own program activities and where to get information about alcohol program efforts. Other pamphlets are used to describe various local treatment programs, on-campus and off-campus, as an aid to early-intervention efforts. Educational pamphlets about how to drink in a responsible fashion have been developed by some programs, such as the University of Southern California (Kataja, 1977), California Polytechnic State University, the University of Texas, and the University of Michigan (USDHEW, 1976). Some educational pamphlets are population-specific, such as the pamphlet on "Drinking Fraternity Style" developed by the University of Florida (Goodale & Gonzalez, 1978). Others are topic-specific, such as pamphlets on party planning that have been developed by the University of Iowa (Strange & Miller, 1978) and the University of Massachusetts (Kraft, 1978), or a "bar guide" developed by the University of Iowa (Strange & Miller, 1978). Notebooks and manuals collecting resource materials have been developed by such groups as the Office of Greek Affairs, Ohio State

University (Tootle, 1977), the national Lambda Chi Alpha Fraternity (NIAAA, 1977a), and the Housing Office of the University of Wisconsin at Stevens Point (Committee for Making Health Decisions, 1977). Training manuals have also been devised in conjunction with various programs, including the University of Florida (Goodale & Gonzalez, 1978) and Iowa State University (Kraft & Moore, 1978).

5.1.1.4. Newspapers. College and community newspapers have been used in three separate ways by many programs. General news accounts about campus programs have been used not only to advertise program activities but also to raise awareness about various drinking problems and to give some factual information about their solution. Special feature articles or editorials have been used on some campuses to give specific information about alcohol-related topics, such as drinking and driving, party planning, drinking and accidental injuries, and the high-risk factors associated with chronic alcohol problems. A third use of newspapers has involved "advertisements" about responsible decision-making themes, such as those developed by the U.S. Jaycees "Operation Threshold" (U.S. Jaycees, 1975).

5.1.1.5. Radio and Television. Campus and community radio and television stations have been used in the same three ways as newspapers. News or public affairs broadcasts frequently publicize alcohol project efforts and can give basic information that may help some people think about their drinking habits. Special shows have been devoted to alcohol topics, either short 1- to 5-minute "tips" on various problems or longer 30- 90-minute versions. Many shows involve interviews or presentations on alcohol topics, such as a radio series developed by Nassau Community College (Pressley, 1978). Other shows use an entertainment motif and intersperse alcohol-related messages, quizzes, and the like, such as the University of Massachusetts's "Dr. Salsa's Medicine Show" (NIAAA, 1977b). Some television shows have been used on campuses with their own stations, especially closed-circuit television outlets. The use of advertisements has generally taken the form of "public service announcements," or PSAs. Such PSAs, when produced attractively, have been quite popular on some campuses, including the University of Massachusetts (Kraft, 1978), and reach a larger audience than single long shows. The NIAAA has also produced both radio and television PSAs, which may be available through the National Clearinghouse on Alcohol Information.

5.1.1.6. Special Displays. Most college programs have used special displays in one way or another. *Bulletin boards, pamphlet racks, or display cabinets* are frequently used to give information and advice about alcohol-related topics. Special *alcohol information centers* have been established at a number of campuses, including the University of Florida

(Goodale & Gonzalez, 1978), Michigan State University (Oliaro *et al.*, 1978), Nassau Community College (Pressley, 1978), the University of Rhode Island (Temple & Vincent, 1978), and the University of Wisconsin at Stevens Point (CMHD, 1978). Periodic special displays have also been tried at a number of campuses, including *Breathalyzer displays* near campus pubs or selected parties, to help students learn the association between blood alcohol levels and legally safe driving limits (Kraft, 1978b); *special tables or booths* in highly visible locations, such as the student union or lobbies of large residence halls, to distribute literature and show films that provide useful information; and *beverage displays* or *mixology presentations*, such as at student orientation programs, or information fairs, to provide examples of attractive nonalcoholic food and beverages and their recipes for use at future campus parties.

5.1.1.7. Films. Two different types of films have been used by various programs. Most commonly, full-length or feature-length films have been shown to a large audience in special presentations. Depending on the purpose of the meeting, the film may focus on the story of a chronic alcoholic, (for example, *The Secret Love of Sandra Blain*), on family problems caused by alcoholism, or on physiological and social factors related to alcohol use (for example, *America on the Rocks*). Some shorter films have also been produced and cover more limited topics, such as alcohol physiology (for example *Booze and You's* by Indiana University) and drinking and driving (such as *A Snort History* by the Denver Alcohol Safety Action Program).

The second type of film that has been used is the so-called trigger film. These one-to five-minute films are designed to depict typical situations that pose a problem, without giving a solution. The film is used to "trigger" or start a discussion about the situation and possible solutions. With a skillful discussion leader, these short films can be quite effective in helping to focus the topic under consideration. A number are described in the *Whole College Catalog about Drinking* (USDHEW, 1976).

5.1.1.8. Special Presentations. Many college programs involve some form of special presentation, including guest lectures, panel discussions, seminars, special contests, or orientation programs. Most of these strategies are used to educate large groups of people in a relatively short one- to two-hour time frame—except for seminars, which may last up to a week. Some special programs are run as part of freshman orientation.

A slightly different form of special presentation involves a so-called alcohol awareness day or week. This special time generally involves a variety of activities and programs, including campuswide publicity leading up to the events, numerous activities during the day or week, and often a big-name speaker either to begin or to end the special time.

Some examples have been described for Dallas County Community College District (Shaw, 1978), the University of Texas (Duncan, Hill, & Iscoe, 1978), and Washington University in St. Louis (Marsh, 1978). To be successful, alcohol awareness days or weeks must be carefully planned in order to exclude presentations with inconsistent messages or activities. For example, programs that view "alcohol as a drug" often have employed ex-alcoholics or "nondrinking alcoholics" as special speakers, who in turn have made presentations that are not compatible with the overall philosophy of the sponsor.

5.1.1.9. Single- and Multiple-Session Discussions. Small discussion groups can be used to help students and student groups examine their own beliefs, attitudes, and behavior in light of new knowledge. Many campuses use specially trained peer educators (i.e., students trained to spend some of their time educating their peers) to lead the discussions, including the University of Florida (Goodale & Gonzalaz, 1978), Indiana University (Engs, 1978), the University of Massachusetts (Kraft, 1978), and the University of Rhode Island (Temple & Vincent, 1978). Most peer education programs use a combination of topic-focused information with "values clarification" techniques. For example, a general discussion session about alcohol might use the exercise "20 Loves" (Simon, Howe, & Kirschenbaum, 1972) to point out to participants the number of activities they enjoy that involve drinking and/or large amounts of money. The exercise can be used to raise questions about a person's own behavior and what keeps him/her from doing things he/she enjoys, especially things that include little or no alcohol. The use of such discussions can also point out alternative forms of behaviors that may help reduce overdrinking episodes.

5.1.1.10. Academic Lectures, Courses. One- or two-session presentations within existing courses as well as special courses solely devoted to alcohol issues have been employed by most programs (Goodale & Hewitt, 1978). The format can vary from didactic lectures to small-group discussions. Depending on the extent of the sessions, the purpose and skill of the presenters, and the involvement of course participants, such academic offerings can help students both examine their own practices and beliefs and test out new behaviors, such as through role plays of how to refuse an alcoholic beverage in a social situation. Courses have also been developed to help heavy drinkers learn about ways to change their own behaviors in a responsible manner. Some colleges and universities also permit a limited number of student-led colloquia to be held for one or two credits, in which students trained in alcohol education techniques can then work with other groups of students as part of their own course requirements.

5.1.1.11. Alternative Activities. Many programs encourage students and student groups to consider increased participation in alternative activities that involve little or no alcohol use. Some campus groups have actually devised booklets about nondrinking events or activities and how to do them, as well as party-planning guides or pamphlets. However, since most booklets or planning guides are used by persons in the university other than the drinker him/herself, they are discussed more fully below.

5.1.1.12. Other. Individual campuses have developed somewhat novel ideas for changing the drinking behaviors of individuals and groups. Washington University in St. Louis has successfully employed writing contests, with prizes, to encourage students to consider their own drinking behavior (Marsh, 1978). The University of Texas has a "Telephone Tape Program" that allows students to call 24-hours a day and listen to tapes on a number of topics, including alcohol topics (Duncan *et al.*, 1978). California Polytechnic State University has employed a "Health Hazard Appraisal," completed by most entering students, that includes a number of questions about drinking attitudes and behavior.

5.1.2. Changing the Reactions to or Consequences of the Drinking Behaviors of Individuals and Groups

Many college and university programs seek to *change the reactions* of individuals and groups to problem-drinking behaviors. Some programs also seek to help individuals and groups *change the consequences* of drinking behaviors. The same methods are generally employed as outlined above for changing drinking behaviors. However, some additional ideas and activities are available. In general, the intent is to "increase the awareness and reactions" of individuals and groups regarding potential or actual problem-drinking behaviors while simultaneously "decreasing the intensity of the reactions' or "decreasing the probability of adverse consequences." For example, people might show concern to someone who frequently exhibits drunken behavior without assuming that everyone who occasionally gets intoxicated is an alcoholic.

5.1.2.1. Surveys. Most college surveys focus some questions on the context of drinking behaviors. Certain types of surveys, such as structured interviews, have been used to help respondents become aware of their own role in permitting overdrinking to occur and of how to modify such practices, such as by offering attractive nonalcoholic foods and beverages.

Other surveys can also be useful intervention tools. For example, two surveys employed by the University of Massachusetts program have proved to be important methods of changing reactions to drinking behaviors as well as of evaluating program results (Duston, 1978). Structured interviews of a random sample of heads of residences (HRs) have heightened the HRs' awareness of environmental and non-alcohol-specific factors that contribute to high levels of dormitory damage after parties, such as poor planning for nonalcoholic food and beverages. A periodic survey of medical clinic visits for alcohol-related contacts has led to increased awareness by medical and nursing staff of the association between overdrinking episodes and various medical problems, so that they can alert students to the role that their drinking has played in their medical problems and ways to prevent recurrences (Kraft, 1979).

5.1.2.2. Posters and Pamphlets. Most educational posters and pamphlets are used to encourage friends to take care of other friends who may have drunk to excess, such as the NIAAA theme, "Friends don't let friends drive drunk." The attempt is to raise peer-group consciousness about other people's behavior and to modify peer norms away from a purely individualistic "whatever he/she does is his/her own business," toward helping each other not to act irresponsibly. These themes have extended to booklets for individual students on "responsible party hosting," including the suggestion to let drunken persons sleep over rather than drive home, and on "how to help a problem drinker." Some campuses have extended the idea to booklets for student bartenders and party monitors (Kraft, Duston, & Mellor, 1978b).

Posters and pamphlets are commonly used to advertise various programs, seminars, and courses designed to train various personnel to recognize and help persons with alcohol problems. The intention of such materials is to attract people into the various programs and activities.

5.1.2.3. Manuals. Many training manuals have been developed. Some training manuals are designed for use with various college and university personnel, such as HRs and residence assistants; they are cited in later sections. Other manuals are specifically designed to train counseling personnel to help students and others with alcohol problems, such as the one published by St. Mary's University in Texas (Bush, 1978).

5.1.2.4. Newspapers, Radio, and Television. These media are used in the same way as described above, except that the contents of the messages are intended to change the reaction to drinking behaviors. *Program articles and interviews* about activities or plans are used to raise awareness about places friends or helpers can learn how to reduce drinking problems. *Feature articles, shows, or radio/television presentations* emphasize various ways that friends, acquaintances, and helping personnel can reduce alcohol problems or refer problem drinkers to helping agencies. Some of these features may give information helpful to party planners, bartenders, party monitors, potential automobile drivers, recreational enthusiasts, and others about how to prevent alcohol problems among friends. *Advertisements and public service announcements* utilize some of the same themes discussed above. Most available PSAs aim at changing the reaction, encouraging friends to help drunken friends or to help problem drinkers get treatment assistance. Specific programs meant to change drinking behavior generally involve messages aimed at changing reactions as well.

5.1.2.5. Special Displays and Special Presentations. The same methods described above are employed here. However, the content may focus more specifically on how to recognize various types of problems and how to deal with specific situations.

5.1.2.6. Single- and Multiple-Session Discussions. These methods are widely used to help groups of students learn ways of helping friends in problem situations. Role-playing party situations, practice in being assertive, and the development of ways to urge persons to slow down their rate of alcohol consumption are well suited to group discussions. "Trigger" films can be quite useful in such settings. Techniques of confronting friends who may have drinking problems can also be developed and practiced. Programs that have involved these approaches are cited above.

5.1.2.7. Academic Lectures and Courses. More formal lectures and courses are used to help peers learn ways to intervene early in potential problem situations without overreacting, similar to the methods outlined for discussion groups. Lectures and courses are also widely used for training paraprofessional and professional counselors to help problem drinkers. Courses with small numbers of participants have the advantage of giving longer periods of time to help students and student staff learn various techniques, such as community development techniques to develop concerted peer pressures against overdrinking and negative behaviors while supporting moderate levels of drinking. Other course designs teach students to lead their own minicourses, or colloquia, seeking to help students not only change their own drinking but also to develop ways of changing reactions to the drinking behaviors of others.

5.1.2.8. Activities. The main example of the use of activities to change the reaction to drinking behaviors by individuals and groups involves planned social events where people enjoy themselves and get to know each other without drinking as a prominent focus. Such activities often break down the stereotypes that various groups may have of others, such as fraternity or sorority house residents versus students living in residence halls, so that overreactions are minimized and sensible reactions are encouraged. No program descriptions have specifically noted these methods. Other activities planned by individuals or groups take place in locations where certain adverse consequences of drinking behavior are minimized. For example, on-campus party locations are used for residents, to minimize the need for anyone to drive home.

5.1.3. *Insulating the Behavior from the Potential Problem Situation or Reaction by Work with Individuals and Groups*

Most methods of *insulating behaviors* from reactions are covered in Section 5.2., where organizational and institutional responses are outlined. However, individuals and groups often use one method of insulation based on common sense: parties are often planned for locations, such as parks, where moderate levels of noise will not bother community residents. Some party hosts/hostesses also arrange for guests who overdrink to stay overnight rather than driving home. Still other groups of friends ride together to parties and designate one person to drive the group home: the designated person agrees to drink moderately that night; in return, he/she will not need to worry about consumption at subsequent parties until his/her turn to drive comes up again. Any of these and other methods of insulating potential problem behaviors can be included in the various educational strategies described above, especially those involving small groups of students. Citations of such approaches are included above under other program descriptions.

5.2. Methods Focused on Organizations and the Institution

Program efforts are frequently aimed at various organizations or agencies within the university community as well as at the university itself. Many desired environmental or social changes require college or university sanction, if not strong support. Although some of the methods and materials described for use with individuals and groups are also helpful in producing organizational and institutional changes, other methods have also been described.

5.2.1. *Changing Drinking and Related Behaviors through Organizational or Institutional Means*

Many organizational approaches to reducing alcohol problems focus on changing drinking behaviors. Although some campuses have tried imposing regulatory approaches without any concurrent educational efforts or without "the consent of the governed," most have used regulatory and environmental approaches along with preventive educational programs for individuals and groups.

5.2.1.1. Task Force. Most college and university programs that seek to prevent or reduce alcohol problems on campus utilize task forces or committees with broad representation from the university community. The task force is used both to collect information about the extent of alcohol problems and to disseminate information about needs, priorities, and programs for the campus. Some task forces meet for a limited amount of time and then disband, such as at the University of Massachusetts (Kraft, Duston, & Mellor, 1977). Other groups are ongoing and give continuing support and guidance to alcohol education activities, such as at the University of Rhode Island (Temple & Vincent, 1978) and the University of Wisconsin at Stevens Point (CMHD, 1978). Because of the far-reaching effects and involvements of alcohol problems on campus, some effort to involve students, staff, and faculty representatives in campuswide programs seems very important.

5.2.1.2. Surveys. Many campuswide programs survey campus agencies and university personnel for various reasons. Student leaders, faculty, and staff may be surveyed to determine the types and extent of perceived alcohol problems. Campus health and counseling agencies may be questioned about the number of students seen with alcohol problems. Dormitory and fraternity and sorority personnel may be asked about the nature of alcohol use and abuse in their living areas. And campus helping agencies may be polled regarding the services they can provide and the limitations of those services. Quite often the surveys are informal and impressionistic. However, they may lead to heightened sensitivity toward alcohol problems. Such surveys formed the basis for most programs described in *A Monograph on Alcohol Education . . . Programs at Selected American Colleges* (Goodale & Hewitt, 1978). The surveys may also alert various campus agencies to interest in alcohol problem reduction and can disseminate some information about current developments, especially if a personal interview technique is employed.

Surveys may lead to *perceived* increases in drinking behaviors because of heightened awareness of drinking problems soon after the initial survey. Surveys may also help other efforts to coordinate various campus programs aimed at reducing campus problems.

5.2.1.3. Alcoholic Beverages Policy. The most obvious way that campus organizations and the college or university as an institution seek to affect drinking behavior is through alcoholic beverage policies. Unfortunately, some campuses have no such policies. Others have policies that are so restrictive that they are not followed. Still others have policies that are so vague that they are not enforceable. Most campuses have policies that merely restate the federal, state, and local laws, such as restrictions on serving minors and intoxicated individuals and rules governing the sale of alcoholic beverages (Milgram, 1978).

A few campus programs have become involved in developing clear, reasonable, and enforceable alcoholic beverage policies that seek to minimize adverse consequences from overdrinking without becoming unnecessarily restrictive of reasonable social behaviors. Michigan State University instituted a policy within its residence halls that sought to respect the rights of hall residents and to place reasonable limits on the conduct of parties in the dormitories, including the provision of at least 25% nonalcoholic beverages at parties (Oliaro *et al.*, 1978). The University of Rhode Island revised its campuswide policy to limit the way in which parties are advertised and to require that nonalcoholic beverages be served (Temple & Vincent, 1978). Most recently, the University of Massachusetts has instituted a comprehensive policy that places strong restrictions on large campuswide parties to ensure adequate planning and conduct of the events and that encourages all party planners to learn and use safe procedures through a series of pamphlets, training sessions, and regulations (Kraft *et al.*, 1978b). No doubt, other examples exist that are not cited in the literature. The effect of such policies when combined with extensive educational efforts awaits future evaluation. However, since these policies seek to regulate behavior rather than to prohibit drinking and were devised with the active participation of student representatives, such policies seem to have an excellent chance of reducing the occurrence of certain alcohol problems.

5.2.1.4. Training Programs. Staff training programs have been used at many campuses to help university personnel learn what responsible decision-making about drinking means and how it can be encouraged. For example, residence hall staff are frequent targets of training about how to plan parties or other activities that will be attractive and fun for students but do not encourage overdrinking or do not even involve alcohol at all, such as the activities described for the University of Wisconsin at Stevens Point (CMHD, 1978). Campus pub personnel have been trained at some campuses to set up and arrange pub facilities that maximize socialization and minimize overdrinking, such as by providing places for people to sit down and talk, serving attractive nonalcoholic food and beverages, and providing entertainment that has a broad appeal without attracting heavy drinking crowds. Orientation programs for incoming students, mentioned above, have been institutionalized at many schools and encourage sensible drinking behaviors, especially within the living units of the schools. Student activities office personnel, who generally monitor certain student organizations and supervise various campus activities, have learned ways to encourage safe drinking practices and activities that do not focus heavily on drinking *per se*.

5.2.1.5. Party Planning. Since much drinking at college occurs at parties, many campuses have made considerable effort to try to influence the planning and conduct of parties. Policies and regulations affecting parties at certain campuses have been discussed above. In addition, some colleges and universities have designed training programs for residence hall personnel, courses and discussion groups for party planners, and special materials for hosts/hostesses, bartenders, and party monitors (bouncers), to educate such student personnel about sound principles to help them with their jobs. Educational efforts generally focus on the size of the event, the amount of alcohol consumption that might be reasonable, ways for party staff to work together to control persons who begin to get out of hand, ways to work with campus police and health personnel in the event of problems, and ways to ensure the safety of attendees and party staff alike. Ideas for party activities and attractive nonalcoholic food and beverages have also been provided, such as in the University of Massachusetts party-planning brochure (Kraft *et al.*, 1977) and the University of Southern California booklet "The Compleat Imbiber" (Kataja, 1977).

5.2.1.6. Peer Education Programs. Many campuses have established active peer education programs, designed primarily to train students to work with other students to change drinking behaviors and norms in the direction of responsible decision-making about alcohol use. The peer educators may be a recognized student organization, as at the University of Florida (Goodale & Gonzalez, 1978), or they may be associated with the student health service, as at the University of Massachusetts (Kraft, 1978) and the University of Rhode Island (Temple & Vincent, 1978). Other programs might choose to affiliate with the campus counseling service or the residential hall office. The main focus of the peer educator activities is prevention, with referral to counseling agencies of any problem drinkers.

5.2.1.7. Peer Counseling and Support Groups. A number of campuses now have peer counseling services for students with drinking problems, some of which include peer support groups. The institutions include East Stroudsburg State College (Bortz, 1978), Haskell Indian Junior College (Woodard & Coffey, 1978), the University of Rhode Island (Temple & Vincent, 1978), and St. Olaf College (Roberts, 1978). Some of the peer counselors function to help students become aware of their problems and seek help through other counseling agencies. Some peer counseling organizations work in conjunction with existing Alcoholics Anonymous and Al-Anon groups, and others work independently.

5.2.1.8. Employee and Student Assistance Programs. Many campuses have established employee assistance programs (EAPs) as an outgrowth of their student programs, as at the University of Rhode Island (Temple

& Vincent, 1978), based on the assumption that students are influenced to some extent by the drinking habits of staff and faculty. In addition, some campuses have adapted EAP models for use by students who are showing decreased academic or work performance, as at Washington University of St. Louis (Marsh, 1978). These activities have an early-intervention focus.

5.2.1.9. Treatment Resources. Most campuses have made sure that adequate treatment resources are available both on-campus and off-campus to help students with drinking problems. Most commonly, the resources include health services personnel (medical and mental health staff), counseling-center staff, community alcoholism services, and Alcoholics Anonymous and Al-Anon groups. Whatever the resources, coordination between the various resources is highly desirable, to permit cross-referral of clients and support of campus efforts. Although some programs do not agree with prevention approaches based on the "alcohol-as-a-drug" or the "alcohol-as-a-food/beverage" models, as was documented at the University of Iowa (Strange & Miller, 1978), most alcohol and alcoholism programs *can* agree on certain common elements and work together for the good of students with drinking problems.

5.2.1.10. Campus Pubs. The number of on-campus pubs is growing (Shaw, 1974). The establishment of on-campus pubs or taverns is one method employed by some campuses to change drinking behaviors. Not only do such pubs frequently reduce some "town–gown" frictions, but they also provide settings where students can learn safe drinking habits, as at the Senior Club at Notre Dame (USDHEW, 1976). Since many campus pub personnel identify closely with the educational mission of the university and most pubs are prohibited from making a profit, the on-campus pub can serve as a powerful tool to help some students change drinking behaviors. Unfortunately, few alcohol personnel seem to have worked closely with such pub personnel, and few reports exist regarding their effectiveness as an educational setting or strategy.

5.2.1.11. Alternative Activities. Certain campuses have increased the number of non-alcohol-specific activities available to students. These activities include not only sanctioned sports and recreational events but also programs that use meditating, jogging, biofeedback, assertiveness training, and other stress management techniques to help students cope without resorting to excess alcohol use. Other campuses have established "coffeehouses" where no alcoholic beverages are served but good food and entertainment are available. Alcohol-specific activities, such as wine-tasting and wine-and-cheese parties, have also been sanctioned by some schools in an attempt to integrate sensible drinking into popular activities. Although the effectiveness of alternative activities in modifying problem drinking continues to be questioned, most comprehensive programs focus some efforts on such approaches.

5.2.2. *Changing the Reaction to or Consequences of Drinking Behavior through Organizational or Institutional Means*

Most organizational or institutional methods of *changing the reactions to or the consequences of* drinking behavior have involved efforts to train various staff and student groups to become more sensitive to problem situations and to respond appropriately. However, a few other methods, involving environmental responses, have also been used.

5.2.2.1. Task Force. A campuswide task force can provide an important impetus to efforts designed to raise the consciousness of the college or university community about potential alcohol problems at the same time that they minimize fears that "all students are alcoholics." The tone of campus programs is frequently set by such a group: the group can help or hinder efforts, depending on how coordinated are the various viewpoints and interests of the committee members. Most of what was said above about using a task force to change drinking behaviors applies to the task force's functioning to change reactions.

5.2.2.2. Training Programs. The majority of students and staff training programs have focused on early identification and intervention strategies for problem drinkers and situations. In fact, some campus programs rely almost solely on such techniques, including Dallas County Community College District (Shaw, 1978), Haskell Indian Junior College (Woodard & Coffey, 1978), Southern Methodist University (Martin, 1978), and the University of Texas (Duncan *et al.*, 1978). Personnel from residence halls, counseling services, health services, campus police, and related student services are trained to recognize potential problem drinkers, to confront them about their behaviors, and either to treat them or to refer them to other treatment resources. In general, the training seeks to increase staff and student sensitivity to problems related to alcohol without overreacting, such as by automatically implying that the person is an alcoholic. The training often includes learning the principles of safe drinking as well as ways to minimize the probability of situations where overdrinking will be harmful.

A few programs include training that modifies reactions or consequences by focusing more directly on the problem situation itself. For example, drunken students who plan to drive home are assisted either to go home in a taxi or with a friend who is not intoxicated or to stay overnight at the site of the party. Drunken students who would ordinarily walk home across a dimly lit campus are driven home to avoid accidental injuries. Intoxicated students who show up at the health center with accidental injuries are given follow up appointments, where the association between overdrinking and such injuries is discussed. Students seeking counseling concerning disrupted relationships are questioned about their drinking habits and any role that excessive alcohol consumption might play in such situations. Or students arrested for vandalism while drunk are held liable for the property damage and encouraged to seek help for the overdrinking if the student feels that the drinking is the problem—without the campus policemen accusing the student of being an alcoholic.

Unfortunately, few college and university program citations included specific outlines of the content of staff and student training sessions.

5.2.2.3. Campus Pubs. The establishment of campus drinking establishments can frequently help efforts to change reactions to or consequences of drinking behaviors. Pubs within walking distance of residence areas can cut down on driving by drunken students. The controlled atmosphere of each pub can also reduce the potential for excessive drinking by large numbers of students, provided it also attracts the same students who would otherwise go off-campus. The location on-campus could also reduce certain reactions, for example, by town police or town residents, since campus police and residents have (presumably) received better training in dealing with potential adverse consequences due to student drunkenness.

5.2.2.4. Environmental Designs. Campus attempts to provide *lighted walkways* between residences and drinking establishments can assist efforts to reduce some accidental injuries (strains, sprains) related to overdrinking. The use of *nondestructible outdoor lighting fixtures* can cut down on some of the property destruction by rowdy students—some of whom may be drunk! *Repair of worn-out bathroom fixtures and furniture* in public facilities can often cut down on a certain amount of property damage blamed on drunken students who may use the facilities. The purchase of *sturdy furniture* for student lounges where parties frequently occur could also assist in reducing alcohol-related property damage. The *campus pub* should be accessible by stairways that are safe for use by intoxicated individuals. Although these and other examples have not appeared in any known descriptions of alcohol programs, they have been used at some campuses and provide a practical way to change some reactions or consequences of certain alcohol-related behaviors.

5.2.2.5. Transportation to Off-Campus Bars. In places where on-campus pubs are not feasible, or otherwise not widely used, the provision of bus or taxi service between popular off-campus bars and student residences has cut down on drunk-driving incidents, such as the "Quickie Shuttle Service" at Notre Dame (USDHEW, 1976). The method at least keeps drunken students, as well as other people on the highway, alive. It is particularly useful in states where the legal drinking age is 21 years and students drive long distances to drink in neighboring states.

5.2.3. *Insulating Behavior from Potential Problem Situations or Reactions, through Organizational or Institutional Means*

Few programs have described ways to insulate problem behaviors from potential reactions. However, some methods have been employed through the use of common sense.

5.2.3.1. Party Locations. A frequent occurrence at most campuses is to locate large and/or potentially noisy parties away from community residences, so that the noise will not cause any problems. Similarly, locations away from busy roadways are generally chosen, to prevent unnecessary pedestrian accidents.

5.2.3.2. Pub Locations and Hours. The physical location of pubs, as well as any other drinking establishments should be removed from potential problem areas, such as churches or other places where people might be offended by loud behavior in the pub. The hours the pub serves alcoholic beverages should not encourage nonhealthy drinking practices by students, such as staying open late on weeknights or serving alcoholic beverages early in the morning (although most state laws already prohibit these practices to some extent).

Some of the other techniques mentioned above as ways of changing the reactions to or the consequences of the drinking behavior might also be considered ways of insulating the behavior, for example, bus service to off-campus bars and environmental designs that place indestructible lights in public places.

6. Evaluation of College Programs

Most college programs are now building evaluation strategies into their designs. Program staff regularly describe the *effort*, or "what was done," including types of activities, numbers reached, and the number of staff hours required. Many college and university programs also describe the *process* of alcohol program efforts, that is "how" the activities were conducted and what participants and other observers thought of the activities. A few programs attempt to measure the *effects* of various efforts, or the "outcome" of alcohol activities. Constraints of the program setting usually make the utilization of experimental and even quasi-experimental evaluation designs very difficult. The most comprehensive description of an evaluation plan for a university alcohol education program was given for the University of Massachusetts (Duston, 1978), although the actual effects of the program have been reported only in a preliminary fashion.

6.1. Effort

Most programs describe the ways they keep track of the efforts expended. Most commonly, each program activity is described, often with an outline of the specific goals and objectives of the activity. Records are maintained of the number of students contacted by each activity and the number of hours of exposure of various students, to give student-contact hours (i.e., number of students times number of hours of contact with each student equals student-contact hours). The number of staff hours involved is also recorded.

The amount of effort put into specific program activities can give an initial impression of how adequately the program objectives were attained. For example, programs that are designed to change the drinking behaviors of all students but reach only 2–3% of the student body every year probably are not going to change campuswide behaviors significantly. On the other hand, programs designed to counsel problem drinkers that reach 2–3% of the student-body each year are probably doing quite well.

Few programs described in the literature cite the actual numbers reached by various activities, except for the programs at the University of Massachusetts and Michigan State University. The University of Massachusetts has conducted surveys that show that up to 70% of a random sample of students recall seeing a specific poster and that 4% reported attending an educational session sponsored by the alcohol project in the previous year (Kraft, 1978). Although we recognize the limitations of the *post hoc* survey, this finding compares favorably with the project's goal of helping all students become aware of alcohol-specific information and of reaching between 5% and 10% of students each year with intensive educational efforts. In one of its surveys, Michigan State University found that over 40% of a sample of residence hall students reported seeing posters, pamphlets, or other materials developed by their project—a proportion that pleased them when compared to their goals (Oliaro *et al.*, 1978).

6.2. Process

Estimates of how well a particular program or activity was conducted are generally obtained from presenters, participants, and other observers. Program *presenters* often give some assessment of a particular intervention either by using standardized process criteria or by describing the events of the educational or counseling session. Most commonly, *participants* in various activities are asked for their reactions to a given activity immediately after the activity and/or a few weeks or months after the activity. For example, peer counselors trained by East Stroudsburg State College are asked to rate the training program in terms of both how it was conducted and what it taught (Bortz, 1978). Clients treated by the Haskell Indian Junior College are "tracked" to find out how well they progress through the stages of the program (Woodard & Coffey, 1978). Participants in educational programs at Iowa State University fill out written forms at the completion of various programs to evaluate the activities (Krafft & Moore, 1978). Key administrators at the University of Massachusetts were asked to give their impression about the alcohol education project efforts and whether or not the program was working: most comments indicated that the administrators believed that the project efforts were well designed and well received and, therefore, had led to an increased awareness about alcohol use and abuse and a decrease in certain problems related to drinking (Kraft, 1978).

6.3. Effect

The measurement of the results of various programs has generally relied on three types of data: survey information self-reported by samples of the target audience, direct observations of selected behaviors, and unobtrusive measures of the occurrence of certain alcohol-related incidents. Frequently, survey instruments used to establish baseline levels of drinking and problem behaviors are repeated periodically, usually annually, to determine trends in alcohol-related knowledge, attitudes, and behaviors, such as at the University of Massachusetts (Kraft, 1978) and the University of Wisconsin at Stevens Point (CMHD, 1978). Surveys are also given to smaller groups of program particpants, to measure changes due to program efforts, such as a two-month follow up of peer counselors trained at East Stroudsburg State College (Bortz, 1978). A few surveys match control groups with the experimental subjects, as in a survey performed at Indiana University, which showed that an alcohol education module significantly increased knowledge over at least a three-month period but did not produce behavioral changes in the same period of time (Engs, 1977).

Some programs conduct surveys of other campus personnel to determine program effects. The most thorough attempt described in the literature is from the University of Massachusetts, where survey methods include structured interviews of a random sample of heads of residence halls, to determine changes in dormitory behaviors, and special surveys of medical and mental health professionals, to determine the number of students with alcohol-related problems seen during one-week periods of time each semester. The use of behavioral observers in the dormitories during selected periods of time, to determine trends in alcohol-related behaviors, and customer counts in the campus pub, to determine the average amount of alcohol consumed during certain time periods, have also been attempted (Duston, 1978).

Other commonly used indices of program effects are so-called unobtrusive measures. Statistical data are gathered to determine the number of arrests for alcohol-related crimes, the number of clinical contacts for health problems related to alcohol use, property damage reports, and student judiciary reports on alcohol-related infractions. Colleges and universities reporting the use of such measures include the University of Massachusetts (Duston, 1978), Michigan State University (Oliaro *et al.*, 1978), the University of Rhode Island (Temple & Vincent, 1978), and the University of Wisconsin at Stevens Point (CMHD, 1978). The obvious limitations of such unobtrusive measures are the inconsistencies and inaccuracies of such "counts" and the inability to attribute causality directly to program interventions.

The wide variety of different campus approaches makes global statements about the effects of current programs impossible. Certainly, many colleges and universities not only have indicated the need for programs to reduce alcohol problems but also have established active programs with whatever resources were available. Each of the programs that have reported their activities feel that their services have been widely used, and many campuses have surveys that show widespread acceptance by students of efforts to prevent as well as to treat alcohol problems. A couple of studies have shown positive changes in alcohol-related knowledge and attitudes as the result of program efforts, and some schools are reporting decreasing rates of certain adverse consequences of drinking, such as property destruction and vandalism. However, no reports have yet documented desired changes in alcohol-related behaviors. It is still too early to tell if failures to document behavioral changes mean that current alcohol education methods are ineffective, that the measurement techniques are still too crude to detect desired changes, or that the nature of the beast prevents reliable documentation. In general, the nature of educational designs, the flexible application of educational techniques, and the complex psychosocial variables of recipients severely threatens the external validity of program evaluations. Indeed, it is even difficult to control programs sufficiently to minimize threats to the internal validity of evaluation schemes.

Certainly, much more rigorous evaluation of alcohol programs, especially of the effects of such programs, is necessary. Attempts to measure behavioral changes rather than merely knowledge and attitude changes are commendable, although more work needs to be done to determine which behaviors to measure, how to measure them, and what analytic techniques can offset the lack of feasibility of equivalent experimental groups.

7. Summary and Conclusions

College programs embody a number of different strategies designed to reduce alcohol problems. In some cases, the strategies employed depend on the college or university's assumptions about alcohol, whether drinking is a vice, alcoholism is a disease, alcohol is a drug, or alcohol is a food or beverage. Although many programs contain approaches consistent with two or more of these assumptions, the predominance of one view of alcohol versus another will determine whether the program's efforts are geared mainly to locate and treat problem-drinking students (secondary prevention) or to educate all students about how to make responsible decisions about drinking and nondrinking (primary prevention).

Strategies used in most programs seek to use various combinations of education and regulation to accomplish program goals. Educational approaches generally rely on communication models that postulate that behavior change can be achieved through knowledge and attitude changes. Regulatory approaches rely on either behaviorist models or practical experiences that indicate that changing or limiting behaviors directly does lead to some desired changes, irrespective of knowledge and attitudes.

Specific strategies can be aimed either at individuals or affiliative groups of individuals or at organizational and institutional representatives. In each case, methods can be employed that (1) change the drinking or attendant behaviors, either through alcohol-specific or non-alcohol-specific measures; (2) change the reaction to or the consequences of the drinking behavior; or (3) insulate the drinking behavior from the potential problem situation or reaction. Various college programs use mixtures of these approaches by employing different sets of techniques.

Strategies directly focused on individuals and groups generally rely on surveys; media and materials, including posters, pamphlets, and newspaper, radio, and television articles, features, and advertisements; special displays, at highly visible places, using mixtures of media and materials and various gimmicks such as Breathalyzer demonstrations;

films, including both feature-length and "trigger" films; special presentations, lectures, panels, or guest speakers; single- or multiple-session discussion groups; academic courses and lectures; and various other activities. Strategies focused on organizations and institutions generally rely on task forces; surveys; alcoholic beverages policies; training programs, for both student helping-agency personnel as well as students who are staff in certain programs; party-planning efforts; peer education and peer counseling programs; employee and student assistance programs; treatment resources, both on-campus and off-campus; campus pubs, including locations, hours, and programming; alternative activities; environmental designs of campus buildings and pathways; transportation to off-campus bars; and safe party locations. Most colleges and universities use a combination of strategies aimed at individuals and groups and at organizations and institutions.

The evaluation of college and university programs relies on measurements of what was done (effort), how it was done (process), and what resulted (effect). Most current programs rely mainly on effort and process data and seem to show encouraging results for their program efforts. The few programs that attempt to measure the effects of program efforts do show desired changes in the knowledge and attitudes of individuals. Certain adverse consequences related to drinking also seem to be decreasing at various campuses, most notably property damage. However, no schools have yet documented significant behavioral changes due to program efforts, although the newness of many of the programs may prevent accurately assessing lasting behavior changes until more time passes.

In general, college programs offer a broad array of approaches and programs. However, the broad array frequently leads to confusion in implementing contradictory goals and objectives.

In general, the following conclusions seem justified:

1. Strategies to reduce alcohol problems should rest on one primary assumption about alcohol and its use, and activities should be constructed accordingly.
2. Campuses need to consider the relative importance of prevention versus the early identification and treatment of alcohol problems. In all cases, adequate treatment resources in the community should be available to help students with their drinking problems.
3. A mixture of methods involving individuals and groups, and organizations and institutions seems to offer the best chance for success, especially if prevention is a major aim of the program.
4. A mixture of educational and regulatory approaches seems most

likely to offer success in effecting campuswide changes, assuming the two approaches are consistent with one another.

5. Evaluation strategies need to be built into every campus program, especially strategies that attempt to measure the effects of various programs on behavior.

With the growth in support for college programs designed to reduce drinking prolblems among students, many excellent programs have been implemented. The immediate effects on most college students are now being assessed by many of the programs. The longer-term effects on both college and university institutions and society as a whole remain to be seen.

References

Ajzen, I., & Fishbein, M. Factors influencing intentions and the intention–behavior relationship. *Human Relations*, 1974, *27*, 1–15.

Blane, H. T. Education and the prevention of alcoholism. In B. Kissin & H. Begleiter (Eds.), *The biology of alcoholism. Vol. 4; The social aspects of alcoholism.* New York: Plenum Press, 1976.

Blane, H. T. Symposium on drinking among college students: Scope of the problem. Paper presented at "Symposium on Drinking among College Students," sponsored by The Medical Foundation, Inc., March 1978, Boston.

Bortz, D. R. East Stroudsburg State College drug and alcohol abuse prevention program—Affective model. In T. Goodale & K. Hewitt (Coordinators), *A monograph on alcohol education and alcohol abuse prevention programs at selected American colleges.* Gainesville, Fla.: Office for Student Services, University of Florida, 1978.

Bush, W. T. Competency-based, modularized instructional program for counselor training in substance abuse services, St. Mary's University, San Antonio, Texas. In T. Goodale & K. Hewitt (Coordinators), *A monograph on alcohol education and alcohol abuse prevention programs at selected American colleges.* Gainesville, Fla.: Office for Student Services, University of Florida, 1978.

Cahalan, D. *Problem drinkers: A national survey.* San Francisco: Jossey-Bass, 1970.

Cahalan, D., & Cisin, I. H. Drinking behavior and drinking problems in the United States. In B. Kissin & H. Begleiter (Eds.), *The biology of alcoholism. Vol. 4; The social aspects of alcoholism.* New York: Plenum Press, 1976.

Cahalan, D., & Room, R. *Problem drinking among American men.* New Brunswick, N.J.: Rutgers Center of Alcohol Studies, 1974.

Caplan, G. *Principles of preventive psychiatry.* New York: Basic Books, 1964.

Committee for Making Healthy Decisions. Teaching Responsible Drinking—A Comprehensive Alcohol Education Program. Compiled by The Committee for Making Healthy Decisions, Housing Office, University of Wisconsin at Stevens Point, 1977.

Committee for Making Healthy Decisions. Alcohol education: Responsibility and alternatives, University of Wisconsin at Stevens Point. In T. Goodale & K. Hewitt (Coordinators), *A monograph on alcohol education and alcohol abuse prevention programs at selected American colleges.* Gainesville, Fla.: Office for Student Services, University of Florida, 1978.

Duncan, J. P., Hill, F. E., & Iscoe, I. An interagency alcoholism prevention program, the University of Texas at Austin. In T. Goodale & K. Hewitt (Coordinators). *A monograph on alcohol education and alcohol abuse prevention programs at selected American colleges.* Gainesville, Fla.: Office for Student Services, University of Florida, 1978.

Duston, E. K. Evaluating an alcohol education project, University of Massachusetts, Amherst. In T. Goodale & K. Hewitt (Coordinators), *A monograph on alcohol education and alcohol abuse prevention programs at selected American colleges.* Gainesville, Fla.: Office for Student Services, University of Florida, 1978.

Engs, R. C. Drinking behaviors among college students. *Journal of Studies of Alcohol,* 1977, *38,* 2144–2156.

Engs, R. C. Indiana University's booze and you's program module. In T. Goodale & K. Hewitt (Coordinators), *A monograph on alcohol education and alcohol abuse prevention program at selected American colleges.* Gainesville, Fla.: Office for Student Services, University of Florida, 1978.

Favazza, A. R., & Cannell, B. Screening for alcoholism among college students. *American Journal of Psychiatry,* 1977, *134,* 1414–1416.

Fishbein, M. Attitude and the prediction of behavior. In M. Fishbein (Ed.), *Readings in attitude theory and measurement.* New York: Wiley, 1967.

Girdano, D. D., & Girdano, D. A. College drug use—A five-year survey. *Journal of the American College Health Association,* 1976, *25,* 117–119.

Goodale, T., & Gonzalez, G. Alcohol abuse prevention program, University of Florida. In T. Goodale & K. Hewitt (Coordinators), *A monograph on alcohol education and alcohol abuse prevention programs at selected American colleges.* Gainesville, Fla.: Office for Student Services, University of Florida, 1978.

Goodale, T., & Hewitt, K. (Coordinators). *A monograph on alcohol education and alcohol abuse prevention programs at selected American colleges.* Gainesville, Fla.: Office for Student Services, University of Florida, 1978.

Hanson, D. J. Drinking attitudes and behaviors among college students. *Journal of Alcohol and Drug Education,* 1974, *19,* 6–14.

Hanson, D. J. Alcohol consumption among college students: 1970–1975. *College Student Journal,* 1977, *11,* 9–10.

Johnson, G. F. S., & Leeman, M. M. Analysis of familial factors in bipolar affective illness. *Archives of General Psychiatry,* 1977, *34,* 1074–1083.

Kataja, E. (Ed.). The compleat imbiber: USC student guide to responsible drinking. Pamphlet produced by the Student Health and Counseling Services, University of Southern California, 1977.

Kopplin, D. A., Greenfield, T. K., & Wong, H. A. Changing patterns of substance use on campus: A four-year follow up study. *International Journal of the Addictions,* 1977, *12,* 73–94.

Krafft, J., & Moore, J. Alcohol education programming at Iowa State University. In T. Goodale and K. Hewitt (Coordinators), *A monograph on alcohol education and alcohol abuse prevention programs at selected American colleges.* Gainesville, Fla.: Office for Student Services, University of Florida, 1978.

Kraft, D. P. College students and alcohol: The 50 plus 12 project. *Alcohol, Health and Research World,* 1976, Summer, 10–14.

Kraft, D. P. Follow up of a federal effort to encourage campus alcohol abuse prevention programs. *Journal of the American College Health Association,* 1977, *26,* 150–153.

Kraft, D. P. The demonstration alcohol education program at the University of Massachusetts, Amherst. In T. Goodale & K. Hewitt (Coordinators), *A monograph on alcohol education and alcohol abuse prevention programs at selected American colleges.* Gainesville, Fla.: Office for Student Services, University of Florida, 1978.

Kraft, D. P. Alcohol-related problems seen at the student health services. *Journal of the American College Health Association,* 1979, *27,* 190–194.

Kraft, D. P., Duston, E., & Mellor, E. T. Establishing effective alcohol program efforts on a university campus. Paper presented at the Annual Convention of the American College Health Association, Denver, Apr. 1976. (Abstract, *College Student Personnel Abstracts,* 1977, *12,* 502)

Kraft, D. P., Duston, E., & Mellor, E. T. Addendum to Third Annual Report on a University Demonstration Alcohol Education Project, NIAAA Grant 3–H84–AA02331–03, unpublished report, Sept., 1978. (a)

Kraft, D. P., Duston, E., & Mellor, E. T. Alcohol education programming at the University of Massachusetts, Amherst, and evaluation of results to date. Paper presented at Annual Convention of the American Psychological Association, San Francisco, Aug. 1977. (Abstract, *Resources in Education* (ERIC), 1978, *13,* No. 7 (ED150–506)). (b)

Kraft, D. P., Duston, E., & Mellor , E.T. Third Annual Report on a University Demonstration Alcohol Education Project. NIAAA Grant 3–H84–AA02331–03, unpublished report, Aug. 1978.(c)

Kuder, J. M., & Madson, D. L. College student use of alcoholic beverages. *Journal of College Student Personnel,* 1976, *17,* 142–144.

Lester, L. F., & Perez, P. Dimensions of college student behavior. Paper presented at Annual Convention of American College Health Association, Philadelphia, Apr. 1977. (Abstract, *College Student Personnel Abstracts,* 1978, *13,* 369–370)

Lippitt, R., Watson, J., & Westley, B. *The dynamics of plannned change.* New York: Harcourt, Brace & World, 1958.

Looney, M. A. Alcohol use survey on campus: Implications for health education. *Journal of the American College Health Association,* 1976, *25,* 109–112.

Marlatt, G. A. Training responsible drinking with college students. Paper presented at Annual Convention of the American Psychological Association, Chicago, Sept. 1977.

Marsh, M. S. Campus assistance program, Washington University, St. Louis. In T. Goodale & K. Hewitt (Coordinators), *A monograph on alcohol education and alcohol abuse prevention programs at selected American colleges.* Gainesville, Fla.: Office for Student Services, University of Florida, 1978.

Martin, C. Alcohol and you at SMU, Southern Methodist University. In T. Goodale and K. Hewitt (Coordinators), *A monograph on alcohol education and alcohol abuse prevention programs at selected American colleges.* Gainesville, Fla.: Office for Student Services, University of Florida, 1978.

Milgram, G. G. Implications of college policy on campus drinking practices. Paper presented at the Annual Convention of the American College Health Association, Philadelphia, April 1977. (Abstract, *College Student Personnel Abstracts,* 1978, *13,* 405)

Miller, W. R., & Muñoz, R. F. *How to control your drinking.* Englewood Cliffs, N.J.: Prentice-Hall, 1976.

Morrill, W. H., Oetting, E. R., & Hurst, J. C. Dimensions of counseling intervention. Technical Report Number 1, 1972, Colorado State University, Grant No. RO1-MH18007, National Institute of Mental Health.

National Institute on Alcohol Abuse and Alcoholism. Large fraternity runs alcohol program. *NIAAA Information and Feature Service,* No. 39, Sept. 8, 1977.(a)

National Institute on Alcohol Abuse and Alcoholism. Radio show uses music in alcoholism education. *NIAAA Information and Feature Service*, No. 41, Oct. 31, 1977.(b)

Oliaro, P., Heckler, D., & Olson, B. The Michigan State University alcohol education project for resident students. In T. Goodale & K. Hewitt (Coordinators), *A monograph on alcohol education and alcohol abuse prevention programs at selected American colleges*. Gainesville, Fla.: Office for Student Services, University of Florida, 1978.

Penn, J. R. College student life-style and frequency of alcohol usage. *Journal of the American College Health Association*, 1974, *22*, 220–222.

Pressley, G. Prevention education training, Nassau Community College. In T. Goodale & K. Hewitt (Coordinators), *A monograph on alcohol education and alcohol abuse prevention programs at selected American colleges*. Gainesville, Fla.: Office for Student Services, University of Florida, 1978.

Roberts, B. B. A community approach to alcohol related problems and alcohol education, St. Olaf College. In T. Goodale & K. Hewitt (Coordinators), *A monograph on alcohol education and alcohol abuse prevention programs at selected American colleges*. Gainesville, Fla.: Office for Student Services, University of Florida, 1978.

Rouse, B. A., & Ewing, J. A. Student drug use, risk-taking, and alienation. *Journal of the American College Health Association*, 1974, *22*, 226–230.

Shaw, J. S. Have some (legal) Madeira, m'dear? Campus drinking is changing. *College and University Business*, 1974, *56*, 46–47.

Shaw, V. A community college based alcohol education program, Dallas County Community College District. In T. Goodale & K. Hewitt (Coordinators), *A monograph on alcohol education and alcohol abuse prevention programs at selected American colleges*. Gainesville, Fla.: Office for Student Services, University of Florida, 1978.

Simon, S. B., Howe, L. W., & Kirschenbaum, H. *Values clarification: A handbook of practical strategies for teachers and students*. New York: Hart Publishing, 1972.

Strange, C., & Miller, B. Alcohol abuse prevention: A systematic campus approach, University of Iowa. In T. Goodale & K. Hewitt (Coordinators), *A monograph on alcohol education and alcohol abuse prevention programs at selected American colleges*. Gainesville, Fla.: Office for Student Services, University of Florida, 1978.

Straus, R., & Bacon, S. D. *Drinking in college*. New Haven, Conn.: Yale University Press, 1953.

Temple, H. A., & Vincent, D. M. Education, the catalyst for comprehensive student alcohol programs, University of Rhode Island. In T. Goodale & K. Hewitt (Coordinators), *A monograph on alcohol education and alcohol abuse prevention programs at selected American colleges*. Gainesville, Fla.: Office for Student Services, University of Florida, 1978.

Tootle, B. J. Booze Nooze: Alcohol Education Program Plans and Intervention Strategies for College Fraternities. Compiled by the Office of Greek Affairs, Ohio State University, 1977.

U.S. Department of Health, Education and Welfare, *Second Special Report to the U.S. Congress on Alcohol and Health from the Secretary of Health, Education and Welfare*. Washington, D.C.: U.S. Government Printing Office, 1974.

U.S. Department of Health, Education and Welfare. *The Whole College Catalog about Drinking: A Guide to Alcohol Abuse Prevention*. Washington, D.C.: U.S. Government Printing Office, 1976.

U.S. Jaycees. Threshold Print Media Kit. Available from Products Division, United States Jaycees, Box 7, Tulsa, Okla., 1975.

Winokur, G., Reich, T., Rimmer, J., & Pitts, F. N. Alcoholism. III: Diagnosis and familial psychiatric illness in 259 alcoholic probands. *Archives of General Psychiatry*, 1970, *23*, *104–111*.

Woodard, M., & Coffey, C. Alcohol education programming at Haskell Indian Junior College. In T. Goodale & K. Hewitt (Coordinators), *A monograph on alcohol education and alcohol abuse prevention programs at selected American colleges*. Gainesville, Fla.: Office for Student Services, University of Florida, 1978.

11

U.S. Military Alcohol Abuse Prevention and Rehabilitation Programs

John E. Killeen

1. Introduction

The misuse of alcoholic beverages among our youth has a significant impact on American institutions, including the military services. The number of young people who drink alcoholic beverages appears to be increasing. The age at which our youth begin to drink appears to be continually decreasing. By the 12th grade, a majority of young people drink alcoholic beverages, and, predictably, many experience problems associated with this drinking. Alcohol continually surfaces as a factor in highway fatalities, homicides, accidents, and suicides among the young. In fact, nearly 8,000 young Americans between the ages of 15 and 24 years die each year in alcohol-related accidents. This constitutes more deaths at this age for alcohol-related reasons than for any other cause. Additionally, 40,000 young people each year are injured in drinking and driving accidents (Initiatives for Alcohol Programs for Youth, 1978).

Most evidence indicates that alcohol-related problems other than alcoholism occur with the greatest frequency between the ages of 18 and 24. These are precisely the ages when young people enter the military

John E. Killeen, Major, USAF • Office of the Assistant Secretary of Defense (Health Affairs), Department of Defense, Washington, DC 20301.

services. In fact, over one-half of the personnel on active duty in the armed services are below the age of 25 years. Clearly, if society at large needs coherent and effective social policies and programs to address the consequences of the misuse of alcohol by young people, the military services have an even more pressing need. The charter of the Department of Defense to maintain a high state of military readiness and proficiency demands that the abuse of alcoholic beverages by members of the military be prevented as much as possible and that the impact of misuse upon service people and the military mission be limited.

Although small-scale alcohol-abuse control programs were instituted in the military as early as 1965, the services really began to systematically confront the challenge posed by alcohol misuse during 1971. Each of the military services has been developing and refining alcohol abuse prevention, treatment, and rehabilitation programs since that time.

Below, the nature of the alcohol-abuse prevention challenge in the armed forces is discussed. The programs of all of the military services are briefly outlined, and an in-depth review of the U.S. Air Force program is presented.

2. Nature of the Prevention Challenge

The structure of the military services and the varying nature of their missions confer both advantages and disadvantages on those who design programs to control the abuse of alcohol among our members. On the advantage side of the register, the military services remain one of the American institutions with a strong tradition and sense of community. The sense of responsibility for "taking care of our own" is strongly established.

Standards of appearance, behavior, and performance are explicit and are continually reinforced. The degree of supervision of and interaction with younger people by older members is significantly more intense than in civilian pursuits, particularly for the young persons living on military installations. Recreational alternatives are extensive. Unemployment does not exist. The military chain of command is structured to permit rapid and thorough response to perceived problems, accountability for results is an institutional fact of life, and with 94% of the commissioned officers possessing college degrees, the leadership is well educated.

The primary disadvantages of the military structure to the design of alcohol-abuse prevention programs center on the size, demography, dispersal, and complexity of the military services.

2.1. Size of the Military Services

Military alcohol-abuse and alcoholism prevention, treatment, and rehabilitation programs provide varying degrees of service to over 8 million members, employees, or dependents. Approximately 2 million persons serve on active duty in the armed forces. Over half of these persons are under the age of 25; 94% are male; approximately 40% are single. These members bring their drinking habits, both good and bad, into the services with them. In addition to these active-duty members, military programs serve nearly 3 million dependents, 1 million civilian employees, and another 2 million National Guard and reserve personnel. The extent of prevention, treatment, and rehabilitation services provided varies substantially among these groups, with the most comprehensive programs targeted at active-duty military.

2.2. Distribution of the Military Services

The 8 million persons associated with the military are dispersed world-wide at over 200 major installations and many more small sites, units, detachments, and ships at sea. Each of these locations is immersed in a unique cultural, environmental, and social milieu. Approximately half a million active-duty personnel are serving overseas at any one time. Approximately a quarter of a million dependents are stationed with their sponsors in these overseas areas. Most of the active-duty members are working under complex, demanding duty conditions. At some locations, after-duty boredom poses problems; at others, long work hours are necessary. Reassignments, temporary and prolonged separation from families, and immersion in unfamiliar cultures with widely varying attitudes toward both alcohol and Americans are an acknowledged part of military service life. In effect, the Department of Defense could be accurately described as the largest and most complex multinational corporation in the world, with all the problems that attend the management of an institution of such scope, complexity, and environmental variation.

2.3. The Challenge

The challenge presented to military alcohol-program managers has been to develop coherent, effective alcohol-abuse prevention, treatment, and rehabilitation programs of worldwide scope for a diversified population with differing cultural, social, and family values. While primarily responsive to local needs and differences, these programs remain subject to supervision, evaluation, and continual improvement from a central point of responsibility. A brief description of the programs designed to meet that challenge is provided below, followed by a more comprehensive look at the U.S. Air Force program.

3. The Military Programs

3.1. The Office of Drug and Alcohol Abuse Prevention

The peak of the military alcohol-abuse-prevention organizational pyramid resides in the Office of Drug and Alcohol Abuse Prevention, part of the Office of the Assistant Secretary of Defense for Health Affairs. This office sets broad policy direction for the services, gathers and analyzes program data, monitors prevention and training programs, and generally coordinates service efforts. A Department of Defense (DOD) Drug and Alcohol Abuse Advisory Committee composed of key program managers from each of the military services, other appropriate DOD personnel, and a Veterans Administration representative is chaired from this office. This committee advises on policy and helps coordinate service programs.

Each of the military services also has a headquarters staff equivalent to the Office of Drug and Alcohol Abuse Prevention.

The military services are charged with implementing DOD policy for program management. Over 1,900 trained persons are dedicated full time to alcohol abuse prevention, treatment, and rehabilitation. Approximately three times that number work with facets of alcohol abuse programs on a part-time basis. These include unit commanders, chaplains, medical personnel, lawyers, recreation program managers, law enforcement officials, and media specialists. Headquarters staffs are kept as small as possible. The programs are structured to place the bulk of the manpower in the field, where program implementation and person-to-person work must be accomplished.

3.2. The Army Alcohol Abuse Prevention and Control Program

The Army Alcohol Abuse Prevention and Control Program is based upon the industrial alcohol program model. The Deputy Chief of Staff for Personnel has primary responsibility for program plans, policy, budget formulation, management, coordination, law enforcement, and behavioral research. However, the day-to-day responsibility for actual program operation rests on individual commanders at the grassroots.

Involvement of leaders and supervisors at the grassroots has proved to be the key to the program. Special training for middle managers is required and is being intensified. Alcohol and Drug Control Officers who manage the local programs are assigned directly to local commanders.

The Army Surgeon General supports the program with clinical manpower, facilities, technical assistance, and medical research. Detoxification services, clinical consultation, medical counseling, and treatment are provided by medical personnel. The Academy of Health Sciences provides training in alcohol abuse prevention and control to physicians and other medical specialists in their basic training courses. They also train alcohol and drug control officers, counselors, and others working in the alcohol program.

From the inception of the program, the U.S. Army has conducted prevention education, treatment, and rehabilitation programs for alcohol and other drugs of abuse within the same facility and with the same resources. This approach was adopted because it was determined to be the most economical way to provide quality services in the U.S. Army, and it permits effective response to the reality of polydrug abuse.

The U.S. Army has alcohol facilities and services available at all installations and activities. Prevention education takes place at each installation, with educational models provided for the entire family and with Teen Involvement Programs for dependent children. Public information programs are extensive. Early intervention when alcohol problems develop has been a critical component of army programs. Alcohol abusers are identified by commander or supervisor referral, medical referral, and self-referral, and as a result of alcohol-related conflict with law enforcement officials (e.g., driving under the influence and fighting). Rehabilitation programs are operated as outpatient facilities. Because of the ability of the U.S. Army to identify alcohol problems early and intervene, inpatient detoxification has been necessary in less than 1% of the cases. Active-duty military, U.S. citizen civilian employees, dependents of active-duty military, and retirees are all eligible to participate in the alcohol programs.

The management of the U.S. Army's alcohol program is regularly monitored and evaluated through staff assistance visits from higher headquarters and through Inspector General program inspections. The program has also been evaluated for several years by the General Accounting Office, and the civilian alcohol program is reviewed by the Civil Service Commission. Additionally, a comprehensive assessment of the Army Alcohol and Drug Abuse Prevention and Control Program was initiated in December 1977. The results of this review are expected by the end of 1979 and are expected to facilitate further program improvement. Effectiveness evaluation is considered critical and is a continuing, integral component of the program.

3.3. The Navy Alcoholism Prevention Program

3.3.1. Background

The Navy Alcoholism Prevention Program (NAPP) began in a small way in February 1965, when the first U.S. Navy-sponsored Alcoholics Anonymous group, called Drydock No. 1, was established at Naval Station Long Beach, California. By 1967, Drydock No. 1 had grown into the navy's first alcoholism treatment center, run by the Bureau of Medicine and Surgery. In August 1971, the navywide program was initiated by the Bureau of Naval Personnel. These early programs have grown into a network of inpatient, outpatient, early-intervention, and prevention education programs that provide services to U.S. Navy, Marine Corps, and Coast Guard units around the world.

The NAPP relies somewhat more heavily on inpatient treatment than do the programs of the other services. This emphasis largely results from the structure of the U.S. Navy and the nature of the naval mission. The U.S. Army and U.S. Air Force, with permanent posts and bases, find it effective to conduct primarily outpatient programs. Each location has readily available medical support and a stable environment. On the other hand, a large proportion of naval personnel serve on ships and move from port to port around the world. When alcohol problems develop, members are best referred to a central treatment facility for care.

In the early years of program development, the U.S. Navy's program focused primarily on treatment and rehabilitation. As experience accrued, increasing emphasis has been placed on the early-intervention and prevention components of the program. The present structure of both the NAPP and the more early-intervention–oriented Navy Alcohol Safety Action Program (NASAP) are summarized below.

3.3.2. The Navy Alcoholism Prevention Program (NAPP)

As indicated above, the NAPP began slowly in 1965. In 1971, navywide programs were initiated. As of 1979, the worldwide system consists of 78 facilities with a maximum annual treatment capacity of approximately 20,000 persons per year and an extensive staff-training capability. Treatment services are also provided for the U.S. Marine Corps and the U.S. Coast Guard.

These extensive programs are a joint line-of-the-navy and medical corps responsibility under the overall direction of the Chief of Naval Operations, the senior military authority of the navy. The NAPP is managed at headquarters level by the Assistant Chief of Naval Personnel for Human Resources Management. The Bureau of Medicine and Surgery provides medical support, liaison, and technical guidance and also funds and operates more than 20 Alcohol Rehabilitation Services, which are located in naval hospitals.

The goals of the Navy NAPP center around the determination that alcoholism is an illness, not a character defect; that alcoholism imposes unacceptable costs upon the navy; and that persons who drink alcoholically can be cost-effectively treated and restored to productive duty. The formally stated goals of the NAPP are shown in Table 1.

The U.S. Navy treatment facilities consist of 3 Alcohol Rehabilitation Centers (ARCs), 4 large Alcohol Rehabilitation Services (ARSs), 18 smaller Alcohol Rehabilitation Services (ARSs) installed in naval hospitals, and 53 Counseling and Assistance Centers (CAACs). The ARCs are self-contained, residential treatment centers with capacities of 70–90 beds. They are commanded by nonmedical officers from the line of the navy, although physicians serve on the staff. These ARCs provide six weeks of treatment, including education, medical care, paraprofessional counseling, and spiritual services. Antabuse (disulfiram) is administered daily. Individual and group counseling, alcohol awareness education, and physical fitness programs are provided. Attendance at Alcoholics Anonymous (AA) meetings, both in the local area and in the ARC, is required. The large ARSs have 40–80 beds and are located in the Naval

Table 1. Goals of the Navy Alcoholism Prevention Program (NAPP)[a]

1. To promote attitudes of responsibility with respect to alcohol in those persons who choose to drink and the social acceptability of an individual's decision to not drink.
2. To achieve general acceptance of alcoholism as an illness that is preventable and treatable.
3. To remove stigmatic effects associated with alcoholism, which militate against proper referral for treatment and subsequent restoration to full duty.
4. To teach supervisory personnel how to detect alcoholism in its early stages and how to induce the alcoholic person to seek treatment, and to provide knowledge of the treatment facilities available.
5. To acquaint personnel with the most effective methods of treating alcoholism.
6. To enhance overall operational readiness of the U.S. Navy by providing facilities for early identification, remedial education, treatment, and rehabilitation for alcoholics and alcohol abusers.
7. To promote the acceptance of the recovered alcoholic person as a useful, reliable member of the military community.

[a] Source: New Headings, 1976, pp. 10–11.

Regional Medical Centers in Long Beach, California; Portsmouth, Virginia; Great Lakes, Illinois; and Newport, Rhode Island. These well-known navy medical programs provide the same treatment regimen as is outlined above. Moreover, the ARSs serve as the critical training facilities for key leaders in navy alcoholism programs. Over 500 physicians have completed the highly regarded two-week alcoholism treatment orientation course taught at ARS Long Beach. Additionally, another 350 health care specialists, chaplains, administrators, and senior officers have completed the same course.

The 18 smaller ARSs are units with 15–30 beds and are located in naval hospitals around the world. Sixteen ARSs are located in the United States, six are overseas. These are actually smaller versions of the ARCs and are headed by a medical officer. The treatment programs at all of these facilities are similar. The programs in the 53 CAACs are designed to meet the needs of the local areas served, and their treatment regimens are more variable. About one-third of the CAACs have from 5 to 20 beds. The remainder are exclusively outpatient programs. The CAAC programs vary in length from 4 to 12 weeks, with longer periods of follow-up support. All programs stress participation in Alcoholics Anonymous. These programs are lowest in cost to conduct, ensure command involvement, and result in early return of the patient to productive work.

Follow-up from all navy alcohol programs is facilitated by a volunteer referral network of Collateral Duty Alcoholism Counselors (CODACs), who, in addition to their regular duties, help local commands with local alcohol programs. This network of nearly 2,000 recovered alcoholics and nonalcoholic professionals (e.g., lawyers, physicians, and chaplains) work part time to provide prevention education, to assist with follow-up support to the rehabilited, and to serve as program advisers to local commanders.

The U.S. Navy has developed a sophisticated staff training network that, in addition to building a strong treatment staff, is progressively disseminating enlightened attitudes concerning the use and abuse of alcohol throughout the fleet. The large Alcohol Rehabilitation Services provide training and orientation to medical personnel and other senior officers. The Alcohol Training Unit (ATU), a division of the Alcohol Rehabilitation Center in San Diego provides a 10-week training course for alcoholism counselors selected to work at NAPP facilities. This ATU also offers a two-week course for all other personnel involved in conducting navy alcohol programs. Nearly all alcoholism counselors who work in ARCs and ARSs are recovered alcoholics with a minimum of two years' sobriety before they are selected for training. The majority of the commanders and key staff of the ARCs are also recovered alcoholics.

The navy has historically sought recovered alcoholics for these positions because of the belief that their experience, their motivation to help other alcoholics, and their close involvement with Alcoholics Anonymous renders them the best qualified to conduct alcohol treatment programs. The U.S. Navy does not have a designated career field for alcoholism counselors, and most return to their original military specialties after working for several years in the alcoholism field. The turnover and the training load resulting from this policy are thought to be compensated for by the diffusion of skilled, alcohol-aware counselors throughout the fleet and by their incorporation into the Collateral Duty Alcoholism Counselor program.

The staffs that man the Counseling and Assistance Centers (CAACs) are exclusively paraprofessional, with no clergy or medical personnel assigned. Normally, a line officer directs the center and a staff of enlisted paraprofessional counselors with training in drug and alcohol dependencies conduct the programs. Normally, one or two of these counselors are recovered alcoholics who have been trained at the 10-week course at the San Diego Alcohol Training Unit.

Since the inception of the formal U.S. Navy program in 1971, nearly 73,000 active military members (mostly U.S. Navy, Marine Corps, and Coast Guard) have entered treatment and rehabilitation programs. Approximately 26,000 of these members were treated in residence; the remaining 47,000 were outpatients. The navy considers rehabilitation effective if after return to the fleet, the member's level of performance is acceptable, the individual is recommended for promotion or reenlistment, or the member is separated with an honorable discharge. The program success rate has been found to vary substantially, based on the age and the career status of the rehabilitated person. Based on a two-year posttreatment follow-up study, effectiveness for those aged 26 and older (essentially career personnel) was 83%. On the other hand, effectiveness for those under age 26 was only 44% (Borthwick, 1977, p. 15). A full discussion of the reasons for this difference would be both complex and beyond the scope of this article. Suffice it to say that, in the author's opinion, most of the variance is accounted for by the career status of the older members and their greater investment in their military careers.

A cost–benefit study (Borthwick, 1977, p. 17) conducted for the navy on their in-residence alcoholism treatment programs showed that rehabilitation has an overall two-to-one cost advantage over separation of the member and replacement with a recruit. For career personnel, the benefit-to-cost ratio increased to six-to-one. The Presearch study also documented a threefold decline in hospitalization rates of alcoholic members after treatment (Borthwick, 1977, pp. 20–21).

Up to this point, discussion of the navy's alcohol program has focused largely on treatment and rehabilitation. This parallels the focus of the navy's programs during the first few years. However, as understanding of the nature of the alcohol problem grew and as experience in providing rehabilitation for younger members suggested that more varied approaches were needed, it became apparent that prevention *per se* required more emphasis.

3.3.3. *The Navy Alcohol Safety Action Program (NASAP)*

In recent years, the U.S. Navy has substantially expanded its programs designed to prevent alcohol abuse. These prevention efforts include promulgation of directives for the operation of clubs and messes ashore that prohibit abusive drinking practices, expanded education and publicity campaigns, and other initiatives. However, one of the most obviously effective prevention programs they have implemented is the Navy Alcohol Safety Action Program (NASAP). The NASAP started as a pilot project at Naval Air Station, Pensacola, Florida, in 1974 and has grown rapidly since that time. It is an adaption of the Department of Transportation's Alcohol Safety Action Projects, which were designed as countermeasures to drunk driving. The navy's version expanded beyond drunk driving to incorporate all alcohol-related offenses, including fighting, safety violations, hospital emergency-room admissions, unauthorized absences, and other breaches of discipline. It is specifically targeted at the early identification and the remedial education of alcohol abusers and the referral for treatment of alcoholics.

Alcohol-related incidents are recognized as being possible indicators of deeper alcohol problems. They are used to precipitate a crisis that permits intervention at the time an individual is most motivated to accept remedial education or treatment. With the cooperation of local law-enforcement officials, shore patrols, judges, and commanding officers, alcohol offenders are ordered into the NASAP, where counselors screen them either into treatment or into a remedial education program. The screening is done by a paraprofessional counselor, normally a recovered alcoholic trained to evaluate the severity of alcohol involvement. Depending on the severity, the individual is assigned to one of two levels of the program. Level I, the remedial alcohol-education program, is targeted at the alcohol abuser, not the alcoholic. These abusers appear to be developing problem-drinking behaviors, but they have not yet lost control. They attend a 36-hour off-duty course designed to explain the effects of alcohol, to show the consequences of abusive drinking patterns, and to provide the tools to change these patterns. Level II, treatment, is the formal treatment and rehabilitation provided by the Navy Alcoholism Prevention Program described in Section 3.3.

NASAP offices are now operating at 25 locations around the world. Over 18,000 persons have been referred to the programs. About 20% of the referrals enter treatment. The remaining 80% complete the 36-hour course. The NASAP has grown to a throughput of over 12,000 persons per year.

Although many of the NASAP programs are new and thorough evaluation of long-term results is just under way, several benefits have become apparent. Because of the focus on early intervention, the average NASAP student is two years younger than the average patient in a treatment program (Brownell, 1978). Before the NASAP, about 25% of the alcoholism treatment beds were filled with nonaddicted problem drinkers. There simply was no alternative means of providing them assistance. With the advent of NASAP remedial education, more treatment spaces are available for actual alcoholics. Costs are also significantly lowered. The cost for a NASAP student is estimated to be approximately $200; the patient cost for treatment is estimated to be $3,000. Initial follow-up studies indicate that the alcohol-incident recidivism rate of NASAP graduates is less than 7%.

In summary, the U.S. Navy operates a comprehensive alcoholism prevention and treatment program that has been shown to be cost-effective. The balance of prevention policy, education, intervention procedures, inpatient and outpatient treatment, and follow-up support is designed to fit the unique needs of a seagoing navy. The research and evaluation of program results permit program managers to continually assess and improve program effectiveness. Moreover, the outcome and cost–benefit research conducted by the navy offers critical, scientifically validated information concerning alcohol programs to all agencies involved in providing alcohol abuse and alcoholism services.

3.4. The Air Force Alcohol Abuse Control Program

3.4.1. *Background*

A comprehensive review of the Air Force Alcohol Abuse Control program is provided below. The U.S. Air Force program is singled out for more in-depth attention because of the author's greater knowledge of both the program and the thinking that went into its design.

Like the U.S. Navy program, the Air Force Alcohol Abuse Control program began in a small way with the opening of one alcoholism treatment center. This center, at Wright-Patterson Air Force Base in Dayton, Ohio, was opened in 1966. From that time until 1970, fewer than 400 persons were treated in that facility. In 1972, alcohol-abuse control programs were formally established at 140 installations around the world. Since that time, the programs have grown in both quantity and sophistication. Now, on every U.S. Air Force installation U.S. Air Force members, their dependents, and civilian employees of the Department of the Air Force have alcohol-abuse prevention information, education, treatment, and rehabilitation services available to them.

The year 1976 proved to be a watershed for the development of U.S. Air Force alcohol programs. From 1972 through 1975, alcohol abuse and alcoholism prevention and treatment programs were functioning adequately at most installations. Regulations and guidelines were provided that were based on the latest information available in the alcohol field. However, the quality of the programs varied substantially from base to base. This variance appeared to result in large measure from the varying personal abilities of alcohol-abuse control staff members to organize resources, to persuade commanders to support their programs, and to integrate community programs. Briefly put, the quality of the base alcohol programs depended largely on the personality, dedication, and ability of local program managers. At the headquarters, program designers were faced with a critical question: "How do we structure our programs to ensure that they will remain responsive to local needs, yet ensure uniformly high-quality control around the world?" The central challenge to be met was to design a means to guide, evaluate, and continually improve all programs Air Force-wide without stifling individual program ownership and creativity with bureaucratic strictures. The decision was made in early 1976 to use a systems management approach. The systems approach had proved so successful in organizing human efforts to develop high-quality weapons systems that it was decided to adapt it to organizing the human resources committed to ameliorating the impact of alcohol abuse and alcoholism on Air Force people.

Implementing the sytems approach to managing the Air Force alcohol program involved four primary steps. First, a clear, unequivocal statement of corporate policy had to be disseminated. All Air Force members had to know precisely what the alcohol program was designed to accomplish. Moreover, a systematic means of implementing the policy had to be developed and publicized. Second, a formal system had to be established to institutionalize the involvement of all persons with key roles (e.g., commanders, chaplains, medical officers, law enforcement officials) in the alcohol program. Third, those persons with responsibility for any components of the program had to have clear and specific objectives to meet. These objectives were to be measurable and were to be developed by local program managers whenever possible. Moreover, these objectives were to be self-renewing to ensure continual progress.

A management-by-objectives system was incorporated into much of the program. Clear time elements were established for meeting objectives. These time elements pertained both to the personal progress of persons in treatment and rehabilitation and to the progress of program managers in improving their programs. Finally, a continuing, institutionalized system for evaluating program results had to be developed to provide regular and routine self-correcting feedback to all levels of program management. This cybernated evaluation system had specifically to avoid fragmented evaluations using varying methodologies that would render results noncomparable over time. Moreover, the evaluation system had to include direct measures of job performance that could be easily used in cost–benefit analyses.

The following sections discuss Air Force policy, organizational structure, and program objectives, along with the actions taken to accomplish them and the evaluation system.

3.4.2. Policy

Succinctly stated, it is Air Force policy to prevent alcohol abuse and alcoholism whenever possible. When prevention fails, alcohol abusers and alcoholics are provided treatment and rehabilitation in order to restore them to effective functioning. When an Air Force member cannot or will not respond to rehabilitation, the Air Force assists him or her in making a smooth transition to civilian life. These policies apply to all military personnel on active duty. Varying elements of these policies apply to U.S. Air National Guard, U.S. Air Force Reserve, Department of the Air Force civilian employees, and military dependents. The objectives of these policies are to ensure that military standards of behavior, performance, and discipline are maintained and that the impact of alcohol abuse and alcoholism on Air Force people is minimized.

3.4.2.1. Prevention Policy and Implementation. The prevention policy is implemented in several ways. The first step in preventing alcohol-abuse–related problems is the recruitment of high-quality personnel. The enlistment and commissioning standards of the Air Force remain very high. Extensive experience and research have shown that a strong correlation exists between completion of a high school education and incident-free, honorable service. In the Air Force, those who have not graduated from high school tend to experience problems, including alcohol-abuse–related problems, more frequently than do high school graduates. Over 95% of the enlistees in the Air Force have completed high school. While these high enlistment standards certainly do not eliminate alcohol problems or even begin to address alcoholism, they do tend to statistically reduce the prevalence of alcohol-related problems in the force.

A second phase of the prevention program centers around widespread, relevant education programs. The Air Force began conducting alcohol education in 1972. In 1973 and again in 1975, education program evaluations were conducted. As a result, five types of training programs were developed, each targeted at a specific audience during a time in Air Force members' careers when they are most receptive to learning. All of the training programs are designed to be presented to small groups. Course outlines reflect standard policies, definitions, and concepts but are structured to permit localization and personal embellishment by instructors. Critiques are built into most of the courses to ensure feedback to the instructors and to provide a means of periodically evaluating education program effectiveness Air Force-wide.

The first of these training programs is provided at all Air Force entry points (e.g., basic military training, officers' candidate school, medical officer orientation, chaplains' orientation, and the Air Force Academy). The specific curricula are targeted at the level and sophistication of the new entrant. As the new entrants complete their initial training and enter the operational Air Force, they attend one of two mandatory four-hour seminars. The first of these two, the four-hour Substance Abuse Seminar, is the Air Force's general substance-abuse education program. Every Air Force member who is not a supervisor attends this seminar each time he or she reports to a new assignment. The seminar teaches Air Force alcohol-abuse policies and programs as they are applied at the new base. It also identifies conditions existing in the local vicinity of the installation that have an impact on substance abuse problems. Considerable emphasis is placed on individual responsibility, values clarification, and Air Force expectations. The course is taught by trained drug and alcohol abuse specialists.

All supervisors reporting to a new base attend the second of these four-hour seminars, the Drug and Alcohol Awareness Seminar for Commanders, First Sergeants, and Supervisors. This seminar is targeted at management and supervisory personnel. Specific emphasis is placed on enhancing the awareness and understanding of Air Force drug and alcohol-abuse control programs and policies. The respective roles of commanders, first sergeants, and supervisors on that base are clearly defined, and a face-to-face meeting and the start of a working relationship with the drug and alcohol staff occur.

The fourth type of training is focused on those supervisors and managers who show high potential for future development. The Air Force conducts an extensive program of Professional Military Education (PME). Schools included in the PME program include the Noncommissioned Officers Leadership Courses, the Noncommissioned Officer Academy, Squadron Officers School, the Air Command and Staff College, the Air War College, and others. These schools focus on preparing supervisors and leaders for their next level of responsibility in the Air Force. Alcohol education programs tailored to the needs of the students are presented at each of the schools. A Special Alcohol Education Program for Senior Officers is also provided; it is discussed in more detail in ensuing sections.

The fifth type of alcohol-abuse control education has a somewhat different focus; it combines both primary and secondary prevention elements. This is the eight-hour off-duty Alcohol Awareness Seminar. The seminar explores alcohol abuse, problem drinking, and alcoholism in a very personalized format. Instructors provide assistance in the self-evaluation of drinking habits and patterns and facilitate self-analysis of the impact of alcohol abuse on career, lifestyle, and significant others. The seminar is available to all Air Force members, civilian employees, and dependents on a voluntary basis. However, attendance is mandatory for any military member who is apprehended for driving under the influence of intoxicating liquor or drugs or for any other alcohol-related incident. For these military members, the eight hours of awareness training are part of a formal screening and evaluation process that includes medical examination, social evaluation by alcohol counselors, remedial driving training (if appropriate), and a review of recent duty performance. If the evaluation results in a diagnosis of alcoholism or there are persuasive indications that a drinking problem exists, the member is entered in the alcohol rehabilitation program.

Other elements of the Air Force alcohol-abuse prevention program include the promotion of alternatives to alcohol abuse, firm alcohol beverage control policies designed to deglamorize the use of alcohol, strong law-enforcement practices (particularly for driving while intoxicated), the enforcement of military standards of discipline and behavior, counseling programs, and the provision of a crisis intervention capability on each major installation. A more thorough description of the nature of these prevention programs is provided in Section 3.4.4.1.

3.4.2.2. Rehabilitation Policy and Implementation. The Air Force policy of providing treatment and rehabilitation to alcohol abusers and alcoholics in order to restore them to effective functioning is implemented through a five-step process. These steps can be labeled identification, detoxification, medical evaluation, treatment and rehabilitation, and follow-on support.

Air Force people are usually identified for entry into rehabilitation from one of four sources. These sources are (1) self-identification, (2) commander/supervisor referral, (3) medical referral, and (4) other sources (e.g., military police, civilian police, safety incidents). In all cases where rehabilitation is needed, members are formally entered into the program by their commanders. Each entrant receives an intake interview. This interview is conducted by a drug and alcohol specialist. During the interview, the rehabilitation program is explained to the participant, and information is gathered to assess the extent of the participant's drinking problem and to begin the design of the rehabilitation regimen. As soon as possible thereafter, a medical evaluation is performed by a physician. Those members suffering from acute intoxication or physical dependence are admitted to an Air Force hospital for detoxification. Whether detoxification is required or not, each member is given a physical examination, his or her condition is diagnosed, and medical treatment is begun. Shortly thereafter, a rehabilitation committee meets. The committee consists of the member's unit commander, immediate supervisor, evaluating physician or mental health officer, and the drug and alcohol specialist. They review and evaluate the participant's case history, including medical, job performance, and other relevant data, and collectively design a regimen tailored to the needs of the participant. The rehabilitation committee confers regularly, formally evaluates the member's progress, decides when to enter the member into follow-on support, and decides when the member is ready to graduate from the rehabilitation program.

The Air Force relies primarily on local programs to provide treatment and rehabilitation. Local rehabilitation is the most cost-effective means of delivering rehabilitation services. It minimizes the time the member is off the job and out of the environment to which he or she must eventually readjust, and it is compatible with the Air Force base structure since medical, spiritual, alcohol specialist, and other rehabilitation support is readily available. The existence of a designated military career field for drug and alcohol specialists, who are highly trained in managing these programs, is a key ingredient in the success of the local outpatient programs.

Local rehabilitation regimens are multifaceted and use many locally available resources. The intensive part of the program is intended to be short-term, usually lasting between 45 and 90 days. The desired outcome is modification of the participant's drinking pattern, including abstinence for alcoholics, so that consumption of alcohol no longer adversely affects the member's duty performance, behavior, or health. Rehabilitation regimens include any combination of individual, group, job-related, spiritual, marriage, family, financial, nutritional, medical, or legal counseling. Progress evaluations and feedback to the participant are based on specific behavioral observations. Recreational programs are integrated into the regimens, and participation in Alcoholics Anonymous is strongly stressed. When the rehabilitation committee determines that the member has successfully completed local treatment and rehabilitation, he or she is advanced to follow-on support. Those who do not progress satisfactorily through local treatment and rehabilitation may be recommended for transfer to one of the 10 Air Force alcohol treatment centers.

Follow-on support is the last and most crucial phase of the rehabilitation program. The follow-on support phase must be successfully completed if the member desires to remain on active duty with the Air Force. It is in this phase that members have the best opportunity to demonstrate their ability to function without impairment, to perform their duties, to meet their responsibilities, and to be fully reintegrated into the Air Force community. Emphasis on participation in Alcoholics Anonymous continues. The duration of follow-on support varies, depending on the participant's diagnosed condition on entry into rehabilitation, the mode of treatment, and the participant's progress. Normally, follow-on support does not exceed one year. Progress in follow-on support is formally evaluated by the member's rehabilitation committee at least every 90 days.

Members who have not responded to the local treatment and rehabilitation regimens may be recommended by their rehabilitation committee for transfer to the closest regional alcohol treatment center for inpatient treatment. Table 2 shows the location and the opening date of these 10 centers. Prior to transfer to any of the centers, participants undergo a five- to seven-day detoxification, if necessary. They are then transferred in temporary duty status as inpatients for the duration of the residential program.

Table 2. Air Force Regional Alcohol Treatment Centers

Date opened	Location
1966	Wright-Patterson AFB, Ohio
1971	Eglin AFB, Florida
1971	Lackland AFB, Texas
1972	Travis AFB, California
1972	Sheppard AFB, Texas[a]
1973	Lakenheath Royal Air Force Station, England
1973	Wiesbaden AB, Germany
1973	Scott AFB, Illinois
1974	Clark AB, Philippines[a]
1975	Andrews AFB, Maryland

[a] 14-day programs (all others 28 days).

Of the 10 centers, eight conduct 28-day programs and two conduct 14-day programs. Table 3 outlines the regimens at the treatment centers. Upon completion of a central treatment program, participants are returned to their duty stations and enter the follow-on support phase of the program already described.

Since 1975, the Air Force has entered approximately 22,000 active-duty military into alcohol rehabilitation. This constitutes a penetration rate of 1% of the active force each year. Approximately 17,000 have continued in the Air Force or have separated at the end of their normal term of service. This equates with a success rate of approximately 77%.

3.4.2.3. Separation Policy and Implementation. Air Force members who cannot or will not respond to rehabilitation are separated from the Air Force and referred for longer-term treatment. While administrative separation action is being taken, the member continues in the Air Force rehabilitation program. During the separation process, the person is provided referral contact points with Veterans Administration alcohol treatment centers and other treatment agencies near the location where the person intends to reside. Separation action is not based on alcoholism but is based either on the specific behaviors that have rendered the member unsuitable or unfit for Air Force service or, if appropriate, on health reasons.

3.4.3. The Formal System of Involvement

As mentioned in Section 3.4.1., Air Force alcohol program designers sought to establish a formal system that would institutionalize the

Table 3. Air Force Alcohol Treatment Centers

Standard 28-day programs		Standard 14-day programs	
A.	Group psychotherapy	A.	Group psychotherapy
B.	Individual psychotherapy	B.	Individual psychotherapy
C.	Dietary regimen	C.	Dietary regimen
D.	The milieu (group living and ward government)	D.	Occupational and recreational therapy
E.	Occupational and recreational therapy	E.	Educational/didactic sessions
F.	Educational/didactic sessions	F.	Electrostimulation aversion (ESA)
G.	Alcoholics Anonymous	G.	Alcoholics Anonymous
H.	Antabuse (required at Travis Center)	H.	Relaxation techniques
I.	Closedcommunity approach (Lackland Center only)	I.	"RECAP" follow-up

involvement of all persons with key roles in the alcohol effort. The system designed to accomplish this consists of three primary, integrated subsystems. One subsystem functions at each base, another functions at the headquarters of each of the major commands, and the third functions at Headquarters, U.S. Air Force.

At the base level, the primary component of the system is the Drug and Alcohol Abuse Control Committee (DAACC). The DAACC is chaired by the commander or the vice-commander and consists of representatives from all agencies with responsibility for aspects of the drug and alcohol abuse control program. Members include the drug and alcohol-abuse control officer, the base legal officer, the director of base medical services, the chief of the Office of Special Investigations, the chief of Security Police, the base chaplain, the director of personnel, and others. The DAACC has responsibility for drug-abuse threat assessment, for alcohol-abuse problem assessment, and for monitoring the effectiveness of the countermeasures designed to combat both problems. It reviews incident reports, customs reports, arrest and investigation trend data, safety reports, inspection reports, anecdotal reports from informed sources, alcohol beverage serving policies, alcohol deglamorization activities, and other sources of information. It monitors the effectiveness of countermeasures to substance abuse problems, which include public information and community action programs, intensified identification programs (e.g., use of roadside Breathalyzers), education programs, rehabilitation programs, and others. The members of the DAACC manage their areas of responsibility in drug and alcohol abuse control, and they provide status reports and briefings to the commander. Within Air Force policy guidelines, DAACCs formulate their own local program goals and objectives and monitor progress through a modified management-by-objectives approach. In essence, the DAACC functions as a board of advisers on drug and alcohol abuse issues to the senior installation commander. It meets at least quarterly, and the minutes of the meetings are forwarded to the respective major air commands.

A DAACC also functions at each major air command (MAJCOM). The scope of responsibility for this subsystem is primarily regional or commandwide threat assessment and design of countermeasures. Membership consists of the major command counterparts to the staff agency participants named at the base level. The MAJCOM drug and alcohol-abuse control office coordinates the DAACC's efforts and manages the day-to-day program at this level. Management and assessment tools at this level are extensive. They include DAACC meeting minutes and assessments from each subordinate base, monthly rehabilitation-program statistical reports, quarterly narrative analyses of drug and alcohol program developments, computerized rehabilitation-program data, staff-assistance visit reports, law enforcement reports, safety reports, inspection reports, reports of disciplinary trends, and other indicators. The countermeasures employed include staff assistance visits, education/information program intensification, inspection visits, adjustment of the resources allocated to the problems, law enforcement initiatives, and other management actions.

At Headquarters, U.S. Air Force, the Drug and Alcohol Abuse Control Office is the focal point. The scope of responsibility is worldwide and includes regional problem assessment and the development of countermeasure policies and programs. The assessment tools available are the same as those used at the major commands, but they provide worldwide information. Additionally, this office works closely with other federal agencies to coordinate the Air Force program with other elements of the federal effort.

This three-level system provides a comprehensive, responsive means of assessing substance abuse problems at all levels of command, and it assists commanders in managing the responses to substance abuse problems. The structure of the system requires that each staff agency chief with any degree of management responsibility for programs impacting on drug and alcohol abuse inform the senior commander regularly on the progress being made in the area of responsibility. Thereby, management involvement is institutionalized, and progress toward goals is regularly monitored by key commanders.

The system discussed above addresses the need to involve key leaders in terms of program management. However, that system does not adequately address the need to personally involve commanders and key supervisors in the rehabilitation process itself. Historically, many alcohol programs have functioned under confidentiality rules that excluded "the boss" from involvement in the process. The manager merely referred troubled employees to an agency that would treat them confidentially and return them to the job at a later date, restored, hopefully, to normal functioning. Because of the critical nature of the military mission and the requirement to be ready to respond 24 hours a day, military rehabilitation programs simply could not exclude the commander from the rehabilitation process. Commanders had to know the status of the people assigned to their units at all times. Therefore, the decision was made not only to advise the commander of treatment progress but to involve him or her in designing the treatment and rehabilitation regimen and in monitoring the member's progress. This decision resulted in the development of a policy that requires rehabilitation committees to oversee the rehabilitation process. These committees are chaired by the unit commander. Membership consists of the participant's commander, his or her immediate supervisor, a drug/

alcohol specialist, and a medical representative. A lawyer or chaplain or other appropriate official may sit on a rehabilitation committee if circumstances warrant. These committees evaluate the member's degree of involvement, prescribe a rehabilitation regimen, confront denial when necessary, follow treatment and rehabilitation progress, and formally determine when the process is successfully completed. These committees have evolved into the key factors in rehabilitation program success. They provide a means of systematically correlating the job performance, counseling, and medical elements of the rehabilitation process. The focus on specific standards of expected behavior, understood and agreed to by all committee members and clearly communicated to each participant, reduces the opportunity for manipulation. The experiential education and sensitizing of commanders and supervisors to the nature of alcohol problems and their personal involvement in achieving rehabilitation successes have substantially decreased the problem of stigma, have improved alcohol awareness, and have added credibility to the rehabilitation process.

The Drug and Alcohol Abuse Control Committees, the rehabilitation committees, and other agencies working with drug and alcohol problems develop local goals and objectives within the policy guidelines established by Headquarters, U.S. Air Force. To update and extend these policy guidelines, Headquarters, U.S. Air Force, convened an Ad Hoc Task Group on Alcohol Abuse in 1976. The Ad Hoc Task Group developed a series of initiatives, goals, objectives, and programs that still provide the policy framework for local base programs. The final report (Ad Hoc Task Group on Alcohol Abuse, 1976) of this group provided clear and specific objectives to meet, many of them subject to measurement. Responsible agencies were designated and clear time elements for implementation of actions were established. Most of the initiatives were designed to be self-reviewing. Brief descriptions of some of the major initiatives are provided below.

3.4.4. *Alcohol Program Initiatives and Objectives*

3.4.4.1. Primary Prevention. One of the principle findings of the Ad Hoc Task Group on Alcohol Abuse was that more systematic efforts had to be expended in primary prevention. As a result, five specific initiatives were established. As a first step, more definitive guidelines for fostering responsible decisions about the use of alcohol were developed and promulgated via regulatory publications. Air Force Regulation (AFR) 30-2, Social Actions Programs, was revised to include these guidelines for responsible decisions about drinking. AFR 215-1, Volume XVI, "Procurement, Use, and Sale of Alcoholic Beverages and 3.2 Beer," also incorporated specific guidance. A publicity campaign was launched to promulgate the guidelines, and they were incorporated into the mandatory alcohol education seminars.

The second initiative focused on deglamorizing the use of alcohol in the Air Force and reasonably controlling its availability. AFR 215-1, Volume XVI (referenced above), was further revised to include 26 specific rules for deglamorizing and controlling the use of alcoholic beverages. These rules limited "happy hours," required food to be served when alcoholic beverages are served, eliminated traditional glamorizing practices, specified limits on alcoholic content in drinks, provided advertising guidelines, prohibited free gifts of alcohol as prizes, prohibited drinking contests, established maximum hours of operation for beverage sale outlets, and provided other specific guidelines for controlling the use of alcohol.

The third prevention initiative launched a self-renewing alcohol-awareness campaign. This included designation of an alcohol awareness month. In conjunction with this effort, three film segments were developed, well-known consultants were sent to bases, posters and decals were distributed, radio and television spots were created, and innovative local efforts were encouraged and rewarded.

The fourth prevention initiative consisted of upgrading alcohol education programs. Most of these programs have been discussed in sufficient detail above. However, the USAF Special Alcohol Education Program for Senior Officers requires further elaboration. In this program, newly selected brigadier generals and selected wing commanders are sent to one of six leading civilian alcoholism treatment centers for a one-day intensive learning experience. The educational program is scheduled in conjunction with the General Officers' Orientation Course, a course designed to teach newly selected general officers those things that are considered essential for them to know to function as generals. The education program is conducted annually, and it has been highly successful in increasing alcohol awareness among senior Air Force leaders.

The fifth prevention initiative focused on promoting alternatives to alcohol abuse. Morale, welfare, and recreation program managers, chaplains, social actions personnel, medical personnel, media experts, and consultants developed a series of continuing programs to focus on alternatives to alcohol abuse.

3.4.4.2. Early Intervention. A particularly critical initiative focused on improving the identification of persons who are experiencing problems with alcohol. Training of physicians about alcohol abuse was intensified. A comprehensive alcohol-countermeasures program, described in detail in Air Force Pamphlet 30–33, *The Air Force Alcohol*

Abuse Countermeasures Program, was developed. Alcohol training programs for medical technicians were expanded. On-site training by consultants and in-residence training at leading alcoholism training centers were provided for drug and alcohol specialists. These training efforts are continuing. The Air Force version of the alcohol safety action program, the alcohol awareness seminar that was previously described, was implemented. Breathalyzers began to be used to detect drunk drivers. These expanded early-intervention efforts are continuing.

3.4.4.3.Treatment and Rehabilitation. A comprehensive alcohol-abuse control program requires sound treatment and rehabilitation components. The structure of the treatment and rehabilitation process has been discussed, but several initiatives resulting from the Ad Hoc Task Group warrant highlighting. First, treatment and rehabilitation resources were expanded. Medical resources dedicated to the alcohol program were reallocated to provide more in-depth coverage. A campaign was launched to secure more active use of Alcoholics Anonymous. Media materials to be used in educational portions of treatment were purchased. Standard office-space and facility requirements for alcohol programs were established. Emphasis was placed on using volunteer resources, wherever possible, to broaden the rehabilitation program.

Second, an intensive campaign to destigmatize treatment and rehabilitation for alcoholism was begun and is continuing. Personnel policies were reviewed to eliminate stigmatizing practices. Testimonials from successfully recovered alcoholics were solicited and publicized. Recovered alcoholic civilian dignitaries were invited to speak on Air Force bases. Research concerning treatment outcomes was conducted and published (Killeen & Lynde, 1977). Publicity emphasizing that alcoholism is preventable and treatable was targeted at all bases. A special, worldwide inspection involving every base in the Air Force was conducted specifically to identify practices that intensify the stigma associated with alcoholism and to recommend ways to decrease the stigma. These efforts are continuing, with each base formulating its own goals and objectives to implement these initiatives.

A third important initiative involved increasing the assistance provided to families. Project Concern, a special ongoing program targeted to involve wives' clubs was begun. A family assistance pamphlet was published. A comprehensive family-assistance program, described in Air Force Pamphlet 30–28, *Now, What about the Family . . . ?*, was implemented. Advanced training in delivering services to families was begun and continues to be provided to alcohol program staff.

All of these initiatives were implemented through the use of a modified management-by-objectives approach. The initiatives were distilled into discrete goals and objectives at Headquarters, U.S. Air Force.

Specific offices with primary responsibility for meeting the goals were named. Completion dates were established. The initiatives were introduced to the field through a worldwide series of regional workshops and were incorporated into staff training programs. At the major command and base levels, the Drug and Alcohol Abuse Control Committees were charged to develop local goals and objectives that would implement the initiatives. Progress is monitored by each of the three Air Force subsystems: the base, the major command, and Headquarters, U.S. Air Force.

This brief summary suggests the level of effort dedicated to combating alcohol abuse in the Air Force. However, the most important question has not yet been discussed. Does it work? To answer this question as definitively as possible, the Air Force has established a comprehensive management-information and program-evaluation system.

3.4.5. *The Management-Information and Program-Evaluation System*

Alcohol abuse, alcoholism, prevention effectiveness, treatment and rehabilitation effectiveness, sound program management, cost–benefit questions, and other related questions merge into complex phenomena that defy precise measurement. To deal with this complexity, a comprehensive management-information and program-evaluation system had to be established that employed the proper mix of human judgment, rigorous scientific inquiry, and institutionalized outcome measures suitable for day-to-day management use. The Air Force has established such a system, organized to fit the structure of the three-subsystem organizational framework discussed above. Although the system is still being refined, it even now provides a comprehensive means of evaluating the effectiveness of Air Force alcohol programs.

Continual management oversight of the drug and alcohol programs at all levels is provided by the Drug and Alcohol Abuse Control Committees discussed above. Additionally, staff assistance visits from major commands and Headquarters, U.S. Air Force, provide onsite guidance to program managers. Particularly useful management effectiveness evaluations are conducted by major commands and the Air Force inspectors general. Headquarters, U.S. Air Force, and most of the larger major-command inspectors general have trained and experienced drug and alcohol specialists assigned to their staffs. These inspectors conduct no-notice inspections, usually annually, of base-level programs to evaluate management effectiveness. Formal inspection reports are written, and the actions taken to correct weaknesses are carefully followed up.

A rigorous scientific evaluation of the Air Force alcohol program by Rand Corporation was initiated in 1977 and is expected to be completed in late 1979. The Rand study will first determine the prevalence of alcohol abuse in the Air Force and compare it with abuse rates in the other services and the civilian population. Second, Rand will determine the effectiveness of existing alcohol-abuse control programs, including identification, education, and treatment. Finally, all of these elements will be drawn together and a cost–benefit assessment will be provided. The study is expected to provide valid and reliable information that can be used for future program development.

The final component of the Air Force management-information and program-evaluation system is built on an existing computerized personnel system. The Air Force operates a centralized personnel-management system in a complex, geographically dispersed environment. The heart of this management system is a computer network called the Advanced Personnel Data System (APDS). The APDS links each major Air Force installation via remote computer terminals with its respective major air command headquarters and with the central data-processing and storage unit at the Air Force Military Personnel Center. The APDS permits rapid personnel accounting and data reporting, provides current management information in useful report formats, and creates the capability to conduct long-term analyses and research.

The alcohol-abuse information, management analysis, and research system is built into the APDS. The level of information available corresponds to the three primary subsystems discussed throughout this chapter. Each subsystem has access to information that meets management needs at that particular level of operation.

At the base level, the system permits automatic reporting to higher headquarters of alcohol-abuse identification trends and demographics. It also helps ensure that the participant receives proper care and regular progress evaluation during rehabilitation. Moreover, the base-level subsystem permits thorough analysis of the local rehabilitation program. The alcohol program manager, but no other base agency, can design analysis formats to suit his or her needs and can receive the computer analyses one day after request. The data fields are tightly controlled and are not available to any agency that is not directly involved in rehabilitation. On successful completion of rehabilitation, the computer file is wiped clean, and there is no further indication in the base-level system that the member was in alcohol rehabilitation.

Major-air-command alcohol-program managers have access to most of the same data as base-level managers. However, there are differences. The major air command subsystem does not contain names or social security account numbers. Therefore, at this level, managers have access to all trend and demographic data, but they cannot identify the individuals who are participating in rehabilitation. This information is not needed at this level. The subsystem at the major command eliminates costly manual reporting, permits the development of computer-generated analyses, and greatly expands the management information available to program directors.

The Headquarters, U.S. Air Force, subsystem is the most comprehensive of the three levels. It consists of two distinct, but linked, files. These are the alcohol file and the alcohol research file. The alcohol file provides the same information as that available to the bases and the major commands. It includes data from each base and major command. The data are used for reporting, analysis, and policy development. They include information on all who entered rehabilitation during the current year. As at the base and the major command, the data are protected and are eliminated from this system after the completion of rehabilitation.

The alcohol research file is a long-term history file that is created annually. This tightly controlled system tracks program graduate-year groups with complete data profiles for five years after the completion of rehabilitation. The same data are collected on a matched control-group sample. The primary purpose of this research file is to provide valid, long-range analyses of the posttreatment performance of rehabilitated alcohol abusers. This file is the only computerized record of alcohol rehabilitation participation that persists beyond the year in which a member completes rehabilitation. The file is tightly controlled, with no access to it except by the Headquarters, U.S. Air Force, alcohol-abuse control office. As a matter of policy, no inquiries are made regarding individuals. The file is employed to obtain aggregate statistical information, and this information is used for authorized research projects only.

Although this computer-based system is still being developed and refined, an initial large-scale study has been completed (Killeen & Lynde, 1977). That study of 1,992 active-duty enlisted personnel who completed treatment at one of the 10 Air Force centralized alcohol-treatment centers between 1971 and 1975 revealed that a substantial number of highly qualified people were restored to effective duty. Their posttreatment performance improved on nearly every variable evaluated. Finally, considering replacement costs alone, the rehabilitation of these individuals resulted in a 3.15-to-1 return on monies invested.

In summary, the Air Force mixture of management assistance visits, no-notice inspections, long-term scientific program evaluation, and computer-based reporting and analysis of current trend information and long-term results provides a comprehensive means of evaluating program effectiveness.

4. Summary and Conclusions

The misuse of alcoholic beverages imposes a substantial cost on all of the institutions in our society. The military services are not exempt from this negative impact. In fact, because of the high concentration of young, unmarried males, the services have a particularly strong need for sound prevention and, when necessary, rehabilitation programs. The structure of the military services provides some advantages and some disadvantages in combating alcohol abuse.

The primary challenge to military alcohol-program designers has been to design coherent, effective programs that are flexible enough to be responsive to very diverse local needs but remain subject to systematic oversight, evaluation, and continual improvement. Each of the services has designed and implemented comprehensive programs targeted at its specific needs. Each of the services has particularly strong components in its program. As thorough evaluation of the effectiveness of the programs continues, the strengths of the programs are being shared and the weaknesses strengthened throughout the Department of Defense. The already comprehensive programs are growing even more sophisticated, and the results of effectiveness evaluations currently taking place will contribute greatly to the existing body of knowledge of alcohol abuse and alcoholism prevention, treatment, and rehabilitation.

References

Ad Hoc Task Group on Alcohol Abuse (Final Report). Washington, D.C.: Department of the Air Force (AF/MPXH), Oct. 13, 1976.

Borthwick, R. B. *Summary of cost–benefit study results for Navy alcoholism rehabilitation programs*. Arlington, Va.: Presearch, Inc., 1977.

Brownell, S. M. *The Navy alcoholism prevention program—Worldwide*. Unpublished manuscript, 1978.

Initiatives for Alcohol Programs for Youth (Draft Report). National Institute on Alcohol Abuse and Alcoholism, July 12, 1978.

Killeen, J. E., & Lynde, R. H. *Analysis of post-treatment performance of rehabilitated alcohol abusers*. Washington, D.C.: Department of the Air Force, (AF/MPXH), 1977.

New Headings, Navy Alcoholism Prevention Program (NAVPERS 15302). Washington, D.C.: Department of the Navy, Bureau of Naval Personnel, 1976.

12

Behavioral Strategies for Reducing Drinking among Young Adults

Peter M. Miller

1. Introduction

Traditionally, alcoholism *treatment* programs have been geared toward middle-aged and older chronic alcoholics. For example, the median age of clients treated in the alcoholism treatment centers of the National Institute on Alcohol Abuse and Alcoholism (NIAAA) throughout the United States is 45 years (Armor, Polich, & Stambul, 1976). Alcoholism *prevention*, on the other hand, has been aimed at the younger, school-aged segments of the population in the 12- to 17-year category.

The group that has received little alcoholism prevention *or* treatment is composed of young adults between the ages of 18 and 25 years. This is especially unfortunate since drinking in this age group is increasing. In addition, when compared with other age categories, young adults are much more likely to experience significant life problems because of their heavy drinking (NIAAA, 1974). One can only speculate why young adults have not been the target of alcohol intervention efforts. A major reason may lie in the fact that they do not fall neatly into the prevention or the treatment camps. Professionals in the prevention area use primarily an educational model that seems most appropriate for junior and senior high school students. From a practical standpoint, students are a "captive" population and, because of their youth and geographical

Peter M. Miller • Department of Behavioral Medicine, Hilton Head Hospital, Hilton Head Island, South Carolina 29928.

stability, are relatively easy to study and follow up using longitudinal analysis. Young adults in the community are much more difficult to reach with educational programs, and the results of such programs are more difficult to assess.

While treatment providers have acknowledged the existence of drinking problems in the young adult population, their efforts to modify programs to meet the needs of youth have been minimal. Recently, there have been increasing efforts to provide programs geared toward young adult drinkers. One of the most recent and most comprehensive prevention efforts has been conducted by the Jaycees, a nationwide organization of more than 320,000 young men between the ages of 18 and 35 years. Known as Operation Threshold, this program has set out to educate members about alcohol, using a responsible-drinking as opposed to an abstinence theme. Because of the apparent lack of success of strictly educational efforts, other programs have focused on modifying alcohol use among young adults via social policy. Rather than directly educating consumers, variables affecting alcohol consumption, such as legal drinking age and hours of operation of liquor stores and bars, are manipulated.

In this regard, behavior modification strategies may offer new tools of prevention or treatment for these young adults. Unfortunately, most applications of behavior modification procedures to alcoholics have been used with older, chronic individuals. There is, however, a small but growing body of literature focusing on young adults.

2. Behavioral Formulation of Alcohol Abuse

Historically, behavior modification explanations of alcohol abuse have undergone a series of developmental changes. Initially, behavioral theories of alcoholism were based on a simple drive-reduction model (Conger, 1956; Kingham, 1958). Simply stated, this "tension reduction hypothesis" involves the notion that alcohol, through its depressant and anesthetic properties, reduces the anxiety and tension related to social and environmental stress. Scientific findings have led to a rejection of any simple conditioning explanation by behaviorists. Contemporary behavioral researchers and clinicians contend that drinking behavior is a learned behavior pattern that is acquired and maintained through a wide array of sociological, psychological, and physiological factors in an individual's life (Miller, 1976). Intervention focuses on four sequential and functionally related events: (1) stimulus control factors (i.e., antecedent cues); (2) mediational variables (i.e., cognitions and attitudes); (3) drinking behavior *per se*; and (4) outcome variables (i.e., consequences of behavior). Within a social-learning framework, abusive drinking is a function of the relationship among these variables at any one point in time. Thus, a detailed description of antecedent events, cognitive expectations, and consequent events could lead to an understanding of the mechanisms controlling drinking behavior. The antecedents and the consequences of drinking generally fall into the following categories: (1) situational (e.g., beer advertisements, favorite neighborhood tavern); (2) social (e.g., coaxing from friends to have a drink) (3) emotional (e.g., boredom, depression); (4) cognitive (e.g., self-derogatory thoughts); and (5) physiological (e.g., withdrawal symptoms, chronic back pain). Any one or a combination of these factors may precipitate abusive drinking. Consequent events occurring immediately after drinking (e.g., attention from friends for being the "life of the party" or reduction in unpleasant feelings such as anger or tension) may help to maintain it via positive and negative reinforcement.

The goals of behavioral intervention consist of modifying social-environmental antecedents to lessen their influence, teaching more adaptive responses to these antecedents, teaching self-management techniques to reduce alcohol consumption, and arranging a system of contingencies to reinforce abstinence or moderate, responsible drinking.

3. Modifying Drinking Skills

Behavioral techniques that have been developed to teach controlled drinking skills may be particularly relevant for young adults. From a prevention standpoint, it seems sensible that training novice social drinkers to drink responsibly would lessen the chances of their becoming problem drinkers. This approach remains to be evaluated experimentally and, indeed, has been challenged by proponents of other theoretical orientations (most notably, Alcoholics Anonymous).

Teaching controlled drinking skills as part of a treatment process has been even more controversial in spite of the evidence that some alcoholics have returned to patterns of moderate drinking (Armor *et al.*, 1976; Pattison, 1974; Sobell & Sobell, 1973). Young problem drinkers with a brief history of alcohol abuse and with a social environment that supports moderate drinking may be excellent candidates for this approach.

3.1. Components of Responsible Drinking Skills

Prior to developing strategies for teaching responsible drinking skills, it is necessary to assess the specific components of these skills.

That is, what constitutes moderate, responsible drinking? One method of determining the answer to this question is simply to set an arbitrary limit on the amount of alcohol an individual should drink in a specified time period. While this rather gross measure has been used by behavioral clinicians, there is little agreement on what this limit should be. For example, Sobell and Sobell (1973) defined controlled drinking as 6 ounces or less per day; Vogler, Compton, and Weissbach (1975) used a criterion of less than 50 ounces of absolute alcohol per month and no more than one uncontrolled drinking episode (blood alcohol concentration greater than 80 mg%) per month; Strickler, Bigelow, Lawrence, and Liebson (1976) used two "drinks" per hour with a maximum of six drinks per episode; Miller (1979) used no more than two drinks per occasion consumed in at least 30 minutes per drink; and Miller (1978) used less than 20 standard ethanol units (1 standard ethanol unit equals 15 ml of pure ethanol) per week or never exceeding a blood alcohol level of 70 mg%. It seems rather amazing that, as yet, no standard definition of responsible drinking has been developed. The absolute amount consumed does not seem sufficient when such factors as rate, situation, and reasons for drinking are also important. Perhaps most important of all, this definition does not take into account individual differences in response to alcohol. Quality-of-life factors such as job performance and marital happiness are also important but may not always be relevant within a prevention framework. Arbitrary limits set by clinical investigators, although they bear some relationship to what we know about the rate of absorption of alcohol in the body, may be more related to the drinking norms of the individual setting the limit than to any socially useful criterion.

A more empirical approach involves the observation of drinking patterns in controlled-drinking and uncontrolled-drinking populations. In one of the earliest studies of this nature, Schaefer, Sobell, and Mills (1971) obtained baseline drinking information on alcoholics and social drinkers in a simulated bar situation. Subjects were observed in small groups and allowed to consume a total of six ounces of liquor or its equivalent in beer. Both alcoholics and social drinkers ordered approximately the same number of drinks (5.3 and 5.2). Alcoholics ordered more straight as opposed to mixed drinks and took much larger sips of their drinks than the social drinkers. For example, when drinking mixed drinks, sips for social drinkers ranged from 0.2 ounces to 0.4 ounces, while the range of alcoholics was 0.35 to 1.20 ounces.

In another investigation by the same group (Sobell, Schaeffer, & Mills, 1972), 26 alcoholics were compared to 23 social drinkers. In this study, the drinkers were allowed to order up to 16 ounces of 86-proof liquor. By increasing this limit, noticeable differences were observed in the total amount of alcohol consumed by the two groups, with alcoholics drinking a mean of 15.27 ounces and social drinkers 6.65 ounces. Differences between mixed versus straight drinks and sip magnitude were similar to those obtained in the previous study. Finally, social drinkers drank more slowly, consuming a mixed drink in a mean time of nearly 26 minutes as compared to a little less than 10 minutes for the alcoholics. It is interesting to note that these same differences in drinking style have been reported for New Zealand alcoholics and social drinkers (Williams & Brown, 1974).

The difficulty in establishing drinking norms in experimental situations is that drinking behavior in a laboratory may be quite different from drinking in a more naturalistic setting. In an attempt to examine this possibility, Kessler and Gomberg (1974) observed 53 males in various community bars. The mean number of drinks ordered per subject was 2.41. Most subjects drank beer and consumed each drink in almost 20 minutes. In the Sobell *et al.* (1972) study, the social drinkers drank significantly more drinks but tended to drink them more slowly. However, Kessler and Gomberg's bar patrons were much more like Sobell's social drinkers than like the alcoholics.

Social and situational variables within the drinking environment influence drinking behavior and must be taken into account when norms are being established. For example, in bar settings, drinkers in groups consume more alcohol than drinkers alone or with one other person (Cutler & Storm, 1975; Rosenbluth, Nathan, & Lawson, 1979). It is interesting to note that Cutler and Storm (1975) reported that this phenomenon was not related to an increased rate of consumption with groups but rather to an increased amount of time in the bar. With a younger population of 18- to 22-year-old college students, Rosenbluth *et al.* (1979) found that drinking in groups increased the rate of consumption as compared to drinking alone. These investigators also found significant differences between the drinking of males and females. Generally, men consumed more alcohol and drank at a faster rate than women. An interaction effect was also noted between sex composition of the drinking group, sex of the drinker, and alcohol consumption. For example, men drank more alcohol and drank at a faster rate when with men than when they were with women. Women's drinking was influenced by male companionship, so that they drank more with men than with other women.

Thus, situational factors must be taken into account when establishing norms for drinking skills. In addition, studies of this nature must be kept in perspective by distinguishing between social drinking and controlled or responsible drinking. As Pattison, Sobell, and Sobell (1977) have noted, the term *social drinking* "is a vague and ambiguous term which merely states that one drinks among other people" (p. 201). In fact these writers suggested that *social drinking* is no longer an appropriate phrase and that its scientific use should be discontinued.

Using the limited data that are available and realizing that more normative drinking information is needed, behavioral scientists have begun to develop methods of teaching drinking skills. These methods include (1) a component skills-training approach; (2) operant approaches; (3) blood-alcohol discrimination training, and (4) aversion-conditioning procedures.

3.2. A Skills-Training Approach

Behaviorists assume that drinking is a learned behavior pattern and that responsible drinking represents a skill that can be taught. It is interesting to note that our society has no standard means of teaching these skills to novice drinkers. Behavioral clinicians have developed methods of teaching behavioral skills in other areas. For example, through instruction, performance feedback, behavioral rehearsal, and modeling, clients are taught assertiveness, marital interaction skills, and self-management skills. The same behavioral training strategies may be applicable to responsible drinking skills.

Miller, Becker, Foy, and Wooten (1976) examined the influence of instructions and practice on modifying the components of drinking behavior of three alcoholics. These investigators were primarily interested in studying the process of training and the interrelationships among drinking components. Each patient was seated in a room furnished to resemble a living-room setting. A coffee table near the patient contained a glass, a liquor bottle containing 100 cm^3 of bourbon, and a pitcher containing 200 cm^3 of water. The patient's behavior was monitored via a closed-circuit television system. For the first three sessions, patients were instructed to drink as they normally would. During this baseline phase, each patient drank in a style that would be considered an "alcoholic" as opposed to a responsible pattern. For example, each consumed all 100 cm^3 of bourbon in less than 30 minutes, took very large sips (e.g., Subject 3 had a mean of nearly 40 cm^3 per sip of straight bourbon), and drank very rapidly (approximately 60–90 seconds between each sip). In a sequential fashion, patients were given instructions on changing specific components of their drinking. During Phase 1, patients were instructed to practice taking smaller sips of each drink. No instructions were given on any other drinking component. All patients substantially reduced sip amount. For example, Patient 1 decreased sip amount from a mean of 23 cm^3 to a mean of 10 cm^3 and maintained this pattern over 15 drinking sessions. With subsequent instructions and practice, the patients learned to drink at a slower rate and learned to mix much less potent drinks (within a range of 20–40% bourbon to 60–80% water). Finally, by modifying their style of drinking, the patients also reduced the total amount of alcohol consumed. Two of the three patients reduced their total consumption by 50% each session, even though more alcohol was available to them.

In the process of modifying the drinking behavior of these patients, the investigators noted a reciprocal relationship among drinking components. When some components such as sip amount were modified in a direction toward responsible drinking, other components such as number of sips changed in the direction of an abusive drinking pattern. For example, when one patient began to take smaller sips of each drink, he also began to drink at a faster rate and to mix more potent drinks. Of course, as training progressed, these components were changed in the proper direction. All of the patients claimed that they were unaware of these reciprocal changes since they were concentrating solely on one change at a time.

This finding is particularly important in this type of training since modification in only some but not all components may lead to a different but equally inappropriate drinking pattern. For example, reducing sip amount may result in an individual's mixing more potent drinks and taking numerous small sips in rapid succession. Thus, individuals learning responsible drinking skills must be taught *all* drinking components, with each one being monitored closely during training to determine the reciprocal effects of change in one on the others.

Guided practice in responsible drinking not only teaches the behavioral components of responsible drinking but also influences cravings for alcohol. In a hospital setting, Hodgson and Rankin (1976) gave an alcoholic daily practice in consuming a relatively small amount of vodka (40 cm^3) without further drinking. After consuming the drink, the patient was instructed to resist the desire to drink further. Throughout the remainder of the day, measures were taken on mood, subjective estimates of tremor and desire for a drink, pulse, and blood alcohol concentration. As the practice sessions continued, the patient's cravings for alcohol gradually diminished. After the sixth session, he experienced no further cravings after his "drink." Clinically, a six-month follow-up was undertaken. During this time the subject drank on only six occasions, each time terminating his drinking soon after he began. This voluntary cessation of drinking or controlled drinking pattern had never occurred during the three years prior to this training. The investigators view this "cue exposure" training as an extinction procedure that decreases arousal to alcohol and thus decreases the probability of excessive drinking.

3.3. Operant Approaches

Operant conditioning approaches have also been used to teach patterns of controlled or responsible drinking. Several studies have indicated that alcoholics will maintain a moderate, controlled drinking pattern in an inpatient hospital setting if reinforced for this behavior with money and/or privileges (Cohen, Liebson, & Faillace, 1971; Cohen, Liebson, Faillace, & Speers, 1971). However, the outpatient application of operant strategies with young adult drinkers is lacking. While the principles of reinforcement would be similar in these cases, the exact nature and implementation of these strategies would be much more complex. Reinforcements must often be social in nature, which involves the cooperation of a spouse or a friend. For example, Miller (1972) used a written behavioral contract between a husband and a wife to schedule reinforcement for moderate drinking by the husband. Prior to the initiation of the reinforcement contingencies, the husband was consuming 4–6 pints of bourbon per week. According to his reports, his wife's critical comments and disapproving glances in reference to even moderate drinking tended to increase his consumption. Under the terms of the behavioral contract, the husband agreed to limit his consumption to between one and three "drinks" (defined as 1½ ounces of liquor straight or mixed) per day in the presence of his wife. This moderate drinking pattern was reinforced by increased attention and affection by his wife, together with an avoidance of paying his wife $20 (to be spent frivolously on a nonessential item) for his excessive drinking. The husband agreed to reinforce his wife in the same manner if she refrained from all negative verbal or nonverbal responses related to his drinking. His drinking declined gradually over the first 30 days of the contract and then stabilized at a moderate level and remained there for up to six months when a follow-up was conducted.

In one of the few applications of operant procedures with young adults, Miller (1975) reported the use of a similar contract with a 23-year-old heavy drinker. In the same manner as described above, the client's wife agreed to provide such reinforcers as increased affection and special meals contingent on abstinence or moderate drinking. Such reinforcers were withheld for a brief time period following an episode of excessive drinking. At a four-month follow-up, drinking was reduced to no more than two beers per day.

3.4. Blood-Alcohol Discrimination Training

Blood-alcohol discrimination training was originally devised by Lovibond and Caddy (1970) as a method of teaching drinkers to become more aware of the intoxicating effects of alcohol and, hence, to control and moderate their drinking. During this training, clients are instructed to drink alcohol in a disguised form (e.g., pure alcohol mixed with organge juice). Usually, a fixed amount of alcohol is provided and the client is asked to estimate his blood alcohol level after a 20- to 30-minute time interval. Clients are provided with a list of the bodily sensations associated with various blood alcohol levels to help them estimate accurately. A breath analysis is then conducted to determine the client's exact blood alcohol concentration. The results of the breath test are provided to the client, and any discrepancy between the estimate and the actual blood alcohol level is discussed. Reasons for errors are examined in reference to the specific internal cues to which the client responded.

This type of training has particular relevance for young adults since it is geared toward the moderation of drinking skills. Also, much of the research on this technique has been conducted with young adults as subjects.

Investigators have posed three questions regarding blood-alcohol discrimination training. First, can alcoholics and/or social drinkers learn to estimate blood alcohol levels? Second, by what process do individuals learn to estimate blood alcohol levels? That is, do they use internal cues such as bodily sensations, external cues such as the time interval between drinks, or a combination of both? Third, can social drinkers and/or alcoholics use this estimation ability to modify their drinking patterns?

With regard to the first two questions, it appears that moderate drinkers *and* alcoholics can learn to estimate blood alcohol levels accurately, within .01 to .02%. However, the process by which they make these estimates may be quite different. For example, several investigators (Bois & Vogel-Sprott, 1974; Caddy, Sutton, & Lewis, 1976; Huber, Carlin, & Nathan, 1976) have found that young social drinkers can learn to estimate blood alcohol levels accurately on the basis of internal cues alone. Bois and Vogel-Sprott (1974) trained nine young men between the ages of 20 and 31 years to estimate blood alcohol levels. During the first three training sessions, each subject received a "mint julep cocktail" that contained 0.9 ml of an alcohol solution per pound of body weight. The alcohol was mixed with an equal volume of 7-Up and a drop of peppermint oil to disguise the taste. Subjects were asked to estimate blood alcohol level (based on physical sensations and feeling states) every 10 minutes. Accurate feedback on actual blood alcohol concentration was then provided. Pretraining mean-discrepancy scores between estimated and actual blood alcohol concentration was .022%. During feedback trials, mean discrepancy scores dropped to well below .01%.

This estimation ability was maintained when feedback was no longer provided. During a second phase of the study, the investigators required subjects to use this new skill to control consumption of their "customary" alcoholic beverages (e.g., beer, martinis). That is, subjects were asked to choose a low blood-alcohol concentration level (between .04% and .06%) and then to decide when they had consumed enough alcohol to reach that exact level. Feedback was provided on drinking accuracy. During training, mean discrepancy scores decreased from .02% to approximately .01%. Thus, after training, subjects were able to drink to a predetermined low blood-alcohol level with little difficulty.

Similarly, Huber *et al.* (1976) trained 36 young moderate drinkers to estimate their blood alcohol levels based on either internal sensations or external cues or both. Mean pretraining estimates differed .014%, .021%, and .022%, respectively, from actual assessments on three separate trials. Subjects were divided into three groups. Group 1, the external training group, were trained to estimate blood alcohol level on the basis of (1) dose relationships for their weight and (2) rate of consumption. Group 2, the internal training group, were trained to estimate using bodily sensations, feelings, and clarity of thinking. Relaxation training was used to increase each subject's awareness of internal sensations. Subjects in Group 3 used both internal and external cues in making their judgments. After training, the mean discrepancy estimate was only .009%. It may be noted that this level of accuracy was similar to that obtained by Bois and Vogel-Sprott. No differences in estimation accuracy were noted among the groups. Thus, with social drinkers, blood-alcohol discrimination training is equally effective whether training emphasizes internal cues, external cues, or a combination of both. However, internal cue training appears to be an advantage when the specific amount of alcohol in a beverage is unknown to the drinker. This may be particularly relevant at social gatherings where an individual does not mix his own drinks. Under these conditions, internally trained subjects were especially sensitive to the internal sensations produced by *low* blood alcohol levels, while the externally trained subjects were not nearly as accurate at these low levels.

In a more recent study, Ogurzsoff and Vogel-Sprott (1976) found that the development of these skills bore no significant relationship to age or drinking habits, suggesting that the training technique may be applicable to a wide range of social drinkers. In fact, Henning (1975) successfully trained both heavy and light social drinkers to estimate blood alcohol levels accurately in only one session.

While these data for social drinkers are relatively straightforward, conclusions regarding the ability of alcoholics to learn these skills are less well defined. Lovibond and Caddy (1970), for example, found that outpatient alcoholics can learn to discriminate their blood alcohol levels within ± .01% using internal cues. However, Silverstein, Nathan, and Taylor (1974) were unable to replicate these results with four chronic alcoholics. Their subjects took many hours to discriminate blood alcohol levels accurately and never reached the accuracy of Lovibond and Caddy's subjects. Also, their subjects lost the ability to estimate when external feedback was no longer provided.

In order to examine this training more systematically, Lansky, Nathan, and Lawson (1976) compared internal versus external training with chronic alcoholics. They found that alcoholics can estimate blood alcohol levels accurately only if continuous feedback on accuracy is provided. Once biofeedback is discontinued, only alcoholics who have been provided external reference points are able to estimate blood alcohol level. That is, they must know such factors as amount and rate of consumption for their estimation. These investigators hypothesized that the alcoholic's lack of sensitivity to internal cues might be related to shifting levels of tolerance, a reduced sensitivity of peripheral receptor cells, or cognitive variables.

Unfortunately, prevention and treatment applications of this method to teach self-control over drinking are lacking. Thus, the crucial question of whether these estimation skills are useful in everyday drinking situations remains to be answered. The limited clinical reports of this procedure with chronic alcoholics are not especially encouraging (Caddy & Lovibond, 1976; Ewing & Rouse, 1976). However, applications with younger moderate and heavy social drinkers and less chronic alcoholics are warranted and would seem, on the basis of laboratory studies, to offer considerable promise, particularly in the prevention area.

3.5. Aversive Procedures

A few clinical investigators have evaluated the use of aversion conditioning to teach controlled, moderate drinking skills. In one of the earliest reports, Mills, Sobell, and Schaefer (1971) treated 13 male alcoholics with this approach. Patients were seated at a simulated bar, two at a time, and electrodes were taped to their fingers. They were instructed to order drinks as they would if the situation were occurring in a regular community bar. Patients received a strong electric shock to the fingers if they engaged in any of the following "alcoholic" drinking behaviors: (1) ordered a straight as opposed to a mixed drink; (2) ordered more than a total of three drinks; or (3) gulped rather than sipped the drink (a gulp was defined as any more than one-seventh of the total volume of the drink). While all patients completing treatment evidenced moderate, controlled drinking patterns in the treatment "bar," only two were maintaining these skills in the community at a six-week follow-up.

Sobell and Sobell (1973) included a similar aversive procedure in a more comprehensive treatment regime to teach controlled drinking to alcoholics. While alcoholics who received the total treatment package demonstrated more clinical improvement and more controlled drinking than control subjects after a two-year period, the effectiveness of the aversion conditioning *per se* in teaching drinking skills was doubtful. In fact, as soon as the possibility of shock was removed, the patients reverted back to alcoholic drinking habits even in the experimental bar.

It seems doubtful that aversive conditioning is a viable method for inducing controlled drinking skills.

4. Developing Healthier Habits

One of the most recent trends in behavior therapy consists of teaching "healthy habits" that can serve as alternatives to drinking. This approach may be particularly relevant to young adult drinkers since it can be used within a prevention *or* a treatment framework. Alternative skills that have been used include relaxation and meditation, assertiveness, exercise and physical activity, and self-management skills. These alternatives function in three ways. First, they provide the drinker with responses that are incompatible with heavy drinking. For example, it is somewhat difficult to drink excessively and also maintain a high level of physical fitness via daily strenuous activity. Second, they provide alternative and more adaptive responses to situations that trigger excessive drinking. For example, relaxation can be used to reduce tension, thereby obviating the need for an "alcohol tranquilizer." Third, these alternatives promote better physical and psychological health and provide a wider variety of ways to derive satisfactions from life.

4.1. Relaxation and Meditation

Complete muscular and cognitive relaxation may be a valuable aid in reducing alcohol consumption. There is certainly ample evidence to suggest that relaxation training adds to the effectiveness of behavioral alcoholism programs (Blake, 1967; Lanyon, Primo, Terrell, & Wener, 1972).

Steffan (1974) examined the relationship between relaxation training and drinking behavior in an experimental laboratory. Four alcoholics were taught muscle relaxation training with the aid of electromyographic biofeedback. During training, the patients received continuous feedback on muscle activity in the frontalis muscle of the forehead. Control phases were included during which training was not provided to control for attention–placebo effects. All patients learned to control tension after relaxation training as measured by biofeedback monitoring and self-reports. Drinking was measured before and after both training and placebo conditions by allowing access to an unlimited supply of 86-proof bourbon. Muscle relaxation training resulted in lowered blood alcohol levels and reports of decreased anxiety. Placebo conditions had no effect on drinking.

Meditation also seems to influence drinking behavior. In analyzing data on approximately 1,800 subjects who practiced transcendental meditation on a regular basis, Benson and Wallace (1972) noted that the majority reported a significant decrease in alcohol use after beginning a course in meditation.

Shafii, Lavely, and Jaffe (1975) investigated the effects of transcendental meditation (TM) on drinking, specifically with young adults. Over 200 subjects who regularly practiced TM were compared with a similar group of young adults who did not meditate. Of the meditating group, 40% had discontinued the use of beer and wine in the first six months after beginning TM. During the same time period, none of the controls reported discontinuing the use of beer or wine. In addition, 54% of the meditating group discontinued the use of liquor, while only 1% of the control group reported this occurrence.

In a controlled clinical trial, Marlatt, Pagano, Rose, and Marques (1976) evaluated the influence of different relaxation-training strategies on the drinking behavior of 44 males whose mean age was 23.5 years. All subjects qualified as high-volume drinkers as assessed by Cahalan and Room's (1974) volume-variability index. Subjects were asked to maintain daily written records of their alcohol consumption prior to, during, and after training. Subjects were randomly divided into four groups. Group 1 received the meditational-relaxation technique developed by Benson (1975) emphasizing a passive attitude, muscle relaxation, and the subvocal repetition of a constant sound (such as the word *one*). Group 2 subjects were taught progressive muscle relaxation as developed by Jacobson (1938) and described by Wolpe (1958). Group 3 constituted an attention–placebo control group. Subjects were simply instructed to arrange for daily rest periods during which they were to read pleasant and relaxing books or magazines. Group 4 received all of the assessments of the study but no treatment. Alcohol consumption decreased significantly for all relaxation groups, meditation, muscle relaxation, and rest—but not for the no-treatment group. For example, mean daily ethanol consumption (expressed in standard units of consumption) for the meditation group was reduced by 50%. Although treatment groups practiced relaxation regularly during training, there was a tendency for the meditation group to continue this practice at a two-month follow-up. The regular practice of relaxation, whatever the technique used, was also associated with increased feelings of "internal" control or self-control. Whether reductions in drinking as a function of relaxation training are due to reductions in anxiety, increased feelings of personal power, or other factors is a worthwhile area of investigation. It appears, however, that regular meditation and/or relaxation can reduce consumption levels, particularly in young adults.

4.2. Assertiveness Training

Assertiveness involves the ability to express positive and negative feelings appropriately, to stand up for one's rights, to express differences of opinion, and to refuse unreasonable demands. Several studies have indicated a relationship between lack of assertiveness and excessive drinking. For example, Miller, Hersen, Eisler, and Hilsman (1974) found that chronic alcoholics significantly increased their alcohol consumption on an in-hospital drinking task following stressful interpersonal encounters requiring assertive responses. Social drinkers, on the other hand, decreased their alcohol consumption following these encounters. In a subsequent analysis, Miller and Eisler (1977) found that alcoholics, as a group, were much less assertive behaviorally than psychiatric patients. A significant negative correlation of .63 was obtained between assertiveness and drinking. Thus, those alcoholics who were the heaviest drinkers were also likely to be the least assertive. It seems, then, that assertion training for alcoholics may provide them with an alternative response to situations that are likely to induce alcohol consumption. Whether younger drinkers would show these same deficits is unclear.

However, in one of the few studies in this area with young drinkers, Marlatt, Kosturn, and Lang (1975) found results similar to those with older alcohol abusers. The subjects in this study consisted of 60 male and female college students with a mean age of 22 years. All subjects were characterized as heavy social drinkers (drinking nearly every day, with five or more drinks per occasion at least once in a while, or drinking about once a week with five or more drinks per occasion). Subjects were randomly assigned to three experimental conditions. Subjects in Group 1, the insult condition, were deliberately annoyed and criticized while working on an anagram task. Group 2 subjects were exposed to the same criticism, except they were allowed to "retaliate" by delivering a punishment to the individual who was responsible for the insults. Group 3 subjects constituted the control group. Alcohol consumption was then measured via a taste-rating task (Marlatt, Demming, & Reid, 1973). In this task subjects were instructed to drink wine and rate its taste on various dimensions. Actually, the *amount* of alcohol consumed was being calculated. Subjects who were angered and were provided no opportunity to retaliate drank significantly more alcohol than subjects in the other two groups. Angered subjects who were allowed to retaliate drank much *less* than subjects in the other groups. Thus, even young social drinkers drink more when they are not able to express feelings of anger. It might be inferred from these results that retaliation in real life in the form of assertiveness would decrease the likelihood of excessive drinking. Perhaps an unexpected positive side effect of the upsurge of assertiveness-training workshops in communities across the country is a decrease in alcohol consumption among the participants.

One of the most frequently occurring social situations that requires a drinker to be assertive is pressure from friends to have another drink. The situation is faced by the social drinker dealing with a forceful host as well as by the alcoholic being tempted by his drinking buddies. Teaching drinkers to handle such social pressure directly and assertively and to feel comfortable about their response would seem to be necessary for the maintenance of either moderate drinking skills or total abstinence. This would have particular relevance for young drinkers, since they most frequently consume alcohol with their peer group. In addition, they are more susceptible to influence by peers because of such factors as need for acceptance and fear of social rejection. Recently, Foy, Miller, Eisler, and O'Toole (1976) have developed the procedure of *drink refusal training* to teach drinkers to cope with social pressure more effectively. Prior to training, example scenes were constructed by alcoholics depicting specific situations in which other people had applied pressure to persuade them to accept a drink. These scenes were then role-played with two "pushers" who used various arguments to persuade the patient to take a drink, such as, "One drink won't hurt you," "What kind of a friend are you?," or "Just have a little one; I'll make sure you won't have any more." All scenes were videotaped and the patient's responses were rated. Components of an appropriate refusal response were then taught in a sequential order. For example, patients were taught (1) to look directly at the pusher when responding; (2) to speak in a firm, strong tone with appropriate facial expression and body language; (3) to offer an alternative suggestion such as, "I don't care for a beer but I'd love a Coke"; (4) to request that the pushers refrain from continued persuasion; and (5) to change the subject by introducing a different topic of conversation. Training consisted of a combination of behavioral strategies. Each patient was shown a videotape of a model demonstrating an appropriate refusal response. Specific components of the skills being demonstrated were pointed out. For example, patients' attention was focused on the facial expressions and the eye contact of the videotaped model, and they were instructed to practice these behaviors during subsequent role-playing sessions. Finally, patients were given an opportunity to rehearse refusal skills via role playing. Feedback was provided on the accuracy of performance.

Comparison of ratings of pre- and posttraining videotapes of performance indicated a marked improvement in abilities. Prior to training, patients would often smile inappropriately, look very uncomfortable, or use such halfhearted remarks such as "Well, I really shouldn't have a drink" or "I'm not *supposed* to." One patient felt so emotionally pressured that he actually agreed to have a drink. After training, each patient responded in a firm, straightforward manner, including each component of the refusal response in his reply. At three months, a clinical and a videotape follow-up evaluation was conducted. Patients maintained their refusal skills during the role-played scenes and had used these skills often at home. For example, for the first time in several years, one patient was able to withstand pressure from former drinking companions. Patients also noted that their ability to refuse drinks increased feelings of confidence, self-esteem, and a sense of personal control over their lives.

4.3. Exercise and Physical Activity

The recent nationwide interest in physical fitness has uncovered another possible alternative to excessive drinking. Regular, strenuous physical activities such as running, bicycling, handball, racquet ball, and swimming are both psychologically and physiologically incompatible with regular heavy drinking. Theoretically, if a young drinker could become addicted to physical activity, his alcohol consumption would be reduced. One reason is that alcohol leads to decreased oxygen uptake, reduced heat tolerance, reduced muscle contractile strength, and impaired coordination (Glover & Shepherd, 1978). Thus, the negative consequences of heavy drinking are immediately apparent because they drastically impair fitness and physical performance. This is particularly important from a reinforcement and social learning viewpoint since, in most cases, the negative effects of heavy drinking are so delayed that they have little influence over behavior. Running increases awareness of bodily needs and the importance of physical fitness. Runners usually improve their nutrition, reduce drinking, and quit smoking.

Running tends to reduce anxiety, depression, and feelings of worthlessness, which are often associated with heavy drinking. For example, Gary and Guthrie (1972) reported improvements in alcoholics' self-esteem, anxiety, sleeping patterns, and cardiovascular functioning as a function of a daily physical fitness program in which patients jogged one mile per day. Along these lines, an annual Alcoholics Olympics is held each year in California to promote running as a method of maintaining sobriety.

Fortunately, running can become as addictive as substance abuse. Glasser (1976) has, in fact, advocated the development of running as a "positive addiction" to counteract excessive drinking. Kostrubala (1976), a psychiatrist who uses running as part of his therapeutic plan for patients, points out that running can become a real addiction in the medical sense since (1) it produces a desire in the user to increase the dosage (mileage) and (2) deprivation—that is, the inability to run because of circumstance or injury—produces restlessness, agitation, and irritability much like withdrawal symptoms.

Unfortunately, while much anecdotal evidence on the relationship between phsyical activity and drinking has been reported, scientific evidence is lacking, particularly for young adults. A recent survey of young psychologist runners indicated that participation in a regular program of running reduced alcohol consumption from a mean of 6.1 drinks per week to 4.69 per week (Fowler, 1978). Further research in this area would be extremely worthwhile. It is, indeed, unfortunate that we overlook such basic alternatives to excessive drinking as physical fitness activities and, instead, focus our efforts on the development of complex theoretical treatment systems. Certainly, one advantage of this approach is the current widespread interest in fitness programs throughout the country.

4.4. Self-Management Skills

Self-management skills training is perhaps the most relevant form of behavior therapy for young drinkers even though it has been used very little in alcoholism prevention or treatment. However, this training has been used quite effectively to break overeating and smoking habits (Bellack, 1975; Bernstein & McAlister, 1976), and reports of its use with alcohol abuse are increasing.

Self-management skills refer to those abilities necessary to modify one's own behavior. More specifically, it is "a process through which an individual becomes the principle agent in guiding, directing, and regulating those features of his own behavior that might eventually lead to desired positive outcomes" (Goldfried & Merbaum, 1973).

The most basic form of self-management is self-monitoring. Self-monitoring simply requires the drinker to keep a daily written record of the number and types of drinks consumed, the time of day, the location, the circumstances, and his thoughts and feelings. Drinks are usually recorded before their consumption. With other addictive habit patterns, self-monitoring has been shown to decrease consumption at least temporarily. While this procedure has been used with drinkers as part of a total self-management training package (Miller, 1978), its effectiveness as a single technique in reducing alcohol consumption has not been tested. Since self-monitoring suppresses other habits, however, it would seem that drinking would be amenable to this procedure.

Self-management also involves rearranging environmental cues or life routines to decrease the likelihood of drinking. This might involve simply taking a different route home from work to avoid passing a series of taverns and liquor stores or keeping beer, wine, and liquor supplies low and inaccessible. The drinker must also learn to break the association between drinking and certain situations. The act of drinking can become conditioned to such circumstances as watching television or "relaxing" after arriving home from work. After repeated associations, a particular time of day or a room in the house may trigger cravings for a drink. For example, a drinker would be instructed to schedule new activities at times when drinking is most likely to occur. For example, he might arrange, early in the day, to meet two friends for jogging, to accompany his children on a bicycle ride, or to play tennis with his spouse soon after arriving home from work. This preplanning of activities that are incompatible with drinking begins to build new associations and lessens the chances of drinking.

Mertens (1964) and Miller (1976) described the use of cognitive self-management strategies. In order to make the ultimate consequences of excessive drinking more immediate, drinkers are instructed to list, in writing, (1) aversive consequences of drinking that will occur if excessive drinking continues and (2) positive consequences of drinking that will occur as the result of abstinence or moderate drinking. The drinker is instructed to read and vividly picture each consequence whenever a craving for a drink occurs. For example, he would be instructed to imagine the emotional enjoyment and feelings of accomplishment of a promotion at work following several months of sobriety.

Details of these and other self-management procedures are described by P. M. Miller (1976), Miller and Mastria (1977), and W. R. Miller (1978).

5. Comprehensive Programs

The systematic evaluation of broad-spectrum behavioral prevention and treatment programs used with young adults is very recent. Unfortunately, clinical trials of behavioral techniques have focused almost exclusively on older, chronic, hospitalized alcoholics. Behaviorists have yet to involve themselves in prevention on a significant level.

However, three comprehensive programs that were aimed at relatively young adult problem-drinkers deserve mention. Miller (1975) reported the behavioral treatment of a 23-year-old married male who consumed approximately 5–6 cans of beer per day. Approximately once per week, the patient drank up to two six-packs of beer when out with his friends. He never drank liquor or wine. The patient was concerned about his heavy drinking, in spite of the fact that it had not as yet led to any significant life problems, and wanted to become a more moderate, responsible drinker. Phase 1 of treatment consisted of training in responsible drinking skills. The patient was scheduled for a series of five drinking sessions, during which components of moderate drinking were taught and practiced. Drinking sessions were videotaped and the patient's drinking behavior rated to provide an index of improvement. Through specific instructions, behavioral rehearsal, feedback, and reinforcement, he was taught (1) to take small sips of beer; (2) to slow his pace of drinking by increasing the time interval between sips and by putting his beer can down between sips; and (3) to limit his intake to a total of two beers consumed in no less than 40 minutes on any one drinking occasion. A timer was used to help the patient pace his sips and drinks. With the assistance of his wife, he was also given assignments to practice these skills at home, keeping records of his progress during each session. Concurrently, factual information about the psychological and physiological effects of alcohol were described.

The patient was then given training in implementing various behavioral self-management techniques. He was instructed to drink only in situations that would decrease the likelihood of excessive drinking. For example, he was to drink only in specified locations, such as in his living room, at a bar, or at a party and never in his car, in his garage, or when alone. He was also taught to rearrange stimulus cues that elicited excessive drinking. This involved keeping no more than six beers available in his house at any one time and keeping these beers out of sight, behind other foods in the refrigerator. At social gatherings, he was to drink slowly and to make every other drink a nonalcoholic one. In addition, he arranged to schedule specific alternative activities, such as playing with the children, going for a walk or a bicycle ride, or working on a special project at times when drinking was likely to occur. He was also instructed to record and chart the number of beers he consumed per day and the approximate length of time it took him to consume each. These records were evaluated weekly by the treatment staff.

Drink refusal skills were taught, since the patient often gave in to social pressure from his buddies to have "one more for the road." He was taught these skills in the manner described earlier, rehearsing his new skills in role-played scenes typical of those he usually encountered. Several scenes were practiced, including those in which he refused all drinks and those in which he refused only the second or third drink. To make conditions more natural and to ensure generalization, a priming dose of two beers provided prior to role playing some of the scenes. It was imperative that he maintain the skills necessary to refuse drinks even under the influence of alcohol.

Finally, his wife agreed to assist by reinforcing both moderate drinking and abstinence by means of increased attention and affection. A behavioral contract was written specifying these contingencies. As part of the contract, she also agreed to refrain from making negative remarks regarding moderate drinking (e.g., "There you go again. Why do you have to drink every day?").

Continuous monitoring of drinking behavior revealed that this client developed and maintained a pattern of responsible drinking. His consumption never exceeded 36 ounces of beer per day over a four-month follow-up period. His wife reported that he continued to use the self-management and refusal skills that he was taught.

Strickler, Bigelow, Lawrence, and Liebson (1976) also reported a comprehensive behavioral program to teach moderate drinking. Although their subjects were not all young adults, their methods seem applicable to this population. This training program consisted of a two-hour group meeting, twice weekly, for seven weeks. During Phase 1 of training, a detailed behavioral analysis of each patient's drinking was conducted. Specific stimulus events precipitating excessive drinking were identified, and new behaviors incompatible with drinking were discussed. Patients were given information about alcohol and its effects and were provided with guidelines for responsible drinking. These guidelines were similar to those described in Miller's (1975) study and included such factors as (1) drinking only with other people; (2) at parties, eating something along with drinking; and (3) taking at least 20–30 minutes to finish a drink. Patients were also introduced to relaxation training as an alternative to excessive drinking.

During Phase 2, patients were given supervised practice in moderate drinking in a simulated barroom. During some sessions, patients observed the behavior of a model adhering to the components of responsible drinking and were told to imitate him. During Phase 3, blood-alcohol discrimination training was conducted. During the final training phase, patients were exposed to a party situation and instructed to use their new skills to moderate drinking.

Results indicated that two out of three subjects trained in this manner reduced their drinking considerably from pretreatment levels and had maintained a moderate drinking pattern at a six-month follow-up. The mean number of drinks per day dropped from 11 to 4 for one individual and from 8 to 4 for the other.

Miller and Munoz (1976) recently developed a multimodal behavioral intervention package aimed at problem drinkers. The program includes alcohol education, blood-alcohol discrimination training, drink refusal and assertiveness training, relaxation training, and self-management training (emphasizing both environmental manipulations and cognitive controls). To evaluate this program, Miller (1978) compared three treatment variations: (1) aversive counterconditioning in which self-administered electric shocks were associated with alcohol; (2) behavioral self-control training, including self-monitoring, self-management training, and training in behavioral alternatives to alcohol abuse; and (3) controlled drinking training involving blood-alcohol discrimination training and discriminated aversive conditioning to teach the components of responsible drinking. Clients included court referrals of individuals found guilty of driving while intoxicated and self-referrals from the community who labeled themselves as "problem drinkers desiring to reduce and control their drinking without stopping altogether." Clients were relatively young, the average age being in the mid-thirties. All groups decreased alcohol consumption, but the aversive conditioning group was least improved throughout the first three months after training. In the behavioral self-control group, the mean weekly alcohol consumption was reduced from 34 standard ethanol units (1 unit equals 15 ml of pure ethanol) to 13 units. The controlled-drinking training group reduced consumption from 38 to 15 standard ethanol units per week. This decreased consumption level had been maintained at a 12-month follow-up. However, at 12 months, the drinking of the aversive conditioning group was also lower, even though this result was not evidenced at 3 months. This result may very well have been due to the fact that training manuals describing the self-control procedures used with the other groups were provided to some of these clients immediately after the 3-month follow-up.

In any event, self-control procedures were effective in reducing the alcohol consumption of young problem drinkers. Aversive conditioning and blood-alcohol discrimination training did not add to treatment effectiveness. Overall, the most clinically effective and cost-effective (in terms of time and money) treatment was the behavioral self-control package, in which self-monitoring, self-management, relaxation, and assertiveness were taught. It was also noted by the investigator that some clients seemed to be able to modify their drinking habits simply through the use of a written manual describing self-control techniques.

Other comprehensive behavior modification programs have reported promising results and should not be overlooked. The most notable of these include Sobell and Sobell's (1973) individualized behavior therapy; Vogler, Compton, and Weissbach's (1975) integrated behavior therapy; and Azrin's (1976) community reinforcement approach. All of these approaches, which are similar to those just described, have been shown to be significantly more effective than Alcoholics Anonymous groups or group and individual counseling in well-controlled experimental studies. However, all of these approaches focused on chronic, older alcoholics rather than on the young adult population. While modifications of these methods may prove effective with young clients, this possibility awaits further experimental evaluation.

Generally, comprehensive behavioral programs with young adults appear to be worthwhile. Clinical research is needed to determine which of the many behavioral techniques within the total intervention package contributes most to the overall effectiveness of the program

6. Conclusions

In summary, while behavior modification strategies have only recently been applied to the drinking behavior of young adults, their use with this population shows considerable promise. In fact, specific behavioral techniques such as self-management and controlled-drinking training seem particularly relevant for young adults from both a prevention and a treatment perspective.

These behavioral approaches represent a *training* rather than an information–educational model. That is, young drinkers are not merely exposed to a didactic educational program or to group discussions on values clarification. Rather, they are involved in a systematic training regime in which they learn and practice specific, practical skills related to responsible drinking.

Some behavioral procedures already seem more promising than others. For example, training in the components of responsible drinking via modeling, rehearsal, and reinforcement has been used effectively. While blood-alcohol discrimination training would seem to be useful at first glance, its practical utility must be established through further clinical research. Some recent data indicate that the more simple procedure of teaching external control through modifications in the number and potency of drinks and in drinking style (e.g., rate of consumption) may be sufficient for some individuals to learn responsible drinking skills (Miller, 1978). The time and effort spent in teaching drinkers to discriminate blood alcohol levels based on internal sensations may not be necessary for all drinkers. Clinical trials evaluating external versus internal training separately and in combination are needed. The use of aversive conditioning to teach drinking skills appears to be contraindicated based on current evidence.

Teaching behavioral self-control skills and behavioral alternatives to the antecedents of excessive drinking appears to be a viable prevention and treatment approach. However, simply initiating new responses such as relaxation or physical activities is insufficient for long-term maintenance of changes in drinking behavior. Social and self-reinforcement systems must be provided to ensure the stability of new habit patterns over time. A young drinker may practice relaxation, meditation, or daily running only until the novelty wears off or until the behavioral training program terminates.

In addition to their potential effectiveness, behavioral strategies have the advantage of being relatively straightforward techniques that are simple to teach and simple to learn. In fact, some individuals may be able to modify drinking habits through relatively low-level behavioral intervention, such as self-monitoring of consumption and reading a detailed self-help guide on behavioral techniques. Alcohologists frequently are guilty of "overkill" when it comes to prevention or treatment. That is, all drinkers requesting assistance are lumped together, are labeled as alcoholics, and are exposed to a conglomeration of therapeutic procedures. Young drinkers would seem to benefit more from a hierarchical system beginning with the most pragmatic and cost-effective intervention programs and working up to more intensive ones. Those who do not respond to simple education, for example, would be exposed to a more complex program of skills training. Those who still do not respond would receive a more extensive therapeutic program. Concomitantly, clinical researchers could begin to delineate the specific types of drinkers who respond best to specific types of intervention.

A final advantage of a behavioral self-control approach is that drinking is viewed as a learned, addictive habit pattern akin to other unhealthy consumatory behaviors, such as overeating and smoking (Miller, 1979). Self-control techniques are equally applicable to any habit patterns. In fact, teaching the behavioral control of one habit with this approach typically generalizes to the control of other habits. This is particularly important since with other approaches, decreases in one habit pattern may lead to increases in others. Thus, ex-smokers overeat, ex-drug-abusers drink to excess, and ex-drinkers smoke more cigarettes. This reactivity among habits requires a *total health approach* to prevention and treatment. By reducing alcohol consumption alone, we may be decreasing an individual's chances of cirrhosis, unemployment, and divorce but increasing the likelihood of heart and lung disease from excessive smoking.

A total health approach has a particular advantage with young drinkers, who frequently perceive little relevance between their drinking patterns and the alcoholism education to which they are exposed. This lack of perception, together with the stigma that alcoholism still represents in our society, may lead to the offhand rejection of participation in alcoholism prevention programs. A total health approach may not only have a better overall outcome but may also be more acceptable to the general population. This is not to say that the issues of alcohol use and abuse should be disguised or avoided. Rather, they should be put into perspective with other related social and health programs to achieve maximum impact from intervention efforts.

References

Armor, D. J., Polich, J. M., & Stambul, H. B. *Alcoholism and treatment*. Santa Monica, Calif.: The Rand Corporation, 1976.

Azrin, N. H. Improvements in the community reinforcement approach to alcoholism. *Behaviour Research and Therapy*, 1976, *14*, 339–348.

Bellack, A. Behavior therapy for weight reduction. *Addictive Behaviors*, 1975, *1*, 73–82.

Benson, H. The relaxation response. New York: William Morrow, 1975.

Benson, H., & Wallace, R. K. Decreased drug use with transcendental meditation: A study of 1,862 subjects. In C. J. D. Zarafonetis (Ed.), *Drug abuse: Proceedings of the international conference*. Philadelphia: Lea & Febiger, 1972.

Bernstein, D. A., & McAlister, A. The modification of smoking: Progress and problems. *Addictive Behaviors*, 1976, *1*, 89–102.

Blake, B. G. A follow-up of alcoholics treated by behavior therapy. *Behaviour Research and Therapy*, 1967, *5*, 89–94.

Bois, C., & Vogel-Sprott, M. Discrimination of low blood alcohol levels and self-titration skills in social drinkers. *Quarterly Journal of Studies on Alcohol*, 1974, *35*, 86–97

Caddy, G. R., & Lovibond, S. H. Self-regulation and discriminated aversive conditioning in the modification of alcoholics' drinking behavior. *Behavior Therapy*, 1976, *7*, 223–230.

Caddy, G. R., Sutton, M., & Lewis, J. The role of feedback and internal cues in blood alcohol concentration estimation. Unpublished manuscript, Old Dominion University, 1976.

Cahalan, D., & Room, R. *Problem drinking among American men*. New Brunswick, N.J.: Rutgers Center of Alcohol Studies, 1974.

Cohen, M., Liebson, I., & Faillace, L. The role of reinforcement contingencies in chronic alcoholism: An experimental analysis of one case. *Behaviour Research and Therapy*, 1971, *9*, 375–379.

Cohen, M., Liebson, I., Faillace, L., & Speers, W. Alcoholism: Controlled drinking and incentives for abstinence. *Psychological Reports*, 1971, *28*, 575–580.

Conger, J. J. Reinforcement theory and the dynamics of alcoholism. *Quarterly Journal of Studies on Alcohol*, 1956, *17*, 296–305.

Cutler, R. E., & Storm, T. Observational study of alcohol consumption in natural settings: The Vancouver beer parlour. *Journal of Studies on Alcohol*, 1975, *36*, 1173–1183.
Ewing, J. A., & Rouse, B. A. Failure of an experimental treatment program to inculcate controlled drinking in alcoholics. *British Journal of the Addictions*, 1976, *71*, 123–124.
Fowler, R. Survey of running psychologists. *Running Psychologists*, 1978, *1*, 3.
Foy, D. W., Miller, P. M., Eisler, R. M., & O'Toole, D. H. Social skills training to teach alcoholics to refuse drinks effectively. *Journal of Studies on Alcohol*, 1976, *37*, 1340–1345.
Gary, V., & Guthrie, D. The effect of jogging on physical fitness and self-concept in hospitalized alcoholics. *Quarterly Journal of Studies on Alcohol*, 1972, *33*, 1073–1078.
Glasser, W. *Positive addictions*. New York: Harper & Row, 1976.
Glover, B., & Shepherd, J. *The runner's handbook*. New York: Penguin Books, 1978.
Goldfried, M. R., & Merbaum, M. (Eds.). *Behavior change through self-control*. New York: Holt, Rinehart, and Winston, 1973.
Henning, J. S. Test of the ability to monitor blood alcohol concentration among male heavy drinkers (Dissertation). Ann Arbor, Mich.: University Microfilm, 75-01637, 1975.
Hodgson, R. J., & Rankin, H. J. Modification of excessive drinking by cue exposure. *Behaviour Research and Therapy*, 1976, *14*, 305–307.
Huber, H., Karlin, R., & Nathan, P. Blood alcohol level discrimination by nonalcoholics: The role of internal and external cues. *Journal of Studies on Alcohol*, 1976, *37*, 27–39.
Jacobson, E. *Progressive relaxation*. Chicago: University of Chicago Press, 1938.
Kessler, M., & Gomberg, C. Observations of barroom drinking: Methodology and preliminary results. *Quarterly Journal of Studies on Alcohol*, 1974, *35*, 1392–1396.
Kingham, R. J. Alcoholism and the reinforcement theory of learning. *Quarterly Journal of Studies on Alcohol*, 1958, *19*, 320–330.
Kostrubala, T. *The joy of running*. Philadelphia: Lippincott, 1976.
Lansky, D., Nathan, P. E., & Lawson, D. M. Blood alcohol discrimination by alcoholics: The role of internal and external cues. Unpublished manuscript, Rutgers University, 1976.
Lanyon, R. I., Primo, R. V., Terrell, F., & Wener, A. An aversion desensitization treatment for alcoholism. *Journal of Consulting and Clinical Psychology*, 1972, *38*, 394–398.
Lovibond, S. H., & Caddy, G. Discriminated aversive control in the moderation of alcoholics' drinking behavior. *Behavior Therapy*, 1970, *1*, 437–444.
Marlatt, G. A., Demming, B., & Reid, J. B. Loss of control drinking in alcoholics: An experimental analogue. *Journal of Abnormal Psychology*, 1973, *81*, 233–241.
Marlatt, G. A., Kosturn, C. F., & Lang, A. R. Provocation to anger and opportunity for retaliation as determinants of alcohol consumption in social drinkers. *Journal of Abnormal Psychology*, 1975, *84*, 652–659.
Marlatt, G. A., Pagano, R. R., Rose, R. M., & Marques, J. K. The effects of meditation upon alcohol consumption in male social drinkers. Unpublished research, University of Washington, 1976.
Mertens, G. C. An operant approach to self-control for alcoholics. Paper presented at the American Psychological Association, Sept. 1964.
Miller, P. M. The use of behavioral contracting in the treatment of alcoholism: A case report. *Behavior Therapy*, 1972, *3*, 593–596.
Miller, P. M. Training responsible drinking skills to veterans. Paper presented at the American Psychological Association, 1975.
Miller, P. M. *Behavioral treatment of alcoholism*. New York: Pergamon Press, 1976.
Miller, P. M. *Personal habit control*. New York: Simon & Schuster, 1979.
Miller, P. M., & Eisler, R. M. Assertive behavior of alcoholics: A descriptive analysis. *Behavior Therapy*, 1977, *8*, 146–149.

Miller, P. M., & Mastria, M. A. *Alternatives to alcohol abuse*. Champaign, Ill.: Research Press, 1977.

Miller, P. M., Hersen, M., Eisler, R. M., & Hilsman, G. Effects of social stress on operant drinking of alcoholics and social drinkers. *Behaviour Research and Therapy*, 1974, *12*, 67–72.

Miller, P. M., Becker, J. V., Foy, D. W., & Wooten, L. S. Instructional control of the components of alcoholic drinking behavior. *Behavior Therapy*, 1976, *1*, 472–480.

Miller, W. R. Behavioral treatment of problem drinkers: A comparative outcome study of three controlled drinking therapies. *Journal of Consulting and Clinical Psychology*, 1978, *46*, 74–86.

Miller, W. R., & Munoz, R. F. *How to control your drinking*. Englewood Cliffs, N.J.: Prentice-Hall, 1976.

Mills, K. C., Sobell, M. B., & Schaefer, H. H. Training social drinking as an alternative to abstinence for alcoholics. *Behavior Therapy*, 1971, *2*, 18–27.

National Institute on Alcohol Abuse and Alcoholism. *Alcohol and health*. Washington, D.C.: U.S. Government Printing Office, 1974.

Ogurzsoff, S., & Vogel-Sprott, M. Low blood alcohol discrimination and self-titration skills of social drinkers with widely varied drinking habits. *Canadian Journal of Behavioral Science*, 1976, *8*, 232–242.

Pattison, E. M. The rehabilitation of the chronic alcoholic. In B. Kissin & H. Begleiter (Eds.), *The biology of alcoholism. Vol. 3: Clinical pathology*. New York: Plenum Press, 1974.

Pattison, E. M., Sobell, M. B., & Sobell, L. C. *Emerging concepts of alcohol dependence*. New York: Springer Publishing, 1977.

Rosenbluth, J., Nathan, P. E., & Lawson, D. M. Environmental influences on drinking by college students in a college pub: Behavioral observations in the natural setting. *Addictive Behaviors*, 1979.

Schaefer, H. H., Sobell, M. B., & Mills, K. C. Baseline drinking behaviors in alcoholics and social drinkers: Kinds of sips and sip magnitude. *Behaviour Research and Therapy*, 1971, *9*, 23–27.

Shafii, M., Lavely, R., & Jaffe, R. Meditation and the prevention of alcohol abuse. *American Journal of Psychiatry*, 1975, *132*, 942–945.

Silverstein, S. J., Nathan, P. E., & Taylor, H. A. Blood alcohol level estimation and controlled drinking by chronic alcoholics. *Behavior Therapy*, 1974, *5*, 1–15.

Sobell, M. B., & Sobell, L. C. Alcoholics treated by individualized behavior therapy: One year treatment outcome. *Behavior Research and Therapy*, 1973, *11*, 599–618.

Sobell, M. B., Schaeffer, H. H., & Miller, K. C. Differences in baseline drinking behavior between alcoholics and normal drinkers. *Behavior Research and Therapy*, 1972, *10*, 257–267.

Steffan, J. J. Electromyographically induced relaxation in the treatment of chronic alcohol abuse. *Journal of Consulting and Clinical Psychology*, 1974, *43*, 275–279.

Strickler, D., Bigelow, G., Lawrence, C., & Liebson, I. Moderate drinking as an alternative to alcohol abuse: A non-aversive procedure. *Behaviour Research and Therapy*, 1976, *14*, 279–288.

Vogler, R. C., Compton, J. V., & Weissbach, T. A. Integrated behavior change techniques for alcoholics. *Journal of Consulting and Clinical Psychology*, 1975, *43*, 233–243.

Williams, R. J., & Brown, R. A. Differences in baseline drinking behavior between New Zealand alcoholics and normal drinkers. *Behaviour Research and Therapy*, 1974, *12*, 287–294.

Wolpe, J. *Psychotherapy by reciprocal inhibition*. Stanford, Calif.: Stanford University Press, 1958.

Index

MIX
Papier aus verantwortungsvollen Quellen
Paper from responsible sources
FSC® C105338

If you have any concerns about our products,
you can contact us on
ProductSafety@springernature.com

In case Publisher is established outside the EU,
the EU authorized representative is:
Springer Nature Customer Service Center GmbH
Europaplatz 3, 69115 Heidelberg, Germany

Printed by Libri Plureos GmbH
in Hamburg, Germany